Live&Work
— IN —
GERMANY

SECOND EDITION · Completely revised and updated

Ian Collier

Published by Vacation Work, 9 Park End Street, Oxford
Web site http: //www.vacationwork.co.uk

LIVE AND WORK IN GERMANY

First edition 1992 Victoria Pybus
Second edition 1998 Ian Collier

Copyright © Vacation Work 1998

ISBN 1 85458 184 8 (softback)
ISBN 1 85458 185 6 (hardback)

Publicity: Roger Musker

Cover Design by Miller Craig & Cocking Design Partnership

Printed by **Unwin Brothers Ltd**,
The Gresham Press, Old Woking, Surrey

Contents

SECTION I — LIVING IN GERMANY

RETIREMENT

SECTION II — WORKING IN GERMANY

EMPLOYMENT

STARTING A BUSINESS

Personal Case Histories

MAPS AND CHARTS

Foreword to the Second Edition

Live and Work in Germany is the fifth in a successful series of books which identifies the opportunities for work, starting a business, or retiring. The book is divided into two sections, *Living in Germany* and *Working in Germany* respectively, which between them cover all aspects of such a venture, from how to find accommodation to ideas and procedures for setting up a small business.

At present there are an estimated 150,000 UK nationals living in Germany, many of whom work for British or multinational companies in the large cities such as Hamburg, Munich, Stuttgart, Düsseldorf, Frankfurt and Berlin, all of which have large expatriate communities. The same is true for Americans and Australians, although figures for those populations were not available at the time of writing. Apart from having been posted to Germany there are many good reasons to take advantage of the opportunity to live and work in another country either for your employer or in your own business; aside from the novelty of a new experience. In Germany these reasons include pleasant working conditions, an excellent integrated transport system, a generous social welfare system and the high standard of living. There is also the opportunity to make new friends and develop new interests and while the hard working Germans in your office, factory or shop may seem aloof at first, once the hard nut of German formality has been cracked, durable friendships will blossom.

The German economy may be in the doldrums at present due to the costs of Unification, but it still forms a base line for the new European currency system. Indeed the current depressed state of the Deutsche Mark is an incentive for new investment either in business or in property, as the underlying trends of exports and productivity show that Germany will soon return to its old position as the European economic powerhouse. The EU has rapidly beaten down the barriers between Member States and unleashed an array of opportunities for those seeking jobs and business opportunities. Germany, one of the cornerstones of the EU, has set an example to the rest of Europe with its highly trained workforce and patronage of small businesses. Germany's geographic position coupled with the European Single Market, the open borders of the Schengen Agreement, the Single Currency and the opening of new markets in Eastern Europe all mean one thing: for those wishing to do business in Europe in the next century the place to be is Germany.

Ian Collier MA,
Oxford, February 1998.

Acknowledgments

I would like to thank the following for their invaluable help in compiling this book: The Embassy of the Federal Republic of Germany in London and the staff of the British Embassy and Consular offices in Germany for providing vast amounts of useful information; especially the Consulate-General staff of Hamburg. Thanks are also due to Anke Büttner for her general assistance and for translating information, Sarah Foster for her helpful comments and experiences of Germany, Herr Pfärrer H.W. Büttner for his help in Nürnberg; Mr Barker of Knight Frank, Tim Grant and Simon Conn for their help with the sections on accommodation. Evi, Maike, Almut and Clemens Büttner for answering and translating numerous questions about all aspects of daily life. *Vielen danke* also to Inge Kempfer for her assistance with the German media.

Telephone area code changes

On April 22nd 2000 there are to be a number of changes to certain area telephone code prefixes in the UK. The most important of these is that the current 0171– and 0181– prefixes for London will both be replaced by the prefix 020–, followed by 7 for current 0171 numbers and 8 for current 0181 numbers. Also affected will be Cardiff (numbers will begin 029 20), Portsmouth (023 92), Southampton (023 80) and Northern Ireland (028 90 for Belfast; contact directory enquiries for other numbers in Northern Ireland). In addition, as from the same date the numbers for various special services including freephone and lo-call numbers will begin with 08 and all mobile phone numbers will begin with 07. Telephone operators are planning to ease the transition by running the current 01 numbers in parallel with the new 02 numbers until Spring 2001.

SECTION I

Living in Germany

General Introduction
Residence and Entry Regulations
Setting Up Home
Daily Life
Retirement

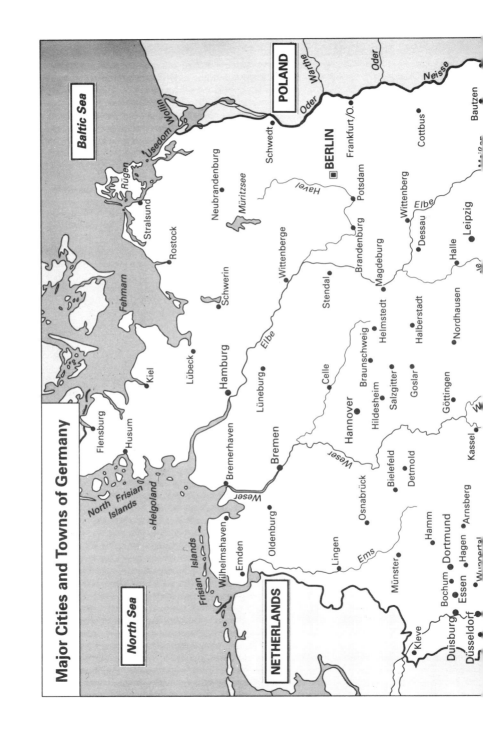

Major Cities and Towns of Germany

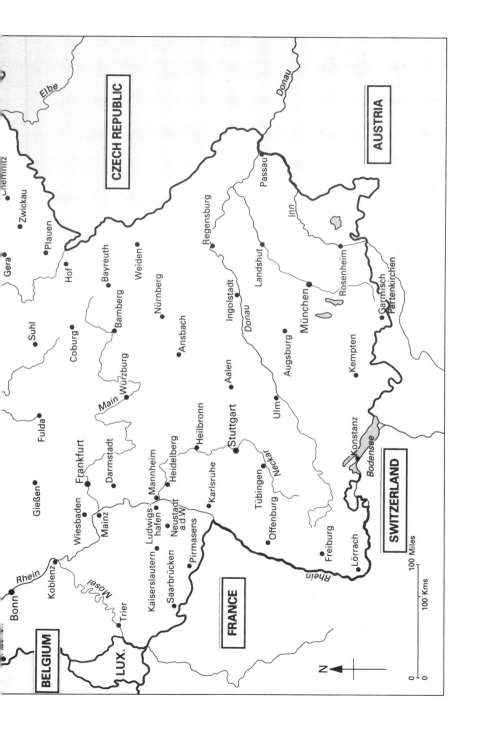

General Introduction

Destination Germany

As the heads of the EU member states continue to indulge in all sorts of political bickering during the run up to monetary union, one might think that the petty tribalism which has underscored much of the mid-nineties would be reflected in the immigration figures across the EU. Certainly given the rantings of Britain's tabloid newspapers during Euro '96 one would think that few Britons would ever leave home for more than a holiday in the sun. However, recent figures put the number of Britons living and working abroad at over ten million and of these British expatriates over one hundred and fifty thousand can be found happily living and working in Germany. The explosion in building sites across the new Federal States (*Länder*) in what was East Germany (there are 17,000 in the Berlin area alone) has certainly meant that the boom years of the '80s for British 'brickies' may be out done yet, but construction is not the only British involvement in Germany.

While Sir Norman Foster has designed the redeveloped Reichstag in Berlin, and factory sites along the Ruhr, Sun Alliance, Boots, Waterstones and Nat West are all examples of British firms investing in Germany. Despite the economic and developmental burden of re-unification with former East Germany since July 1990, Germany still has much to offer in terms of career and business prospects.

Germany is one of the most industrialized countries in Europe with one of the highest standards of living. Along with Denmark, Germany shares a higher element of social welfare in the workplace and the community than any of the other EU countries. Labour and employer relations are amongst the best in Europe with workers having the chance to sit in on committees overseeing negotiations on wages and conditions.

Undoubtedly, given the high rates of unemployment especially amongst the young, in the new Länder in the East and recent fall of the mark against the pound all has not been well. A monumental problem that still lies ahead is the desperate need to restructure the tax and social security system which has recently been held up by political in-fighting within the coalition government. However the German economy is still taken as one of the baselines for European Monetary Union, which is planned for 2001. Even if the current coalition is riddled with in-fighting in the run-up to the general election in 1998, Germany's economic recovery in the Fifties and Sixties should be taken as an omen of how well the country can work when the politicians have a common aim.

Pros and Cons of Moving to Germany

Those intent on living and working in Germany will find that Germany is not only a major player in the European Union but is also home to many multinational companies, allowing the potential expatriate to choose from a wide range of employment and career possibilities. From the employee's point of view there are distinct advantages to working in Germany: high wages; generous fringe benefits and salary related social security payments (see Chapter 6, *Employment*). An unemployed German typically receives two thirds of his last wage in unemployment benefit. In 1996 the average pay for a worker at BMW was DM 60,000 (£27,000) compared to £16,000 for the average worker with Rover in Britain, while the German worker had a shorter week too. So while you may pay a lot for your benefits, you can still take a lot home with you secure in the knowledge that you'll have a decent safety net too. Many Germans in the engineering and electronics industries now work a 35 hour week, while recently Volkswagen agreed a 29 hour week with its employees, thus achieving an old aim of the trade unions to develop a leisure society. Although some of these shorter working weeks are made up of shift work in an attempt to prevent job losses, the practical upshot is that the workers have a good job, good wages and a good part of the week to themselves and their families. Two standard additions to pay packets across Germany are the payments of *Urlaubsgeld* and *Weihnachtsgeld*, the former is an extra months pay for one's summer holiday, while the latter is for Christmas presents.

Even before re-unification Germany was not generally considered to be a country of stylish expatriate living in the manner of France's Provence or the Italian 'Chiantishire'. Perhaps this is due to the clichéd view of the teutonic work ethic, even if this does not sit logically with the many jokes about German holidaymakers and their towels. However, as can be seen from the above, the Germans enjoy one of the most uniformly high living standards in Europe combined with the shortest working week in Europe, and a generous amount of annual leave. Even if the 'ossie' of the eastern länder still feel left behind by their more worldly 'wessie' western cousins, the German government has spent a tremendous amount of money upgrading the infrastructure of the former East Germany. So it shouldn't be too long before the *autoroutes* and *autostrada* are clogged up with 'ossies' alongside the camper vans and space mobiles of Bonn and Frankfurt heading for their holidays.

Setting up home in another country will always cause problems even for proficient linguists as the newcomer gets to grips with slang terms or variations in dialect. The German language is perceived as a bigger problem than most due to its many rules, exceptions and regional variants (see Chapter Four, *Daily Life*); for Britons part of this image is fostered by schools insisting that one should be good at French before one can learn German. However it is comforting to know that most urban Germans are more than proficient at speaking English, and generally will relish the opportunity to practise or 'fine-tune' their grasp of English. For obvious reasons Russian is still the main second language in the new länder, but this is changing and you shouldn't be heading for Germany if you only wish to speak English.

For those seeking an expatriate life in Germany, there is much to recommend it. 82 million people are spread across 357,000 square kilometres, so the population density is less than that of Britain and one is never far from an extraordinary variety of charming landscapes. Driving on the *autobahn* between Nürnberg and Frankfurt one winds through wooded valleys and vineyards perched on steep sided hills.

Public transport is well laid out, often with integrated networks of trains, trams and underground systems in the larger cities. While the German winter is generally colder with more snow than in Britain, due to its continental location, the Germans have houses and heating systems built to cope with it. Not only that but they have both staff and an individual's public duty to help keep the paths and streets clear of snow. German efficiency and social responsibility may be viewed askance by more relaxed cultures, but it means that when snows falls, the trains do not stop because its the wrong type of snow.

The following is a summary of the main pros and cons of living in Germany from the British point of view:

Pros: Germany is one of the most developed countries in Europe.
Germany still has one of the strongest economies in the EU.
Germany has one of the most generous welfare systems in Europe.
German labour laws are amongst the most employee-friendly in the West.
Germany has a pleasant and civilized environment for living and working.
Public services including transport are fully integrated and efficient.
Most cities and large towns have very efficient bus and tram networks.
Many Germans speak English.

Cons: German is one of the most difficult European languages to learn.
Unemployment has risen to over four million since re-unification.
The German economy is suffering under the strain of re-unification.
The German wage deductions are quite high.
The political system with its emphasis on consensus can result in confusion and inactivity.
The Germans can be very formal in their social affairs.
Some Germans are still keen to mind other people's business for them.

Political and Economic Structure

Economic History

The recovery of Germany from the remains of 1945 is one of the economic miracles (*Wirtschaftswunder*) of the twentieth century. As the modern appearance of many parts of Germany's historical cities testifies, they were rebuilt from the rubble resulting from the Allied bombing campaign. In 1945 the defeated Germany could not have been in a worse state: amongst the rubble of some of their finest cities, the people of Germany were faced with a collapsed infrastructure and chronic food shortages.

Under the agreement of the London Protocol of 1944, Germany was to be divided up by the Allies. This partition was originally to have been into three zones, but after the surrender in 1945 this was expanded to four occupation zones. The British took charge of the industrialized north-west, the Americans policed the south including Bavaria, Württemberg and Hessen, while the French, oversaw territories adjacent to their borders: the Saarland, Baden and areas in the Rhineland and Palatinate, which appropriately perhaps, included some of the finest wine-growing regions. These zones including the western zone of the partitioned city of Berlin, were democratized in about four years. The whole process began immediately after the fall of the Nazi regime when democratic forces emerged under the auspices of the Western powers and were transmuted into the BRD (Bundesrepublik Deutschland). The Russians had control over East Berlin and those parts of Germany east of a line running from Lübeck on the north coast in a rough curve to the Czech border, from which the GDR (German Democratic Republic) or East Germany was born.

With the descent of Churchill's *iron curtain* and the sovietising of the recently liberated Eastern Europe the West was obliged to shore-up the financially shattered BRD as an integral part of the policy to create a new stronger Europe in order to counterbalance the threat of communism from the east. Thus they did not exact war reparations in the crippling way that occurred after the First War, and which many experts agree was one of the major factors that allowed the rise of Nazism. Instead West Germany was allowed to go straight back into manufacturing. Stalin however, wanted reparations in payment for Soviet losses after the invasion of 1941 and proceeded to move all the available industrial equipment back to Russia. Despite the picture of devastation conjured up by descriptions of post-war defeat, the fact remains that most of Germany's industrial production plants were unscathed by the devastation that afflicted the civilian populations of the great cities. Germany thus had a solid base from which to recommence manufacturing. Germany was also permitted to benefit from the Marshall Aid Plan and by 1947 this much needed injection of capital was producing a modest economic improvement. The other linchpin of economic recovery was the currency reform of 1948. The brainchild of the German economist Ludwig Erhard, the reform involved the creation of a new bank which was to become the Deutsche Bundesbank. The inflationary Reichsmark was abolished overnight and replaced with the new Deutsche Mark. Germans were allowed to exchange their Reichsmarks for the new currency at the rate of 60 Reichmarks for one new mark. On the face of it perhaps a bad deal, but with the increasing stability of the Deutsche Mark it turned out to be a blessing in disguise as the reform spurred an economic revival.

In Berlin the signs of success of the post-war economy in West Germany served only to heighten the discrepancy between the Allied and Russian (i.e. Communist) zones. In June 1948 Stalin used the introduction of the Deutsche Mark as a pretext to blockade Berlin, the Russians sealing the exits from east to west with a view to swallowing up the whole city into East Germany; which they then demanded be recognised as the capital of East Germany. The Allies countered with the famous Berlin airlift which kept the citizens of West Berlin from starvation and finally forced the Russians to abandon their siege of West Berlin in April 1949. This show of solidarity forged a partnership between the western powers and their former enemies.

The tensions between the western powers and the soviets had been building since 1945 and while the siege of Berlin was one symptom another was the re-drawing of boundaries. As eastern Poland and the pre-war German region of Könisberg were absorbed into Russia a large chunk of pre-war Germany east of Stettin and Frankfurt/Oder was given over to Poland. This coupled with the expulsion of ethnic Germans from Czechoslovakia and Hungary saw over seven million people deported into West Germany. These coupled with the numbers of Germans fleeing communism or trying to rejoin families in the west saw the population of West Germany swell by an estimated thirteen million which provided Germany with an almost inexhaustible supply of cheap labour which was a vital element in the recovery of the economy. With cornerstones of the recovery in place Germany was ready to accept a challenge that few nations have ever had to face: to rise from the debris of utter defeat (*der Zusammenbruch*) in a new form — a challenge that was taken up with unparalleled zeal.

Germany's post-war economic recovery was on a scale unmatched by any other European nation. From 1950 to 1964 GNP tripled. By 1960, the BRD was producing 50% more steel than had the enlarged pre-war Germany. Germany had few reasons for gratitude to Hitler, but the Volkswagen car, pioneered under the Nazis, became the greatest symbol of the German post-war export boom.

Other factors contributing to the success of the post-war economy were the self-imposed wage restraints practised by the workers and the relatively small number of unions (sixteen) which avoided the demarcation disputes that so hampered the British post-war industrial relations, and thus the economy.

By the 1960's recession, slight by today's standards, had crept into the German economy producing an unemployment figure of 700,000.

By the 1970's Germany's economy suffered like others in Europe from its reliance on imported energy sources and the oil price rises occasioned by various Middle East crises including the Iranian revolution of 1979. Meanwhile, expenditure on social welfare had risen from 38% of GNP to 51% by 1980. Unemployment reached 8.5% in 1982 and inflation 6.5% in 1981. By 1986, thanks to the widespread boom of the eighties, Germany's budget deficit had fallen from 4.5% in 1982 to an astonishing 1.5%. Inflation was zero.

However, the unemployment figure which was two million in 1986 has grown, in part through the acquisition of the former East Germany and the need to reorganise its industry so as to make it economically competitive. Workforces were trimmed to bring the factories into line with western working practices, however, the high wage deals of West Germany were then applied to companies in the new länder and caused many to fold quite soon after. Currently 4.5 million (11%) German workers are unemployed and this strain on the economy and the high labour and other costs to industry currently mean that the German economy is still in recession while the rest of the EU nations are on an economic upswing. Hence the recent attempts by Chancellor Kohl's coalition government to cut business and personal taxes, especially the Solidarity tax, levied to assist the regeneration of the eastern länder.

For many years the Mark was seen as a token of regeneration, prosperity and socially enlightened capitalism, and many Germans are loath to give it up, yet the German economy forms one of the benchmarks for European Monetary Union. Thus the German government is faced with the inter-twined problems of bringing the economy back into line, while preparing for monetary union and keeping the electorate happy as the 1998 General Election casts a shadow ahead of it. These woes have not been helped by the recent climb of the pound against the mark to a twenty year high. Yet even with all these troubles the German economy is still one of Europe's strongest and the light may well be shining at the end of the tunnel as recent reports show that the number of business deals recorded in the Spring of 1997 involving more than DM1 billion more than doubled the figure for the same period in 1996.

Recent Political History

In modern times, unlike Britain and France, Germany has not enjoyed a continuity of government or even borders. Before 1815, Germany was a jigsaw of little states and principalities ruled by an absolutist aristocracy, the names if not all the boundaries of which are echoed in some of the sixteen present day Länder such as Bavaria, Thuringia and Saxony. In 1871 the first unification of Germany was orchestrated by Bismarck and dominated by a cohort of aristocrats and the legendary army of Prussia, a state which ceased to exist after the end of 1939-45 War. Around Prussia, the smaller satellite states clustered, as if seeking protection. This Imperial period lasted until the end of the Great War when having lost all credibility in the eyes of ordinary Germans it was replaced by the Weimar Republic. This lasted until 1933 when Hitler was elected Chancellor and shortly after created a one-party state. It was a tragedy for the Western world that the experimentally democratic Weimar republic proved so weak and unstable, thus allowing the demonic forces of Nazism to wreak so much havoc across Europe.

The political vacuum left by the obliteration of Hitler and the Nazis was filled by the Allied occupational forces who oversaw the democratization of Germany. The short-lived so-called 'denazification' whereby the Allies supposedly rooted out from public institutions many of those who had held power in the Nazi era was in fact limited to those well-documented cases where people could be proved to have carried out their duties in a particularly brutal way. It is truer to say that a large percentage of Germans holding office were not Nazi fanatics, they had merely gone along with Nazism until it proved a total failure. It became quickly apparent to the Allies that if they barred all former Nazis from holding office, there would be no-one left to run the country. A compromise was reached whereby those with dossiers against them were penalized and the rest were able to retain their posts after the war.

Between 1945 and 1947 the Russians and the Allies set about re-organizing their respective zones into Länder. The commanders of the Russian and Allied zones permitted the formation of four main political parties.   The KPD, CDU, SPD (see Political Parties below) and the Liberal Democratic Party. As the Cold War became an increasing reality, the Allies concentrated their efforts on rapid stabilization of West Germany as a bulwark against the spread of Communism.

In 1946 the Russians forced a merger of the KDP and SPD in their zone into the SED (*Sozialistische Einheitspartei*, Socialist Unity Party) hoping to prompt a similar merger in the Western zone, thus producing a ruling party strong enough to carry out a re-unification of Germany which would remain in the Russian sphere of influence. In the event the attempt was a failure and the Russians' interest in a re-united Germany declined thereafter.

Government

On May 23rd 1949 under a new constitution (the Basic Law), the liberal and democratic Federal Republic of Germany was inaugurated. Full sovereignty was not achieved until May 5th 1955 as the interim occupation regime had to be dismantled in stages. Under the Basic Law Germany is a democratic republic made up of federal states based on the rule of law and social justice. Germany as a whole is governed by a Parliamentary system comprising an upper house, the Bundesrat and a lower house, the effective legislature of the country, the Bundestag. While its Federal status means that Germany, is made up of the sixteen German Länder which reflect features of the political and legislative framework of the nation in their regional administration. So each of the Länder has its own legislature elected by popular vote on the same terms as the Bundestag.

An elected Federal President (*Bundespräsident*) is the Head of State, while the Government is led by the Federal Chancellor (*Bundeskanzler*). The office of Federal President is elected by a Federal Convention made up of members from the Bundestag and others elected by the state parliaments. The Presidential term of office is five years, with re-election allowed only once. It is the President who suggests to the Bundestag a candidate for the office of Federal Chancellor taking into account the party political majority in the Bundestag, the Chancellor is nominated by the President and elected by the Bundestag. In effect the Chancellor is the elected government as it is the Chancellor who creates a Cabinet by proposing members of the Bundestag for the various ministerial posts, their appointment as Federal Minister is the decision of the President. The Federal President at the time of writing is Roman Herzog, while the post of Chancellor is currently held by Helmut Kohl as head of a coalition government which has been in power since 1983.

Following the reunification of Germany the Bundestag voted by a small margin to move the parliament and government from Bonn to Berlin, while the Bundesrat will remain in Bonn for the time being as will eight federal ministries. The ministries which remain in Bonn will have offices in Berlin and those which move to Berlin will do likewise. Moving the main government to Berlin will probably cost DM 20 billion and the process should be completed during the parliamentary recess between 1999 and 2000.

The Bundesrat

The Bundesrat represents the sixteen federal states, and has a part in the legislative process as more than half of all bills need its formal approval especially those concerning the financial or administrative affairs of the states. The senators are not directly elected to this house by the people but are usually cabinet members of the Länder governments. Voting in the Bundesrat is made up of 68 votes split between the various states according to their population. The Bundesrat can object to a particular bill, but this can be overruled by the Bundestag, if an agreement can not be reached then a mediation committee made up from both houses will attempt to resolve the problem. The President of the Bundesrat, elected annually is in effect a deputy to the Federal President.

The Bundestag

The Bundestag, the lower house of 656 seats is elected every four years by universal suffrage, although the number of seats may vary to reflect the electoral situation. The electoral system is a combination of proportional representation and direct election of the candidates nominated by their respective parties. In order to ensure that government can function properly, only parties which poll at least five per cent of the vote or, win three seats under the first-past-the-post system may have representatives in the Bundestag. It is the Bundestag which provides the main check on government affairs as it is this chamber that draws up most legislation. While the Federal Government generates most of the bills, the others being introduced by ordinary members of the Bundestag or Bundesrat, each bill has to face three readings before a vote is taken to pass it or not. Of the 7,500 bills put before the German parliament since 1949 4,600 have been passed into law.

The Electoral System

The conversion to democratic rule, has proved more traumatic for Germany than other European nations. Germany's first attempt at rule by political parties was the Weimar Republic (1919-1933) which was undermined by the iniquitous terms of the Versailles treaty, aggravated by the French occupation of the Ruhr and the crippling burden of war reparations, which left many people sceptical of government. The combination of these factors made a democratic consensus difficult and instead favoured the rise of extremist factions. For all its problems, the Weimar Republic did work for the first ten years. Its fate was ultimately sealed by the world economic crisis which proved to be the last straw. The recession gave rise to the situation where the small National Socialist German Workers Party (NSDAP) from Bavaria could gain votes in northern Germany due to the dissatisfaction of the voters. Eventually this party grew in strength and Hitler came to power, initially as Chancellor of a coalition, President Hindenburg remained distrustful of this undemocratic process which saw the other parties disbanded. On

Hindenberg's death Hitler promptly merged the roles of president and chancellor. The Third Reich benefited by contrast with the turmoil of the Weimar years from a period of economic stability, until Hitler's dreams of an empire plunged Germany into World War.

With the demise of the NSDAP or Nazis, it was left to the Allied Powers to nurture the seeds of German democracy which had lain hidden or imprisoned and from their efforts emerged an extremely stable system. The German political system has several checks to prevent a repeat of the instability of the Weimar period. One of these is the five percent clause, by which only parties gaining at least five percent or three constituency seats can be represented in parliament. Although this hurdle is waived for national minorities such as the Danish minority which has a seat in the Schleswig-Holstein parliament.

Anyone in Germany who is 18 or over and has held German nationality for at least one year may vote or stand for election in parliamentary elections. Bundestag elections are based on a system of personalised proportional representation, each voter has two votes. The first vote is for a constituency candidate, and election is on a first-past-the-post basis from the number of votes cast, the second vote goes to a candidate picked from a list put up by the parties. The votes from constituency and state lists are offset so that the party political composition of the Bundestag reflects the votes for the parties across the constituencies.

Political Parties

The last general elections were in 1994 and so 1998 may see a change in the political landscape. Listed below are the political parties which make up the current Bundestag, with the numbers of seats held in brackets:

CDU (244) & CSU (50): Formed after the war the Christian Democratic Union operates in all the Länder bar Bavaria where its sister party, the Christian Social Union (CSU), operates. The CSU operates solely in Bavaria, although the CDU and CSU act as joint parliamentary group in the Bundestag, and therefore this pair is the largest party. In contrast to the Catholic Centre Party of the Weimar years, these parties draw support from Catholics and Protestants. A former CDU leader was Adenauer the first post-war chancellor and its current leader is Chancellor, Helmut Kohl.

SPD (252): The German Social Democratic Party (*Sozialdemokratische Partei Deutschlands*) is currently the main opposition party though it has coalesced with as well as opposed the CDU. Originally a radical left-wing party its origins go back to 1875 and the formation of a Socialist Labour party compounded from the German General Workers' Association and the Social Democratic Workers Party. After the Second World War the SPD shifted towards the centre in order to court popularity amongst the electorate, although its share of the vote has dropped with the advent of the Greens. The SPD was the party of the much venerated foreign minister of the sixties, Willy Brandt who pioneered the concept of *Ostpolitik* (detente with the East).

FDP(47): The Free Democratic Party (*Freie Demokratische Partei*) a small but influential centre party which has formed coalitions with both the CDU/CSU and the SPD during its history. A firm supporter of liberalization of criminal law and pro-abortion, the FDP was also committed to the support of Ostpolitik. Since 1982 the FDP has been in coalition with the CDU/CSU thus holding the balance of power in the government. Its most prominent member was the foreign minister,

Hans-Dietrich Genscher who resigned in April 1992 after eighteen years in office amid rumours of a growing rift between the FDP and Chancellor Kohl's CDU party.

Alliance 90/The Greens (49): The green movement which began in Germany in the 1970's developed a higher profile in Germany than in any other European country. Some pundits attribute this to the greater need of younger Germans to rebel against the excessive materialism and industrial success of their over orderly nation. The Green Party was formed in 1980. After several victories at Länder level they achieved representation in the Bundestag in 1983 and the European Parliament in 1984. The Greens failed completely at the polls in 1990 only gaining representation by sharing with Alliance 90, the eastern civil rights campaign with whom they have since merged. However they seem likely candidates for a ruling coalition with the SPD after the 1998 elections, especially given their current power-sharing position in 12 of the 16 Länder.

PDS (30): Is the successor to the Socialist Unity Party (SED) which once ruled East Germany although it hasn't been able to establish itself very well in a united Germany. In the 1990 election it only gained seats through the exception to the five percent clause given to the eastern länder. However in the 1994 elections they gained four constituency seats in Berlin.

The current Bundestag is made up of 672 seats due to the share of direct votes within the proportional system. There are other parties which can be found holding seats in the länder parliaments which can climb to greater prominence given the rules of the German political system. Some of these are listed below:

DVU: (Deutsche Volksunion). In common with France, Germany is experiencing the worrying phenomenon of the rise in popularity of extreme right-wing politics. The DVU won six seats in the Bremen state parliament in 1991 and hopes to notch up further success, notably in Schleswig-Holstein. Campaigning on a platform of clamping down on fake asylum seekers of which Germany has had more than its fair share, the success of the DVU has so far largely been at the expense of the SPD, as can be seen from its recent gains in the Hamburg elections.

Republicans: The Republicans are Germany's right wing radical party of the south and in the April 1992 Land elections they polled nearly 11% of the vote at the expense of the CDU. This result was viewed as a protest vote against liberal government policy toward asylum seekers.

Geographical Information

Following reunification in 1990 Germany now occupies an area of 137,777 sq miles/ 356,844 sq kms, geographically, almost at the heart of Europe. Germany is bordered on the west by the Netherlands, Belgium, Luxembourg and France; on the south by Switzerland and Austria, on the east by the Czech Republic and Poland and on the north by Denmark. To the north west lies the North Sea while the Baltic washes the northern beaches. Generally, the north of Germany is formed of the flat North German Plain, while the Central Upland Range of hills and mountains effectively divides north and south Germany as the ground rises towards the Alps. The upland areas of south west Germany are cut by the valleys of the Mosel, the Main and Rhein (Rhine), which water the vineyards of these terraced hills. While further south the land rises again into the slopes of the Schwarzwald (Black Forest) it dips briefly into the Lower Bavarian Plain before rising into the Alps along the Swiss border. More highlands occur in the Bavarian Alps of south east Germany. There are several important navigable rivers including the Donau (Danube), the Mosel, the Rhein, the Elbe and the Weser.

Regional Divisions and Main Towns

The Federal Republic of Germany comprises sixteen Länder, six of which were formed from the former East Germany. The länder including the city of Berlin and the Hanseatic Cities of Bremen and Hamburg are (in German): Baden-Württemburg; Bavaria (Bayern); Brandenburg; Hesse (Hessen); Lower Saxony (Niedersachsen); Mecklenburg-West Pomerania (Mecklenburg-Vorpommern); North-Rhine-Westphalia (Nordrhein-Westfalen); Rhineland- Palatinate (Rhineland-Pfalz); Saarland; Saxony (Sachsen); Saxony-Anhalt (Sachsen-Anhalt); Schleswig-Holstein; Thuringia (Thüringen).

The Länder and Capitals

Land	Capital	Population in Millions	Area in Sq Kms
Baden-Württemberg	Stuttgart	10.3	35,751
Bayern	Munich	12	70,554
Berlin	.....	3.5	884
Brandenburg	Potsdam	2.5	29,059
Bremen	.....	.68	404
Hamburg	.....	1.7	755
Hessen	Wiesbaden	6	21,114
Mecklenburg-Vorpommern	Schwerin	1.8	23,838
Niedersachsen	Hanover	7.8	47,338
Nordrhein-Westfalen	Düsseldorf	17.8	34,071
Rheinland-Pfalz	Mainz	4	19,849
Saarland	Saarbrücken	1.1	2,570
Sachsen	Dresden	4.6	18,337
Sachsen-Anhalt	Magdeburg	2.8	20,445
Schleswig-Holstein	Kiel	2.7	15,729
Thüringen	Erfurt	2,.5	16,251

Population

Germany's population is the largest of any European Union country with 82 million people living there at the end of 1996. The next largest national populations are Italy's 58 million and Britain's 57 million. This figure divided by the area of Germany (357,000 sq km) compared with that of France (56 million people spread over 544,000 sq km) explains why Germany is one of Europe's most densely populated countries with 229 people per square kilometre. The reason for such a density of population can be attributed to the influx of 14 million German-speaking refugees who fled from Eastern Europe after the Second World War, and the high numbers of refugees and asylum seekers from Vietnam and the former Yugoslavia. Thus the population count includes some 7.2 million non-Germans. Many ethnic Germans have returned to Germany from countries which were once German territory, in the three years up to 1992, 2.3 million immigrants of German origin arrived, and this migration is still occurring, in 1996 the number of migrants entering Germany including immigrants of German origin was 252,000.

The population is not evenly distributed across Germany, as can be seen from the table below, only a few cities have more than a million inhabitants, yet the industrialised area of the Rhine-Ruhr is home to 11 million. Here though the towns and cities have a tendency to merge into one long urban sprawl making town population counts difficult. The west of Germany is the more densely populated region having 16 of the 19 towns inhabited by more than 330,000 people, while in the east one fifth of the population live on roughly one third of the land. However, only 26 million people live in the 84 cities of more than 100,000 inhabitants, the majority of Germans live in small towns and villages.

Oddly enough there also seems to be an inverted parallel of the North/South divide across Britain, with the Bavarians taking the part of the Scots; i.e. very careful with their money but fond of a good party. However this idea of Southern Germans being friendlier to strangers will depend on who you talk to. In the cities where populations tend to be mixed and sophisticated, this north/south stereotype tends to break down.

As mentioned above the indigenous German population is interspersed with many foreign nationals. Some of these are guest workers (*Gastarbeiter*) or their relatives, who began arriving in the 1960's and 70's to provide much needed labour for burgeoning German industry. In 1995 the German government claimed that 'Foreigners stimulate every sector of the economy' with 28 percent of welders and 25 percent of hotel staff being foreign given as examples. At one time welcomed for their usefulness to German Industry the gastarbeiter have never really integrated into German society. What will happen to relations between Germans and them now that there are over 4 million Germans in need of employment remains to be seen.

Populations of the Main Cities:

Berlin	3,472,000	Frankfurt	652,000
Bremen	549,000	Hamburg	1,706,000
Cologne (Köln)	964,000	Hanover	526,000
Dortmund	601,000	Leipzig	481,000
Dresden	474,000	Munich (München)	1,250,000
Duisburg	536,000	Nuremberg (Nürnberg)	496,000
Düsseldorf	573,000	Stuttgart	589,000
Essen	617,000		

Climatic Zones

Germany lies on the western edge of the European continent, in the moderately cool west wind zone between the influences of the North Atlantic weather systems and continental climate of the East. Continental influences from the south also make themselves apparent with the regular appearance of the warm alpine Föhn. The driest months are April and October but otherwise precipitation is evenly distributed around the year, although as was seen in July 1997 this can vary. Admittedly much of the flooding then was caused by heavy rains over the uplands of Poland and the Czech Republic. Summers can be especially hot with July being the warmest month with average temperatures ranging between 18-20°C. Germany usually has notable Indian summers brought on by the high pressure systems which normally prevail at that time of year, and winters vary in severity depending on the area. The region crossed by the Rhine and its tributaries generally has an average winter temperature of 1.5°C while the higher points of the Bayerische Wald can drop to -6°C and in the Alps to -10°C. The temperature in Nürnburg in the week around Christmas 1996 varied between -19°C at night and -5°C at noon. However, the open plains of the north are also prone to cold winters lying as they do between the North and Baltic Seas. In the higher altitudes of the German Alps snow-free periods only occur in the summer months. The snow-blanket in the highest range, the Zugspitze, is over six feet thick from December to May.

Average Temperature Chart

Area	January	April	August	November
Berlin	min -12°C/10°F	-2°C/28°F	7°C/46°F	-3°C/25°F
	max 8°C/48°F	22°C/72°F	31°C/88°F	12°C/55°F
Frankfurt	min -10°C/14°F	0°C/32°F	8°C/48°F	-2°C/27°F
	max 10°C/50°F	23°C/75°F	8°C/48°F	-2°C/27°F
Hamburg	min -2°C/28°F	3°C/38°F	12°C/54°F	2°C/37°F
	max 2°C/36°F	12°C/55°F	22°C/72°F	2°C/37°F
München	min -5°C/23°F	3°C/38°F	12°C/55°F	4°C/40°F
	max 1°C/35°F	13°C/56°F	22°C/73°F	13°C/56°F

Regional Guide

Like the shires of England and the States of America, Germany's regional differences are defined not so much by the political divisions of the Länder, each with its own Parliament, but by historical differences, regional dialects and accents. Although the Länder all bear historic-sounding names, only a few, most notably Bavaria and the free cities and regions of Hamburg and Bremen have kept their historical boundaries intact. Others are jigsaws of former duchies and kingdoms, pushed together first by the Prussians and then the Allies. It is for this reason that local identity is strongest in the historically unaltered Länder, and that the modern German's concept of *heimat* (homeland) comes from the region they live in rather than the concept of a German fatherland. Examples of these historic and regional differences can be found in the anti-prussian jokes of the Bavarians, which are mostly aimed at Berliners, these are told in the same manner as jokes in Scotland about the English. Not all of these differences are based on history, to many western Germans with relatives in the East, the accent of a Saxon brings back memories of the GDR's Border Guards. However, these memories appear to be fading, especially as so many physical traces of the iron curtain are being built over.

It is a myth that the greatest visible regional differences are between the north and south: the hackneyed tourist images of fairy-tale castles and medieval towns of half-timbered buildings may be found equally in the north (e.g. Lemgo (Lümeberg), Hamelin (Hameln), Goslar etc.) as in the heavily promoted south (e.g. Bavaria's Schloss Neuschwanstein). After the war it was probably true to say that the north-west was more industrialised than the south, but decades of development mean that both north and south now have their share of industrial areas. Likewise while the heavy industries of East Germany were a blight on the land, the eastern länder are now much cleaner and greener than in the early nineties. More information about the länder of Germany, including maps, can be obtained from German Tourist offices or from a good map and travel guide shop.

Useful Addresses:
German National Tourist Office: 65 Curzon Street, London W1Y 8NE; tel 0171-493 0080. Brochure Request & Information Line 0891-600 100 (Premium rate) Web-site http://www.germany-tourism.de
Edward Stanford Ltd: 12-14 Long Acre, Covent Garden, London WC2E 9LP; tel 0171-836 1321.

Baden-Württemberg

Main cities: Stuttgart, Mannheim, Karlsruhe, Freiburg, Heidelberg, Ulm, Heilbronn.

Baden-Württemberg is one of the two big Länder that make up the south (the other being Bavaria) and is one of the newest states having been formed in 1952. The region is made up of two distinct historical entities with divergent cultures. Baden is the region to the west which includes most of the Black Forest and whose largely Catholic inhabitants are generally more laid-back than those of Württemberg (often known as Swabians after the local mountain range), who embody more of the stereotypical hard-working, houseproud German who keeps a watchful eye on the purse strings.

The south of Germany is often referred to as the 'sunbelt' and is traditionally less industrial than the north. However this is perhaps truer of Bavaria than Baden-Württemberg whose industrial base grew up in the nineteenth century. But the modern state manages to earn its income from work and pleasure, given that more tourists visit Baden-Württemberg each year than it has inhabitants, it is Germany's third largest wine producer, yet it is also the location for the headquarters of Bosch, Daimler-Benz and Porsche. Since the 1970's a successful drive to keep up with new technology has paid dividends and Baden-Württemburg boasts no fewer than 130 research institutes and a dozen science parks where university professors work part-time for companies they have been encouraged to set up themselves. Daimler-Benz has its biggest plant in Germany at Sindelfingen just outside Stuttgart and the mighty IBM corporation has its European headquarters nearby. Publishing is also a major industry, with 40 percent of all German books being published here.

In addition to the scenic attributes of the Swabian Alps and the Black Forest Baden-Württemberg includes the northern shores of Lake Constance (Bodensee) which forms part of the border with Switzerland and Austria. It is also home to Germany's oldest university, Heidelberg and eight others, including Tübingen, which are equally at home with venerable traditions and the latest high technology research. A high speed data link is being constructed to link the universities, so it shouldn't be too long before Baden-Württemberg produces modern scholars to rival those of the past such as Schiller, Hegel or Heidigger.

The regional capital Stuttgart experienced something of a building crisis in the early nineties, brought on by the unsuitability of its hilly environs for building on. This forced prices for land and property in Stuttgart to an all-time record for

The Länder and Regional Capitals of Germany

DENMARK

Baltic Sea

North Sea

Kiel

SCHLESWIG-HOLSTEIN

MECKLENBURG-WEST POMERANIA

Schwerin

Hamburg

NETHERLANDS

Bremen

LOWER SAXONY

BRANDENBURG

Berlin

Hannover

Potsdam

POLAND

NORTH RHINE-WEST PHALIA

SAXONY-ANHALT

Halle

Düsseldorf

Erfurt

SAXONY

Bonn

Dresden

BELGIUM

HESSE

THURINGIA

RHINELAND PALATINATE

Wiesbaden

LUX.

Mainz

CZECH REPUBLIC

Saarbrucken

SAARLAND

BAVARIA

Stuttgart

FRANCE

BADEN-WÜRTTEMBERG

München

SWITZERLAND

LIECH.

AUSTRIA

ITALY

◉ City State

| 0 | 100 miles |
| 0 | 150 km |

anywhere in Germany, however, Munich has since taken this lead. As a consequence of this, people in their thousands and industries in their hundreds have been relocating to smaller towns nearby.

Mannheim in the north-west corner of the region is a masterpiece of seventeenth century town planning; it was laid out in 1607 on the grid pattern (later exported to America), which admirers of Lisbon in Portugal, will appreciate. Throughout the nineteenth century, Mannheim became steadily industrialised. It is the home of the Benz automobile company whose founder demonstrated his prototype here in 1886 and named the car after his daughter, Mercedes. Heavily bombed, Mannheim has unfortunately lost much of its original charm. This cannot be said of Heidelberg, 18 kms distant, which was spared the attention of the bombers it is said, largely because of its pre-war popularity with Americans. Even today there is a large resident community of Americans in Heidelberg.

A former state capital of Baden, Karlsruhe (Charles' Rest) is positively a neophyte in the line-up of historic German cities. It did not exist before 1715 and like Mannheim is a fascinating example of town-planning. The central point is the Schloss from which the main avenues radiate outwards like the rays of a sun. Karlsruhe is chiefly important as the seat of the two highest courts of Germany: the Federal Court of Justice and the Federal Constitutional Court.

Freiburg im Breisgau, usually referred to as just Freiburg, is a historic university town near the border with France. It has a retained a relaxed and lively atmosphere, which it owes to its Austrian overlords the Habsburgs, who held sway here for over four centuries until 1805. It's cosmopolitan atmosphere is derived in part from the university and in part from its proximity to both France and Switzerland, this atmosphere combined with its convenient position for visits to the Black Forest including the famous spa of Baden-Baden, make this city interesting enough for serious consideration as a place to live and work.

Bavaria (Bayern)

Main cities: München, Nürnberg, Augsberg, Regensburg, Würzburg.
The largest of the Länder, and home to 12 million people, the Bavarian state dates from the 6th century and its people are noted for speaking a pronounced dialect. Bavaria is also home of Germany's highest mountain the Zugspitze (2,962 metres). The clichéd view of Bavaria of jovial, beer-swilling, wurst-gorged, inhabitants and mad kings is most relevant to the south of the region around the capital Munich (München). Also found in the south are the Swabian Alps (south west), a string of lakes (Ammersee, Starnbergersee or Würmsee, Walchensee, Tegernsee and Chiemsee) and the Bavarian Alps which form the boundary with Austria. The perfection of this idyll is seldom marred except by the dreaded Föhn, a warm, dry, headache-inducing wind that blows on the German side of the Alps. The River Danube (Donau) flows from the west right across central Bavaria and for 240kms/ 149 miles beside it from Ulm to Regensburg is a well-worn cycle route. To the north of the Donau lies Franconia (Franken) and the main northern city of Nürnberg. To the east lies the untamed swathe of the Bavarian Forest and ultimately the border with the Czech Republic. Until the 1950s Bavaria was primarily an agrarian state, while agriculture and forestry still play key roles over 90 percent of the state's gross domestic product comes from the production and service sector.

The former kingdom of Bavaria was ruled by the Wittelsbach dynasty, first as Dukes then as kings, from 1180 to 1918. Bavarians are very conscious of their long history of autonomy and their national flag proclaims *Freistaat Bayern* (The Free State of Bavaria), somewhat inaccurately since they are now firmly part of

Germany and separatism is not a serious issue, although Franconians will point out that they are nothing like Bavarians. Bavaria does however have a reactionary image stemming from the brief communist government of Munich in 1919, and the 1920's when it was the headquarters of the Nazi party. These tendencies were echoed in the strong electoral support in the north of the state, mainly amongst the peasantry, for the extreme right during the 1960's. Bavaria is also notable for its cultural events such as the Munich Oktoberfest, and the Bayreuth Festival with its season of Wagnerian Opera, not to mention the Passion Plays of Oberammergau, which have occured every ten years since 1634.

The regional capital could hardly be elsewhere than the important city of München which is stylish, extremely hedonistic and friendly, with a frenetic business tempo which belies the jolly rustic, Bavarian image. Despite the CSU predominance in rural Bavaria, München itself has always been, and is, staunchly 'red' (i.e. SPD voting and thus ruled). Recently however extreme right-wing movements have also made some electoral inroads in München.

During the Second World War, München endured over 70 air raids but unlike many German cities managed to adhere to aesthetic principles in its rebuilding and reconstruction, which add much to the city's appeal. Host to the ill-fated Olympic Games of 1972, Munich has splendid sports facilities. Other plus points include one of the best integrated public transport systems in Europe and a huge new airport which opened in 1992. München is popular with foreigners as a place to live and work and currently around 20% of its 1.25 million population is estimated to be non-German. Despite a lively cultural scene, München's most celebrated annual event remains the Oktoberfest, a two-week orgy of beer-drinking and merry-making that takes place in marquees (*Bierzelte*) on the Theresien Meadow under the gaze of a 60 foot statue, the Goddess Bavaria. This rowdy and enjoyable custom dates from 1810 though it would appear that the majority of participants these days are from Australia. It isn't all beer and pig knuckles though as München is home to six million volumes in one of the largest libraries in Europe.

Bavaria's other most famous city is the medieval city of Nuremberg (Nürnberg), sadly still inextricable in many people's minds from pre-war Nazi rallies and post war Nazi trials. Although most of the Nazi era architecture has been destroyed and built over, especially during the expansion of the city in the 1950's, some does remain and is used to teach school parties to avoid the mistakes of the past. Apart from the remarkable castle (*Burg*), the city is notable for the twin churches of St Sebaldus (*Sebalduskirche*)and St Lawrence (*Lorenzkirche*) which sit on the slopes either side of the river Pegnitz. Both of which have been restored from almost complete ruin during the war. In the fifteenth and sixteenth centuries Nürnberg was a flourishing centre of Renaissance arts and was the home of Hans Sachs and Albrecht Dürer; who's house is now a museum in a street below the Burg. Modern Nürnberg has an industrial centre developing between it and nearby Fürth, so that soon an industrial conurbation will form, focusing on electrical and mechanical engineering, plastics and toys.

Augsburg, situated on the Romantic Road, is one of the Germany's oldest cities having been founded in 15 B.C. It is renowned chiefly for its Renaissance art and architecture. It is also an important manufacturing centre for a variety of industries from textiles to automobiles.

The historic city of Regensburg is situated on the Donau and has been inhabited since Roman times when it was known as *Castra Regina*. Its main attractions are the intact medieval architecture, including the Stone Bridge dating from 1146, and innumerable beer gardens popular with the large student population.

Würzburg, a city situated on the River Main in the north west of Bavaria, is the capital of the wine district of Franconia. Wurzburg which lost much of its architectural heritage in one air raid, was once the seat of Bishop Princes and their former palace is renowned for one of the most beautiful staircases in the world. These days the city can boast a busy electronics industry and Bavaria's three largest vineyards.

Berlin

From Imperial capital to bombed-out wreck and bridge between ideologies, Berlin is a city that has seen more drama and adversity in its 125 year life than most European cities of greater lineage. So it is hardly surprising that the reunification of the two halves of Berlin has come to symbolize the reunification of Germany itself. Until November 1989 West Berlin was an isolated enclave of West Germans situated deep in East Germany with the Berlin Wall, erected almost overnight in 1961, dividing the city between Democratic West and Communist East Germany. On November 9th 1989 the GDR government abandoned all border checkpoints in the city and amidst scenes of great emotion the *Wessis* (West Germans) and *Ossis* (East Germans) danced on the Wall, the politicians, including the patriarchal Willy Brandt, arrived to shed tears at the Brandenburg Gate and the dismantling of the concrete remains of the Berlin wall began. Reducing the psychological wall will take longer as there are still tensions between east and west in this city of contradictions; flamboyant yet coy. Heartland of a dictatorship, and home to those who resisted it, East German capital while West German city, the inhabitants still take a great deal of pride in Kennedy's famous phrase 'Ich bin ein Berliner', while pointing out that it can also be read as 'I am a doughnut'.

Modern Berlin is all change as thousands of building sites transform what was once no-man's land into apartments and offices. A City which lost ninety percent of its buildings in the war is now a gleaming catalogue of modern architectural practices. Where Checkpoint Charlie stood on the Friedrichstrasse, is now a new business centre, Alexanderplatz, once a grim Stalinesque square, is to become a precinct of shops and offices. In 1994 it was estimated that 20,000 new apartments were being built a year, however, even this was estimated to be short of the housing pool needed for Berlin. Hopefully this will be remedied before the Government moves there, but at present good accommodation is in demand.

In 1991 it was decided that Berlin would once again be the German capital provoking the flood of new buildings to house the ministries and their 12,000 staff. Now much of the necessary infrastructure has been completed, and the actual movement of the government ministries is planned to happen between now and the year 2000. While the old seat of the German parliament, the Reichstag has been redeveloped by Sir Norman Foster, Germany's largest pre-war synagogue has been rebuilt on Oranienburgerstrasse, and the British and American Embassies are transferring their main offices here from Bonn.

Berlin now has twelve Technology and Business Incubation Centres, the first being created by enterprising academics, which provide advice and financial assistance for fledgling companies. Once an industrial city the home of Siemens and AEG, with Daimler-Benz and Sony developing new sites, Berlin is also rapidly developing its service sector. In addition to this it is also home to 250 research institutes and three universities (the Humboldt, Free and Technical) giving it Germany's largest student population with 147,000 students living and studying there.

As well as the recent draping of the Reichstag by Christo, and the collection of the works of 130 artists in the Age of Modernism Exhibition, Berlin is the site for a new branch of the Guggenheim Art Museum. Musically Berlin is home to several major orchestras and three opera houses, not forgetting the cultural event of the year for many young Germans; the Love Parade in the summer, arguably the world's biggest open air rave, and while some Berliners complain about the amount of rubbish it generates others are happily counting the DM 2 million of extra revenue it brings. Berlin may be famous for the bars and cabarets, some of which are building on the exotic club life of the twenties, but the city is also famous for its many beer halls and more than a few Irish pubs, most of which are actually run by Irishmen.

Brandenburg

Main cities: Potsdam, Frankfurt an der Oder, Brandenburg.
Brandenburg surrounds Berlin but has a smaller population spread over a greater area, even so they recently voted against merging with Berlin, contrary to the plans of both parliaments. This stubborn nature may go some way to explain how the people of this area came to be a major European power. Characterized by marshland and massive pine forests this area was once written off as barren and useless owing to an over-endowment of lakes. This was changed 250 years ago, at the behest of Frederick II, by the engineering skills of the Dutch who drained much of the marsh to create the Oderbruch (the scene of recent flooding as the dykes collapsed after unimaginable flooding of the river Oder), an area which was to become Berlin's vegetable garden. Prior to the creation of Prussia, the area was the largest electoral province ruled by the Hohenzollern dynasty, in 1685 the 'Great Elector' Frederick William signed an edict granting religious tolerance and freedom from persecution to 20,00 hugenots, lutherans and jews, in contrast to later views of the state he helped create. Under Frederick II, Prussia became a European military power, his home was the magnificent Sanssouci Palace, designed by him but based on Versailles.

The main city, Potsdam is situated on the Havel river and was a royal seat of the Hohenzollern Electors of the Brandenburg March, the city still has many Baroque palaces from this period. In 1945 the Cecilienhof Palace was the site of the 1945 Potsdam Conference at which the Allies met and agreed upon the division of nearby Berlin, into four zones of occupation.

Brandenburg's traditional agricultural output has been market vegetables for Berlin, rye and oilseed, however the economy is expanding into the electronics and optics markets, with over 120 major investors. There are many canals linking waterways across northern Germany and the world's largest ship elevator can be found on the Oder-Havel canal. Other revenues come from tourism and wildlife as there are numerous nature reserves in the woods (Uckermark, Elbtalaue, and Spreewald). The area around the lakes is a popular recreation area and tourist attraction.

Potsdam is not just a museum town for tourists, but also the centre of an industrial area of chemical, textile and clothing factories. Oil refineries and lignite-fired power stations are the major blots on the landscape, particularly the latter which claim to be the largest of their kind in the world. While Frankfurt an der Oder is home to the Viadrina University where Kleist and the von Humboldt's studied.

Hansestadt Bremen

The Free Hanseatic city of Bremen is, like Bavaria, Hamburg and Saxony a political entity which existed prior to 1945. A Land in its own right, situated on the river Weser within Lower Saxony, it is, after San Marino, the second oldest city republic in the world. A bishopric since 787 and granted the rights of a free city in

1186 Bremen joined the Hanseatic League in 1358. Its subsidiary city the sheltered, deep water harbour of Bremerhaven which lies 65 kms to the north was founded in 1827 at the mouth of the Weser.

The economic life of Bremen revolves around trade and shipping, each year 10,000 ships link Bremen with 1,000 ports around the world. Bremerhaven is Europe's largest container terminal, while the Bremen Securities Exchange has been in operation for over three hundred years. In addition to this Bremen is noted for ship-building, luxury foods and also has a key role in aerospace component manufacture.

In addition to the university with its emphasis on engineering and natural sciences Bremen has five research institutes conducting work on subjects ranging from Polar Ecology to Applied Beam Technology.

With its historic squares of renaissance buildings and gothic cathedral Bremen attracts many tourists and the 960 year old Bremen Free Market on the Bürgerweide is one of Germany's largest fairs.

Hansestadt Hamburg

Germany's second largest city and as mentioned above a state in its own right, Hamburg is also Germany's principal seaport even though it is situated 90kms inland on the Elbe. Founded in 811 it began to flourish in the twelfth century and was one of the founders of the Hanseatic League. Hamburg has always maintained a policy of structural change, which coupled with some disastrous fires and the war has left little of the old city standing. The most notable building is the baroque St Michael's Church, locally known as 'Michel' it is the city's landmark. Most great ports have a red-light district but Hamburg's Reeperbahn would appear to be world renowned.

Hamburg is a focus for trade with the east with around 370 firms from Asia trading here, amongst the 3,000 firms engaged in the import and export business. Hamburg also has a thriving service industry, the city is the banking and insurance capital of northern Germany. As well as trade Hamburg is famous for ship-building and the attendant port industries of refining and processing raw materials. The city is also a major media centre, being home to several publishing groups and broadcasters, employing over 50,000 people. Although some of them may move to Berlin when the government moves there, at present 15 of the largest circulation magazines are produced here and Hamburg based editions account for 50 percent of German press circulation.

New developments helped by Hamburg's own Business Development Corporation created 20,000 jobs in one five year period. The city has also benefited from reunification in regaining its traditional hinterland which now means that goods can move across north Germany for export through Hamburg. In the mid-eighties the city developed links with Scandinavia to replace this lost trade, which now means that it benefits both ways while Rostock in the east has lost out. Another development is the construction of the Transrapid levitating train to run between the city and Berlin.

Hamburg might be Germany's second largest industrial centre but it is at the same time an incredibly green city with almost half of its land area being given over to arable crops and private gardens or to public parks and heaths. Landscape and nature reserves account for 28 percent of the city's area.

The city was the site of Germany's first opera house and as well as hosting Handel's first opera, the international career of the Beatles was launched here. Brahms is another famous son and Hamburg was home to the publisher of Heinrich Heine's novels.

Hesse (Hessen)

Main cities: Wiesbaden, Frankfurt am Main, Darmstadt, Kassel, Marburg.
Hessen with its population of six million is Germany's fifth largest state and is composed of a group of formerly autonomous states. Before Bismarck's unification the region encompassed four, principalities and the free city of Frankfurt, which were absorbed into Prussia with the exception of the Grand Duchy of Hesse-Darmstadt. In 1945 the American military government merged the Duchy with the recently Prussian territory to form this new Land. The Land parliament occupies the former Ducal Palace of the Duchy of Nassau in the regional capital, Wiesbaden. Hessen is phenomenally prosperous thanks to a combination of industries and banking. The region is focused on the dynamic city of Frankfurt, Germany's answer to Manhattan and home to the German Stock Exchange, the Deutsche BundesBank, and more than 400 other banks. Frankfurt also has Germany's premier airport and is home to the national carrier Lufthansa.

Historians might refer to Hesse as a unity born from diversity but geographers would consider it a colourful jumble of uplands and valleys with the rivers Main, Wetter and Eder cutting through the upland ranges of the Tanau and Vogelsberg. In addition to the wide Rhine (Rhein) valley along which the state border with Rheinland-Pfalz runs. Hessians speak a marked dialect and the local cuisine has developed to be accompanied by the regional wines. The Bergstrasse and Rheingau are among Germany's best fruit and wine growing areas, as this is the home of the Rheinwein and Reisling.

With four major industries represented by Hoechst, Degussa, Volkswagen and Opel (i.e. chemical, motor vehicle, mechanical and electrical engineering) and the financial heartland of Germany it is little wonder that Hesse's gross domestic product is over DM 50,000 per capita. The Rhein-Main airport just outside Frankfurt employs over 60,000 and is one of Europe's busiest. Frankfurt is also famous for hosting several trade fairs of which the autumn Frankfurt Book Fair (Frankfurter Buchmesse) is the world's biggest, drawing over 9,500 companies from a hundred countries, and an estimated 270,000 visitors.

The cities of Wiesbaden, Frankfurt and Darmstadt are all clustered together in the southern corner of Hesse, while the north of Hesse is less heavily populated. Kassel is the main town here, home to the Brothers Grimm Museum while the old university city of Marburg, one of Germany's finest medieval gems lies to the south west of Kassel.

Lower Saxony (Niedersachsen)

Main Towns: Hannover, Braunschweig, Göttingen.
The modern Lower Saxony was based on former kingdom of Hannover with some duchies and principalities tacked on, so that it is now the second largest state in Germany. However, it is the least populated, with 7.8 million people spread across 47,388 square kilometres stretching between the North Sea and the Harz Mountains. Much of Lower Saxony is taken up by the North German Plain and is therefore rather flat and windswept. In between the sea and the mountains lie remote heathlands, the metropolitan area of Hannover, and the Hildesheimer Börde an area of the most fertile soil in Germany. The East Frisian islands, the coast, the mountains, the Teutoberg Forest and the Lüneberg Heath (Germany's oldest nature reserve) provide recreation for millions of Germans who swell the population on holiday each year. Brunswick (Braunschweig) was one of the four major metropolises of the Late Middle Ages, the royal house of Hannover

provided England and Wales with King George I, and it was on the Lüneberg Heath that the German surrender was signed in 1945.

The anglicised versions of some the city names of Lower Saxony should be familiar to British readers too. Until recent changes, many pubs across Britain were called the Brunswick Arms, Hamelin (Hameln) and its rodent clearing flautist should also be familiar from childhood memory for most readers.

While two thirds of the state's economy is agricultural, Lower Saxony provides one fifth of Germany's natural gas, and Wolfsburg is the home of Volkswagen and the famous Beetle. Over 50 million cars have been built by Volkswagen to date, with MAN producing trucks here too. While the levitating Transrapid Train route is being built across the state to run between Hamburg and Berlin, the train itself is being built and tested in Emsland. Transport figures heavily in Lower Saxony as the state has the most extensive network of cycle paths in Germany. Wilhelmshaven, which was once home to the Imperial German Navy is now Germany's deepwater super-tanker port. Brunswick is home to Central European Time at the Federal Institute of Physics and Metrology, and the Brothers Grimm, in addition to their work on folk tales began compiling the Deutsches Wörterbuch (a comprehensive German dictionary) at Göttingen University in 1838. The last volume of this was completed in 1961.

Mecklenburg-West Pomerania (Mecklenburg-Vorpommern)

Main cities: Schwerin, Rostock, Neubrandenburg Greifswald.

The Land of a thousand lakes, Mecklenburg-West Pomerania with its island of Rügen, is probably most well known through the art of Caspar David Friedrich, the state's most famous son. The state forms Germany's northern coast, the Mecklenburgische Seenplatte, on the Baltic and is noted for its scenic beauty. The many lakes set amidst gently rolling hills, forests and meadows make this an area popular with both holiday makers and wading birds. Of the large lakes (Müritz, Schwerinersee, Plauersee and Kummerowersee) the Müritz is the largest in Germany, with an area of 117 square kilometres. Off the Pomeranian coast is the large island of Rügen with its stunning white cliffs, to the west of which is the island of Hiddensee, which is popular with naturalists. Pomerania was historically Swedish territory before becoming the Prussian state Pommern, while Mecklenburg an independent part of the German Empire, spent three hundred years divided into two states; Mecklenburg Schwerin and Mecklenburg Strelitz. The region is mostly remarkable for the dialect spoken which is actually Low German (*Plattdeutsch*).

Four of the state's cities are Hanseatic towns from the period when the area dominated trade with Scandinavia, a tradition which meant that Rostock became the home of the GDR's biggest shipyards. Ship-building is still a major industry in the city, but luxury foods, engineering and construction are beginning to take larger shares in the state economy. Nonetheless agriculture has always dominated the region, with 80 percent of the land being tilled to produce grain, oilseed and potatoes.

As noted earlier tourism is a major industry with over 2 million visitors a year to the state's lakes, cliffs, reserves (there are nearly 400 nature and landscape reserves) and the three national parks.

The Land capital, Schwerin was founded in 1160 and is situated on the southern end of the Schwerinersee and was once home to the Grand Dukes of Mecklenburg-Schwerin, whose palace is now home to the länder parliament. The city is also notable for its Brick Gothic cathedral. While Rostock is a university city and is actually larger than Schwerin, it is best known for its seaside resort of Warnemünde and the festive Hanseatic Port Days. Rostock was also home to Field Marshal Blücher, who commanded the Prussian force at Waterloo.

North-Rhine-Westphalia (Nordrhein-Westfalen)

Main cities: Düsseldorf, Münster, Dortmund, Duisberg, Bonn, Essen, Köln, Aachen.

The most populous of the länder North Rhine-Westphalia has twice the population of Bavaria but only half its surface area. The Rhine-Ruhr conurbation, with no less than fifteen cities is one of the most built-up areas in Europe, in one area of the map the cities of Duisberg, Essen, Bochum and Dortmund simply merge into one urban strip 60 kilometres long by 25 kilometres wide. The Ruhr with its 30 power stations is Germany's main source of energy, although there is less heavy industry in the area since the clean up campaign of the sixties to cut pollution and there is a pastoral fringe to the area with lakes and wooded valleys. Although the Federal Capital, Bonn, is just south of Cologne (Köln) the regional capital is at Düsseldorf, which also has another of Germany's main airports.

Modernisation and a desire to clean up industry has led to a great diversification in the state's economic structure, where once the coal and steel industry employed one in eight workers they now employ one in twenty-five. In addition to this there are over 1,600 firms focusing on environmental technology in the area, and half the land is given over to agriculture and forestry. New industries such as media and culture employ 230,000 people as part of the 60 percent of the state's workforce employed in the service sector, almost half of Germany's top 100 firms have their headquarters in the region. Düsseldorf is one of Germany's banking centres, while Duisberg on the Rhine is the world's largest inland port, controlling cargo traffic from the North Sea to Switzerland. One might assume that the move of capital to Berlin would signal Bonn's decline, but Bonn has been designated the federal city for science and communication, home to Deutsche Telekom and the Centre for Advanced European Studies And Research (CAESAR). Bonn is also home to Haribo's Gummi-Bears (*Gümmibärchen*), the little jelly teddy bears which generate two billion deutschemarks of income per year.

One of the great cities of Germany is Cologne (Köln), founded by the Romans in 33 BC, which owes much of its importance to being accessible from the North Sea via the river Rhine on which it is situated. Cologne was practically flattened by wartime bombing, but miraculously the famous cathedral (the *Dom*) survived and ironically the bombing allowed the discovery of much of the roman city beneath the medieval buildings. One of the charms of Köln is that its inhabitants (*Kölner*) are easy going and friendly, even if the Kölsch dialect is almost incomprehensible to outsiders. Düsseldorf, after Frankfurt, is a major centre of international finance and banking, while Dortmund is home to Becks beer and has overtaken München as a brewing centre. With its 99 theatres, 15 opera stages, and 390 museums any culturally minded individual would enjoy life in the region which gave birth to Beethoven.

Rhineland-Palatinate (Rheinland-Pfalz)

Main cities: Mainz, Ludwigshafen, Koblenz, Trier

Home to Gutenberg, Karl Marx and Martin Luther's Reformation, the Rheinland-Palatinate is used to dramatic change. The most recent being the amalgamation by the French of several disparate parts of Germany into one new länder in 1945. This picturesque landscape, crossed by the Rhein and Mosel, is probably Germany's most famous wine producing area. Many of the cities spread out along the Rhine are some of Germany's oldest: Koblenz, Mainz, Worms and Speyer can each boast 2,000 years of occupation, while Trier on the Mosel (near the border with Luxembourg) has the spectacular Roman remains of the *Porta Nigra*. At the confluence of the Rhine and Mosel stands the city of Koblenz. The stretch of the Rhine from Koblenz to Mainz cuts through slate mountains crowned with the picturesque ruins of many castles. This is the haunt of the Lorelei and other characters of German folklore. It was at Mainz that Johannes Gutenburg developed mass printing techniques which have since had such an incalculable impact on modern civilization.

To the south west, flows the Mosel whose banks are dotted with vineyards and villages like Bernkastel and Piesport, familiar to German-wine lovers. Unfortunately the Wine road (*Weinstrasse*) which runs from Schweigen on the French border to Bockenheim is a heavily publicised tourist industry in its own right and should therefore be avoided in high season. Although the wine festivals in September are worth braving the crowds for. Just as inspirational in its own way but considerably less trampled and less river-oriented, is the lower part of the Rhineland-Palatinate, including the modest Hunsrück mountains and the Pfalz which is heavily forested. This area enjoys a certain popularity with the Germans but few foreigners have heard about it and its wooded tranquillity makes it an ideal escape.

While the region is Germany's largest wine producer, there are other heavier industries present. Ludwigshafen is one of the few blots on the Rhineland-Pfalz with its many factories, including the chemicals giant BASF, which form an industrial belt linking up with Mannheim across the Rhine in Baden-Württemburg. The current chancellor of Germany, the affable Helmut Kohl is about the best thing to have come out of Ludwigshafen which is his home town. While Mainz still maintains its links with the media, the land capital is home to Europe's largest television network ZDF and its rival SAT1.

Saarland

Main cities: Saarbrücken, Saarlouis.

Of the German States Saarland is the smallest Land of all, only the three city states are geographically smaller. For much of modern history the Saarland has been fought over, like two dogs over a bone by the French and Germans. French until 1815, it then passed into German hands until the end of the Great War when in 1920 under the terms of the armistice its administration was in the hands of the League of Nations. In 1935 the people voted to return to German rule, an act which was repeated twenty years later in 1955, when the region again voted for integration with Germany having been under French administration since the Second World War. This small area which provided a prototype for re-unification in the fifties, now seems to be repeating the procedure on a European level with the cross-border activities of the Saar-Lor-Lux mega-region. This is an initiative undertaken by the Saarland, Luxembourg and Lorraine in France to 'Think European: Act Local' in an attempt at mutual integration. In fact the area has been central to Franco-German and European politics since the Middle Ages, when the Dukes of Burgundy lived here.

The Saarland takes its name from the river Saar a tributary of the Mosel, which meanders through a picturesque countryside of sloping vineyards. Once prized for its coal and iron ore deposits the area's major exports are now the fine reislings grown along the Saar. Although cars and steel still take a share of the state's output, much of the local workforce commutes across one border or another thus clouding the employment and productivity statistics.

Saxony (Sachsen)

Main cities: Dresden, Leipzig, Chemnitz, Zwickau.

Home to the renowned Meissen pottery in Dresden, Saxony is the most densely populated of the new Länder. The Free State of Saxony was ruled by a dynasty of Saxon kings from the fifteenth century up to 1918. Saxony has been a home to much of Germany's cultural history; Bach, Strauss, Wagner and Schumann all worked on and performed famous pieces here. During the reigns of Augustus the Strong (1694-1733) and Augustus III (1733-1763), the capital Dresden became North Europe's centre for art, music, literature, and architecture earning the title 'Florence on the Elbe'. The other great city of the east, Leipzig is also in Saxony. In the eighteenth century Leipzig was a lively commercial city with strong artistic trends, especially in music: Johann Sebastian Bach, who worked there from 1723-1750, is probably the city's most illustrious maestro.

Many of the region's factories were shut down following unification but the region is on an economic upswing. The former Trabant factory has been taken over by a private enterprise and now turns out autoparts for Mercedes amongst others. Dresden may attract five million tourists a year to its architectural glories and the Meissen pottery works but it is also home to many modern innovations. The first reflex cameras were produced here and at Scharfenstein the first CFC-Free fridge was developed. Since unification Saxony has seen much investment from global operators; Shell, BP and Phillips have all begun to operate here and the electronics giant Siemens is investing in a microelectronics centre in Dresden. Volkswagen has an automobile plant at Zwickau with an engine plant at nearby Chemnitz.

In the thirties Chemnitz, Dresden and Leipzig formed a triangle of industrial activity, and suffered immensely for it during the war. Dresden still bears many scars (the investment in reconstruction and restoration currently exceeds 24 billion DM) but the Semper Opera House and Zwinger and Taschenburg Palaces have been reconstructed and plans are in hand to rebuild the famous baroque buildings of the city, including reassembling the Frauenkirche. Once the most imposing Protestant church in Germany it has been, for fifty years, a memorial in rubble to a day and a night of bombing.

Leipzig has always had a large book trade and it is now home to the most modern large scale mail order house in the world, while the number of banks opening branches here are likely to turn the city into Germany's third major financial centre. The former airport has been converted into a conference and business fair centre and the annual book fair in March is liable to rival Frankfurt's. Leipzig's University was founded in 1409 making it one of Germany's oldest institutions. and Chemnitz has eastern Germany's second largest Technical University.

Saxony may once have been home to some of the worst sites of industrial pollution, but much has been cleaned up, and while the region's wineries were decimated by years of neglect there still remain 310 hectares of vineyard producing some fine Weissburgunder wines.

Saxony-Anhalt (Sachsen-Anhalt)

Main cities: Halle, Magdeburg, Naumburg, Dessau.

Saxony Anhalt has only a brief recent history, its territory (the Altmark to the north, the Magdeburger Börde, the Harz mountains and Anhalt to the east) is a patchwork of older regions ruled by other states; Anhalt was a minor princedom founded by the Ascanian princes and flourished in the 18th Century under the Princes of Anhalt-Dessau. Ranging from the Harz mountains to the North German plains Saxony Anhalt is a region of extraordinarily scenic landscapes. The state capital, Magdeburg, on the banks of the Elbe dates from 805 and is home to the first Gothic cathedral built in Germany. Saxony Anhalt was the heart of the Reformation with Martin Luther's birthplace at Eisleben and the church in Wittenberg where he nailed up his theses, here. A major industrial city of the east, Halle has the honour of being the birthplace of Georg Friedrich Händel in 1685, and is notable for its cathedral church and Red Tower.

The south of the state was the industrial region, with Dessau being home to both the first all metal commercial airliner (in the Junkers Ju52) and the first colour film in the 1930s. Heavy machinery and vehicle construction are still dominant in the economies of Magdeburg and Dessau. The Bitterfeld chemical works were once a synonym for industrial pollution, but chemical production in the Halle-Mersburg-Bitterfeld triangle has occurred since the 19th Century and continues today, although using cleaner technology. The old heavy industry and disregard for the environment have caused a major clean-up problem but intense investment in this area is helping to reduce the problems.

Agriculture has a fair share of the economy as the Magdeburger Börde and Harz foreland contain rich, fertile loess soils. Grain, sugar-beet, potatoes and vegetable crops all grow well here and Germany's northernmost vineyards are to be found along the Saale.

The state is rich in art and architectural history, apart from being the home to the Nazi's Stuka aircraft. Dessau was the home of Walter Gropius and the Bauhaus movement thought of as degenerate by Hitler, but lauded by architects around the world; the town's Wörlitz Park has one of Europe's finest English-style gardens. In the Harz mountains Naumberg is the site of the art-historically important 13th Century statues of Ute and Ekkhard, remarkable for their life-like faces and Quedlinburg has 1,200 half timbered houses in its Old Town, making the town a UNESCO World Heritage site.

Schleswig-Holstein

Main cities: Kiel, Lübeck, Flensburg.

Bordered by the North Sea and the Baltic, Schleswig-Holstein is Germany's most northern state, and home to an ethnic mix of inhabitants. Hence one can hear conversations in German, Low German, Danish and Frisian, as the state includes the Frisian Islands off its western coast and is home to over 50,000 Danes. From the red cliffs of Helgoland, across the islands of Sylt, Föhr and Amrum and to the mud flats of Wattenmeer National Park, the region is a holidaymaker's and nature lover's paradise. Further inland are the lakes of 'Holstein Switzerland' and the open air museums of Molfsee and viking Haithabu. With such scenic beauty it is not unsurprising to find the area is home to many of modern Germany's finest authors, such as Günter Grass, Siegfried Lenz and Sarah Kirsch.

The Kiel Canal links the Baltic with the North Sea and Kiel was the pre-war home of the German Navy: hence heavily bombed. Lübeck was luckier and the 'Queen of the Hanseatic League' retains many fine medieval buildings, so that it is now a World Heritage Site.

For many years the region depended on agriculture and fishing, while Kiel's life revolved around its shipyards; these have survived by specialising in the types of ship built, while the rest of the state has embraced new technologies. Schleswig-Holstein is home to more than 1,000 wind turbines making it Germany's main supplier of 'green' electricity, while 4,000 firms are involved in information and communications technology. With three universities and four polytechnics employers in the area can draw upon a skilled workforce.

Thuringia (Thüringen)

Main cities: Erfurt, Weimar.

The geographic heart of Germany, The Free State of Thuringia is a land of forests and mountains crossed by the rivers Saale, Werra and Weisse Elster. This is a fairy-tale land, perched on the Harz mountains and covered by the Thuringian Forest. The capital Erfurt, reinforces this image with its perfectly preserved medieval and renaissance town houses in a pedestrianised centre. Apart from Erfurt and the forests of the Thüringen Wald, the main attractions of the Thuringia region are the two historic cities of Eisenach and Weimar. Eisenach is overlooked by the ancient fortress of the Wartburg, where Luther translated the New Testament into German and which was also the inspiration for Wagner's opera Tannhauser (based on a troubadours' singing contest that took place in the Middle Ages). The Wartburg also gave its name to the sister automobile to the GDR's Trabant. Eisenach itself is the birthplace of Johann Sebastian Bach. In 1919 Weimar was the seat of the constitutional assembly of a briefly liberal republic, and also the first home of the Bauhaus movement, but its golden age was earlier; when in the 18th century it was the home of Goethe, Schiller and Wieland. Sadly only ten kilometres from Weimar is Buchenwald, the antithesis of German enlightenment. An infamous Nazi concentration camp where over 50,000 Jews, gypsies, homosexuals and communists were incarcerated or killed; Buchenwald is now a national monument to the victims of fascism.

Industrialisation in Germany began in Thuringia, with the mining of Potash, followed by gunsmithing, glass making, and machine tool manufacture. The famed German optics industry is based upon the Zeiss and Schott works in Jena, Eisenach once home to the laughable Wartburg now turns out cars for Opel. Half of Thuringia is agricultural land producing grain, rape, potatoes and sugar beet.

Germany's oldest hiking path winds through the Thüringen Wald, and the region has a wealth of mineral springs and resorts for the footsore traveller. The 'Thuringian Classical Route' is a 300 kilometre long tour of the state's beauty spots, palaces and cultural history, remembering the period when the region was the centre of German intellectual life, not just the geographical centre.

Residence and Entry Regulations

The Current Position

A large workforce of immigrant *gastarbeiter* (guestworkers) and liberal immigration laws have been the power behind German reconstruction since the early fifties. However, times have changed and the German economy has been under pressure since the unification of East and West and the recession of the early nineties. Unemployment and economic sluggishness are making ordinary Germans unhappy and this is putting pressure on the authorities to tighten work, entry and residence regulations.

The need to restructure the labour intensive industries of the former East Germany, a general economic downturn and the high costs to employers of Germany's generous wage regulations have helped put nearly five million people out of work. This in turn has put pressure on the government to crack down on immigrant workers, many of whom happily work for less than the minimum guaranteed to a German. While this problem is centred on the construction industry, with a general election looming, many politicians are using it to lambast the Kohl government about the economic situation as a whole. Thus at the time of writing the German authorities are cracking down on building sites and companies in a drive to ensure that cheap labour isn't inflating unemployment statistics.

At the same time some of Germany's problems stem from the generous benefits system which pays out at the previous rate earned, and this can dis-incline some workers from taking up a new job. These problems are not helped by Germany's continuing popularity with refugees, asylum seekers and other immigrants; even with recent changes to limit the numbers in order to ease tensions, over 420,000 immigrants arrived in Germany in 1996.

So while these recent problems paint a grimmer picture of the opportunities to live and work in Germany, than was the case a few years ago, UK citizens are perfectly entitled to live and work there (in fact entry is easier now) and many opportunities to do so still exist, especially for those in the Information Technology industry.

Settling in Germany is as much about getting all the paperwork sorted out as finding a job there. To register as a citizen, obtain your tax card, health insurance and a residence permit all takes time. While the EU may seem to be a scary network of civil servants trying to legislate against everything, being a citizen of an EU state has many benefits. Not least of which are the rights of work and residence in any EU state, thus making entry and residence easier for UK nationals.

The most important factor to note is that while attempting to get a job and register yourself in Germany might seem like being asked to climb a bureaucratic mountain, the officials of the German authorities are very thorough, and they will try to make it as painless as possible; unfortunately they are also very busy. It helps if you have done your homework first and this book and your local consulate in Germany can help. The offices in the cities with most applications (e.g. Berlin) tend to open early, to help speed things up. So sit back and be patient, the Germans may not be quite as bad as the clichés make out but they are very efficient and you can be sure all paperwork will be dealt with as quickly as possible. Of course if you feel you are being shuffled between offices by unfriendly officials then it always helps to ask the name of the person you are dealing with. If they know that you will say who sent you when you get to the next office, then they will be more helpful, but on the whole, German civil servants tend to be just that.

Please note that all the competent diplomatic authorities emphasise that you need to be able to speak some German if you intend to find work in Germany.

Entry for British and EU Nationals

British nationals or citizens of other EU member states wishing to visit Germany for three months or less require only a valid passport endorsed with the words 'Holder has the right of abode in the UK', 'UK Citizen' or 'European Community'. Under EU agreement these regulations also apply to an individual's family members (spouse and children up to 21 years of age), irrespective of their nationality. However your passport should be valid for at least four months after your arrival in Germany.

Residence Permit

British nationals and others planning to stay in Germany for longer than three months need to obtain a residence permit; these have different names depending upon the type required, but *Aufenthaltsgenehmigung* is the umbrella term. If you are entering to work then you should obtain one as soon as you begin work. These are issued free of charge. While you can stay for up to three months whilst looking for work, you are effectively a tourist, so it helps if you are looking for work while living there to clarify your position by registering as an 'Alien' with the local citizens administration (*Einwohnermeldeamt*), (see below *Useful Terms*) who will issue a Certificate of Registration (*Anmeldebescheinigung*). Ideally you should obtain this certificate within ten days of arriving in Germany, you will need to take it with you when you need to obtain a residence permit, and you can apply for that as soon as you have a job offer. You can then take this certificate to the local office of the Foreign Nationals Authority (*Ausländeramt*) where you will be issued your *Aufenthaltsgenehmigung*. It should be noted that the system as described is based on the entry regulations for citizens of EU States and the USA, and this is easier than for citizens of other countries.

At the *Einwohnermeldeamt*
The local office will also be listed in the telephone book under the heading *Stadtverwaltung*. They will give you a registration application form (*Meldeschein*) which must be completed with proof of residence (i.e countersigned by a landlord, hotel manager or estate agent). The *Meldeschein* must be presented to the registration authority, who will issue the *Anmeldebescheinigung*. (It should be noted that any change of address must be reported to the registration authority within one week, you should also inform them if you leave Germany permanently).

At the *Ausländeramt*
To obtain your residence permit take the Certificate (*Anmeldebescheinigung*) to

the local Foreign Nationals/Aliens Registration Authority (*Ausländeramt*) which can be found in the Town Hall (*Rathaus*) or the Area Administration Centre (*Kreisverwaltung*). In smaller towns the Rural District Office (*Landratsamt*) is usually located in the town council building (*Stadverwaltung*). Residence application is free of charge and must be accompanied by evidence of means of subsistence and/or that employment has been taken up, two passport photos, proof of identity (a passport will suffice) and proof of medical insurance. For non-EU citizens it may also be necessary to undergo a medical examination. The German authorities will issue a temporary residence permit, valid for two months, if an applicant has not secured employment at the time of request. The residence permit lasts for five years and is renewable. The permit is no longer endorsed in passports but instead separate cards are issued by the registration authority. These are not identity cards and therefore are not valid for crossing frontiers. However, they should be carried with your passport when you are entering or leaving Germany. Further information on the application procedures is available from the German Embassy in your country.

Entering to Work

European Community regulations allow for the free movement of labour within the EU, hence UK citizens do not require a work permit to work in Germany. Although British nationals looking for employment can enter the country on a valid passport they must apply for a residence permit if they intend to stay and work for more than three months (see above). Job applicants should have proof that they have registered with the local authorities. To work in bars, restaurants and similar establishments it is necessary to have a health certificate (*Gesundheits-zeugnis*). This can be obtained from the local health department (*Gesundheitsamt*), but can take a few weeks to be processed.

Entering to Start a Business

EU Nationals are free to enter Germany on a valid passport and set up a business. The German authorities welcome new enterprises and the Federal Ministry of Economics (*Bundesministerium für Wirtschaft*) acts as a first point of contact for new enterprises. They can provide information about the correct ministries and länder development agencies to contact. The Legal Department of the German-British Chamber of Commerce in London also offers help and information for prospective entrepreneurs planning to move to Germany. The procedures for officially establishing a business are detailed in Chapter Seven *Starting a Business*.

Entering on a Self-Employed Basis

While the information above applies to any Briton seeking work in Germany there are additional formalities which a self-employed worker needs to complete **before** leaving for Germany. As most self-employed Britons seeking work in Germany are taking up work in the construction industry, it is essential, in the light of recent problems with dubious building agencies, that they have prepared the correct documents. In order to work in Germany as a self-employed worker you will need to register with the local Chamber of Handicrafts office (*Handwerkskammer*), to be registered you will need to provide a Certificate E101 and a certificate of experience.

The E101 is a document which shows that you have been paying self-employed National Insurance contributions in the UK and that you will remain in the UK NI scheme. A British worker who is normally self-employed in the UK can remain in the UK insurance scheme for up to one year while working in Germany. For advice on your entitlement to an E101 you can telephone the Department of Social Security on 0645 154811, or write to their International Services Department (International Services, DSS Longbenton, Newcastle-Upon-Tyne, NE98 1YX). Details of Certificates of Experience can be obtained from the British Chamber of Commerce (Certification Unit, British Chamber of Commerce, Westwood House, Westwood Business Park, Coventry, CV4 8HS.), at the time of writing the cost for a certificate was about £80. Current information on the regulations concerning self-employment for non-Germans can be obtained from the Embassy or the Legal Department of the German-British Chamber of Commerce.

Entering as a Student:

Further details can be found in Chapter Six under *Studying in Germany*, and from the various Student Exchange agencies. The most authoritative is the German Academic Exchange Service (*Deutscher Akademischer Austauschdienst*) which publishes a very useful guide for students as well as lists of scholarships and sources of funding. In order to study in Germany you will have to prove that you are sufficiently competent in the language to make study there worthwhile. Any place offered will only be open for the duration of one semester rather than an academic year as German universities, unlike those in Britain, work on the semester system, although you can apply to extend your study. These run from September-February and March-August. The main universities have their own Foreign Student Offices (*Akademisches Auslandsamt*), which you should contact at least 6 months, preferably a year, in advance of your planned start date for studying. These offices in conjunction with the DAAD will be able to advise you on all aspects of entering Germany to study.

While entering Germany to study is easier for EU and American nationals the basic requirements for entry are that you have documentary proof of your place at a German university, a passport which will remain valid for the entire period of your stay, proof that you have sufficient funds to support you during your studies and if necessary the correct visa. The DAAD recommend that you arrive with at least 300 DM on you to cover the various expenses of the first few weeks of term, they also recommend that you should allow between 1,000-1,300 DM a month for living expenses. On registering at the Aliens Registration Office with your various documents and passport photos (see above) you will be issued with a Student Residence Permit (*Aufentsbewelligung*), this is only valid for study and does not permit the holder to take up any temporary work between semesters.

Entering with Retirement Status:

Since 1 January 1992 pensioners from EU Member States have been able to live wherever they choose in the new boundary-less European Community. As stated above people intending to retire to Germany require a residence permit (*Anmeldebescheinigung*), in compliance with the Foreign Nationals Act (*Ausländergesetz*). It will have to include pension details, proof of adequate medical insurance cover and supply evidence that individuals have 'sufficient' funds to support themselves without working. Under European Union regulations if you work in two or more EU states you will be able to combine state pension contributions paid in each country; for up to date information on this contact the Department of Social Security. UK pensions can be paid directly to individuals resident in Germany, and if your retirement scheme includes health insurance you should have the right to have the same cover as a retired German. To obtain these benefits you should inform your pension authorities of your planned move and obtain a form E121 from your health authority, this should be handed to the relevant authorities in your new homeland.

German Residency

The residence permit is renewable every five years, and provided you give a satisfactory reason for remaining, residence in Germany on such a permit can be indefinite. A renewal may be restricted to 12 months if the applicant has been out of work for more than one year. A permit will automatically expire if the holder gives up his or her residence in Germany for more than six months, except in the case of compulsory national service in the home state. Actually obtaining the permit should not take more than an hour or two, so long as you turn up with the right paperwork, and can speak German well enough to understand the process. A UK or EU State citizen is entitled to the same rights as a German national, with the exception of voting in German elections. As local affairs will affect all residents, any EU national living in a country other than their own can vote in municipal elections, and elections for local Members of the European Parliament. However, they may only vote in one European election, either where they currently live or where they came from. Thus British nationals retain the right to vote in UK general elections, while being able to vote in German municipal elections, although they should clarify their position with their local consular authority. EU citizens may even stand for election to municipal bodies, although you will need to confirm this with the local election regulations.

Should you decide to leave Germany on a permanent basis you must notify the local registration authority (*Einwohnermeldeamt*) before leaving.

People resident in Germany for more than ten years are entitled to apply for citizenship. Applicants must meet certain criteria. These include: no prior criminal convictions, and a sufficient knowledge of spoken and written German. However, German laws do not generally allow for dual citizenship. Marriage to a German national guarantees residency in Germany but does not ensure naturalization.

Non-EU Nationals

US, Canadian, New Zealand and Australian citizens do not require a visa for visits of up to three months. It is possible to extend such a visit to a maximum of six months by application to the local Authority for Foreigners (*Ausländerbehörde*) when in Germany. However the validity of the traveller's passport should exceed the length of their visit by at least four months.

At present due to the treaties concluded between Germany and the USA, US citizens have practically the same status as EU Citizens when looking for work in Germany, in that they can stay for up to three months while looking for work and once a job has been obtained the authorities have to issue a residence permit.

Australians and Canadians coming to work in Germany need to obtain a visa before leaving their homeland, for which proof of employment in Germany must be provided.

Non-EU nationals who intend to work or establish themselves in business (or other self-employed activities) require a residence permit. To apply it is first necessary to obtain a visa. This must be done before entering Germany and application forms are available from the Visa Section of the nearest German Embassy. Nationals of EEA countries (Finland, Iceland, Norway, Sweden and Switzerland) can apply after entry. The form must be completed in triplicate and submitted with a valid passport, three passport photos, written confirmation of work from your prospective employer and proof of medical insurance cover. If the application is approved a visa will be issued. The visa can only be issued in the country of application, and it cannot be forwarded to Germany. After entering Germany the applicant must register immediately with the Foreign Nationals Authority (*Ausländeramt*), who will issue the residence permit. The permit is valid for up to five years, or the duration of employment, and is renewable.

Useful Terms:

Einwohnermeldeamt: Citizens Administration Office.
Akademisches Auslandsamt: Foreign Student Office.
Anmeldungen/Abmeldungen: Registration/De-Registration.
Aufenhaltsgenemihung: General Residence Permit.
Aufentsbefugnis: Refugee's Residence Permit.
Aufentsbewelligung: Student Residence Permit (no paid work permitted).
Aufentserlaubnis: Residence Permit for Workers.
Auskunfte: Information (Help Desk in an Einwhonermeldeamt).
Ausländerangelegenheiten: Foreigner's Affairs
Bescheinigungen: Certificates of Residence etc.
Einreisen: Immigration into Germany.
Firmenvisa/Geschäftsvisa: Business/Trade Visa.
Kinderausweis: Child's Identity Card.
Lohnsteurkarten: Tax Cards.
Melderegister: Registration of Citizens.
Personalausweis: Identity Card.
Reissepässe: Passport.
Umzugleichtgemacht: Information Sheets for new arrivals, essentially 'Move Made Easy'.

Useful Addresses:

German Embassies and Consulates in the UK:

Embassy of the Federal Republic of Germany: 23 Belgrave Square/Chesham Place, London SW1 8PZ; tel 0171-824 1300; website: http://www.german-embassy.org.uk
German Consulate General: 16 Eglinton Crescent, Edinburgh EH12 5DG; tel 0131-3372323.
German Consulate General: Westminster House, 11 Portland Street, Manchester M60 1BY; tel 0161-237 5255.

British Embassy and Consulates in Germany:

At the time of writing it is planned that the British Embassy will move to Berlin in November 1999.
British Embassy: Friedrich-Ebert-Allee 77, D-53113 Bonn; tel 0228-91670; website http://www.britbot.de
British Embassy (Berlin Office): Unter den Linden 32/34, D-10117 Berlin; tel 030-201840.
British Consulate General: Yorckstr. 19, D-40476 Düsseldorf; tel 0211-94480.

British Consulate General: Bockenheimer Landstrasse 42, D-60323 Frankfurt am Main; tel 069-1700020.
British Consulate General: Harvestehuder Weg 8a, D-20148 Hamburg; tel 040-4480320; fax 040-4107269; website http://www.british-dgtip.de
British Consulate General: Bürkleinstrasse 10, D-80538 München; tel 089-211090.
British Consulate General: Breite Strasse 2, D-70173 Stuttgart; tel 0711-162690.

US Embassy and Consulates in Germany:

US Embassy: Deichmannsaue 29, D-53179 Bonn; tel 0228-3392286
US Embassy (Berlin Office): Neustädtische Kirchstr. 4-5, D-10117 Berlin; tel 030-238 5174.

Australian Embassy in Germany:

The Australian Embassy: Godesberger Allee 105, D-53175 Bonn; tel 0228-810 3160.
The Australian Embassy (Berlin Office): Uhlandstrasse 181-183, D-10623 Berlin; tel 030-880 0880

Canadian Embassy in Germany:

The Canadian Embassy: Friedrich-Wilhelm-Strasse 18, D-53113 Bonn; tel 0228-9680; fax 0228-968 3904.
Office of the Canadian Embassy-Berlin: Internationales Handelszentrum, 23rd Floor, Friedrich Strasse 95, D-10117 Berlin: tel 030-261 1161; fax 030-262 9206.

Other German Embassies:

USA
Embassy of the Federal Republic of Germany: 4645 Reservoir Road, NW Washington DC, 20007-1998, USA; tel 202-298 8140.
German Consulate General: 460 Park Avenue, New York, NY 10022, USA; tel 212-308 8700; website http://www.germany-info.org/

Canada
Embassy of the Federal Republic of Germany: 1 Waverly Street, Ottawa, Ontario, KZP OT8; tel 013-232 1101; website http://www.docuweb.ca/Germany/

Eire
Embassy of the Federal Republic of Germany: 31 Trimelston Avenue, Booterstown, Blackrock, Dublin 31, Eire; tel 031-2693011.

Honorary Consulates:

The German Embassy represents and promotes German interests in the UK. However, Germany is further represented by a number of honorary consuls throughout the country. These include:
Consul for Germany: 12 Albert Street, Aberdeen AB1 1XQ; tel 01224-643379.
Consul for Germany: c/o AVX Ltd, 1 Ballyhampton, Larne/Belfast BT40 2ST; tel 01574-60777.
Consul for Germany: 111/117 Victoria Street, Bristol, BS1 6AX; tel 0117-9298040

Other Useful Addresses:

American Chamber of Commerce in Germany: Rossmarkt 12, D-60311 Frankfurt am Main, Germany; tel 069-929 1040.

German-British Chamber of Industry and Commerce: Mecklenburg House, 16 Buckingham Gate, London SW1E 6LB; tel 0171-976 4100; website http://www.ahk.london.co.uk

British Chamber of Commerce in Germany: Severinstrasse 60, D-50678 Köln, Germany; tel 0221- 314458.

Department of Social Security: International Services, DSS Longbenton, Newcastle-Upon-Tyne, NE98 1YX.

Deutscher Akademischer Austauschdienst (German Academic Exchange Service): 34 Belgrave Square, London, SW1X 8QB; tel 0171-235 1736; fax 0171-235 9602.

Federal Ministry of Economics (Bundesministerium für Wirtschaft): Foreign Investor Information Centre, Scharnhorststrasse 36, D-10117 Berlin, Germany; tel 030-20147751/55; website http://www.bmwi.de

Setting Up Home

There are over 150,000 UK nationals currently living in Germany of whom the majority are there for work or for family reasons. Unlike southern Europe, Germany, does not attract sun-worshipping British house buyers looking for a holiday-villa, retirement home or investment opportunity. But, while the spacious and practical German house may lack the romantic courtyards and fountains of a Mediterranean villa, they are built for living in rather than for social cachet. Thus anyone who wishes to entertain friends is unlikely to have to worry about their guests hitting any low beams, most German town houses and flats are built to a scale usually found only in the more prosperous areas of suburban Britain. Should you obtain property outside of a town then its location, if not the design, will still be fairly romantic, by contrast with much of Britain.

Most workers sent on a foreign assignment can expect to have the company help with setting up a new home, given the costs involved. One reputable research organisation that many companies use is The Economist Intelligence Unit (15 Regent Street, London, SW1Y 4LR; tel 0171-830 1000; fax 0171-491 2107) which carries out worldwide cost of living surveys. These carefully researched reports make statistical comparisons of various facets of living in one country or another and give an accurate indication of the likely costs or savings to be faced by an employee if transferred to another location.

While the Germans are much like the British in wishing to own their own homes, relatively high property prices make this an expensive option. This fact coupled with the probable reasons for being in Germany mean that most expatriates will rent their accommodation while there. However the high prices of property (see Table 1 on p60) and the costs of borrowing mean that most Germans rent their houses and flats for a very long time.

The biggest problem with much accommodation in Germany is in its externals, the flats are generally airy and spacious to live in, and even a two-bedroom council flat is likely to have storage space in the attic or basement, possibly both. However, because of the need to house people quickly after the devastation of the war many apartment blocks and housing schemes from the fifties and sixties are rather drab and uniform looking when seen from the outside. Unlike similar schemes in Britain however, the Germans have had the room and sense to plant lots of trees and grass around them to enhance the area, and some cities encourage the painting of colourful murals on end walls to brighten things up.

Property buying and renting procedures are bound to be unfamiliar to the majority of expatriates and this chapter outlines the main processes involved. It is essential to take expert professional and local advice before any financial commitments are made. Such advice is easily obtainable from relocation agencies, many of whom will happily research possible houses and flats for you as part of the service. Other possibilities are estate agents (*Makler*) property agents (*Immobilien*), other expatriates, building societies (*Bausparkassen*) and of course the mortgage banks (*Hypotheken*)

How do the Germans Live?

There are about 35 million dwellings in Germany, ranging in size from single rooms to mansions through the usual range of flats and family houses. Of these roughly 42% in western Germany are owner occupied, with the remainder being rented. This contrasts with Britain where the percentage of home owners is around 70%. In the eastern Länder the ratios are 26% and 74% respectively. While flats have traditionally been rented out privately, 17% of those in western Germany are subsidised by the Federal government, this 'social housing' is mostly for the elderly, disabled and low income families. With the German population increasing by around four million between 1989 and 1994 the demand for housing, and consequently the prices of real estate and accommodation rose sharply. Even with fairly extensive building projects prices rose, and the search for affordable property increasingly resulted in a shift to satellite towns and villages. Another reason for moving out of the cities is that Germans are demanding more living space. Meanwhile those who do have city flats tend to hang on to them (both as owners and tenants), because a change of tenancy means an increase in rent, with the result that the amount of property in circulation is comparatively small. At present the amount of building work under way in Berlin, and the move of Government offices there from Bonn, means that it is likely that the availability of houses and flats in these cities is going to fluctuate quite a lot in the next few years, as the staff of the various ministries leave their old homes for new ones.

In east Germany the standard of accommodation is poorer than that in the west, for a variety of reasons, mostly due to the hasty construction of the post-war years and a lack of maintenance since. The focus of effort was on new building rather than looking after the existing stock. Unlike western Germany, eastern Germany did not tear down buildings left standing after the war and more than 51% of east German housing stock pre-dates 1948, compared with 19% in western Germany. The average available living space per individual is smaller in the east than the west 29.8 square metres compared to 37.4. While these conditions are slowly changing, it should be borne in mind that many western businessmen have seen the east as a territory to exploit. Under the communist regime there was no pressing reason or spare cash for saving up, which meant that most eastern Germans do not have the same kind of savings 'cushion' that their western cousins have; thus in the property market they are hamstrung. This situation means that when a block of flats is for sale only a 'wessie' is likely to buy it, and in order not to lose money on such a large investment the rents will rise, often quite steeply.

Relocation Agencies

The increasing globalisation of industries and markets has meant an increase in the numbers of staff being sent on assignment to subsidiary or partner firms in foreign countries. This in turn has lead to a boom in the relocation business, as companies are set up to help executives and others settle in new homes in different cultures. A good relocation agency can cover a lot of ground for you, saving you time in finding a home, a good school for your children, a local medical practice and even a social life. Relocation companies are either global networks of offices or national companies providing services for trans-national clients. The companies listed below are mostly based in Germany and offer a range of service packages for the would be expatriate. Most of them will, in addition to finding you accommodation, provide you with assistance with registering and getting through all the administrative tasks on arrival. These services are either charged for individually or included in a package offer, either way their activities on your behalf can be tailored to suit your needs and pocket, whether you are an individual or a company wishing to send staff to Germany.

It should be noted that at present the German relocation industry is unregulated, however there are two regulatory bodies which have members operating in Germany, these are the British Association of Relocation Agents (ARA) and the United States Employee Relocation Council (USERC). The ARA is a professional body which requires full members to have been trading for two years and to abide by rules of conduct and professional standards for relocating clients. The ARA runs courses for accreditation and professional development and will arbitrate in any disagreements with member firms. At present the ARA is trying to develop a European wide professional body to regulate and set professional standards for relocation companies. Those companies listed on their website which are not ARA members are firms which have expressed some interest in setting up the pan-European association.

Association of Relocation Agents: Premier House, 11 Marlborough Place, Brighton, BN1 1UB; telephone 01273-624455; fax 01273-623098; e-mail address info@relocationagents.com website http://www.relocationagents.com

Please note that some companies are not members of the ARA (denoted by ARA), but are listed by them (denoted by L).

Accent Relocation: (L) Ohlestrasse 46f, D-22547 Hamburg; tel 040-832 5985; fax 040-832 6188 and Haydenstrasse 154, D-40822 Mettmann; tel/fax 02104-16396. This Hamburg based relocation agency specialises in relocating British and

American executives for companies in the Hamburg and Niedersachsen region.

Arriva relocation services: (ARA) Ingrid Henke, Glesebrechtstrasse 10, D-10629 Berlin; tel 030-882 4830; fax 030-885 4558; e-mail arriva@berlin.shafu.de

International Business & Relocation Services: (L) Nanda Leick, Rosenstrasse 7, D-80331 München; tel 089-231 1380; fax 089-2311 3811. In business since 1990 and helping companies such as Motorola and Coca Cola relocate executives and premises to Germany, this Bavarian based company has a multilingual staff (English, French, Italian and Japanese are spoken) to help you move in. Their services include support with moving, registering, settling in and moving home again after your stay in Germany.

Entrepreneurial Management Services International (EMSI): Breitscheider Weg 115, D-40885 Ratingen; tel 02102-731066; fax 02102-39657. Will tailor an individual information package according to your needs. The basic information package costs around 300 DM for individuals and 880 DM for businesses.

Erding Relocation: (L) Gabrielle Schmid, Freisinger Str. 45, D-85435 Erding; tel 08122-84393; fax 08122 84315; e-mail RELOCATION@t-online.de Based at the München's new airport, this company offers start-up, housing and ongoing services for those moving to Bavaria. These services range from meeting you on arrival, (eg registering you, obtaining residence permits and tax cards) to helping out with school meetings and finding a good plumber.

Key to Bremen: Carolyn Messerknecht, Hans-Thoma-Strasse 3, D-28209 Bremen; tel/fax 0421-347 8798; e-mail smesserknecht@messerknecht.de Specialising in the Bremen area, but with partner firms in other cities across Germany, this relocation company provides extensive assistance for English speaking clients. City orientation, banking assistance, cultural orientation, househunting and permit, customs and registration assistance are some of the services offered. Help is also available for locating schools, and English speaking doctors and lawyers. Five service packages are offered or you can negotiate your own package according to your needs.

RSB Deutschland GmbH: (ARA) Dreieichstrasse 59, D-60594 Frankfurt am Main; tel 069-6109470; fax 069-611759. In business since 1987 RSB can assist clients to settle in more than 40 German cities, and offers relocation services for transfers of staff: to Germany, within Germany, from Germany elsewhere and from one country to another.

Start-Up Services GmbH: Helga Bailey, Stefan George-Ring 2, D-81929 München; tel 089-939 4520; fax 089-930 2445; e-mail hbaley@t-online.de USERC member company.

Purchasing Property

In Germany the method of buying a house is radically different from the system in Britain. For a start the Estate Agents (*Immobilien-Makler, Haus-Makler,* and *Wohnungsvermittler* are the German equivalents of estate agents.) are a lot harder to find, and speculative browsing of houses on the market is likewise a lot harder; you can't just stroll down the high street looking in windows at potential purchases. While there are some British firms who deal in the German property market such as Knight Frank or Jones Lang Wootton these firms specialise in commercial property rather than residential, unless you fancy a castle or vineyard. Another hurdle for the prospective house buyer is the cost, in buying a house the deposit at around 40% excludes all but the well-off from taking out a mortgage until they have spent several years saving towards it (see the section on Bausparkassen below).

Most German estate agents are either independent brokers working from home or they operate from very office-like offices, rather than the office cum shop of their British counterparts. Finding them is more a case of searching the press and yellow pages. If anything the German estate agent could be regarded as secretive, but this is due to the way that houses are sold. If you buy a house, through them you will pay them an introduction fee (*Nachweissgebühr*), so they do not particularly wish to risk losing sales by giving out information willy-nilly, after all for all they know you could be another *Makler*. However, once you have arranged an appointment to discuss buying a house and the type of house you're looking for they can be quite professional, just don't expect the house details to be as extensive as those produced in Britain. What you should expect is a very large bill on top of the house purchase price for all the expenses of the house buying process. As stated above the estate agents charge a fee and this can range from 3-6% of the purchase price of the house, so it is prudent to ask what the rate of commission (*Provisionssatz*) is before engaging their services.

Once you have found a property that you wish to buy and have been introduced to the seller, the sale process begins; you have to instruct a notary (*Notar*). Unlike the solicitors engaged by both parties in a UK house sale, the Notar works for both parties, at the same time. The Notar's role is to be the fair and even handed representative of the state, overseeing the legal side of the house sale. So while this can be very fair, you do not have the security of having a legal representative who is definitely working on your behalf. The Notar is responsible for drawing up and witnessing the legal document (*Urkunde*) containing the sale and purchase details. As stated the house purchaser engages the Notar, and thus pays their fees, these are between $\frac{1}{2}$ to $\frac{3}{4}$% of the house price, this is on top of the agent's fees for introducing you to the seller. Added to which is the German equivalent of Stamp Duty; this Land Purchase Tax (*Grunderwerbsteuer*) is 3.5% of the house price. So by the time you have completed the formalities of buying a house you can expect to have to add on roughly 10% of the house price to cover the fees and taxes.

It is possible to cut out the makler by consulting the property and classified pages of your local German newspaper, and dealing with the house sellers directly. However, many of these adverts may have been placed by makler, so you'll have to ask around. The British embassy and consulates across Germany are also a useful source of information on local housing conditions, and which local newspapers are the best for adverts.

Useful Addresses

British consulates in Germany:

British Embassy: Friedrich-Ebert-Allee 77, 53113 Bonn; tel 0228-91670.

British Embassy (Berlin Office): Unter den Linden 32/34, 10117 Berlin; tel 030-201840.

British Consulate General: Harvestehuder Weg 8a, 20148 Hamburg; tel 040-4480320.

British Consulate General: Bockenheimer Landstrasse 42, 60323 Frankfurt am Main; tel 069-1700020.

British Consulate General: Bürkleinstrasse 10, 80538 München; tel 089-211090.

British Consulate General: Yorckstr. 19, 40476 Düsseldorf; tel 0211-94480.

Association of German Estate Agents (Verband Deutscher Makler): Head Office, Riedemannweg 57, D-13627 Berlin; tel 030-38302528; fax 030-38302529

Finance

It is a hard life for the expatriate worker who wishes to purchase property, most of the information aimed at expatriates seeking properties or mortgages would appear to have been written under the misapprehension that all expats are only concerned with buying houses to return home to, or as investments to be rented out in your absence abroad. Financing the purchase of a non-UK property is harder to arrange than you might expect, given that most expatriates are earning very good salaries. However, the mortgage situation for non-UK residents is now improving and details of how one can go about arranging a mortgage locally or through a UK mortgage lender are given below.

German Home Loan Societies (*Bausparkassen*)

Unless they have sufficient funds so that they can afford to buy outright, any foreigner wanting to enter the German property market will have to consider taking out a loan with a German home loan society *Bausparkasse*. There are 34 Bausparkassen across Germany, 21 private and 13 public, the public ones are operated by the Länder banks, while the private bausparkassen are run by share groups (*Aktien Gesellschaft*) and so have the AG suffix. Of the 13 Landesbausparkassen 4 are legally independent operations, the remainder are subsidiaries of the state banks. In practice this division means that you may find offices of all 21 private Bausparkassen in your home town, with the only apparent competition for them coming from the offices of the Landesbausparkasse. However, while each Landesbausparkasse can only operate in its home state, contracts with them can be arranged through any local *Sparkassen* bank office (*Sparkassen* are a variant of Landesbanks in that they are backed by city or regional councils).

Bausparkassen are credit institutions which have developed from the same roots as the British building society system, however, they operate in a different manner to the British model, and the two should not be confused. Where British building societies operate on the 'open' system; taking savers deposits as a 'float' to trade in stocks and shares in order to finance loans and mortgages, the Bausparkassen utilise the 'closed' system. This entails the collection of savers to form a pool of funds from which loans can be drawn. Some 20 million Germans hold a *Bauspar* savings agreement, and two-thirds of German homes are co-financed by this method.

Unlike in Britain where you start savings accounts as soon as you wish, with only a vague notion of when you might want to buy a home, the German Bauspar system is geared towards buying right from the start. Unlike British banks and building societies Bausparkassen will only lend money to savers, and these loans will only be made for the purchase of houses, flats, building land or the business extras required in building properties for accommodation. The Bauspar system works by identifying members as savers (creditors) or borrowers (debtors), as you are either saving money with them or paying back an amount borrowed. The potential home buyer enters into a savings contract (*Bausparvetrag*) with the Bausparkassen, this sets out how much they wish to borrow to finance their purchase and how much they need to save each month and for how long, until they will be issued the loan. While Bausparkassen will lend up to 80% of the purchase price, the typical amount the saver needs to build up before recieving the loan is 30-50% of the amount required. The benefits of this system are that the interest rates tend to be low on the loans (varying between 4.5% and 6.5%), by comparison with British savings schemes though, the Bauspar savings do not attract very good interest rates, typically being between 2.5-4.5%. The amounts you can borrow, and so the amounts you need to deposit each month will vary according to the individual Bausparkasse and the tariffs and loan periods that they offer. In some respects the modern Bausparkasse is a more customer friendly institution than in the past, and you can obtain loan agreements which are much more tailored to your needs should you wish to, and waiting times for loans have come down in recent years. The differences between Bausparkassen and mortgage banks (*Hypotheken*) are that as a saver you have a legal right to the loan, it being part of your Bauspar contract, the interest rates of the loan do not vary with market fluctuations, and as a Bauspar saver you obtain certain safeguards through the land registry.

The main types of Bauspar agreements are Fast, Standard, Long-Term and Options. The Standard tariff is aimed at medium level savings for 7 years with interest accruing at 2-3.5%, with a loan repayment period of 11 years, with interest on the loan of around 4.5%. The Long-Term agreement involves a longer savings period with lower monthly deposits at 4-4.5% interest, followed by a longer repayment period where interest is at 6-6.5%. The Options tarif is tailored to the individual customer's requirements and the Fast agreement speaks for itself as an option for those with sufficiently high income. According to the Association of Private Bausparkassen (*Verband der Privaten Bausparkassen e.V*, Postfach 15 01 55, D-53040 Bonn; website http://www.bausparkassen.de) the upper and lower time limits on loans are 6.5 and 18 years respectively. In all these cases however, there will be differences between individual tariffs and the interest and repayment levels they will operate at.

There are also facilities available to those customers wishing to purchase or renovate property at short notice, and whose bauspar agreement has not yet 'matured'. It is possible to provide funding for saving or pre-financing of an agreement with a loan from another credit institution (eg a hypothek or bank loan), this loan is free from redemption payments until the allocation date of the Bauspar loan, which is then used to repay the other loan. This is also the most advantageous financial mixture for housing purchases; the combination of bauspar loan and mortgage. It is not uncommon now for banks, Bausparkassen and Hypotheken to work together, so that the procedure from application to redemption is simplified by package services, often including insurance policies.

Mortgages with German Banks

In addition to the loans offered to savers in the Bauspar system, mortgage banks (*Hypotheken*) exist in Germany as well as the German version of the standard high street bank. The range of services available from either of these institutions with regard to the prospective house buyer, will vary from bank to bank. At present there are some 35 mortgage banks with offices across Germany. Unlike the Bausparkassen they will lend money for any purpose, but only to a maximum of 60% of the purchase price. The mortgage banks give mortgages and municipal loans by raising funds through the issue of bonds, therefore, the rates and terms will vary according to market conditions.

Offshore Mortgages

Many expatriates would like to be able to obtain mortgages with the high street institutions that they are used to dealing with, however, being a non-UK resident often makes it very difficult to obtain mortgage funding. This is especially the case should you apply for a mortgage to buy a property outside of the UK. While some building societies do arrange financing for properties in France, Spain or Italy, this is not yet the case for Germany. Most of the information aimed at expatriates about obtaining a mortgage, has the purchase of a UK property in mind, either for letting out to obtain income, or as a home to move into on your return. Hence the lender can accept that as security for the loan, because in the event of your defaulting they can easily dispose of the property. However, this does not necessarily preclude you from using your assets, a domestic or foreign property to help secure finance for a house purchase and advice on these matters can be sought from financial consultants. One such firm is Conti Financial Services (see below), who can advise you on foreign purchases. It should be noted that as well as risking your home if you can not maintain repayments on any mortgage or loan secured on it, you are also at risk from exchange rate variations with foreign currency mortgages.

Useful Addresses

Conti Financial Services: 204 Church Road, Hove, BN3 2DJ; tel 01273-772811; e-mail contifs@compuserve.com website http://www.inatos.co.uk/conti; fax 01273-321269. Conti have 17 years experience of arranging finance for clients in Britain and abroad wishing to purchase property around the world. They are also an independent mortgage broker and can arrange financing in several currencies. As members of the Federation of Overseas Property Developers, Agents and Consultants, and affiliate members of the Association of Relocation Agents this firm is a specialist in overseas residential mortgages.

TWG Estates Ltd: 36-37 Maiden Lane, Covent Garden, London, WC2E 7LJ; tel 0171-240 0300; e-mail twg.estates@virgin.net; fax 0171-836 1500. Are a relocation agency who also provide a comprehensive service for those wishing to sell or rent their home while working abroad, or even those wishing to purchase property for letting while overseas. They can arrange mortgages for property in the UK and overseas as required.

Housing Incentives

The German government provides assistance for homeowners through the Home Assistance Act (*Eigenheimzulagenesetz*) which came into force in December 1995, this amends a previous Home Ownership Bonus Act (*Wohnungsbau-Prämiengesetz*). In effect every Bauspar investor receives an additional 10% from the government towards their annual savings, up to a maximum of 1,000 DM for single savers and 1,600 DM for married couples. These bonuses are given on the proviso that taxable income thresholds are not exceeded in that year: 50,000 DM for a single person and 100,000 DM for married savers.

Additionally the government provides assistance for those wishing to build or buy their own home by encouraging working people to develop assets. This is a home buyer/builders bonus which amounts to 5% of the assessed price of new buildings (up to a maximum 5,000 DM) and 2.5% for older buildings (maximum 2,500 DM), with an increase in income thresholds and an additional 1,500 DM per child. The laws incorporating these bonuses also contain an ecological element in the promotion of energy efficient homes.

There are also housing supplements available for those who can not afford their rent, but as with Britain's Housing Benefit these are subject to income thresholds. In the eastern states modernising the older buildings has so far cost 6 billion DM in government grants, these are aimed at renovating sanitary and heating systems as well as the building's fabric.

Renting Property

Given the prices of real estate in Germany, the majority of inhabitants rent rather than buy somewhere to live and Germany has strict and complicated rent-control and tenancy laws which are fairer to tenants than is the case in Britain. Most German accommodation for rent is understandably rented unfurnished, so that tenants can furnish it how they wish with their own stock of furniture. This is especially true with regard to the kitchen, more than a few expatriates have been surprised to move into their new flats only to find that the kitchen is an empty concrete box without even a sink or any taps. Furnishing and decorating the flat are entirely the domain of the tenant, except that the tenants must have enough money to spare to redecorate to the landlord's wishes when they move out, unless the new tenants are happy with the existing decor. In which case all that is needed is for the house or flat to be cleaned prior to returning the keys. It is always wisest if your company is not arranging accommodation to take a few days holiday well in advance of your new posting to make the arrangements for renting a flat or house. More often than not you will be able to find temporary furnished accommodation to last you until you can get a flat or apartment of your own.

Some of the rent figures noted below and in the *Housing Reports from the Main Cities* (see below) have been taken from The Economist Intelligence Unit's *Worldwide Cost of Living Survey* carried out in the Spring of 1997. This surveyed five cities in Germany compared with London and included details of average house sizes and rents. Thus a 2 bedroom unfurnished apartment in London will range in cost between £1,105 ($1,782) and £2,383 ($3,844) to rent per month and have between 210-690 square feet (or 20-64 square metres) of floorspace. A similar apartment in Düsseldorf would cost between 1,300 DM ($755) and 1,750 DM ($1,017). and have around 100-120 square metres of floorspace. Hence while much is made of accommodation being expensive in Germany, on the whole it is larger and cheaper than its UK equivalents. The housing surveys consulted various expatriate groups to consider living arrangements, as well as studying several districts of each town studied.

The Costs of Becoming a Tenant

There is considerable capital outlay involved in renting an apartment. If the apartment has been located by an agency, the agency commission will be at least two months rent. According to the Economist Intelligence Unit's report the fees charged by agencies vary from two to three months rent, or even 25% of the annual rent (Berlin).

Once the prospective tenant (*Mieter*) has located a flat he or she will have to sign a contract with the landlord (*Vermieter*) or owner (*Hausbesitzer*). Leases are generally for one or two years, but can be for up to five. Tenants have to pay at least a month's rent in advance, plus a refundable deposit the *Kaution* (usually equivalent to three months rent) against damages. The damages deposit must be paid into an account and the tenant receives it back, plus interest if there are no damage charges on departure. If you add up all these expenses before you even move in, then it works out that you will have paid at least four to seven months worth of rent without actually spending a night in your new home. And of course you will have had to conclude a deal with the previous tenants with regard to the kitchen, unless you have a sink unit and cupboards of your own to fit. 90% of the time the previous tenants will take the kitchen with them. Do not bank on being able to pop down to Ikea either, although this chain exists in Germany, the current waiting time for kitchen units is between six weeks and three months, at a cost of around 8,000 DM.

Tenancy law is based on freedom of contract and is aimed at establishing a fair balance between the interests of tenants and landlords. No tenant need fear unjust and arbitrary eviction or excessive rent increases. A landlord can only give notice to a tenant who is meeting their contractual requirements in the event that 'justified interest' can be proven (eg if they need the accommodation for themselves). Rents may rise at the end of each contract providing it does not rise above that charged for comparable housing in the same area. It is always worth having a German friend, your relocator or your company's legal department take a look at any tenancy agreement as they will spot any dodgy clauses, and it only takes about a quarter of an hour to read through the lease. Most leases are fair, but occasionally landlords will try and get you to sign a lease with a clause adding 8% to the rent each year, or one that states that if you don't notify them two years before the contract expires it will run on for another five years automatically. However, if at the end of a five year contract the landlord wishes to sell the property, the tenants have first option on buying it.

Housing Reports from the Main Cities

Many towns and cities have active tenants associations (*Mieterverein*), in return for an annual subscription they will help negotiate for you in disagreements with landlords and advise on rent rates and leases. However, please note that these are clubs and so will only advise members. Other than your own search through the classified adverts, you can also try to find accommodation through an estate agent (*Makler*). Unlike the British high street agency with windows full of houses and flats for rent, almost like a shop window, these are more office based and you will need to make an appointment first. The prospective tenant should also clarify the terms for the agent's fees as it is the party renting who pays the agent's commission.

Berlin: As the German Government is moving from Bonn, even with the current building boom, it is inevitable that prices and rent rates will soar as the demand for accommodation for government employees builds up. While some large companies have talked about moving to Berlin the main movement at present seems to be outward. The city is losing 20,00 people a year, as they flock out of the city and into suburban houses with gardens. All of which adds up to a confusing picture. Information on accommodation can be obtained from the accommodation office (*Wohnungsamt*) for the district where you plan to live, or from the *Mitwhonzentralen* agencies, (Küfurstendamm 227-8, D-10719 Berlin; tel 030-883051) one of which (Holsteinische Str. 55, D-12163 Berlin; tel 030-861 8222) has women only apartments available. General accommodation information can be obtained from the Senatsverwaltung für Arbeit und Frauen (Storkowerstr. 97, D-10407 Berlin; tel 030-4214 37 13). The best local German newspaper in which to look for property adverts is the Sunday newspaper *Berliner Morgen Post am Sonntag*. The Berlin equivalent of the Citizen's Advice Bureau, the *Verbraucherzentrale* (Lützowufer 11-13, D-10 Berlin; tel 030-214850) may also be able to advise foreigners looking for accommodation.

The Economist Intelligence Unit Cost of Living Survey studied eight areas of Berlin and found that a two bedroom apartment would cost between 1,250 DM and 2,200 DM for 75 square metres of floorspace. While the typical advance payments were three months rent up front and a similar figure for the kaution, with it taking over 30 days to move in. Temporary furnished accommodation is available, but costs between 70 DM and 180 DM per day.

Bonn: Bonn has always had a shortage of accommodation because of its huge population of diplomats, bureaucrats and politicians, this should ease now that some of those will now be moving to Berlin. The most exclusive areas (e.g. Bad Godesberg, Venusberg) are understandably very expensive. Cheaper houses, both to rent and buy may be found in Meckenheim 40 minutes west of the city by bus. The local tenants' association (*Mieterverein e.V. für Bonn:* Kaiserstr. 22, D-53113 Bonn; tel 0228-222035; fax 0228-219848) produce a list *'Mietspiegel'* of local rent rates as well as assisting with tenancy problems. The current edition of the Mietspiegel dates from 1994 but a new edition is to be produced in early 1998. According to the last figures a good quality flat in a good area would cost between 13 and 15 DM per square metre, according to the age of the building.

The local daily newspaper *General Anzeiger* (Wednesday and Saturday editions) is the main source of advertisements for accommodation to let, but there is also the tri-weekly *Annonce* (3 DM), a classified ad paper which carries accommodation adverts, including some in English.

Düsseldorf: Accommodation in Düsseldorf is often difficult to find, flats are snapped up as soon as they are advertised so it is advisable to do your house hunting on the spot, or use a Makler. The Cost of Living Survey estimates that current Makler fees in Düsseldorf are around the equivalent of two months rent, while the Consulate General's information sheet, estimated it at about three months worth. Accommodation is publicized in the local daily newspapers, with the peak days being Wednesday and Saturday. The main daily is the: *Rheinische Post*. Other widely read local newspapers include the *Westdeutsche Zeitung*, *Neue Rhein-Ruhr Zeitung* and the *Westdeutsche Allgemeine Zeitung*. Furnished temporary accommodation is available for 400 DM per month.

At the time of writing the average rent on a two bedroom flat would cost between DM 1,300 and 1,750 and have around 100-120 square metres of floorspace. The advance payments work out as a month's rent and three months' worth for the kaution. The good news is that moving in takes only two to ten days.

The British Consulate General in Düsseldorf (Yorckstr. 19, D-40476 Düsseldorf; tel 0211-94480.) produces a leaflet *Living in Düsseldorf* which contains hints on residence permits and accommodation. The main Mieterverein can be contacted at Oststrasse 47, D-40211 Düsseldorf; tel 0211-169960.

Frankfurt: The centre of Frankfurt is primarily a banking and commercial area, and therefore contains limited accommodation. Unfurnished accommodation currently costs between 10-20 DM per square metre, the cheapest two-room flat in the centre would cost about 1,100 DM per month, plus bills, according to the local consulate. The costs of a two bedroom apartment can vary between 1,300 and 2,100 DM, for between 70-120 square metres. While the time taken to move in can be from ten days to a month, although only a month's rent is required in advance. Of the five cities surveyed Frankfurt is the only one where the generally available accommodation is furnished. Areas where accommodation prices are likely to be lower, are Bochenheim (near the university) and Bornheim (north of the centre). The best newspaper for accommodation to let advertisements is the *Frankfurter Rundschau* and in particular the Saturday edition which comes out at 2pm on Fridays, but all the adverts are quickly followed up.

Short term accommodation may also be obtained through the City Mitwohnzentrale (An der Staufenmauer 3, D-60311 Frankfurt/Main; tel 069-5975561) or other agencies of which a few are listed in the consulate's brochure. There is also other temporary furnished accommodation which can be from 500 to 1,500 DM per month.

The Frankfurt Tenants' Protection Association (*Mieterschutzverein Frankfurt a.M. e.V.*) is located at Eckenheimerlandstr. 339, 60320 Frankfurt am Main; tel 069-560 10 57; fax 069-56 89 40.

Hamburg: Hamburg is the most Anglophile city in Germany with an estimated British population of around 6,000 and many British expatriate clubs. German unification has put the famous Hanseatic port of Hamburg right back at the centre of trade with eastern Europe through its regained eastern hinterland of Mecklenburg-Pomerania. Evidence of this can be seen in the record number of traders and companies in the process of setting up in Hamburg. This influx has caused an unprecedented demand for business and residential premises which has pushed up property prices beyond the reach of many Germans and foreigners wishing to start up small businesses. Buying property is therefore likely to be out of the question for most expatriates, unless they go at least one hour from Hamburg city centre.

According to the 1995 Mietenspiegel produced by the Hamburg Mieterverein, a good quality flat will range between 13.4 and 21.9 DM per square metre in the 60-90 square metre space range (the low end of the two bedroom flat size range in Germany), according to the age of the building. Some of Hamburg's accommodation stock is pre-1918, but this tends to be less than 65 square metres.

The survey in the Spring of 1997 by the Cost of Living team estimated that a two bedroom flat now begins at 2,395 DM and tops out at 4,300 DM a month for between 80-120 square metres. Luckily the advance rent and kaution only add up to four month's worth but moving in takes between ten and thirty days. The temporary furnished accommodation that is available is not cheap either at a rate of 385 DM per week, or 2,350 per month.

The best newspaper for accommodation advertisements is the *Hamburger Abendblatt*, which is published daily around mid-morning. The Wednesday and Saturday editions carry extra property supplements.

Anyone having difficulties with their landlord or in need of preliminary advice about renting accommodation, could contact the Hamburg Tenants' Association (*Mieterverein zu Hamburg*, Glockengiesserwall 2, D-20095 Hamburg; tel 040-322541). As well as the *Living in Hamburg* brochure the British Consulate General in Hamburg produces brochures for Bremen, Kiel and Hannover.

Munich: According to the consulate small to medium sized flats are difficult to find and so are expensive, the surveyors found rents beginning at 2,500 DM, for a two bedroom apartment. While moving in can take as little as two days, the advance rent can be between one and three month's worth. There is some temporary accommodation, but at a price; 1,500-2,900 DM per month. A quick look at the München row in the table below will indicate that the city is probably the most expensive place in Germany for accommodation.

The main newspapers for accommodation advertisements are the *Süddeutsche Zeitung* (Wednesday and Friday editions); the *Abendzeitung* and *Tageszeitung (TZ)* (Friday and Saturday editions). Other useful publications include *Taking up Residence in Bavaria* a seven-page leaflet produced by the British Consulate in Munich and an American-run newspaper *Munich Found*. The Ring Deutscher

Makler is able to put enquirers in touch with estate agents (Ring Deutscher Makler, Landesverband Bayern e.V., Theatinerstrasse 35, D-80333 München; tel 089-2908200).

Below is the 1997 table of rent and purchase prices put together by the Association of German Estate Agents (*Verband Deutscher Makler* Head Office, Riedemannweg 57, D-13627 Berlin; tel 030-38302528; fax 030-38302529). This lists prices for flats and houses from a variety of cities and towns across Germany. These give some indication of the likely cost of housing and, on careful analysis, some clues as to how much accommodation is actually available to rent or buy. The table is divided fairly obviously into columns according to the type of accommodation available. The last two columns deserve special attention as they list the 1997 prices for building land **(A)** indicates building land for a family house, while **(B)** is building land for the construction of an apartment block or business premises which can then be rented out.

Table I — Rent and Property Prices in Deutsche Marks.

Table compiled by the Verband Deutscher Makler (Association of German Estate Agents).

City/Town	Flat Rental 70-80m. sq. (DM/m. sq.)	Flat Purchase 60-90m. sq. (D/M m. sq.)	Terraced House c. 100-140m. sq. (in thousand DM)	Detached 1 Family House, 150-200m. sq. (in thousand DM)	Building Land (A) incl. service mains (DM/m. sq.)	Building Land (B) incl. service mains (DM/m. sq.)
Aachen	7.5-16	1,200-4,000	200-440	340-800	300-600	370-800
Aschaffenburg	7-15	2,500-5,200	390-680	500-1.2 million	600-850	700-800
Augsburg	6-13	2,000-5,000	350-650	480-900	300-900	500-950
Berlin	5.5-19	1,800-5,500	250-850	350-2 million	250-2.1 million	300-2.8 million
Bielefeld	7.5-15	1,800-4,700	290-580	330-700	250-500	350-500
Bochum	7.5-15	1,800-4,100	250-600	400-1 million	350-650	400-750
Bonn	9-18	2,200-5,000	300-580	400-950	320-550	450-900
Brandenburg	5-8	2,000-2,800	180-300	280-500	150-270	100-200
Braunschweig	7.5-15	1,300-3,800	280-700	280-700	180-350	150-350
Bremen	8-15	1,650-2,300	170-450	380-900	170-400	450-600
Celle	7-11	1,800-3,000	220-400	260-400	150-250	150-250
Chemnitz	6.5-14	650-4,500	80-480	100-550	120-300	200-400
Cottbus	8-12	1,500-3,500	180-400	150-450	100-270	100-270
Darmstadt	9-17.5	1,800-5,200	400-640	450-1 million	600-1 million	750-1.1 million
Dortmund	8-16	1,750-4,800	265-520	350-900	300-600	300-900
Dresden	8-17	2,500-5,000	200-580	350-650	120-450	220-850
Duisburg	7-15	1,3000-4,300	230-480	280-600	280-500	220-450
Düsseldorf	9-22	2,200-7,900	300-800	400-2 million	400-900	400-1.5 million
Erfurt	7-18	2,000-5,200	250-600	250-750	200-450	250-600
Essen	8.5-18	2,000-6,000	400-650	450-1 million	450-700	300-800
Flensburg	8-15	1,500-4,000	200-360	300-500	100-300	100-300
Frankfurt/Main	10-19	2,800-6,300	400-650	450-1.5 million	700-1.1 million	900-2 million
Freiburg/Br.	11-20	2,800-5,600	420-800	500-1.5 million	500-1.2 million	500-1.1 million
Gelsenkirchen	5.5-13	1,500-3,800	200-430	350-800	350-500	300-450
Görlitz	7.5-12	2,500-3,300	120-280	150-320	80-160	50-120
Göttingen	8-15	1,800-3,200	240-400	350-650	350-600	300-370
Halle/Saale	10-14	2,800-3,900	270-500	350-420	200-250	00-900

Hamburg	12-20	2,500-7,500	300-850	350-2.2 million	250-800	500-800
Hannover	6-12	1,800-2,600	270-500	350-1.2 million	280-600	300-700
Heidelberg	9.5-17	2,400-4,500	420-700	500-1.2 million	380-1.1 million	550-1.6 million
Hildesheim	7.5-11	1,200-2,200	180-450	350-650	200-400	250-450
Homburg/Saar	8-14	1,500-3,000	230-600	250-450	180-280	160-250
Ilmenau	6-13.5	1,200-3,500	110-330	120-360	110-170	110-200
Ingolstadt	8-13	2,000-4,800	420-580	400-900	450-650	500-900
Jena	8.5-19	2,300-3,500	200-450	220-580	220-430	300-500
Kaiserslautern	7-15	1,700-3,500	240-380	250-500	250-400	300-500
Karlsruhe	8-15	2,700-5,000	380-690	450-1.2 million	480-1.1 million	500-1.1 million
Kassel	6-12.5	1,500-3,800	200-360	270-580	180-300	300-650
Kiel	8-18	2,000-4,600	250-470	330-650	170-320	350-520
Koblenz	7-12	2,400-3,600	250-480	300-600	260-500	600-900
Köln	11-19	2,600-6,000	290-600	360-1.8 million	300-800	400-1 million
Leipzig	6-17	2,200-5,000	200-500	250-500	90-300	200-800
Leverkusen	8-16	1,800-4,500	330-550	450-1 million	400-500	380-700
Ludwigsburg	10-16	3,100-5,500	450-800	500-1.2 million	650-1 million	650-1.2 million
Ludwigshafen	9-14	2,600-4,400	300-500	380-600	450-600	600-800
Lübeck	8-17	1,800-4,600	240-460	310-640	170-320	350-520
Magdeburg	8-15	2,000-3,800	270-330	260-450	180-350	350-650
Mainz	10-18	2,800-5,400	400-600	550-800	550-950	500-850
Mannheim	8-15	2,800-4,800	360-650	380-1.2 million	500-1 million	500-1.1 million
Mönchengladbach	7.5-17	1,600-4,000	270-480	380-900	600-900	300-550
München	12- 28	3,800-8,500	500-1.1 million	850-3.2 million	900-2.2 million	900-2.1 million
Münster	9-16	2,400-4,800	350-520	430-900	400-700	750-1.2 million
Neubrandenburg	6-15	1,100-2,900	220-350	250-500	120-130	150- 180
Neuss	9-14	1,700-4,500	320-500	380-700	340-600	600-1.2 million
Nürnberg	8-15	2,000-5,500	350-600	500-1.5 million	600-900	500-900
Offenbach	9-16.5	1,800-5,000	400-600	400-900	650-900	700-900
Oldenburg	8-13	1,600-3,900	210-360	250-490	170-190	290-420
Passau	8-11	2,000-3,900	260-390	380-600	280-400	250-380
Potsdam	5-19	2,000-5,000	270-400	350-600	300-600	400-800
Regensburg	7-15	2,500-5,800	330-600	350-1 million	400-700	500-700
Reutlingen	8-16	2,500-4,800	290-650	420-1.2 million	420-850	750-1 million
Rostock	10-16	2,500-4,400	220-350	250-500	100-210	190-700
Saarbrücken	9-15	1,700-4,500	270-500	300-600	250-400	250-380
Schwerin	8-16	3,000-4,200	250-520	300-520	80-200	150-1 million
Stendal	5-11	2,500-3,300	160-320	280-500	80-130	150-300
Stuttgart	11-24	2,900-11,000	550-1.1 million	750-2.9 million	900-2.7 million	1.5-3 million
Trier	8-14	2,200-4,200	300-500	320-650	300-500	500-1.1 million
Ulm	7-13	2,000-4,400	300-590	400-1 million	280-900	350-900
Weimar	8-21	1,700-4,500	200-410	200-540	270-450	360-480
Wiesbaden	10 -19	2,800-6,400	460-720	500-1.5 million	700-1.2 million	1-1.8 million
Wolfsburg	8.5-11.5	1,800-3,000	250-400	330-600	200-300	no figure available
Würzburg	8-13	2,400-4,600	380-800	450-950	400-800	450-800
Wuppertal	7.5-16	1,700-4,500	320-500	450-1 million	350-500	350-700

Occupants' Obligations and Hausordnungen

In many parts of Germany, tenants of apartment buildings are obliged to participate fully in the maintenance of the common areas (e.g. grounds, paths, cellar/basement, corridor, landing etc). Legal requirements include that the occupant of a house with a chimney, should engage the services of a chimney sweep two or three times a year. The occupant is also required to keep the public pavement outside the dwelling, clear of ice or snow during winter. There are usually restrictions on noise levels outdoors and on bonfires.

Being a tenant in Germany involves adhering to a set of fairly strict indoor *Hausordungen* (house rules). These may include such unfamiliar restrictions as how late or early you can take a bath, restrictions on the decibel level of televisions, music centres etc. and a precise time for locking outside doors.

Useful Abbreviations and Terms:

Abstellr. (Abstellraum): storeroom (for hoover etc.).
Altb.(Altbau): old building.
App.(Appartement): apartment.
Atelierwhg. (Atelierwohnung): studio flat.
Aufzug: lift.
Bad (pl. Bäder): bathroom(s).
Baugrundstück: building estate.
Bes. (Besichtigung): viewing.
Bj. (Baujahr): year of construction.
Blk. (Balkon): balcony.
beziehb.(beziehbar): ready for occupation.
bzf.(bezugsfertig): ready to occupy.
Dachgarten: roof garden.
DG (Dachgeschoss): attic floor.
Dachgeschosswohnung: attic flat.
3-Zi-Komf-DG-ETW (Dreizimmer-Komfort-Dachgeschoss-Etagenwohnung): three-roomed, luxury attic flat in an apartment block.
EBK(Einbauküche): fitted kitchen.
EG (Erdgeschoss): ground floor.
EFH (Einfamilienhaus): family home.
eig. (eigen): own.
Ein-zimmer-wohnung mit Bad/Dusche: single-room flat with bath/shower.
Esszi.(Esszimmer): dining room.
ETW (Etagenwohnung): flat (in an apartment block).
excl.(exclusiv):
Fahrstuhl: lift.
Fertigst.(Fertigstellung): to be completed.
freist. (freiestehend): free standing/detached.
Gehmin. (Gehminuten): minutes walk.
gepfl. (gepflegt): well maintained.
Gge.(Garage): garage.
gr.(gross): large.
Grd.(Grund): ground.
he. (hell): light, airy.
Hzg.(Heizung): heating.

die Kaution: security deposit against damage. Usually two months rent.

Kaltmiete: rent minus heating.

Keller: cellar/basement.

kl.(klein): small.

kompl.einger.(komplett eingerichtet): fully furnished.

Kü.(Küche): kitchen.

Lage: site, situated.

langfristig zu vermieten: long-term let.

leer: unfurnished.

Maklercourtage: agent's commission.

die Miete: rent.

die Mietdauer: period of lease.

die Mieteinnahme: revenue from rent.

die Mieterhöhung: rent increase.

der Mietvertrag tenancy agreement.

möbliert: furnished.

Monatsmiete: monthly rent.

nähe/nh.: near/close to.

Nebenkosten: maintenance charges (for a block of flats).

Neub.(Neubau): new building.

Nfl.(Nützfläche): usable space.

OG (Obergeschoss): upper floor.

reizv.(reizvoll): charming.

renov.(renoviert): renovated/newly decorated.

ruh./rhg. (ruhig): quiet.

Schlafzi.(Schlafzimmer): bedroom.

sep.(separat): separate.

Spitzenlg.(Spitzenlage): prime site.

S-Lage (Südlage): south facing.

Stellpl.(Stellplatz): parking place.

Stck. (Stock): floor (storey).

Terr. (Terrasse): terrace/patio.

TG (Tiefgarage): underground parking.

überd. (überdacht): roofed.

UG (Untergeschoss): cellar/basement.

VB (Verhandlungsbasis): guide price.

Verkehrsgünstig: convenient location.

voll einger. (voll eingerichtet): fully furnished.

von Privat: private let/sale, i.e. no agent's fee.

Warmmiete: rent including heating (e.g. *1400 DM Warm*).

Wfl./Wohnfl.(Wohnfläche): living area.

Wokü/Wohnkü. (Wohnküche): kitchen/diner.

Whg.(Wohnung): flat/accommodation generally.

Wohnzi.(Wohnzimmer): sitting room.

zentrale Lage: central situation.

Zhg. (Zentralheizung): central heating.

das Zimmer: room.

2-Zi-Whg: (Zweizimmerwohnung): two-roomed flat; (also *2Zimmerige Wohnung*).

zzgl.(zuzüglich): plus, including.

Insurance

Owing to the legal responsibilities of householders for accidents occurring to a third party on their property: falling on the icy pavement or footpath outside the building, loose tiles, hazards caused by children's toys etc. it is advisable to take out third party or liability insurance (*Haftpflichversicherung*) while living in Germany. Cause any damage, or have a child run riot and you will be liable for the cost of repairs. It is not a question of going to court as it is all settled by insurance claims. Apart from the insurance possibilities offered by the main German insurers, or any relocation agency that you engage, you can engage an insurance broker (*Versicherungsmakler*) to obtain the best deal for you ; one such is:

Cathy J. Matz: Burgerstrasse 10, D-61476 Kronberg; tel 06173-2897; fax 06173-4497; e-mail cathyjmatz@aol.com. An independent financial advisor who's offices are based near to Frankfurt am Main, services available include insurance and investment advice. Through a network of insurance companies, both foreign and domestic, insurance cover is available for health, disability, life, liability, household, car and legal fees.

Of course while you are in Germany you will also need to insure your property, and likewise maintain the insurance on any property that you leave behind. If your goods are in storage then your storage company will probably have some form of liability cover against damage, or you may wish to save yourself this trouble by engaging a house-sitter, or letting your property out (see below) in which cases these options may well pay you while looking after anything that you don't take with you. One of the problems of leaving your home empty while you are away is that many insurance companies exclude water damage from policies in cases where property is empty for more than 30 days. While the insurance market has been soft recently the problems that much of Britain faced from storm damage means that many companies are taking a harder line again. One way around this is to take out insurance with a specialist firm, two such are:

Europa: Provender Mill, Mill Bay Lane, Horsham, RH12 1TQ; tel 01403-263860. Can offer insurance cover for vacant properties, but discounts on buildings insurance are offered if the property is tenanted (ie house-sat). These discounts start at 7.5% on an insured sum of £65,000, they also have a tenant theft component in case you are unlucky with your choice of sitter.

Jardine Group Services: Threefield House no. 7, Threefield Lane, Southampton, SO14, 3QH;tel 01703-228277. This empty property insurance is arranged in conjunction with the law society, so a solicitors assistance will be needed.

House Sitters

Many families with homes who have to move abroad for work purposes find that one way of ensuring that their home and possessions are safe, is not to store them but to pay for house-sitters or even rent out their home and make some extra cash (see below). This certainly means that if you can not take furniture with you then at least you don't have to sell it or worry about it mouldering in storage. House sitters are also a useful bargaining tool when discussing your new situation with your insurers. Even if you empty all your furniture into storage and leave your own home empty while renting accommodation abroad, you run the risk of burst water pipes, squatters or vandals causing damage in your absence. Aylesbury based Homesitters have arranged up to 15% discounts on home insurance policies, and have a list of insurers and brokers with reductions available to their clients. Fees are usually calculated by the house-sitting company on a daily basis, beginning at about £20 per day. The house-sitters are usually middle aged and have had extensive background checks carried out on them by the agencies.

However it is still necessary to exercise caution in this matter, any company which does not accept responsibility for its employees actions should be avoided, fidelity bonding which protects owners from rogue sitters is an assurance of risk cover and is offered by the main agencies. Below is a list of some of the most reputable companies:

Homesitters: Buckland Wharf, Buckland, Aylesbury, HP22 5LQ; tel 01296-630730; fax 01296-631555. Incorporated in 1980 to provide low-cost caretakers for private houses, Homesitters vets all employees meticulously. Peace of mind is guaranteed by fidelity bonding, and the fact that all sitters are directly employed staff. Guardian, Norwich Union and Eagle Star are some of the insurers who will reduce policy premiums if a house sitter is used, and these range from 5-10% of buildings and contents insurance.

Housewatch: Little London, Berden, Bishop's Stortford, CM233 1BE; tel 01279-777412. Are a nationwide house-sitting company in business since 1985. Although the main operation is holiday house-sitting, arrangements can be made to look after your property should you have to move abroad before selling it, or if a property becomes vacant in your absence overseas. The sitters taken on to watch your house in these circumstances will therefore, remain until all the legal procedures of sale or probate are completed, giving you the reassurance that all is well in your absence.

Universal Aunts: PO Box 304, London, SW4 0NN; tel 0171-738 8937. In operation since 1921, this company will arrange sitters as necessary, depending on the owners requirements, for up to a year and possibly longer by arrangement. Their sitters will only leave the house for two hours a day to shop or walk any pets, and light garden maintenance (eg watering plants) is included in the daily rate. Sitters will undertake actual gardening on your behalf, and look after larger pets, even livestock, subject to negotiation.

Letting Your Property

One way of helping pay towards your new accommodation in Germany is to rent out your own home, this has the added benefit of also covering your current mortgage costs without putting you to the time ands trouble of selling before you leave, and gives you somewhere to come back to when your assignment ends. If at the end you don't wish to return home then you can think of it as an investment, although of course you should check with the tax authorities with regard to your liability with regard to taxes in your home country. In Britain if you are looking to let your property then you should check that the agent is a member of ARLA (Association of Residential Letting Agents, Maple House, 53-55 Woodside Road, Amersham, HP6 6AA; tel 01494-431680.), this association only admits businesses over two years old and members are bound by a code of conduct including indemnity insurance and a fidelity bond to cover insolvencies. Around half of all letting agents are members of this association, which stipulates that rent has to be forwarded to the owner within ten days of payment. ARLA have an information hotline (01923-896555) which will help find an agent in a particular area of the UK.

At present if an owner is not registered for UK taxes the agents have to retain funds as a provision for tax at source, but any interest on these monies should be forwarded to the owner. Agency fees are usually around 10% for supervising letting and 15% for full property management. The differences between the two services are that the former is really just administering the collection of rent and arranging contracts, so that should there be any problems the tenants would be passed on to the landlords to deal with them. Full management essentially means that the agency acts as the landlord's representative, ideal for those landlords overseas. If any problems arise the agency will deal with them, hiring contractors or repairmen as necessary.

Chestertons Residential: 40 Connaught Street, London, W2 2AB; tel 0171-262 5060. Have 15 offices around London dealing with London area properties. Their Landlord's Information Pack contains details of services, rates and a London area rent guide.

Countrywide Residential Lettings: tel 01372-843811. Have offices across the UK

Finders Keepers: 73 Banbury Road, Oxford, OX; tel 01865-311011; fax 01865-56993. This property management agency has been in business for 26 years, and is a member of the National Association of Estate Agents. They have offices in Swindon, Banbury, Abingdon, Witney and so deal with properties in Oxfordshire and Wiltshire.

TWG Estates Ltd: 36-37 Maiden Lane, Covent Garden, London, WC2E 7LJ; tel 0171-240 0300; e-mail twg.estates@virgin.net; fax 0171-836 1500. Are a relocation agency who also provide a comprehensive service for those wishing to sell or rent their home while working abroad, or even those wishing to purchase property for letting while overseas. They can arrange mortgages for property in the UK and overseas as required. Their main operational base is London and the Home Counties (roughly speaking the commuter belt up to $1\frac{1}{2}$ hours travel around London).

Utilities

It is important for anyone looking for accommodation in Germany to note that most rents do not include charges for water, gas and electricity which are expensive commodities, all of which are metered so you only pay for what you use (or what you think you use, see below). At present German electricity is the most expensive in Europe. In addition to natural gas (see below), Germany also has substantial reserves of coal and lignite (*Braunkohle*). Germany subsidizes its coal industry quite heavily, half of this subsidy comes from a levy on electricity consumers who pay the generating companies the difference between the price of the 50 million tons of domestic coal used and the price of coal on the world market.

Most local supply companies will have application forms available at the Einwohnermeldeamt, so that new residents can inform them as quickly as possible, in order to maintain supplies. If this isn't the case look up *Stadtwerke* in the telephone book. The cards produced by one such local company in Nürnberg allows those moving in and moving out to arrange their supplies not to mention reporting meter readings for billing!

On the subject of which it is worth noting that most Germans pay their domestic debts by a monthly debit direct from their bank accounts. These come under the general heading of *Nebenkosten* in most household accounts. These payments cover municipal rates for street sweeping and rubbish collection, as well as monthly payments to cover energy, water and sewerage bills. Of course some towns will have more expensive utilities than others. Thus in Berlin the average monthly expenditure on energy alone will be around 200 DM (these figures are based on moderate usage by a family of four, in a survey taken by the Economist Intelligence Unit), while in Frankfurt electricity, gas and water will cost 70 DM, 100 DM and 55 DM respectively; totalling 225 DM. Compared to these large cities, Nürnberg would appear to be nearer the average for a German town in its cost of 125 DM per month for all the services (this figure is based on the Nebenkosten of a family of five). Although the charges are deducted on a monthly basis, these deductions are based on an estimate of your usage, these estimates are either derived from meter readings or extrapolated from the size of your house and family calculated against use patterns. How often your meter is actually read will depend upon the practices of your local supplier, however, if you undershoot their estimates, you will either receive a rebate or be charged less for the next year.

Electricity

Electricity is supplied by regional networks which enjoy lucrative local monopolies, these can be small city based companies or big regional concerns of which Viag, Bewag (Berliner-Kraft-und-Licht AG), RWE, Preussen Elektra and Bayernwerk are examples. For the time being Germany is a captive market and so prices are artificially high, however, EU regulations are set to change that, as by 1999 outside competition must be allowed on the domestic supply market. Germany's electricity is 60% generated from conventional sources and 33% nuclear, with an increasing ratio of supplies coming from 'green' technologies. Around 21 nuclear power stations are currently in operation in western Germany, and around 3,500 wind turbines.

Consumers can request free wiring checks and also buy recommended appliances from the company supplying their area. The electrical current is 220 volts AC, 50 cycles, two phase, and so different to the UK's 240 volt supply. This means that appliances from the UK will work, albeit sluggishly. However, since there is a risk of damaging sensitive equipment designed for UK electrical specifications, it is important to seek the manufacturers' advice before importing such equipment for use in Germany. There is also the added hassle of having to change all your three-pin plugs for two-pin ones, or buy adapters for those items where the plug is integral with the power cable. Since German electrical equipment is renowned for its durability and high safety standards, it is probably better to buy your equipment once you are in that country. In Germany, electrical goods come with plug attached, a feature of which will almost certainly be made standard throughout the EU in the next few years. German plugs are of the continental two-pin type. Electric light sockets are for screw-type bulbs only.

Electricity is measured by an electricity meter which is usually black in colour and measures usage in kilowatt hours.

Gas

Germany has enough natural gas (*Erdgas*) to supply about a third of domestic needs. The rest is piped in from Holland and Russia. Like electricity, the gas market is run by private companies. Two of the largest are BASF and Ruhrgas. It was a consortium of gas companies with various European investors which began the Russo-German gas pipeline project in the 1980s. Gas is metered by the cubic meter and your gas meter will either be painted yellow or have yellow connections to the supply pipe.

Water

All German houses have water meters fitted as standard and water is charged for each month by the cubic metre used. In addition to this there is a separate charge for sewerage, the rates for which are charged as a set annual fee per person. The current costs (based on figures from Nürnberg) are 2.4 DM per cubic metre for water, plus 7% VAT and 3.7 DM without VAT for sewerage.

Telephones

At the time of writing Deutsche Telekom had just lost its monopoly of the German telephone system, so the costs of installing a telephone may well drop. At present to obtain a phone line from Deutsche Telekom, the installation fee is around 100 DM including VAT. If you take over the previous tenant's telephone number the connection charge drops to 50 DM. Private lines can usually be installed within two weeks of application in most parts of western Germany, basic monthly rental is around 22 DM and bills are rendered monthly. Telephone calls are still charged for by the unit at a base rate of 10 pfennigs per unit, the cost of your call depends on the time of day and distance involved, as these factors affect how much phone time you actually get per unit.

Removals

While those readers moving to Germany for only a short while can get by with renting a furnished apartment, those engaging on long term employment, especially those taking their family with them will have to ship or store almost all their goods, unless they can afford to run two homes, or wish to rent out their home and furniture.

However much of your furniture and household goods that you wish, or can afford, to take with you to Germany, you will need a good removal firm to ship them for you. Lists of these can be obtained either from the Association of International Removers or the British Association of Removers. Or you can pick a company by studying advertisements or surfing the internet.

The Association of International Removers: Unit K, Abbey Wharf Industrial Estate, Kingsbridge Road, Barking, Essex, IG11 0BT tel; 0181-594 7790. Are a specialised professional association and can supply a list of international removers in your area. As they are a bonded association your goods will be delivered by another member should the company you have chosen cease trading for any reason.

The British Association of Removers: 3 Churchill Court, 58 Station Road, North Harrow, HA2 7SA tel; 0181-861 3331 fax; 0181-861 3332. Have an International Removers list, if you contact them with an outline of what you'd like to move they will send you a list of up to 3 companies in your area who are capable of meeting your requirements, which you can then contact for an estimate or more detailed discussion.

Paramount Logistics Ltd.: PO Box 61, Avonmouth, Bristol, BS11 0BD; tel 01179-081418; fax 01179-085564; e-mail sales@paramountltd.co.uk ;website http://www.paramountltd.co.uk Is a global freight company who can tailor any move to the individuals needs, so they will do as much or as little as you wish. This personalised consultative service includes the options of full packing, transhipment and unloading of your goods including cars and pets.

Allied Pickfords: Heritage House, 345 Southbury Road, Enfield, Middlesex, EN1 1UP; tel 0181-219 8000; fax 0181-219 8001; e-mail nd19@dial.pipex-com Can arrange storage and shipment of all types of personal effects, including moving furniture and pets to all parts of Germany. Shipping requirements are discussed in a personal visit and a full packing service is offered.

An alternative to searching for a good remover and having to juggle their costs against your means, is to take up a new option, advertising your job on-line. If you contact Freightpages (07000-484848; website http://www.freightpages.com) you can advertise your removal needs for companies to tender. It acts like an on-line small ad. in that a removal freight company can read your posting and contact you with a service offer and quote.

Redirecting Post

If you are moving house to Germany then there is unlikely to be anyone to forward your post for you, should you accidentally forget to inform anyone of your new address. Or if your stay is not for very long you may find it easiest to just have your post redirected. This option solves both long and short term mail forwarding problems and saves you having to send out lots of change of address notes to friends, family, book clubs etc. British readers can have their post forwarded to them by the Royal Mail's Redirection Service, this service can be arranged either by filling in the leaflet available at Post Offices, which includes a pre-paid envelope; or you can apply on 0345 777 888 (calls charged at local rate), if you wish to pay by credit card. Redirection is available for one, three or twelve months (costing between £12 and £60 at time of writing) and will begin from one week after your application.

Customs Regulations Regarding Household Effects

Since 1993 British and other EU citizens have been able to move household effects around Europe without any customs documentation, although just in case you are stopped on a spot check it is always handy to have proof that you are taking up residence or beginning a job in Germany.

Cars

Importing or Buying Locally: If your residence in Germany is temporary (less than one year) you may drive your car on a British registration for that period. If you are intending to live in Germany for longer than one year you may import a motor vehicle that has been registered in your name for at least six months in your previous country of residence, duty free. You need not pay duty on vehicles from EU countries. However, German safety and anti-pollution laws for motor vehicles are some of the most stringent in Europe and, depending on the vehicle, may necessitate costly modifications. Compulsory items such as warning triangles and first-aid kits should ideally be purchased in Germany to ensure that they are of the required specifications. For instance the German first-aid kit must include impermeable gloves as an anti-HIV precaution.

Another reason for buying locally is that there are considerable savings to be made on the prices of a BMW, Mercedes or Porsche, especially with the current state of the Deutsche Mark against Sterling and the US Dollar. Buying a German model also means that your car has the driver's seat on the correct side of the car for driving on German roads.

The current situation is that a new car bought in Germany attracts 15% VAT, while in Britain this is 17.5% and the British buyer will also need to pay £140 Road Tax (Vehicle Excise Duty).

Licensing, Car Tax and Vehicle Inspection: Cars in Germany should be licensed by the German licensing authority (*Strassenverkehrsamt* or *Zulassungsstelle*). A Briton can bring their own car with them but it can only be driven with its British licence plates for one year, after which it must be re-registered with the German authorities and a new plate fitted. Motor vehicle tax (*Kraftfahrzeugsteuer* shortened to *KFZ-Steuer*) will also need to be paid. The local vehicle registration office (*Landeseinwohneramt*) will be listed under local council offices in the phone book and will advise you on the papers you will need to re-register your car for German licence plates. These will usually be proofs of ownership and insurance and previous registration documents. The registration charge (*Zulassungsgebühr*) is currently 5 DM, while the motor vehicle tax varies according to engine size.

Some new cars entering Germany may need to pass type-approval tests, to ensure that it complies with EU safety and technical regulations. For information on whether or not your vehicle needs type approval contact the Federal Vehicle Office (*Kraftfahrt Bundesamt*), Fördestrasse 16, D-24944 Flensburg.

Every two years (if not a special vehicle), the vehicle must have a mechanical inspection carried out by a Technical Supervisory Agency (*Technischer Überwachungsverein* TüV or DEKRA). The same agencies are now required to perform an anti-pollution test (*AU*) which is even more stringent than the similar test introduced in the UK in November 1991, but which allows low emission cars a tax discount. Before taking your car for its TÜV its wise to have it checked by a reputable garage, and make sure that you have the approved first aid kit and safety equipment in the car, and don't forget your papers (*Fahrzeugschein*). Once inspected, if fit, a disc will be placed on the rear registration plate, this will note the expiry date of the inspection.

Driving Licences: On 1st July 1996 a standardised pink driving licence was adopted across the EU, from this date onwards drivers who change their residence within the EU no longer have to exchange their licence for the national version after 12 months. Licences issued in one member country will be valid in all the others until expiry, even if it is an old national licence. The new EU licences are divided up into categories according to which type of vehicle you are licenced to drive, in Germany some of these categories require the driver to undergo a medical examination in order to qualify, and this will apply to expatriate drivers even if their home state does not require a medical for that category of licence. In Germany it is also a requirement that you carry your log book (*Fahrzugschein*) with you when driving. Further details on licences and local conditions can be found in Chapter Four (*Driving*).

Car Insurance

Car insurance in Germany is more expensive than in the UK. The various premiums are calculated using the following criteria:
1. The period for which the driver has held a licence and for how long he or she has been accident-free.
2. The classification of the car into a class (*Typentarif*) according to the average frequency of damage to that car model.
3. The area in which the owner of the car resides.
4. The proportion of each claim which will be paid by the owner.

In Germany, it is compulsory to have third party insurance. Fully comprehensive insurance also covers fire, theft and damage. No-claims bonuses accrued with British car insurance companies will be taken into account by German insurance companies when setting premiums for UK citizens resident in Germany. You should therefore obtain confirmation of any such bonuses, from your British insurer. The Green Card (International Insurance Certificate) is no longer necessary, under recent EU rules. But, while the provisions of the European Single Market allow you to insure your car with a British insurer and thus save money, a vehicle licensed in Germany has to be insured with a third-party liability insurer 'registered' in Germany, so always check with your insurer first.

Importing Pets to Germany

The British are renowned for being inseparable from their pets, especially dogs and cats. Most removal firms can give you the help and advice needed to take pets with you to Germany. But the main source of information for importing pets into Germany is the Ministry of Agriculture, Fisheries and Foods (MAFF) who receive information direct from their equivalent ministries in Germany. If the owner is transporting his or her own animal to Germany a certificate of health is not normally required. However, some shipping companies and airlines require you to produce a certificate of health to ensure the animal is fit enough to travel. EU nationals within the borders affected by the Schengen agreement can transfer their animals across the borders quite happily once they have been innoculated against rabies.

For dogs and cats, belonging to British citizens, a bi-lingual certificate, issued by a British veterinary surgeon who is registered as an inspector of the Ministry of Agriculture, attesting that the animal has been vaccinated against rabies not less than 30 days, and not more than 12 months, prior to the date of export, must be obtained. In some cases i.e. if more than three animals are involved, or if the animals are not going to the owner on arrival in Germany an import licence may also be required. The ministry of agriculture can supply explanatory leaflets on request. The base guidelines can be found in EU Regulations 92/65/EC and 90/425/EC which have been passed into German Law as the *Binnenmarkt-Tiersüchen-Schutzverordnung* and these also cover the import of American pets into Germany.

Dogs in Germany

Once in Germany, dogs have to be kept on a lead in parks or wherever signs indicate that this is necessary. As a general rule, fighting dogs must be muzzled in public places, and most Germans 'poop-scoop', and will expect you to do so too, in built up areas. For dogs, an annual registration at the Town Hall is required. This *Hundesteuer* is similar to the Dog Licence in Britain, except that rates are set by individual town or city councils. These are generally higher in more built up areas, and while the fee increases with the number of dogs you have the increases are less than you may expect. Thus in Passau the hundesteuer is 50 DM no matter how many dogs you have whereas Aachen charges 174 DM for the first animal, 228 DM for two and 276 DM for three or more. The highest fee for one dog is 276 DM in Köln, while the average appears to be around 150-180 DM, but various discounts are available. Veterinary Surgeons (*Tierärzte),* can be found through the yellow pages, but many people prefer personal recommendation.

Re-importing Pets to the UK

Pets entering the UK must be placed under six months quarantine according to the Rabies (Import of Dogs, Cats and other Mammals) Order 1974. At present a scientific risk assessment is being carried out by MAFF officials, in order to see if the British laws should be relaxed in line with the rest of the EU. For the time being if you wish to bring an animal back to Britain from another country then you should contact the MAFF who will send you the appropriate application forms for an import licence, including a list of Quarantine Kennels and Carrying Agents.

Useful Addresses:
*Ministry of Agriculture, Fisheries and Food:*Animal Health Division, Hook Rise South, Tolworth, Surbiton KT6 79F; tel 0181-330 4411 (Switchboard).
Ministerium für Umwelt, Raumordnung und Landwirtschaft: Abteilung für Veterinärwesen, Schwannstr. 3, D-40476 Düsseldorf, Germany.

Daily Life

Moving to a new country gives rise to one set of problems, living there presents the newcomer with another, subtler, set. The little nuances of daily life and the habits and rituals of shopping, banking and even catching the bus are now a challenge. This chapter is intended to supply sufficient practical information for the reader to get to grips with their new home as quickly as possible. However as Germany is a nation of federal states regional variations will occur, and things may change over the life of this book, so not all the information is uniformly applicable. As in any endeavour being properly prepared will make life easier, whether this means attending a training course, or immersing yourself in all things German at your local library, or by surfing German related websites. However, there are other ways to deal with this and the Embassies and Consulates will have an information office from which you can find out more about Germany if the other options are closed to you.

Be Prepared

Information Resources

A good starting point for information is the German Tourist Office in your home country for a supply of maps, transport information and brochures, or if you are connected the Internet has a wide range of sites about Germany. The German National Tourist Office in London has a premium rate phone line (0891-600100, 50 pence per minute) for ordering brochures or if you can afford it for listening to information about Germany. There is also a phone number given if you would prefer to talk to an operator, if you can not get to their offices. German maps are of a very high standard and are widely available in the UK. Amongst the most widely stocked are Kümmerly and Frey whose range includes a very detailed 1:500,000 one sheet map. Stanfords in London have an up-to-date selection of maps ranging in price from £4.99 according to the publisher and scale.

Alternatively you may want to visit one of the Goethe Institutes who have many centres around the world, and whose aim is to disseminate information about Germany and German culture. Hence the libraries in each Institute are very useful for research before you leave and the institutes can arrange courses for learning the language (see below).

Other useful information to prepare you for your new life can be found on the internet, either specific information relevant to your new home from the various Federal or Länder government websites, or from the wide range of newsgroups and FAQ (Frequently Asked Questions) sites. One of the best of these is the Soc. Culture German FAQ website, which is posted monthly, it can be found at http://www.physics.purdue.edu/vogelges/faq.html.

Another option to prepare yourself for your new life is to attend a training course, there are many of these available, some run by educational charities, or organisations engaged in promoting Germany, while others are run by businesses. One such is the Centre for International Briefing, which can provide customised residential briefings for any country, these are suitable for businessmen or their families, or even home based international managers. The programmes provide in-depth information about the country, including politics, economics and social issues. Practical advice on the business and working environments are given by recently returned businessmen or expatriates, allowing the trainee to prepare their communication and negotiation skills for the new workplace.

Useful Addresses:
German National Tourist Office: 65 Curzon Street, London W1Y 8NE; tel 0171-493 0080. Brochure Request Line 0891-600 100 (Premium rate); website http:/ /www.germany-tourism.de
Edward Stanford Ltd: 12-14 Long Acre, Covent Garden, London WC2E 9LP; tel 0171-836 1321.
The Centre for International Briefing: Farnham Castle, Farnham, Surrey, GU9 0AG; tel 01252-721194; fax 01252-719277; e-mail cib.farnham@dial.pipex.com website http://www.cibfarnham.com
*The Goethe Institut (UK):*50 Princes Gate, London SW7 2PH; tel 0171-411 3400; fax 0171-581 0974; website http://www.goethe.de
Manchester: Churchgate House, 56 Oxford Street, Manchester, M1 6EU; tel 0161-2371077.
Glasgow: 3 Park Circus, Glasgow, G3 6AX, Scotland; tel 0141-3322555. website http://www.goethe.de/gr/gla
The Goethe Institut (Australia): Nat West House, 40 Allara Street, P.B. 186 Civic Square, Canberra City, ACT 2601, Australia; tel 62-474472.
The Goethe Institut (USA): Goethe House, 1014 Fifth Avenue, New York, NY10028, USA; tel 212-439-8700; website http://www.goethe.newyork.org
The Goethe Institut (Canada): 418 Sherbrooke Street East, Montreal, Quebec, H2L 1J6, Canada; tel 514-499 0159; website http://www.goethe.de/uk/mon

Anglo-German Societies

Before actually leaving for Germany it is a good idea to find out if any Anglo-German clubs and societies exist in your area as these organize various social events and seminars will help to soften the blow of culture shock on your arrival in Germany, allowing you to develop potentially useful contacts in the expat community before you get to Germany. Addresses of such societies can be found in your local library or information centre or you can contact the Cultural Department of the German Embassy which should be able to supply a list of such societies. The main German cultural society worldwide is the Goethe Institut (address above) and if all else fails they should be able to point you in the right direction.

The British-German Association (18 Conduit Street, London, W1R 9TD; tel 0171-629 4975; fax 0171-629 5162) exists to promote friendship between the two countries. They arrange social events, seminars and study trips to Germany. There are 60 affiliated organisations in the UK which you can contact through the association or its quarterly magazine *British German Review*.

For businessmen and students there is also the Anglo-German Foundation for the Study of Industrial Society (17 Bloomsbury Square, London WC1A 2LP; tel 0171-404 3137), which aims to support bi-lateral research and links between academics and industry.

The German Language

The main drawback of moving to Germany is having to learn a new language, and German has a fiendishly complicated grammar with many variations and exceptions. Some of the main hazards include gender and case endings of nouns (similar to Latin) and immensely long sentences or compound words. One famous and often cited opinion on this trait of the language is Mark Twain's essay of 1880 'The Awful German Language' which claims that *only the dead have time to learn it* a full text of this essay is available to read on the web and ironically is recommended by several of the language sites on the net, you can find it at http://www.cs.utah.edu/gback/awfgrmlg.htm1#x1. However do not be put off by such comments about these facets of the language, it is not that bad really. While German can create long compound words to give a clear definition of something (e.g. *Donaudampfschiffahrtsgesellschaftskapitänsmütze* meaning Danube tourist steam boat Capitain's hat) such long words are usually paraphrased or avoided, by native speakers. Even the more widely used term *Geschwindigkeitsüberschreitung* (breaking the speed limit) might look like a long winded way of saying it, but the policeman saying it will take no longer to say it as would an English speaker their version.

Pronunciation is less of a problem than grammar. The vowels and vowel combinations can be learned quite quickly. The umlaut (two dots) used above the vowels a, o and u, represents an e. Thus *ä,* is a combination of a and e pronounced like the e in pet, *ö,* is a combination of o and e like French *eu* and *ü* is a combination of u and e as in the French 'tu'. This added 'e' is quite an easy way to get into pronouncing umlauts and is used as a shorthand on the internet, where technology works against the use of accented vowels.

The above refers to Standard German or *Hochdeutsch* which is taught in all German schools and used in the media. There are two main dialect groups: *Plattdeutsch* (Low German) and *Hochdeutsch* (High German). Standard German is a form of High German which means that it is mutually intelligible with other German dialects (e.g. Bavarian, Franconian, Swabian, Hessian, and Saxon). The differences in the dialects are mostly related to regional or cultural oddities and accents. It is very much like the differences in English between a Geordie and a Cockney, both speak English but that doesn't mean that they pronounce it the same way. All of this means that when you arrive in Germany you will not understand the occasional dialect term in any given conversation, but within a few months you'll have picked them up because every time you gave someone a quizzical look they would have explained in Hochdeutsch.

Low German on the other hand has no standard form (other than Dutch) and is a lot less intelligible to someone who only knows Standard German. As a result, these dialects (spoken in the Northern Plains and in the Rhineland) owing to the advance of Standard German, are a lot less thriving than their High German counterparts (although 8 million north Germans speak them) having lost a lot of ground since the Middle Ages when it was the official commercial language of northern Germany. One 1994 debate in Bonn was held almost entirely in *Platt* to prove a point that the language needed more support. However, practically everybody who speaks them will also know good Standard German and will speak that to anybody they do not know. Which means that anyone living and working in northern Germany is unlikely to have problems understanding people face to face.

The main problem for the learner is that German is currently a language in flux, as the researchers of the *Duden* the main German Dictionary needed to find a standardised way of writing and spelling modern German. This reform would standardise the spelling of various new words and would ease teaching and learning of written German, by removing such oddities as the funny 'b' shaped squiggle for double 's' or 'sz'. 1996 saw the German Government's decision on 'the spelling reform of the century' after many discussions with the cultural ministries of the other German language states, Austria, Liechtenstein and even parts of Switzerland and Italy. However 1997 saw a court case in Wiesbaden which may hold up these reforms.

One final point on the subject of German orthography is the numbering system. While the numbers when written by hand show a similarity between 1 and 7, the 1 has a longer downstroke at the top of the stem than in English usage, thus resembling a 7. The 7 being differentiated by a horizontal stroke across the middle of its stem. The most noticeable difference is the use of the decimal point; in German mathematics and the prices of goods or services the system used in English numbering is reversed thus the decimal point **.** is actually a comma **,** until one reaches the level of thousands when it switches around again. Thus one deutschmark and fifteen pfennigs will be written 1,15 and four thousand, five hundred will appear 4.500.

Self-Study Courses

The advantage of self-study courses is that they allow the student to absorb material at their convenience and own learning pace, thus you can fit in some study while working rather than having to arrange your life around a course timetable. The disadvantages are, that a lot of self-motivation is required and it is not possible to practice spontaneous conversation and your pronounciation may suffer. However, these methods are popular, relatively cheap and would not still be available if they were ineffective. Almost all self study courses are available from bookshops and most include tapes to help you train your ear for the sound of German.

The BBC offers learning language materials for adults in fifteen languages and these range from simple survival guides to comprehensive courses. In German this range includes phrase-books, tapes, grammar guides and travel packs which are available in all good bookshops or direct from the BBC, with prices ranging from £2.99 to £12.99. The BBC has also produced some very fine language learning programmes for radio and television. As well as *Deutsche Direkt !* and *Ganz Spontan* for which the books, tapes and videos are still available, there is the latest offering, *Deutsche Plus* which has programmes on BBC2 and Radio 4. The language programmes are designed as multi-media packages, of television and radio programmes coupled with study books and audio tapes. The course *German Means Business* is accompanied by a course book and audio tapes and a special video pack is aimed specifically at those who already have some German and wish to survive in a business environment. Based on location recordings it is aimed to help the business person dealing with German business contracts including cultural differences and the business meal. For the casual visitor or complete beginner there is also the *Get By In* course (currently £29.99) which consists of a book, two audio cassettes, a video and video handbook. The *Deutsch Direkt!* language pack of course book and three audio cassettes is currently £29.99, while the *Deutsche Plus* pack of course book and four cassettes is £39.50, a CD set for the latter is also available.

All the books and tapes can be ordered direct from the BBC from BBC Books (Book Service By Post Ltd, PO Box 29, Douglas, Isle of Man, IM99 1BQ; tel 01624-675137; fax 01624-670923). Overseas readers can order through the BBC Shop in Newcastle, (tel 0191-222 0381; fax 0191-261 9902), however the shop does not offer an enquiry service. Further details and queries about the BBC's language courses can be obtained from the Education Information Unit (BBC White City, 201 Wood Lane, London W12 7TS; tel 0181-746 1111; e-mail Edinfo@bbc.co.uk; website http://www.bbc.co.uk/education).

Linguaphone (head office: Carlton Plaza, 111 Upper Richmond Road, London SW15 2TJ; tel 0181-333 4898; fax 0181-333 4897) also provide a range of self-study courses in over 30 languages to suit different language learning needs. Travel Packs (£9.99 at time of writing) are available from WH Smith, AA Travel Shops and all good bookshops and they cover simple holiday vocabulary. Full Language Courses (£179.90-£399.90 from the head office) aim to teach between 1,500-3,000 words of vocabulary. The Full Courses are available as books, cassettes, CDs and videos, and include a special Business Course.

You can also study on the Internet, Peter Schröders German language site features sections devoted to all aspects of the language and includes sound files to illustrate pronounciation; http://members.icanect.net/peters1/intro.htm.

Language Courses

*Goethe Institut:*50 Princes Gate, London SW7 2PH; tel 0171-411 3400; fax 0171-581 0974. The Goethe Institute offers language courses at its centres in London, Manchester and Glasgow, for details contact their Language Courses on 0171-411 3451. It also has sixteen institutes in major German cities including Munich, Bonn, Berlin, Bremen, Düsseldorf, Freiburg, Mannheim and Frankfurt.

Berlitz (U.K.) Limited: 9-13 Grosvenor Street, London W1A 3BZ; tel 0171-915 0909; fax 0171-915 0222. Another international organization, Berlitz offers language courses in the UK which can then be continued at any of its 330 centres overseas. The Berlitz method involves tailoring the course to the individual's requirements as far as the level and course intensity is required. The cost varies depending on these factors. Further details may be obtained from the above address.

EF International Language Schools: Kensington Cloisters, 5 Kensington Church Street, London, W8 4LD; tel 0171-795 6675; fax 0171-795 6635; website http:/ /www.ef.com EF have run a full-time school in Munich for the last ten years and the mix of students of all ages, nationalities and abilities creates a relaxed and enjoyable learning environment. Teachers use a balanced combination of

written work, role-play, conversation and language laboratory work to develop your fluency. Courses are matched to individual requirements and the fees include accommodation with a local family to help you practice outside your course. EF's courses can last from two weeks to an academic year, and students can prepare for internationally recognised language qualifications.

Euro-academy Limited: 77a George Street, Croydon, CR0 1LD; tel 0181-686 2363; fax 0181-681 8850; brochure line 0181-760 5167. Offer courses for young people and adults across Europe, with 10 sites in Germany alone. They believe that the most stimulating learning method is to 'learn the language on location'. Crash, Intensive and Business courses are available all year and last from two to four weeks. Requests for their brochures 'Learn the Language on Location' and 'Business Class' can be obtained freepost from the above address if the post code CR9 9ER is used.

*Eurolingua Institute:*Eurolingua House, 61 Bollin Drive, Altrincham, WA14 5QW; tel/fax 0161-972 0225; website http://www.eurolingua.com Provides unique opportunities for people of all ages to learn languages in the country where they are spoken. Combined language learning, study, activity and holiday programmes are offered including one-to-one homestay programmes.

Part-time Courses

Most local colleges of further education run evening courses in German, these can be of a formal nature for complete beginners to 'A' level standard; or of a more conversational type for students of varying standards. Information about these courses and costs can be obtained from your local library or college of further education, which usually have a large advertising drive in June or July for courses starting the following September. While most of these courses run along the same timetable as the academic year, some have start up dates in January or are re-run each term. In addition many colleges of further education and local adult education organizations offer personal language tuition on a one-to-one basis which can be very useful if you want to brush up your business vocabulary. Course lengths and prices vary according to the local authority and funding. Another way of finding a private tutor is to check the classified advertisements in the press or through local Anglo-German clubs or societies, although you should make sure of your tutor's qualifications to speak English and German, before you part with any cash.

Courses in Germany

In almost all large German towns, and some smaller historical ones, facilities exist whereby foreigners can attend German courses. Some of these will be run by the German equivalent of a local college of further education (*Volkshochscvhule*) these may be run all year round based at a permanent language institute, e.g. the Goethe Institute, EF etc. (see above), or by universities during the summer vacation. Many of the language courses are run parallel with others on the history and culture of Germany and thus a combined course can provide excellent access to a deeper understanding of the country. A full list of operators of courses throughout Germany can be supplied on request by the Information Centre of the German Embassy (21-23 Belgrave Square, London SW1X 8PZ; tel 0171-824 1300) although this only lists the head offices of these organisations.

Schools and Education

The problem of deciding how and where to send children to school is a perennial one for parents and arises whether they live in the UK or whether they live abroad. Moving abroad with young children need not cause a lot of disruption to their education, since in many ways younger children are far more adaptable when it comes to picking up foreign languages and ways, than older, teenage children. If your offspring are already at boarding school in the UK or USA, it is tempting to leave them there in order to avoid unsettling them. However, they may be passing up an exciting opportunity to broaden their horizons by going to an international or British school abroad, or a German school, with the added benefits of developing international connections and the chance to become fluent in another language. It is however important to maintain continuity in the type of education: thus a child who has already embarked on GCSEs, 'A' level courses or SATs in the UK or USA should ideally attend a British or American school in Germany, where the same curriculum is pursued. Unfortunately with the decline of the military presence in Germany there are relatively few such schools around. A child of primary school age, whose education has not begun in earnest could be sent to a German primary school for one or two years and could then be switched into the UK or American system without any long-term adverse effects which would be likely to result from a later changeover between two curricula. They would also benefit from getting extra tuition in German so that they could mix with the other children. Many parents favour sending their children to an international school, where the emphasis on languages within a rounded education may prove beneficial, especially given the good pupil teacher ratios of classes in these schools. Details of other schools in Germany are given on pages 86-88.

German Schools

British parents living in Germany on a long-term basis who have put their children through the German state education system have been favourably impressed not only with the range of subject matter, especially in international politics, and foreign languages, but with the high quality of teaching. The main differences between the German and British state schools are that unlike in British schools where the emphasis is on developing the whole person, the object of German schooling is only to train the mind; secondly most German schools operate lessons between 8am and 3pm (this can vary according to school and region) after which most children return home to do their homework. School attendance is compulsory for all children between the ages of 6 and 18, based around nine years of full time schooling followed by a further three years of either full-time academic or part-time vocational study (*Berufschule*). As schools are subject to state laws there will be regional differences between the attendance, areas of study and homework required from pupils. An example of this can be found in music lessons, where Berlin has 13 secondary schools teaching music Bremen has none. In the state education sector, after primary education, children are streamed into three types of secondary education depending on ability and aims; these are Secondary Generals, Intermediate and Grammar schools (*Hauptschule*, *Realschule* and *Gymnasium*), each offering a different type of school leaving certificate according to academic prowess. There are also a few Comprehensive Schools (*Gesamtschule*) which offer the same school leaving certificates as the other three types of secondary school. Over 12 million pupils study at more than 52,000 schools across Germany and as in Britain state education is free. The state system accounts for the education of 96% of German children; the remaining 4% attend private schools, these being divided between Grammar, Waldorf and special schools.

Secondary Education and Qualifications

After Primary school children attend an observation level of the various secondary schools or if available an orientation level of a Gesamtschule. Whatever type of school the child enters the observation stage (school years five and six) is a phase of special encouragement to ensure that the child is helped to make the right choices for themselves regarding their future educational path. These school years are taught by a mixture of teachers from each school type to allow for a fair assessment of the pupil on one side and the different schools on the other. Hauptschule and Realschule aim to give children a general basic education with the standards of Realschule being higher, with the Gymnasium being higher again. Hence the different school leaving qualifications (*Abschluss*) or the higher education entrance qualification (*Abitur* or *Zeugnis der allegemein Hochschulreife*) awarded by the different types of school. An important point to note is that like Britain and America schools operate within a catchment area, and all children in this area must attend that school, until they reach Gymnasium level. At this level the child and parents can choose which establishment to attend, for example if the nearest school does not emphasise French as much as another more distant school, the Francophone child may attend the latter for preference.

The stages of the German education system are:

Primary School (*Grundschule*): Grundschule covers the first four years (six in Berlin and Brandenburg) of schooling and begins at age 6. Apart from reading and writing, children receive a grounding in the subjects they will be studying at secondary school namely *Sozialkunde* (social affairs), *Gesichte* (history), *Erdkunde* (geography), *Biologie*, *Physik* (physics), *Chemie* (chemistry), *Mathematik*, *Religionslehre* (religion), *Musik* (music), *Kunsterziehung* (art), *Handarbeit* (needlework) or *Werken* (crafts) and Sport. All subjects are compulsory and the number of weekly lessons varies depending on the year from 20 to 30.

Secondary Schools:

Hauptschule Around a quarter of German children attend Hauptschule for years five to nine of schooling, although a voluntary tenth year is offered in most of the Länder. The subjects studied correspond to the Primary School subjects with the addition of a foreign language (usually English) and *Arbeitslehre* (Working World Practices). In Bavaria *Haushalts und Wirtschaftskunde* (Domestic Sciences) are also studied. In Bavaria, Grundschulen and Hauptschulen are amalgamated into one unit, the *Volksschulen* (Elementary Schools). Hauptschulen are designed for children to begin vocational training after nine or ten years at school, once they have their school certificate (*Hauptschulabschluss*) they can go on to part-time vocational study at *Berufschule*.

Realschule: The aim of the Realschulen is to provide the basis for careers in middle-management and positions at a similar level. In 1994 about 40 percent of all pupils obtained the Intermediate school certificate (*Realschulabschluss*). This enables the holder to go on to full-time vocational school (*Berufsfachschule*) or a vocationally orientated upper secondary school (*Fachoberschule*). The latter allows the student to study for the Polytechnic (*Fachhochschule*) entrance certificate (*Fachochschulreife*). The subject matter and extent of the Realschule curriculum varies between Länder. Learning foreign languages and the general overall higher level of study marks the difference between the Hauptschule and the Realschule, as students are taught a second foreign language (usually French) from year eight.

Gymnasium: Are for the most academically promising and are geared to providing a general education leading to the Abitur for university entrance. The Abitur is generally reckoned to be more rigorous than the UK 'A' levels as it is aimed at achieving a high level in a range of subjects, but is still less difficult than the infamous French baccalaureate. There is also a seven stage Gymnasium for those children who's aptitude only becomes noticeable at the observation level of the other schools. Subjects are divided into three categories: language, literature and art; social sciences; and mathematics, science and technology. For their Abitur, students must take four examination subjects. The Abitur entitles the holder to study the subject of their choice at university or an equivalent institution, subject of course to availability.

German Private Schools: Those Germans who wish their children to attend private schools have a choice of anthroposophical schools (*Waldorfschulen*) based on the system of education founded by the Austrian scientist and humanist, Rudolph Steiner, which looks at the child as a whole rather than a mind to be developed. There are about 80 Waldorfschulen, as well as Montessori schools, where the ideology is 'Help me to help myself', (in fact some state schools have classes based on the Montessori principle) and some private schools run by churches. In general the private schools tend to be patronised by the offspring of German intellectuals and professionals, who can afford the fees. There are also around 20 *Internate* (boarding schools) run along English public school lines. The academic reputation of the private schools is however considerably lower than that of the Gymnasien, which are the only places where a child can take an Abitur.

German Universities

The academic traditions of many German universities reach back several centuries (eg Heidelberg was founded in 1386 and Leipzig in 1409), while others are more recent; to cope with expanding demand more than 20 more have been founded since 1960. In the sixties only eight percent of each age group went to university, nowadays it is closer to thirty; currently around 1,850,000 students are enrolled at universities across Germany. However, even with over 220 universities and polytechnics, and a falling admissions figure many lecture theatres are crammed more than full and courses are over-subscribed by eager students.

Until the middle of this century the academic style of German universities was based on the principles of Wilhelm von Humboldt, who believed that universities should be purely for academic research. So that students were not taught with any future profession in mind. This has changed to reflect the needs of modern society and the individual student, thus traditional universities rub shoulders with technical universities, colleges of education and Fachochschulen.

The modern German university is owned by the regional government but self-governing, headed by a Rector or President. The governing bodies should be comprised of 50% professors and by law, a selection of representatives from all categories including: academic tutors, students and employees.

As in most other European countries it is a constitutional right in Germany, that everyone who attains the university entrance qualification is entitled to enter higher education. However, the straightened circumstances of the nineties seem to have forced an increasing number of *Abiturienten* to reach the conclusion that a university degree is not necessarily a guaranteed career-ticket and consequently, many are pursuing apprenticeships instead. Every third student enrols at a Fachhochschule for a practice related study course, which is of shorter duration than at university. These courses cover such areas as business studies, engineering, design and social work.

It should be noted that with the present overcrowding of classes, a high drop-out rate and a general dissatisfaction with the length of studies, many changes are being proposed. These changes may well include making institutions more responsible for picking the students they enrol and introducing a three or four year first degree, as opposed to the current situation where it can take seven years to obtain a first degree.

There are also a few private institutions which of course charge high fees. For 29,700 DM you can study medicine, or for 7,900 DM a semester you can study at the European Business School, so while the latter course does result in excellent job offers, only 2% of students study at these private institutions. There is also a German equivalent of the Open University for those who wish to study from home or while working, which will soon be moving from its 14 day postal cycle to the internet.

Costs
University tuition is free and students are covered by the institution's health insurance, so the only costs to students are living expenses, books and stationery, which are usually met by their families. There is a little help with this as a child in higher education still qualifies for the German child benefit (*Kindergeld*) until they are 27, however this is not necessarily a large sum. Under the Federal Training Assistance Act students have the legal right to public funding, half of which comes in the form of a grant and the rest as an interest free loan re-payable within five years of the end of the entitlement period. The main cost to students is accommodation, as rents are high and there are few college dormitories, only 55% of students in western Germany have the option of college accommodation, and this figure drops to 10% in the eastern länder.

Period of Study
Those used to the English system of higher education with its fixed terms for completing degrees, may be surprised by the relaxed German attitude to the duration of the study period. The German academic year consists of two semesters which run from October and April. Most study programmes have two stages but their duration is not fixed: you are supposed to obtain a certain number of credits in whatever time it takes you for both stages. Apart from certain subjects including law and medicine, it is possible to perpetuate your studies almost indefinitely. This length of study coupled with increased overcrowding has lead to a rise in the number of students dropping out of their courses. The average time for completing a degree is now seven years. What is more, many students are commencing their studies late, after an apprenticeship or compulsory military service. As for that subject of horror for British students - 'finals', if you flunk them in Germany another attempt is permitted up to two years afterwards. So far, proposals have been made to limit the duration of studies but little has been done by the universities to implement any such measure and thus the overcrowding in the university system will continue for the foreseeable future.

Degrees
The degrees awarded in Germany are the *Magister Artium*, the *Diplom* or *Diplom Ing.* and the *Staatsexamen* according to the course studied. The Magister is a

Masters level degree in Arts and Humanities which is taken by those students who wish to continue their studies as research students and eventually become academics. The Diplom is also at Masters level and is awarded within the Social and Natural Sciences to those subjects which have a practical or professional bent such as psychology, with the Diplom Ing. as an engineering graduate qualification. While the Staatsexam is a professional style qualification taken by those wishing to enter state service e.g. lawyers, teachers, civil servants. There are no BA or BSc degree equivalents in Germany.

Admission

For students wishing to study in Germany admission to a German university depends on a thorough knowledge of German, in addition to the Abitur, or its foreign equivalent. The Federal and State governments are keen to attract foreign students, over 142,000 studied there in 1995. The *Deutscher Akademischer Austauschdienst* (German Academic Exchange Service) listed below can supply the relevant information, including details of its German preparation course. Tuition is free for both first and postgraduate degrees, but as noted above living expenses can be high. For postgraduates there are various grants, details of which can again be obtained from the DAAD, for more details of academic exchanges to study in Germany see *Studying in Germany* in Chapter Six, *Employment*. Another organization useful to students wanting to study at German universities as part of their UK course is the UK Erasmus Socrates (address below). Although they cannot actually arrange placement with a German university they can supply information leaflets on the processes involved. The other branches of ERASMUS in Britain can arrange teacher exchanges anywhere in the EU. For further details of teacher exchanges, see Chapter Six, *Employment*.

In addition to the many German universities there is a complete residential campus of a major American university the University of Maryland, University College at Shwäbisch Gmünd (see below for address). This campus is part of one of the twelve largest public universities in America and now has 300 sites around the world. The college offers US Bachelor's Degrees in eleven subjects to a student body drawn from 36 nations. The university and its host city both offer scholarships to students in financial need and the college operates a rolling admissions policy. Alternatively a budding engineer can study at the Technical University of Braunschweig which has a teaching agreement with the University of Rhode Island, this rewards engineering graduates with a D. Ing. and an American Master's degree.

Useful Addresses:

DAAD: Main Office, Kennedyallee 50, D-53175 Bonn, Germany; tel 0228-8820; e-mail postmaster@daad.de; website http://www.daad.de

DAAD (UK): 34 Belgrave Square, London SW1X 8QB; tel 0171-235 1736; e-mail info@daad.org.uk; website http://www.daad.org.uk

DAAD (USA): 950 Third Avenue, New York, NY 10022, USA; tel 212-758 3223; website http://www.daad.org

UK Erasmus-Socrates: The University, R and D Centre, Canterbury CT2 7PD; tel 01227-762712.

University of Maryland, University College Schwäbisch Gmünd: Universitätspark, D-73525 Schwäbisch Gmünd, Germany; tel 07171-18070; fax 07171-180 732; e-mail tshea@admin.sg.umuc.edu website http://www.sg.umuc.edu

Technical University of Braunschweig: website http://www.tu-bs.de/

Reform Since Re-Unification

As the two German states integrated there was much that needed to be changed; not least was the dogmatic representations of old, which meant that East German school books did not mention West Germany and vice-versa and the limit that only 10% of gymnasium pupils could take the abitur. However most of the hardest tasks are well over and all that is needed is for time to cement the changes into place. Now there are 17 universities and 14 colleges of art and music across the former East, and the geographical spread and academic range of all institutions has been improved. The introduction of 26 Fachhochschulen, a type of institution only recently introduced to the new länder has assisted this and over 52,000 students are now enrolled in these schools. The choice of second language has also been changed, whereas Russian was the norm it is now only an option behind English and French, this change can have ironic benefits. One eastern school which had a twinning arrangement with a western school felt some friction amongst its students during a class exchange, as the arrogant 'wessies' lorded over the 'ossie' hosts with their command of such English terms as 'PC' and 'layout'. Since then the twinning arrangement has eased the tensions, and the partnership has arranged trips to France, where ironically the eastern students fare better; French being their first second language compared to the westerners' Latin. However, even as the sweeping reforms of the east's education system now settle into permanence there are those who lament a couple of the former features of the education system in the east. One is the free kindergartens, invaluable to working mothers, but not provided under the west German education system; the other is the compulsory afternoon sporting and cultural programmes.

Vocation Training in College and the Workplace

Vocational schools are mandatory for anyone under 18 who is not at some other type of school and youth vocational training in Germany is generally acclaimed as the best in Europe. It consists of a variety of apprenticeships, work and part-time study, and full-time vocational study.

Apprenticeships last from two and a half to three years, but are only available in recognised occupations. The apprentice is paid a training allowance which increases annually, and is taught and examined according to regulations laid down by federal ministries, business associations, trade unions and chambers of crafts and trades.

While some teenagers are still taking up apprenticeships the trend in youth training is towards a more formal qualification that blends theory and practice. The State issues the conditions under which vocational training may be provided, but the financial support is largely provided by individual firms from the mega-corporation to the single employer. Vocational training generally occurs under the 'dual-system' whereby practical training on the job with a firm (*Betrieb*) is coupled with theoretical training at a part-time school (*Berufschule*). In 1996 1.6 million young people were training for the 470 types of employment for which recognised training is required.

Trainees are known as *Auszubildende* (or 'Azubis'). Trainees attending a Berufschule must be in the process of undergoing their initial job training or already have a job. The contract for a two or three-year course involves the Azubi receiving general education and specialized instruction in a variety of skills at the Berufschule for up to two days per week. In addition up to three days a week are spent in a firm learning a specific job or trade. The instruction received at the Berufschule is closely related to the training received in firms. Vocational skills acquired in this way may include hairdressing, car mechanics and clerical skills. During the training period, the Azubi receives a small wage from the employer which rises significantly upon the completion of the training period.

In addition to apprenticeships and Berufschule, there are the options of full-time vocational school (*Berufsfachschule*) and vocational secondary school (*Fachoberschule*). Of the two, the former offers vocational courses lasting between one and three years, which can count as part of an apprenticeship or replace it entirely. While the Fachoberschule with its theory classes, workshops and on-the-job training qualifies students for entry to the polytechnics (*Fachhochschule*) which offer practice-related study.

British, European and International Schools

Although the state schools of Germany are very good it is understandable that many parents will prefer their children to be educated in an English language school, especially one that teaches the same syllabus as the children will be returning to if the move to Germany is not a permanent one. Naturally there are only a few British schools offering the National Curriculum in Germany, so many parents will find their choice is between the more prevalent International Schools which offer a range of syllabuses, and the local German schools. With luck they may be able to get their children into one of the European Schools, which have been founded to educate the children of EU staff on placements outside their homeland. Below are details of several schools, new comers to Germany can also obtain information about schools in their area from the nearest consulate office.

In September 1997 two of the British Schools in Germany became International Schools offering the International Baccalaureate Programme from Primary level through to University entrance. As independent schools the fees are high, but pupil teacher ratios are better than in state schools in Britain or the USA. There are at present a dozen international schools in Germany each one offering a variety of curricula including the British National Curriculum, the International General Certificate of Secondary Education and the International Baccalaureate, some also offer American School programmes. For more information about the International Schools in Germany contact The European Council of International Schools (21 Lavant Street, Petersfield, Hants GU32 3EL; tel 01730-268244). Information can also be obtained from their *On-Line Directory of International Schools* (website http://www.ecis.org) which list the schools and gives details of the curriculum types and fees.

The European schools, of which there are two in Germany at Karlsruhe and München, are operated by the EU to provide native language teaching for the children of EU employees wherever they may be employed. There are a limited number of places available each year for children of non-entitled families, application for these is by writing to the Head of the School. These places are fee-paying although some help can be given in cases of hardship. Each school teaches from Primary through to University entrance level, following the syllabus of the International Baccalaureate. Teaching includes one foreign language from the first year of primary school, with another language to be learned from the second year of Secondary school (languages are taken from the range available at each school). More information on the European Schools can be obtained by writing to them directly (addresses below) or from The Central Office of the Board of Governors of The European Schools (Rue de la Loi 200, Belliard 7-1/008, B-1049 Brussels, Belgium).

National Schools:

For details of German state schools in your area contact your local School Authority or youth education office (*Amt für Schule* or *Behörde für Schule, Jugend und Berufsbildung*). Certainly the Hamburg office can provide an English language leaflet giving details of school types and the information offices which can help a child decide which educational direction they wish to go in (Freie und Hansestadt Hamburg, Behörde für Schule, Jugend und Berufsbildung, Postfach 76 10 48, D-22060 Hamburg, Germany).

Note on the entries: 'IGCSE' is the International General Certificate of Secondary Education, 'IB' is the International Baccalaureate and SAT is the American College Board Entrance Exam.

Playgroups:

English Kindergarten: Verein zur Förderung der Englischen Sprache e.V.: Haus d. Jugend, Bebelallee 22, D-22299 Hamburg; tel 040-511 4256. This operates two playgroups; for children aged 3 and over, weekday mornings and on Wednesday afternoons for children aged from 4½ to 7-8.

British Schools:

Berlin British School: Dickensweg 17-19, D-14055 Berlin, Germany; tel 030-304 2205; fax 030-304 3856. Ages 3-13. Opened in 1994 in a former British Services School, the school teaches the National Curriculum, which can be adapted for pupils from other backgrounds.

St George's: The English School of Cologne: Administration Dept. Heisterbacher Str. 121, 53332 Bornheim, Germany; tel & fax 02222-81610. Ages 4-18. Prepares pupils for Common Entrance, GCSE and A Levels, using a termly syallbus so that pupils can advance at their own pace. American and Canadian teaching is also offered.

American Schools:

John F. Kennedy School: Teltower Damm 87-93, D-14167 Berlin, Germany; tel 030-807 2771; fax 030-807 3377; website http://www.kennedy.behive.de Ages 5-19. This German-American community school offers teaching in English and German from Kindergarten or 'Vorschule' up to High School Diploma level in grade 12 or the German 'Abitur' in grade 13. Families paying German income tax do not pay fees for their children's tuition.

European schools:

Europäische Schule: Albert-Schweitzer-Strasse 1, D-76139 Karlsruhe, Germany; tel 0721-680 090; fax 0721-680 0950. Kindergarten to sixth-form. An international, co-educational school with a European curriculum leading to the European Baccalaureate.

Europäische Schule München: Elisa-Aulinger-Strasse 21, D-81739 München; tel 089-630 2290; fax 089-630 22968. The second European School in Germany, teaching is free but places are limited to children of EU staff; other children can obtain places awarded by a lottery, held in April for the coming school year.

International Schools:

Independent Bonn International School: Tulpenbaumweg 42, D-53177 Bonn, Germany; tel 0228-323 166; fax 0228-323 958. Ages 3-13. Formerly the British

Embassy Prep School, the school takes around 220 pupils from the international community of the Bonn/Cologne area. The school folows the Primary and Middle years curricula of the IB, coupled with a range of extra-curricula activities.

International School of Düsseldorf e.V.: Niederrheinstrasse 336, D-40489 Düsseldorf, Germany; tel 0211-94066; fax 0211-408 0774. Ages 4-20. The international curriculum and IB are offered to pupils from kindergarten to High SchoolGrade 13.

Franfurt International School: An der Waldlust 15, D-61440 Oberursel, Germany; tel 06171-20281; fax 06171-202 384; e-mail fis_admissions@fis.cocos.de Ages 4-19. Teaching is in English with German, Spanish and French offered to over 1,500 pupils within an IGCSE and IB syllabus. The school also acts as local test centre for IGCSEs and the SAT. The school itself is 15 km from Frankfurt and offers transportation to it and the branch site at Wiesbaden.

International School Hamburg: Holmbrook 20, D-22605 Hamburg; tel 040-883 0010; fax 040-881 1405. Ages 3-18. Founded in 1957, the first such school in Germany, the school offers the IGCSE and IB, to around 500 pupils in classes of between 10 and 20 pupils. There is also an Early Learning Centre attached to the school for Pre-Kindergarten, Kindergarten and Reception classes. German is offered from grade two onwards.

Franconian International School: c/o America House, Gleissbühlstr. 13, D-90402 Nürnberg. This new international day school should open at the start of the academic year 1998-9 as a grade school. Adding an academic year each year until the school can offer the complete American High School Diploma or IB.

Leipzig International School e.V.: Ratzelstr. 26, D-04207 Leipzig, Germany; tel 0341-421 0574; fax 0341-421 2154; e-mail c-reckhaus@intschool-leipzig.com; website http://www.uni-leipzig.de/ods/lis.html Ages 4-15. This day only school was set up in 1992 as a pre-school and elementary school, with the intention of adding an academic grade every year. Teaching follows the IGCSE and IB syllabuses.

Munich International School: Schloss Buchhof, D-82319 Starnburg, Germany; tel 08151-3660; fax 08151-366 119. Ages 4-18 An independent, co-educational, comprehensive-type day school based on an international curriculum incorporating elements of both the British and German educational systems. Curriculums taught include National Curriculum, IGCSE, American High School Diploma (including SAT Preparation), and IB. Pupils are admitted throughout the year according to class space and ability.

*International School of Stuttgart e.V.:*Vaihinger Strasse 28, D-70567 Stuttgart-Möhringen; tel 0711-718 9161; fax 0711-718 9485; e-mail 100451.3621 @compuserve.com Ages 3-16. Teaching an international syllabus with plans to extend the school by an academic grade each year, the school currently teaches the IGCSE programme and will start with the IB in the school year 1997/8.

International School Wiesbaden: Kohlheckstrasse 43, D-65199 Wiesbaden, Germany; tel 0611-946 7978/79; fax 0611-946 7970. As a branch of the Frankfurt International School, this non-profit co-educational school offers a european, international and American college preparatory programme.

Service Children's Education:
In addition to the above there are some British primary, middle and secondary schools in Germany which are primarily for the education of Servicemen and other entitled personnel working abroad, however, fee paying children of non-service

families can apply to be accepted. Applications need to be sent to HQ Service Children's Education, Building 5, Wegberg Complex, BFPO 40.

Media and Communications

Newspapers

Unlike Britain, but in common with other European countries Germany does not have an array of national daily papers: *Bild*, *Frankfurter Allgemeine Zeitung* (usually shortened to *FAZ*) and *Die Welt* are the only three that can claim a national readership. The traditional basis for the German daily press is the regional or local subscription paper, as can be seen from the table below. The remaining 1617 German newspapers provided by 380 publishing companies, are all regional, though in the cases of one or two, readership may spread over a wide area, again this is reflected in the circulation rates, where the big three do not fare as well as one might expect. For instance the *Süddeutsche Zeitung* based in Munich enjoys wide popularity in southern Germany, while the devoted readership of the sharp-shooting *Frankfurter Rundschau* extends similarly deeply into the Frankfurt hinterland. In addition to the dailies, there is one major weekly newspaper *Die Zeit*. Unlike Britain and North America there is no tradition of hefty Sunday papers, while *Bild*, *FAZ*, and *Die Welt*, put out Sunday editions (eg *Welt am Sonntag*) there is no chance of a German news vendor getting a hernia., except possibly from his large Sontag lunch.

Bild-Zeitung (Bild): A massively popular daily its 4.4 million readership makes it Europe's largest selling tabloid, just ahead of Britain's *Sun* to which it is sometimes compared. Somewhat sensational in content, it probably goes beyond the bounds of what might be considered good taste by Britons. Bild being the German for 'picture' of which there are more than a few, often of young women, in large format. Despite its lurid style, Bild has an element of acute political reporting. Because of its large circulation, politicians have to take notice of Bild, and many of them grant interviews to it. Cover price 70 pfennigs.

Die Welt: Germany's second largest national daily newspaper, and flagship title of the Axel Springer Group. It is published in Berlin but available in 130 countries across the world, making it a useful daily for those preparing themselves for the move to Germany. In Berlin and Hamburg the paper also has extensive local sections. Circulation is 214,000 with a cover price of 1.80 DM.

Frankfurter Allgemeine Zeitung:(FAZ) Is a weighty daily which has no British equivalent. Cautious and balanced, it reflects the opinions of the business world and deals with a range of subjects: political, business and cultural, on a worldwide basis. The business section makes it the business person's favourite newspaper. Like *Die Welt* this broadsheet is popular with libraries, businesses and individuals around the world. The daily circulation figure is around 393,400. Cover price 2 DM.

Die Zeit: Die Zeit, published in Hamburg is Germany's sole weekly newspaper though both Die Welt and Bild publish Sunday editions. Regarded as broadly liberal, it allows different shades of opinion on major issues to be voiced in its columns Circulation is around 494,000 and the cover price is 4 DM. Although it is going through a difficult time at present as many younger readers consider its editorial stance outdated, and hence some reorganising is taking place.

Der Spiegel: Spiegel is Germany's largest weekly news magazine renowned for its investigative journalism and in-depth articles. Its adherents point out that it has good contacts with the movers and shakers of the political world, and through them, humanises politics. The cover price is 5 DM and circulation hovers around 1.1 million in Germany and 5,86 million worldwide.

Focus: A competitor to *Der Spiegel*, this magazine has a slightly more conservative approach, but its in depth articles cover modern trends in German life, business and international politics as well as advances in science and technology. Although only a recent addition to the press market it is reaping a circulation of 780,000. Cover price 4.50 DM.

The Fifteen Daily Papers with the Largest Circulations

Title	Place of publication	Editions sold
Bild	Hamburg	4,643,935
Westdeutsche Allgemeine	Essen	660,000
Hannoverische Allgemeine	Hannover	559,812
Stuttgarter Zeitung	Stuttgart	502,379
Express	Köln	440,000
Sächsische Zeitung	Dresden	426,000
Süddeutsche Zeitung	München	405,424
Nürnberger Nachrichten	Nürnberg	400,000
Frankfurter Allgemeine Zeitung	Frankfurt/Main	393,390
Rheinische Post	Düsseldorf	390,708
Augsburger Allgemeine	Augsburg	373,987
Südwest Presse	Ulm	350,000
Hamburger Abendblatt	Hamburg	294,576
Stuttgarter Nachrichten	Stuttgart	273,000
Berliner Zeitung	Berlin	230,565

Magazines:

The buoyant market for illustrated magazines in Germany (there are some 20,000 titles in circulation) probably reflects the affluence of the Germans. Magazines range from the outrageously lurid but topical *Stern* and its rival *Bunte* to the German equivalents of the women's and teenage press which fill so much newsagents' shelf space in Britain. Despite, or perhaps because of, its unashamedly sensational content, Stern's circulation is a hefty 1,237,000. In the same market are the even more trivial, gossip magazines e.g. *Neue Revue*, *Quick* and *Weltbild*.

Women's magazines (*Frauenzeitschriften*) account for an additional, combined magazine readership of around ten million. The main ones in descending order of circulation are *Bild der Frau* (2 million), *Neue Post*, *Tina*, *Freizeit Revue*, *Brigitte*, *Für Sie* and *Freundin*.

Another market area is the Television guide magazines which have a very wide readership, especially Hörzu which has 6 regional editions. Apart from the various channel listings these weekly titles have a good range of articles from the standard interviews with the stars, behind the scenes reportage and reviews of films, to in the case of *TV Hören und Sehen* articles and advice on family issues. The top five circulation magazines are *Prisma* (circulation 2,978,682), *TV Movie* (2,647,620) priced 2.50 DM, *Hörzu* (2,373,058) priced 2.30 DM, *TV Hören und Sehen* (1,949,309) priced 2.30 DM and *Fernsehwoche* (1,423,499) priced 1.70 DM.

English-Language Publications

Major international English-language newspapers and magazines like *International Herald Tribune, Time, Newsweek, The Financial Times* etc. are all readily available on German news-stands. Most of them have production facilities in Germany, both the 'Trib' and the 'FT' are printed in Frankfurt. At present the former has a German circulation figure of 19,000. British newspapers are available on a daily basis at news-stands and bookshops in major cities. English-language publications available across Germany, or by subscription include:

The Times: Subscriptions Department, PO Box 479, Virginia Street, London, E1 9XY; tel 0171-782 6118. The Times is available on a daily basis in Germany although the time of arrival at news-stands will depend on location as it is produced in London and Belgium. Readers in Frankfurt can get copies as early as 7 am, but those in München or Berlin will have to wait until late morning or lunchtime. The cover price is 4.50 DM and 9 DM for the Sunday Times. , Due to shipping problems the latter is only available at larger shops, stations and airports on the day printed having been flown out. An alternative is to take out an annual subscription, the current rate for the Monday-Friday issues is £474 in Europe, however, you will usually receive issues two to three days later than published.

The Guardian: Subscriptions Department, 164 Deansgate, Manchester, M60 2RR; tel 0161-832 7200. *The Guardian International* is the overseas daily version of the Guardian, and is produced in Frankfurt, and is available at news-stands across Germany. However, it lacks the supplements found in the British version. Die hard readers who don't want to lose out will have to obtain a subscription which costs £1.72 per copy due to the weight when posted. *The Guardian Weekly* is an internationally available round up of the week's events as reported in The Guardian, the cover price for the weekly edition is 4 DM.

The American: 110 Mill Road, Westhampton Beach, New York 11978, USA; tel 516-288 4621; fax 516-288 6284. A colourful weekly tabloid (circulation 25,000) available at shops, news-stands and by subscription across Germany and Europe. Annual subscriptions cost 200.20 DM while copies retail for 5.50 DM. As well as news stories of interest to American expatriates it also carries classified adverts.

Aussenpolitik: Interpress Verlag, Hartwicusstr. 3, D-22087 Hamburg; tel 040-228070. An English-language publication summarising world affairs, produced by a German publisher and aimed at the expatriate market.

The European: 200 Gray's Inn Road, London, WC1X 8NE; tel 0171-418 7777; fax 0171-418 1840. A tabloid weekly round up, this is effectively a useful one-stop for those wanting political, business and cultural information across Europe. Circulation is currently over 120,000 and the cover price is 4.5 DM. At the time of writing there was a raft of changes about to take place although no details were available.

The Economist: 25 St James' Street, London SW1A 1HG; tel 0171-830 7000 and Bettinastrasse 62, D-60325 Frankfurt am Main; tel 069-975 8720; fax 069-975 87221. This highly regarded weekly magazine offers broad international perspectives on business and political affairs, as well as analysing new trends in science and technology. The German edition goes on sale on Fridays with a cover price of 7.90 DM, although an annual subscription is 155 DM. Circulation in Germany is 25,288 and subscriptions can be arranged by contacting The Economist Newspaper Ltd, PO Box 14, Harold Hill, Romford, RM3 8EQ.

Financial Times: Number One, Southwark Bridge, London; tel 0171-873 3000; website http://www.FT.com and Financial Times (Europe) GmbH, Nibelungen Platz 3, D-60318 Frankfurt am Main; tel 069-156850; fax 069-596 4478; subscriptions 069 1568 5170. Britain's premier Financial and business daily has a print site and editorial department in Frankfurt, the circulation in Germany alone is 16,778.

Forces Echo: Is a service oriented English-language weekly, produced in Britain for Germany, covering service news sporting fixtures and results. Copies are available at British base shops and service clubs.

Germany: A Guide to Living and Working in Germany: Rios Werbung GmbH, Eschersheimer Landstr. 69, D-60322 Frankfurt am Main. An A5 magazine put together by an American publishing team, aimed at informing expatriates of how to get the best out of life in Germany.

International Herald Tribune: Barbican City Gate, 1-3 Dufferin Street, London, EC1Y 8NA; tel 0171-628511; fax 0171-628 5533; website http://www.paris-anglo.com/iht and Friedrichstrasse 15, D-60323 Frankfurt am Main; tel 069-726755; fax 069-727310. At the time of writing the 'Trib' was offering a 50% discount on subscriptions hence you could get a 12 month subscription plus 52 free issues for 700 DM (£210).

Metropolis: was a printed magazine in Berlin which is currently only available on the internet: http://www.zitty.de

Munich Found: Munich Found Verlag, Germaniastrasse 11, D-80802 München; website http://www.munichfound.de The oldest and largest English-language magazine for Munich and Oberbayern, is a monthly publication offering articles on politics, culture and useful tips for expatriates. Circulation in Bavaria is 35,000 and the readership is mostly English-speaking professionals. Siemens, BMW, Marriott and Hilton Hotels all subscribe for their employee's benefit.

Sixth Sense: Catterick Barracks, BFPO 39. A weekly publication aimed at service personnel and their families, serving in Germany; with a circulation of 14-17,000 copies. It contains radio and television details, articles about Germany, situations vacant and classified adverts.

Transitions Abroad: PO Box 1300, Amherst, MA 01004-1300, USA; tel 413-256 3414; fax 413-256 0373. Is a bi-monthly magazine with articles on living and working abroad, and active involvement as a guest in the host community rather than as a tourist. An annual subscription presently costs $24.95 in the USA, $29.95 in Canada and $38 around the world.

*USA Today:*12th Floor Swiss Centre, 10 Wardour Street, London, W1V 3HG; tel 0171-559 5900; fax 0171-559 5885. Another American daily available across Germany, international circulation averages 70,000 annually. The cover price is 3.50 DM or 635 DM for a subscription. Friday is the publication day for the weekend edition and classified adverts are carried every Monday, Wednesday and Friday.

The Written Word: Bretzfelder Strasse 5, D-71543 Wüstenrot/Kreuzle; tel 07945-1751. An A5 magazine for English speakers in Baden-Württemburg, containing news, information on local groups, theatre listings and articles of interest to expatriates.

Television

As with education, television and radio broadcasting (*Fernsehen*) is a mixture of public and private enterprise, the public stations are controlled on a regional basis by the Länder. Eleven channels are available, in addition to cable and satellite. German television has over the decades been characterized by its self-imposed censorship which has resulted in it trying to broadcast only what the public will find acceptable. Unfortunately, this, combined with a conscientious objectivity on political issues and an excess of public service broadcasting, has led to accusations of dullness, uniformity and parochialism. However, on the creative side German television has some highlights: arts programmes and documentaries covering the international scene are of high quality.

The largest public channel, ARD (short for *Arbeitsgemeinshaft der öffentlich-rechtlichen Rundfunkanstalten der Bundesrepublik Deutschland*) is a group of eleven regional radio and television companies: Westdeutscher Rundfunk (WDR), Norddeutscher Rundfunk (NDR), Mitteldeutscher Rundfunk (MDR), Ost-deutscher Rundfunk Brandenburg, Radio Bremen (RB), Hessicher Rundfunk (HR), Südwestfunk (SWF), Süddeutscher Rundfunk (SDR), Sender Freies Berlin (SFB), Saarländischer Rundfunk and Bayerischer Rundfunk (BR). This television channel is *Erstes Deutsche Fernsehen* (Channel One). In addition to this the regional companies transmit their own television programmes (Channel Three in each region). The second national public channel is ZDF (*Zweites Deutsches Fernsehen* Channel Two) unlike the ARD consortium, it does not also operate a radio network. It is however, like ARD in that it is run by a consortium of Länder, and is effectively a public service broadcaster, even sharing weekday morning programming with ARD. So while Britons may assume it is broadly similar to BBC1 and BBC2 German television is uniquely German in its organisation The programmes broadcast by both stations are broadly similar in content. The largest elements are Plays and Films (23%), News (11.3%), Children's and Youth Programmes (10%) and Sport (7.6%). Financing comes in part from advertising (20% for ARD and 40% for ZDF), and a licence fee.

As is the case in Britain licences are required for television and radio equipment in Germany. These fees go towards the running costs of the public broadcasters. Usually in a private household only one radio or television set has to be licensed, at the moment the fee is 28.25 DM per month; if you only have a radio this drops to 9.45 DM. The licence only covers one household property so if you live in Frankfurt and have a holiday home in Gelsenkirchen then you will need two licences. Licences can be paid for by direct debit or through post offices, where you will also find application forms and information (but only in German). The administration of licence fees is carried out by the *Gebühreneinzugszentrale* (GEZ, 50656 Köln; tel 0221-506111; fax 0221-5061 2507; e-mail *GEZ#@t-online*). The fees are gathered by GEZ and distributed among the various companies according to listener and viewer density; hence Westdeutscher Rundfunk receives a 25% share compared to Radio Bremen's 1.2%.

Cable television (*Kabelhaushalte*) is now available as are several satellite channels: SAT 1, 3 SAT, PRO7 etc. 3 SAT is a culturally weighted programme broadcast by a consortium of ARD, ZDF and the Swiss and Austrian broadcasters. In any television listings magazine the daily programme guide can be expected to cover from five to eight pages due to the availability of around 22 terrestrial, cable and satellite channels. Much to the consternation of the public broadcasting concerns, new private channels are rapidly augmenting their audience ratings. ARD and ZDF at present each have around a 30% rating. In areas which have cable television the private channels have a fifty per cent rating. The attraction of the private and satellite channels over public broadcasting is a more adventurous style of programme. In addition to serious discussions of hot political issues like abortion, there are less serious programmes with mass appeal e.g. games and quiz shows.

Radio

Germany has an expanding array of radio stations; currently the number is around fifty, as each of the eleven public broadcasters operates four or five regional radio stations, these broadcast a variety of news, light music and entertainment programmes.

English-speaking radio stations include *The World Service*, Radio Luxembourg and Radio E; a consortium of 4 national broadcasters (including the BBC and Deutsche Welle) across Europe with English-language programmes. The British Forces Broadcasting Service (BFBS) and the American Forces Network (AFN) are obviously operated by the military for the benefit of service staff. In addition Radio Stuttgart and Deutsche Welle regularly put out programmes in English, Deutsche Welle transmits three programmes a day in English on 7170 and 9615 Khz.

Deutsche Welle also operates the official German shortwave radio station, which broadcasts in German for Germans abroad and those wishing to find out about Germany before they move there. In addition to the shortwave broadcasts some programmes, such as concerts are recorded for broadcast via satellite to radio stations across the United States. In addition to the website page (http://www.dwelle.de) listing programmes and frequencies including broadcasts in English (of which there is a weekly schedule) they produce a monthly magazine with times and frequencies which is available from:

Deutsche Welle: Öffentlichkeitsarbeit, 50588 Köln; tel 0221-3890; fax 0221-389 4155.
Deutsche Welle: Studio Washington, P O Box 50641, Washington, DC 20091-0641, USA; tel 202-393 7427; fax 202-393 7434.
AFN: Bertramstrasse 6, D-60320, Frankfurt am Main. Broadcasts 24 hours a day on 98.7 FM.
BFBS: BFBS Herford, BFPO 15. Has seven transmitters across Germany broadcasting programmes between 93 and 106 Mhz, 24 hours a day. The aim of the service is to entertain and inform, while maintaining a link with events in Britain.

Post and Telecommunications

In 1995 the German *Bundespost* monopoly on postal and telephone services was broken up when the entire enterprise was split into three companies and effectively prepared for privatisation by the state. The three new companies *Deutsche Telekom, Deutsche Post* and *Deutsche Postbank* all have AG status.

Post: Post Offices (Postämter) are normally open from 8am to 6pm Monday to Friday and 8am to 1pm on Saturdays. Post boxes are yellow and bear the post horn symbol. Large towns also have special airmail (*Flugpost*) boxes which are blue. There are stamp machines outside most post offices, in railway stations etc. and stamps (*Briefmarken*) can be bought in hotels as well as post offices. At the time of writing the cost of sending an ordinary letter to Britain from Germany began at 1 DM, 10 Pf. A Poste Restante (*Postlagernde Sendungen*) service is provided free at the main post office (*Hauptpostamt*) of every town. You should ensure that all mail to be collected thus is clearly marked *Postlagernde Sendungen* by the sender, as Poste Restante is not a familiar term in Germany. Radio and television licence fee application forms can be obtained from post offices.

When addressing mail for Germany, it should be noted that the German address order may differ from what the reader is used to: the name of the recipient on line one, followed on line two by the name of the street and then the building number (on the right), and on line three by the postal code (*postleitzahl*) and then the name of the town or city. An example being:

Anna Cooper,
Lorenz Str. 29,
90422 Nürnberg.

From outside Germany it is helpful to insert a capital D before the postcode.

Telephones: Deutsche Telekom has just lost its monopoly on the German telephone system, so the costs of installing and using a telephone may well drop. At present to obtain a phone line from Deutsche Telekom, the installation fee is around 100 DM, unless you are taking over an existing line number. Private lines can usually be installed within two weeks of application in most parts of western Germany, basic monthly rental is 21.39 DM and bills are rendered monthly. Telephone calls are still charged for by the unit at a base rate of .1043 DM per unit plus VAT (VAT is currently 15% but is set to rise to 16% in 1998-9), the cost of your call depends on the time of day and distance involved, as these factors affect how much phone time you actually get per unit. Note that calls are cheaper after 6pm, five tariff bands operate and a three minute local call at daytime rates will be about the equivalent of two units. However, at the weekends and on public holidays only two tariffs are in operation. The cheapest rate is between 10pm and 6am daily which is why long distance calls are usually made late at night.

In Germany, as elsewhere across Europe most public phone boxes are no longer payphones but need phonecards (*Telefonkarte*) for use. Telephone cards are available at post offices and railway stations and cost 12 DM for 40 units or 50 DM for 200 units. The older telephone booths are easy to spot by their bright yellow colour, newer models are being installed across the country, and are similar to the aluminium and plastic booths now used by British Telecom across Britain. However you would be hard put not to realise what they were, especially given the label *Telefon*. A local call from a phone box should cost about 20 pfennigs for 1½ minutes. You can also telephone from main post offices where there are banks of telephones: after being allotted a booth at the counter, you make your call and return to the counter to pay. If dialling abroad, go to the counter marked *Auslandsgespräche*.

The German yellow pages are known as *Gelbe Seiten*. Listed at the front are the emergency services' numbers, directory assistance numbers and the current postal rates. The ordinary telephone directory (*Fernsprechbuch*) contains personal and business subscribers' numbers as in the UK. While to call Directory Enquiries you ring 01188 (at a charge of 60 pfennigs), International Enquiries are on 00118 and cost 96 pfennigs.

The mobile phone, or 'handy' as the Germans call them, is gaining ground rapidly, and while Deutsche Telekom's subsidiary DeTeMobil is doing its best to retain its monopoly, it is facing some very stiff competition in this market. The rates and services are much the same the world over, and you can find a mobile dealer in most towns, much as you would in Britain or America.

To telephone Germany the International code is 49, prefixed by whatever the international access code is for your location (in Britain and Germany this is 00). To call the UK or the USA and Canada from Germany the international access codes are 44 for the UK and 1 for the USA and Canada, this is followed by the subscriber's number minus the first 0 e.g. to call Vacation Work (01865-241978) from Germany would be: 0044 1865 241978. From Germany you can direct dial most countries around the world.

Emergency Service Telephone Numbers
For the Police call **110**
For the Fire Brigade call **112** this is also the number to call for emergency ambulances.

Main German Telephone Codes

Aachen 0241
Augsburg 0821
Berlin 030
Bayreuth 0921
Bielefeld 0521
Bochum 0234
Bonn 0228
Braunschweig 0531
Bremen 0421
Bremerhaven 0471
Celle 05141
Chemnitz 0371
Cottbus 0355
Darmstadt 06151
Dortmund 0231
Dresden 0351
Duisburg 0203
Düsseldorf 0211
Eisenach 03691
Erfurt 0361
Essen 0201
Frankfurt/Main 069
Frankfurt/Oder 0335
Freiburg-im-Breisgau 0761
Gelsenkirchen 0209
Gera 0365
Hagen 02331
Halle 0345
Hamburg 040
Hannover 0511
Heidelberg 06221
Karlsruhe 0721
Kassel 0561
Kiel 0431
Koblenz 0261
Köln 0221

Krefeld 02151
Leipzig 0341
Leverkusen 02171
Lübeck 0451
Ludwigshafen/Rhein 0621
Magdeburg 0391
Mainz 06131
Mannheim 0621
Mönchengladbach 02161
München 089
Münster 0251
Neuss 02131
Nürnberg 0911
Offenbach/Main 069
Oldenburg 0441
Oranienburg 03301
Osnabrück 0541
Paderborn 05251
Passau 0851
Potsdam 0331
Regensburg 0941
Reutlingen 07121
Rostock 0381
Saarbrücken 0681
Solingen 0212
Starnberg 08151
Stuttgart 0711
Suhl 03681
Trier 0651
Ulm 0731
Wiesbaden 0611
Wilhelmshaven 4421
Wuppertal 0202
Würzburg 0931

The Internet

The global electronic data network is as popular with German computer users, schools and students, as with the inhabitants of any western country. The T-Online internet service provider, a subsidiary of Deutsche Telekom, has 1.7 million subscribers making it Germany's largest network operator, other internet providers operating in Germany are America Online (400,000 subscribers) which is in partnership with German publishers Bertelsmann, Compuserve (300,000 subscribers), and germany.net (240,000 subscribers). Most major cities now have their own websites, in addition to those operated by the government ministries, transport operators, universities and newspapers. The content of German websites is unsurprisingly in German, however, (unlike many websites in Britain or America, which are only in the native language) many sites do have an English language version; even if it is only a one page summary. One example of this is the business newspaper *Handelsblatt* website (http://www.handelsblatt.de), which has selected articles from the newspaper on-line, with a daily summary in English. Around 35% of all businesses employing more than ten staff have access to the internet, and around 13% would no longer be able to do business without it.

The main problem with 'surfing' for German users is the high cost of the telephone connection from their PC to the internet. Part of the reason why T-Online's subscriber base is so large is that it is an off-shoot of Deutsche Telekom, who also provide most of the connections and phone services used for internet access, and who until recently have had a monopoly on telecommunications and thus the prices charged. The opening up of the telecommunications market from January 1998, should see these costs begin to drop.

Recently in an attempt to rationalise the abilities of personal computers (PCs) to download and replay audio and video entertainment, with the status of the public radio and television networks the German government proposed a tax to be levied on PCs. At present it is not known what this tax would be used for, but an estimated figure of the cost of a 'PC Licence' put it at about £120. The tax would be levied on every PC capable of replaying audio and video 'clips' taken from the net, and would probably affect business and individual computer owners.

Cars and Motoring

Germany has one of the most up-to-date and extensive motorway systems in Europe, so it comes as a pleasant surprise that, unlike Italy, France etc, there are no tolls. However the *Autobahnen* (motorways) have another scourge: there is no speed limit. The government recommends that drivers should restrict their speed to 130 kph (78 mph), but this is widely regarded as a joke. Consequently, German executives are inclined to give vent to their killer instincts when behind the wheels of their powerful BMW's, Mercedes and Audis by bearing down on anything in the fast lane. At speeds in excess of 200kph (125mph), lights flashing furiously, they clear the way, before accelerating into the distance. However, just because somebody does this to you, does not mean that it is accepted road etiquette. The police have a tendency to arrest anyone acting in this fashion, especially with the growing incidence of 'road-rage' in Germany. In a drive to stamp out aggression at its source, penalty-point fines can be imposed by the police on drivers considered to be acting in an aggressive manner. Acts which are considered likely to initiate aggressive behaviour include spitting, gesturing and shouting obscenities.

From time to time experiments limiting motorway speed to 100 kph (62 mph) are made, and when the weather is wet or foggy speed limits are posted and these should be adhered to. At any given time a small percentage of Autobahnen have a speed limit in operation but on the whole it seems unlikely that the Germans will bring in a general speed limit in the foreseeable future. The arguments against a speed limit include the fact that only 6% of fatal accidents occur on the motorways, making them the safest roads in Germany. However this probably says more for the high safety standards of German cars than for German driving. Speed limits on other roads are: 50 kph (30 mph) in cities and 100 kph (62 mph) on other roads except motorways. The speed limit for cars pulling a caravan is 80 Kph (50 mph) on ordinary roads and motorways. At crossings and traffic junctions vehicles coming from the right have priority unless otherwise indicated by road signs. Children under 12 years old must be secured by special seats and the wearing of seatbelts in both the front and back of the vehicle is obligatory. Drivers should always bear in mind that most cities have bicycle lanes and these often cross the roads at junctions, so keep your wits about you. You should also bear in mind that bus lanes are strictly for buses and taxis, the exception being when making a right turn, but only at the turn. Added to these hidden dangers are the pedestrian-only zones that some cities are enforcing, as if one-way streets and parking restrictions don't make life difficult enough. The problem is that unless you have kept up with German news and bought the latest street maps, you are likely to blunder into a problem.

Road signs worth noting are: *Umleitung* (detour); *Fahrbahnschäden* or Strassenschäden (damaged road surface); *Kreuzung* (crossroads); *Strasse gesperrt* (road closed); *Steinschlag* (falling rocks); *Hupverbot* (no hooting); *Einbahnstrasse* (one-way street); *Halten Verboten/Halteverbot* (no parking).

Foreign vehicles may be driven in Germany with a foreign licence for up to a year. European vehicles may be driven without time limit as long as the owner takes up permanent residence in Germany. Since July 1996, drivers who change their residence within the EU no longer have to exchange their licences for national versions, as licences issued in one EU State will be valid in any other EU State indefinitely.

Ever pollution conscious, Germany has enforced the fitting of three-way catalytic converters on all new motor cars (except very small ones) since 1986, and leaded petrol is no longer available, unleaded (*bleifrei*) petrol is rated at 91 octane and *super bleifrei* is 95. A free booklet (*Tanken & Rasten*) on the German motorway network is available at all autobahn service areas, or from Autobahn Tank & Rast AG (Andreas-Hermes-Str. 7-9, D-53175 Bonn).

The German equivalent of the AA is ADAC. ADAC, the AvD and other motoring associations run a breakdown service (*Strassenwacht*) on all motorways and main roads. The emergency police service can be summoned by dialling 110 or 112. There are automatic telephones situated at regular intervals along all motorways.

Useful Addresses:
Allgemeiner Deutscher Automobil Club e.V. (ADAC): Am Westpark 8, D-81373 München; tel 089-76760.
Automobilclub von Deutschland e.V.(AVD): Lyonerstrasse 16, D-60528 Frankfurt-Niederrad; tel 069-66060.
Auto Club Europa (ACE): Schmidener Strasse 233, D-70374 Stuttgart; tel 0711-530 3266.

Buying a Car in Germany

Whatever other directives Brussels will seek to impose across all EU borders, it does not appear imminent that the British custom of driving on the left will be converted in the interests of EU standardization. Thus many British expatriates will face the choice of importing their right-hand drive car from the UK, or buying a new one in Germany. Although you may import your car from Britain without paying customs charges, there may be considerable expense, depending on the type of car, in carrying out certain modifications to make it conform to German safety and anti-pollution laws. Unless you are especially attached to your motor car, there is almost certainly less hassle and savings to be made by buying in Germany. For further details on importing a car and buying in Germany, see Chapter Three, *Setting up Home*.

Driving Licences

On 1st July 1996 a standardised pink driving licence was adopted across the EU, from this date onwards drivers who change their residence within the EU no longer have to exchange their licence for the national version after 12 months. Licences issued in one member country will be valid in all the others until expiry, even if it is an old national licence. Hence you do not have to obtain a new licence in your new home country unless you wish to; however, if your licence expires then you must renew it in the state where you are 'normally' resident (normal residence being that place where you spend 185 days per calendar year through personal or occupational ties). This condition also applies if your licence is stolen or you wish to add a new vehicle category to it. Licence applications should be made locally (not centrally as in the UK) to the Strassenverkehrsamt, the new EU-model German licence (*Führerschein*) is planned to be a credit card style document due to its handy size and the difficulties it presents to forgers. The new model of EU wide licence does not exempt expatriate drivers from facing the same checks as local drivers, so your licence may be subject to medical checks. In Germany it is also a requirement that you carry your log book (*Fahrzugschein*) with you when driving.

Drivers who have held a licence for less than two years are still required to register with the local licensing office, as German drivers serve a probationary period. Your licence should be registered with the local office within three months of taking up permanent residence. The licence will still have full validity but should you commit any traffic offences then you will be required to take an improvement course.

MOT and Insurance

Motor vehicles in Germany are licensed by the *Zulassungsstelle* (licensing authority) at your place of residence. Since July 1997 an emission-oriented tax for cars is in force; there is a reduced rate of tax for cars with low emission rates. Vehicles must be inspected every two years by the Technical Supervision Agency (*Technischer Überwachungsverein (TÜV) or DEKRA*). For new cars, the first inspection and anti-pollution test is carried out after three years. Third-party liability insurance (*Haftplichtversicherung*) is compulsory. For details of obtaining insurance and a German driving licence, see Chapter Three, *Setting up Home*.

Transport

You may find that it is possible to do without a car in Germany as the transport system is one of the best in Europe. In many of the larger towns and cities you'll find an excellent integrated local transport system of buses, trams and trains (underground and regional). Since 1991 the Federal Ministry of Transport (http:/

/www.bmv.de) has spent 58 billion DM, upgrading the rail system, roads and waterways under the 'German Unity' transport scheme.

Railways

Deutsche Bahn carries over 300,000 passengers across Germany daily, standard price tickets covering journeys up to 100 kilometres are valid for one day, longer journeys on a single ticket are valid for four days, and return journeys are valid for a month. Due to the size, efficiency and speed of the train service, long distance trains are usually full so it is wise to reserve your seats on the train when you book your tickets. This costs about 6 DM, but is well worth it, as you can still reserve seats, if there is space, on the day of your journey. There are also a wide range of discounts, offers and group tickets which cut the cost of travelling, or you can obtain rail cards (for adults and children) which give you a percentage discount on rail ticket prices.

There are several types of main line trains :

Long Distance
ICE: Inter City Express. For those in a real hurry, the ICE will hurtle you across the landscape at over 200kph (125 mph). The Deutsche Bahn leaflet for 1997 calculates the Hamburg-Nürnburg journey at 4 hours.
IC: Inter City service. Express trains with services including on board public telephones, parent child compartments, and restaurant cars or a trolley service of refreshments. The daily Hamburg to Nürnberg IC 727 *Loreley* service takes 8 hours to cross Germany, stopping at 17 stations on the way.
Euro-City: An international high quality train service usually integrated with the IC network.
IR: Inter regio similar to the IC but the network is larger and they stop at more stations, on most lines there is at least one an hour.

Short Distance
Eilzug: A semi-fast train service, some operate like the ICs while others stop at every station depending upon the route operated.
RE: Regional Expresses stop only at major stations.
RB: Regional Bahn; the slower version of the RE stopping at all stations. An example of the difference is that the RE from Nürnberg to Bamberg takes 45 minutes compared to the 61 of the RB.
SE: Stadt Express. City express service.
S-Bahn: urban trains which service the suburban areas and hinterlands of major towns and cities.

Ticket prices can be obtained from railway stations, tourist offices and railway agents in Germany along with free timetables (*Städteverbindungen*). Deutsche Bahn also maintains an office in Britain for those wishing to make their travel arrangements and buy tickets in advance (Deutsche Bahn UK, Suite 4, 23 Oakhill Grove, Surbiton, KT6 6DU; tel 0181-390 8833. Those with an internet connection can check train times and details from the Deutsche Bahn website (http://www.bahn.de), which while it can take a while to load has information in German and English.

Another new development planned for commuter use in 2004 is the electro-magnetic, levitating *Transrapid* service (http://www.transrapid.simplenet.com). This is planned to run between Hamburg and Berlin at up to 500 kph, with six services an hour. The track is under construction between the two cities, while the train itself is under test in Lower Saxony.

City Transport

U-Bahn: Those who live and work in the cities (especially Hamburg, Frankfurt, München, Bonn, Düsseldorf, Berlin, Stuttgart, Nürnberg and Hannover), will find excellent underground railway (*U-Bahnen*) networks. As with the Paris métro it is cheaper for regular users to buy a book of tickets or multi-ride pass (*Mobikarte*) the latter are especially useful as they allow two people to travel together. The U-Bahn closes down between 1am and 5am.

S-Bahn: Many of the city underground routes are supplemented and overlapped by regional railway routes. These S-bahnen are either operated by the municipal authority or Deutsche Bahn, and serve both the town centres, urban fringe and the surrounding area.

Trams and Buses: In the larger cities bus, tram and U-Bahn tickets are interchangeable and buying a book of tickets or mobikarte is a useful economy measure if you are a regular user of city transport. Confusingly, in all city centres, trams go underground. In some towns there are 'pure' underground lines, but most are mixed surface and underground and go subterranean for only short stretches. Bus services are also useful for reaching the suburbs and bus stops (*Bush-altestellen*) are easy to find.

Be warned that larger cities like München, Hamburg and Frankfurt have an array of fare structures depending on which zone your destination is located in. Fares are graded by the number of zones through which you pass. Having worked out the correct fare, you must not forget to get your ticket cancelled by machines located at platform entrances or inside buses and trams. Machines are generally marked E for *Entwertung* (cancellation). This must be done on each stage of the journey. An oversight can result in a hefty on-the-spot fine.

Taxis: Can be hailed, booked by telephone or picked up at taxi stands. Fares vary between cities and extra is charged for luggage and dogs. Taxis are easy to spot by the regulation off-white paintwork, and in Frankfurt you can even find a few of the famous London cabs (although with a new paint-job of course). Hailing these is probably harder as at the time of writing they are rather a novelty for locals to ride in, and so there is a waiting list in operation.

Municipal Transport Authorities:

Hamburg Verkehrsverbund GmbH: Steinstrasse 7, D-20095 Hamburg; tel 040-325 7750. Operates two U-Bahn, 7 S-Bahn and 8 bus routes throughout the whole Hamburg area (roughly 30 km across). Buses and trains run every five minutes except between midnight and 5 am, when a night bus service operates.

Münchener Verkehrs-und-Tarifverbund GmbH: Postfach D-26 01 54, München; tel 089-2103 3229. Eight S-Bahn and six U-Bahn and vast number of bus lines criss-cross the city and surrounding area, forming a transport area covering around 500 square kilometres. A *Daily* ticket, valid for unlimited travel costs 8 DM for the city and 16 DM for the entire zone.

Rhein-Main-Verkehrsverbund: Am Kreishaus 1-5, D-65719 Hofheim. What was once the Frankfurt Transport authority now covers a much wider area. 24 hour travel tickets are available ranging in price from 9 DM within Frankfurt to 48 DM to travel between Darmstadt and Marburg (a distance of 80 km).

Bus

Unlike Britain or America there is no nationwide network of bus routes. The rail network is supplemented and overlapped by regional buses run by the local transport authorities. In part this is the result of the extensive rail network. On the whole if a town or village is not served by a train or s-bahn regional train line then a bus will run to it, albeit on a limited time-table. Having said that, there are some coach companies running cross-country services on routes such as Berlin-München. However these are not part of any extensive network and so your ability to use them instead of the train is limited.

Boats

Cruising on the great rivers of Germany, the Rhine, the Mosel, the Danube, the Weser and the Elbe, or along the shores of the larger lakes like the Bodensee, can be a very pleasant way to unwind. Ships of the Köln-Düsseldorfer Rheinschiffahrt AG (KD Lines), sail from Rotterdam in Holland through the west of Germany down to Basel on the German-Swiss border as well as the shorter scenic stretches between Köln and Mainz/Wiesbaden and along the Mosel. KD has also operates on the Elbe (see below), and holders of Deutsche Bahn rail cards can get discounts on tickets. On the Danube cruisers go from Regensburg or Passau. The Weser boats take passengers from Hannoversch-Münden to Hameln. For a west east trip, start at Hamburg and cruise the Elbe from Hamburg or Lauenburg to Bad Schandau, south of Dresden. On all these cruises stops are made at various places of interest. The German tourist board can supply further details.

Air

The recently privatised German national carrier is Lufthansa, with its home at Frankfurt; the busiest airport in continental Europe. As well as international flights Lufthansa operates on the main routes between German cities including Berlin, Erfurt, Leipzig, München and Dresden. Some of these flights are in conjunction with British carriers like British Midland, who's flights to Dresden are picked up by Lufthansa from Cologne/Bonn. Recent market changes in the EU have led British Airways into the German domestic flight market with its subsidiary Deutsche BA. These flights are most notable for the attempts of the flight-crew to reduce the tedium of travel for business passengers; ranging from juggling to comedy double-acts. It may seem ludicrous but has so far weaned a 42% share of passengers away from Lufthansa.

There are frequent flights to and from major German cities to the main UK airports, with either Lufthansa, BA, BM or any of the trans-Atlantic American carriers. Lufthansa itself has joined the *Star-Alliance* of airline companies based in the USA, Canada, Scandinavia, Brazil and Thailand, hence entering partnership deals for trans-Atlantic and trans-global flights.

The main German airports for travellers arriving from outside Europe are Frankfurt Rhein-Main, Düsseldorf and München. Other major airports are Cologne/Bonn, Leipzig/Halle, Dresden, Berlin-Tegel and Berlin Templehof.

Useful Addresses:
Lufthansa German Airlines: World Business Centre, Newall Road, London Heathrow Airport, Hounslow, TW6 2RD; tel 0345-737747; website http://www.lufthansa.co.uk
Deutsche BA: Postfach 50 07 48, D-22707 Hamburg; tel 040-309 6630.

Getting There

Apart from the various airlines offering flights to Germany, more traditional and cost effective means of getting to Germany are available, especially if you wish to travel with more than twenty kilos worth of luggage and personal effects. One route is the car ferry, thus allowing you more control over how fast you get to Germany and with what personal affects. Most ferries from Britain to Germany travel in to Hamburg, so if you are relocating there this is a cost-effective option. Most non-europeans will have to have their goods shipped in or pay very expensive airfreight costs, but a relocation company can probably get you a good deal in this area (see Chapter 2 *Setting Up Home*). Another alternative for those who like driving is to take the Eurostar, through the channel tunnel to France and then drive on to Germany.

Students on the other hand, travelling with either a study abroad period or a summer job in mind will need less luggage. Even so planes and ferries can be expensive and you still have to arrange train tickets from your arrival point in Germany. A relatively inexpensive alternative is coach travel from Britain, the major coach firms such as Eurolines run long-distance coaches from Britain to the continent.

Scandinavian Seaways: Germany Direct: Scandinavian Seaways, PO Box 643, Bristol, BS9 1UU; tel 0990-333 000. Awarded five stars by the AA, Scandinavian seaways run a car ferry service between Harwich and Hamburg with fares from £72.

Eurolines: 4 Cardiff Road, Luton, LU1 1PP; tel 0990-143219. One of Europe's major coach operators, 40 services are operated from Victoria Coach Station in London to cities across Germany. Connections with National Express services to London from across Britain can be arranged as one ticket purchase. Prices vary according to the destination required and there are discounts for children and those under 26 or over 60. Cologne and Frankfurt are served daily, and there are regular services to Stuttgart, Munich, Berlin and Hamburg, all at competitive prices. Contact Eurolines for more information or a copy of their brochure.

Banks and Finance

The organization of the banking system in Germany is to a large extent dictated by the principles on which the economy is run and the country is governed. Compared with Britain, the USA etc. only a small percentage of Germany's industry is in public ownership. Both the national government and the Länder dole out billions in subsidies and regional aid packages. To facilitate the distribution of funds on a regional basis, all the Länder governments own large banks. Compared with France, where the banking system is still largely under state control, the German government has extremely limited control over the private sector. The Deutsche Bundesbank is the central bank whose primary function is to act as guardian of the currency. The Bundesbank acts as banker to the federal government, issues banknotes, acts as intermediary for financial transactions and controls the money supply and the amount of credit available to the economy.

Payments Systems, Eurocheques and Credit Cards

The main way of paying for goods and service in Germany is still hard cash, while almost all employees are paid by bank transfer into their accounts, when they spend it, on the whole they'll use bank notes and coins. Payment by cheque is rare, and credit/debit cards have still to gain the widespread use that they have in Britain and America (recent figures estimated that while every American alive has more than one credit card only one in eight Germans has one). The main card in use with Germans is the Eurocard, which is allied to the Mastercard system, Visa and American Express are also accepted. However, while the Eurocard is accepted in more locations than the others the only places you can be certain that any card will be accepted is in the larger shops, railway stations and airports. Deutsche Bahn have recently launched the Bahncard a joint rail discount card and credit card but take up of this has not been as large as might be expected. However if you're willing to pay the interest you can obtain cash using a credit card from most bank cash machines/autotellers (*Geldautomat*). Certainly at the moment holders of Royal Bank of Scotland bank cards can use Belgian cash machines and this availability may spread to Germany in the next few years.

Payments systems (cashless money transfers) are highly sophisticated and automated in Germany. In addition to the major banks' internal systems for payment and data processing, the *Gesellschaft für Zahlungssysteme* (established in 1982) administers all Eurocard and Eurocheque transactions. The main methods of paying for bills in the absence of cheques are the cashless transfers which should be familiar to most Britons reading this. The simplest of these is the Transfer (*Uberweisung*) where you simply fill in the transfer form with the relevant details and hand it in to the bank. Regular payments for bills or rent can be covered by a Standing Order (*Dauerauftrag*) which deducts an agreed sum on an agreed date each month and deposits it in the recipient's account. Should your regular debits vary in size then you can arrange a Direct Debit system (*Lastschriftverfahren*) with the organisation that you are paying. The authorisation for deductions from your account is an *Einzugsermächtigung*. As these arrangements and sums will all appear on your statement so that you can check that all is well, you also have the security of being able to recall these payments up to three months after deduction. However, if you do this with a utility company they will consider your bill as unpaid, and you risk the consequences.

European Monetary Union (EMU)

At present the German currency is the Deutsche Mark, each consisting of 100 Pfennigs. However as part of the drive towards economic and political union the EU intends to launch a Single European Currency, which will replace national currencies and thus save businesses and individuals money that is otherwise lost in exchange rate differences. This single currency would be issued and managed by one independent monetary authority, the European Central Bank. The new currency will be the 'Euro' consisting of 100 Cents. Each nation participating in European Monetary Union will be issued with Euro notes and coinage, which bear their own national symbols, thus allowing individuals to retain a sense of national pride within a greater European community.

At the time of writing the process leading up to EMU has been in progress for several years; as EU member states seek to control their economies in order to be admitted to the 'Euro-club'. Those countries which are economically eligible for EMU will lock their national currencies together in one exchange rate in 1999. Following a period of single monetary policy controlled by the European Central Bank, the new Euro bank notes and coins will be issued in early 2002 and by July 2002 all national notes and coinage would be withdrawn from circulation.

France and Germany are the countries which have most political and economic interest in the creation of the new currency and it is their economies which have been taken as the base line for the eligibility of nations to take part in the single currency. However, recent economic and political events have made German participation uncertain. Chancellor Kohl and his administration are firmly behind EMU, but the recent massive rise in unemployment and the 1998 General Election, to be held in September, may affect this process. At present Germany is still set to take part in EMU, even though more than half of the German population do not wish to give up their 'Mark', and current economic trends are undermining the country's eligibility. The Chancellor's plans for EMU have also been challenged by a group of academics through the Federal Court, and the result of this challenge will not be known until mid-1998. Thus at present we can not say whether Germany will enter the EMU, or not.

Opening a German Bank Account

Opening a bank current account (*Girokonto*) in Germany is a remarkably straightforward and swift procedure needing only the completion of a bank account application form, the presentation of your passport as proof of identity and an initial deposit to open the account. It is recommended that you have the sum ready in cash, as cheques or drafts from your home bank will take a while to be processed, and so hold things up. The whole process need take only a few minutes. The 'big three' banks (Deutsche Bank, Dresdner Bank and Commerz Bank which are privately owned) between them have thousands of branches in Germany. If possible, it is advisable to choose one of their main city branches, rather than a smaller sub or rural branch as the former are more clued-up when it comes to transactions and advice. Many foreigners remark on the high quality of German banking services and the user-friendly environment of most German banks. It is quite usual for clients to have their own personal advisor on whom they can drop in for financial advice or even for a chat. Surprisingly for a country with such a reputation for tight controls on credit lending to companies, clients with personal accounts will be automatically granted an overdraft up to a limit decided by the bank. Generally however, Germans are far more wary of being overdrawn than the average Briton. The main differences between UK and German personal current accounts are that Eurocheque chequebooks and cheque cards are used as the main withdrawal system for personal account holders, unlike in the UK where a separate application is made for such facilities (usually prior to foreign travel), and that German banking, even if you are in credit, is not free. Banks are generally open from 9am to 4pm, with smaller branches closing between 1 and 2.30 for lunch.

Although the system varies from bank to bank, there is normally a monthly charge for maintenance of the account (*Kontoführungsgebühren*). In addition there are charges for withdrawal of funds via both the cashier or the cash machine, for payment of standing orders etc. Although it may pay to shop around for the best deals, be warned that, like the excellent German health service, the first class banking system is subsidized by the consumer.

For most personal banking services it is wise to shop around for the best deal for your money against the cost of maintaining accounts. There are several types of bank, the private banks, of which the big three; Deutsche, Dresdner and Commerzbank are the most well known outside Germany. The state savings banks (*Sparkassen*) which are owned by the regional authorities, the guild banks (*Genossenchaft*) and post office savings accounts. All types of banks are able to transfer money abroad in Deutsche Marks or other currencies which is probably an essential service for most expatriates.

Electronic banking is a new toy in Germany, Deutsche Bank recently launched its internet branch *Bank 24* (http://www.bank24.de). This was launched in late 1996 and in one year has 80,000 customers who's internet banking and brokerage transactions account for 42% of its business.

Useful terms:
die Bürgschaft/Garantie: guarantee.
das Depositenzertifikat: certificate of deposit.
die Hypothek: mortgage.
der Inhaber: bearer.
der kurzfristige Uberziehungskredit: short-term overdraft.
Persönliches Konto: a personal account.
der Saldo: balance.
Scheckheft: a cheque book.
Scheckkarte: cheque card.
die Uberziehung des Kontokorrentkredites: an overdraft.
der verbürgte Kontokorrentkredit: overdraft secured by a guarantee.
der Wechsel: bill.

The three main German banks have branches in London, these are in the main part branches of their corporate investment arm, so you may not necessarily be able to gain any assistance with private bank accounts. Because of the simplicity of the procedure for opening an account, it is not normally necessary to open an account in advance of going to Germany. However the London branches should be able to provide the address of the nearest local branch in Germany.

Useful Addresses:

Deutsche Bank AG: Jürgen-Ponto-Platz 1, D-60301 Frankfurt am Main; tel 069-2630.

Hansard Europe Limited

When in Germany....

Hansard Europe Limited, a Dublin-based offshore company, offers products designed exclusively for the German market.

Hansard German products have been designed to be tax-efficient with regard to German tax and life assurance regulations.

For more information about Hansard Europe Limited or the Hansard Group, please contact Product Support on +353 1 278 1488.

"Dedicated to the orderly creation of wealth."

Hansard Europe Limited, P.O. Box 43, Enterprise House, Frascati Road, Blackrock, Co. Dublin, Republic of Ireland.
Telephone: +353 1 278 1488 Fax: +353 1 278 1499
Internet: http://www.hansard.com
Service-Hotline für deutschsprachige Kunden Telefon/Telefax: +353 1 283 6735
Registration No. 219727 Dublin, Republic of Ireland.

Dresdner Bank AG: Dresdner Bank House,125 Wood Street, London EC2V 7AQ.

Commerzbank AG: London Branch, 23 Austin Friars, London EC2N 2EN.

American Express: Postfach 11 01 01, D-60036 Frankfurt am Main.

Offshore Banking

British citizens who live and work abroad are only required to pay UK tax on income arising in the UK. There is thus an incentive for them to move their assets and savings to an offshore tax haven where they will earn interest gross of UK tax. For those habitual expatriates who move from one foreign land to another for work, there can be considerable advantage in maintaining assets offshore. Anyone living and working abroad should seriously consider this option as it not only allows easy access to their funds, no matter which foreign country they find themselves based in, but can also ensure the first steps towards tax efficiency. Anyone contemplating a move should note that expatriates are entitled to a personal income allowance before tax in the UK of up to £4,045 (1997-8).

With many banks and building societies now opening branches offshore there is an increasing range of facilities available. Expatriates will find a variety of products and services tailored to meet their specific needs: worldwide access to funds, accounts in different currencies, telephone banking, and assistance with insurance and investment to name but a few. The products available range from simple deposit account to index-linked deposits, managed funds, offshore trusts and packages of all these such as that offered by Lloyds Bank Overseas Club. For those with significant funds there is also the option of Offshore Private Banking offering a full investment portfolio management service.

Useful Addresses:

Abbey National Treasury International Limited (Abbey National Offshore): International House, PO Box 545, The Parade, St. Helier, Jersey, JE4 8XG; tel 01534-885000; fax 01534-885050.

Abbey National: 237 Main Street, Gibraltar; tel +350-76090.

Barclays Personal Banking International: Barclays Bank Plc, PO Box 41, St Peter Port, Guernsey, GY1 3BE; tel 01481-723176; fax 01481-715518; e-mail Guernsey@offshorebanking.barclays.com

Hansard Europe Ltd: PO Box 43, Enterprise House, Frascati Road, Blackrock, Co Dublin, Republic of Ireland; tel +353-1278 1488; fax +353-1278 1498; website http://www.hansard.com Launched in 1995 Hansard Europe sell unit linked life assurance policies across the European Union, with variants in their products for France and Germany. These policies include Capital Builder and Retirement Programme.

Hemery Trust and Corporate Services Ltd: 31 Broad Street, St. Helier, Jersey JE4 8XN; tel 01534-630630; fax 01534-630631; e-mail Hemery@itl.net Financial consultants who can offer a range of services including investment advice, for expatriates.

Lloyds Bank Plc: PO Box 12, Douglas, Isle of Man, IM99 1SS; tel 01624-638104; fax 01642-638181.

Lloyds Bank Plc: PO Box 53, St Peter Port, Guernsey, Channel Islands, GY1 4BD; tel 01481-725131; fax 01481-714295.

Lloyds Bank Plc: Jersey Offshore Centre, PO Box 770, Jersey, JE4 8ZG.

Nat West; Expatriate Service Office: National Westminster House, 6 High Street, Chelmsford, Essex CM1 1BQ; tel 01245-292456.

Brewin Dolphin Bell Lawrie Ltd: 5 Giltspur Street, London, EC1A 9BD; tel 0171-246 1028; fax 0171-246 1093; e-mail rlindsay-stewart@bdbl.co.uk Is an amalgamation of two of the oldest names on the English and Scottish stock markets, they offer a wide variety of services including worldwide investment management and financial planning; contact Robin Lindsay Stewart.

Royal Bank of Scotland International: Offshore Banking Centre, PO Box 678, 59-63 Bath Street, St Helier, Jersey, JE4 8YN; tel 01534-24365.

Taxation

Any person who spends more than six months (183 days) per year in Germany has to pay German tax on his or her worldwide income. Taxable income includes income from work, letting and leasing, trade enterprises, returns on investment, annuities and speculative capital gains (except on the sale of a principal residence). However, thankfully, double taxation agreements exist between Germany and the UK, USA and Australia so your income will not be taxed twice. For further details of Income Tax and other salary deductions, see Chapter Six, *Employment*. In addition to tax on wages and unearned income, there are various other taxes including VAT, Land Tax and Church Tax.

Church Tax

Church tax (*Kirchensteuer*) is compulsory unless you make a declaration that you do not wish to be a member of any church. If you do not make such a declaration you will be registered as a member of the local Catholic or Protestant Church which 90% of Germans are (at least for tax purposes). The tax is deducted with income tax and amounts to eight to ten per cent of the income tax to be paid.

Solidarity Tax

Since January 1995 a 7.5% Solidarity Tax has been levied on income and corporation taxes, without any income limits, but there are regulations to prevent multiple taxation and to avoid overburdening those on low incomes. The tax has been levied to help cover the costs of reconstruction in the new Länder, and will be reduced in stages over the next few years.

Local Tax

A land tax (*Grundsteuer*) is levied on the owners of land and buildings, and is calculated on the basis of their rentable value. The level of tax varies between different regions, but is usually modest and deductible for income tax purposes. For acquisitions of real estate there is a transfer tax payable on land and buildings, which is levied on the purchaser.

Other taxes

VAT: (*Mehrwertsteuer* or *MWSt*)is charged at 15% on most goods and services, this is set to rise later in 1998 to 16%. For most foodstuffs, there is a reduced rate of 7½%. The following are MWSt exempt: banking, insurance, education, library services, property sales, medical services and cultural performances. A turnover tax (*Einfuhrumsatzsteuer*) is levied on imports.

Health Care, Insurance and Hospitals

Germany's health care system goes back to Bismarck's time when the foundations for the present system, aimed at the care of industrial workers, was the most progressive of its kind in the world. In the 1990's the system has lost none of its edge. No expense it seems, is spared to equip hospitals and surgeries with the latest technology and well-trained staff. Germans enjoy, free, one of the highest standards of healthcare in the world, but as the system is entirely funded by compulsory contributions, citizens pay for it indirectly and heavily. Although preventative medicine, consultations and hospital treatment are free to those paying into the state health insurance scheme, beneficiaries still have to make token contributions towards the cost of prescribed medicines, spectacles etc. The system involves the doctor, dentist etc. invoicing the sickness insurance fund (*Krankenkasse*) (see below), under a fixed scale of charges, for the treatment administered to the patient. This has generated probably the only complaint about the German health service, that there is a lot of form-filling involved.

As soon as you have taken up employment, your employer will take the necessary steps to register you with social security. You register first with the Krankenkasse which will then inform the competent pension and insurance bodies. You will then be issued with an insurance number which will be used to track your pension and insurance contributions, much like the British National Insurance number. The insurance authority will issue you with a social insurance identity card (*Sozialversicherungsausweis*) The pension authority also will issue you with an insurance book (*Versicherungsnachweisheft*) which you must hand on to your employer while you are working for them. If you have already worked in Germany then you should merely hand over the insurance book to your employer on arrival. The book will be returned when you cease working for your employer.

Since 1995 Germans have also had the chance to take out private health insurance on top of the state system.

Using the Health Care System

Anyone employed by a German firm and earning less than 74,000 DM is required to enrol in one of the state run health insurance schemes (*Krankenkassen*), such as the *Allgemeine Ortskrankenkasse* (*AOK*), *Barmer Ersatzkasse* (*BEK*), and *Deutsche-Angestellten-Krankenkasse* (*DAK*). Nearly 90% of Germans are covered by such a scheme, one of the most comprehensive in the world. All those in employment pay half the health contribution (14% of their income) up to a fixed limit each year, and the employer contributes a similar amount. Foreigners employed in Germany are also entitled to use the state healthcare scheme since they will automatically have contributions deducted from their wages. Dependants of employees making contributions are also entitled to state healthcare. Those employed in Germany by a UK employer for less than a year should apply to the DSS International Services before leaving the UK (see below). In Germany, patients are free to choose their doctors and dentists and often the hospital as well, subject to their doctor's approval. With such an openly competitive system, standards are high as the bad doctors simply go out of business.

Hospitals

The overwhelming number of hospitals, around 83%, are under the control of cities or Länder. The remaining hospitals are run by the churches and part of the Kirchensteuer (see *Taxation*, above) helps to subsidize these, or by private health schemes. For those opting for preferential treatment (single rooms etc) under a private Krankenkasse scheme, church-run hospitals are generally cheaper than the Länder-run ones. Hospitals invoice the Krankenkassen at rates calculated on a daily basis and charges are fixed depending on the level of facilities provided. Although medicine is an extremely lucrative profession in Germany, it is reckoned that, despite the opportunities for abuse of the system, there is minimal dishonesty amongst doctors, even though top specialists, who can invoice the Krankenkassen vast sums for consultations, are suspected of having a tendency to overcharge.

DSS Forms 111, 101 and 102

Forms E111, E101 and E102 are issued in the UK by the Department of Social Security (International Services, Longbenton, Newcastle upon Tyne NE98 1YX; Helpline 0645 154811) or Social Security Agency, Overseas Branch, Commonwealth House, 35 Castle Street, Belfast BT1 1DX (for those living in Northern Ireland). The E111 (allow one month for processing) entitles UK nationals to receive treatment under any EU country state health system for a period up to a maximum of one year, while the applicant still retains temporary status. Those going to Germany to look for a job on spec would be advised to apply for the explanatory leaflet T5 (Health Advice for Travellers) which contains the application form for an E111, or read page 12 of the leaflet SA29 (Your Social

Security Insurance, Benefits and Health Care Rights in the European Community). Generally, the E111 covers hospital treatment, and private travel insurance (see below) will be needed to cover costs for prescribed medicines, specialist examinations, X-rays, laboratory tests, physiotherapy or dental treatment and repatriation back to the UK.

Those who are working in Germany for up to 12 months, but are being paid by a UK employer, will normally still be paying UK national insurance contributions. In such cases the employer should obtain form E101 from the DSS International Services (see above). On arrival in Germany, the E101 should be presented to the relevant local authority in order to gain exemption from that country's national insurance scheme. Should the applicant find that owing to an unexpected change in circumstances they are obliged to continue their employment in Germany for up to another twelve months, he or she should apply at least one month before the expiry of the E101 for an extension (E102). It is necessary also to seek the approval of the German national insurance authorities before applying for continued exemption. The DSS Overseas Branch issues a leaflet (SA29) giving details of social security, health care and pension rights in the European Community.

Private Medical Insurance

Those who are in Germany seeking work, will require private travel insurance to cover the balance of the cost of medical treatment not covered by the E111 (see above). If you already hold private health insurance for the UK, you will find that most companies will switch this for European cover once you are in Germany. With the increase of British and foreign insurance companies offering this kind of cover it is worth shopping around as cover and costs vary.

One of the best known UK companies is BUPA International (Russel Mews, Brighton, BN1 2NR; tel 01273-208181; fax 01273-866583; website http://www.bupa.com/int). BUPA offers a range of schemes to suit most needs. As the standard of healthcare in Germany is uniformly high, private patients' plans are not strictly necessary. However it can cut the waiting time which may otherwise be necessary for some treatments. Other health insurers include:

Expacare: Dukes Court, Duke Street, Woking, GU21 5XB; tel 01483-717800; fax 01483-776620. Specialists in expatriate health care offering high quality health insurance cover for individuals and their families, including group cover for five or more employees. Cover is available for expatriates of all nationalities worldwide.

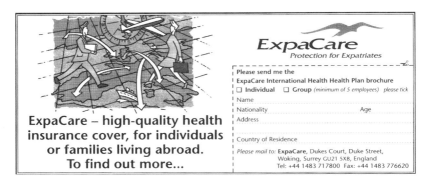

PPP Healthcare: Phillips House, Crescent Road, Tunbridge Wells, TN1 2PL; tel 01892-512345; fax 01892-515143. Offer three levels of insurance package within their International health Plan: Prestige, Comprehensive and Standard. There are no restrictions on age and a medical is not required. Members of the International Health Plan have access to a 24-hr Health Information line staffed by medical professionals.

Local Government

Operating parallel to the Federal Government are two levels of local government: the Länder and various types of Municipal Councils (*Gemeinderat, Stadtrat, Kreisrat, Bezugstag*) according to whether you are an urban or rural dweller. In general the Federal government works without an administrative sub-structure; only the Foreign Office, Defence Ministry and Labour Ministry have their own agencies. Thus it needs to use the administrative apparatus of local government and up to 10% of the Länder staff are employed directly by the Federation.

Länder: As stated in Chapter 1, the 16 Länder are not merely subordinate agencies. They are public entities each with their own limited form of sovereignty, a constitution and the right to self-government. The Länder each have an elected parliament (*Landtag*), a government elected by parliament, their own administrative authorities, and an independent judiciary. The administrative framework of the Länder is clearly defined and under Basic Law they have specific areas of responsibility. Thus, the fields of power that have been decentralized to the states include law and order, education, the administration of justice and measures of public assistance. All Länder have ministries of the Interior, Finance, Economy, Transport, Social Security and Education. Schooling and education provision account for nearly one-third of a Land's budget — the highest single apportionment; the police and judiciary receive 10%. Although it is the function of the national government to make the law, the Länder, through the auspices of the Bundesrat play a substantial role in the federal legislative process (see below). Each state also has its own central bank linked with the Bundesbank, and a network of savings banks.

The Länder are divided into area-states (*Flächenstaaten*) and city states (*Stadtstaaten*). The three city states are Berlin, Bremen and Hamburg. Each has a Senate and senators, led in Hamburg and Berlin by a Chief Bürgermeister, and in Bremen by a Senate President. The area states, which have a Cabinet headed by a Minister-President, are Baden-Württemberg, Bayern, Brandenburg, Hessen, Mecklenburg-Vorpommern, Lower Sachsen, Nord-Rhein-Westfalen, Rheinland-Pfalz, Saarland, Sachsen-Anhalt, Schleswig-Holstein, and Thüringen.

Municipalities: The municipalities (*Gemeinden*) form the lowest tier of public administration, but nevertheless have a special status within the Länder. They elect a council which has the right to self-government, a right that has been enjoyed since the beginning of the 19th century. Municipalities consist of rural counties (*Landkreise*) and town boroughs (*Kreisfreie Städte*), which are generally towns with a population exceeding 80,000. Among the responsibilities of the municipalities are town planning, cultural and educational affairs, public welfare, public transport and the supply of utilities (energy and water). The municipalities also play a prominent role in sports and the provision of recreational facilities accounts for more than one-fifth of a municipal council's budget. Certain tasks of the municipality governments are beyond the capability of all but the largest cities. In such instances as the supply of gas, electricity and water they can form joint undertakings with other boroughs. Revenue for these services comes from local taxation and funding from the state.

Crime and Police

Crime

Germany has witnessed a dramatic rise in the number of reported crimes since reunification, which has been attributed by some social commentators to problems such as unemployment that have arisen from the merger of east and west. Other problems are more generic to the western world, such as a rise in teenage gang related crimes, such as 'tagging' trains with graffiti. The Berlin police arrested over 1,800 youths on graffiti related offences in the first half of 1997. However, on the whole Germany is still a safer place to live and work in than many western countries. The law abiding and orderly nature of the Germans makes the country a very safe place to live. Street crime certainly has a lower incidence than in Britain, or the US, and the busy-body manner of many Germans means that you are unlikely to be ignored if attacked. Germany's greatest problem is cutting down on the flow of illegal immigrants. While some judicial attitudes to the use of 'soft' drugs have been prominent in the media, drug use and supply is still illegal. The main focus of the media in recent years has been on the growing hard drug problem, but most of this news is misleading, rather than pampering drug-users the authorities are trying to stop them killing themselves and ensure that if they can not be weaned off the addiction then at least they won't turn to crime to feed it. The neo-nazi skinhead may grab the headlines with some obscene slogan or action, but if caught by the police he is liable to severe punishment. That the German police do take this scourge seriously can be seen in the reactions of the yobs, arranging rallies using false names or purposes and then changing venues at the last minute to foil any action on the part of the police.

Police

The German (*Polizei*) police officer is little different from other European counterparts and is armed. The police are generally helpful and polite, but tend stick to the letter of the law and at times can be a bit too bureaucratic. While occasional newspaper reports show them as turning a blind-eye to neo-nazi rallies or even of treating ethnic minority groups harshly, this is down to individual officers and is no different to the situation with British or American police forces. In theory it is advisable to carry some form of ID at all times (a passport or driving licence will suffice) as if you are stopped by the police and are without personal documents, they could take you to the police station and keep you for up to six hours. In practice, few Germans, especially the younger generation ever bother to carry any personal identification with this eventuality in mind. As already mentioned, the police are very correct and if they wish to pursue any matter they will do so with great thoroughness. If you are driving a vehicle and you are stopped you will be asked for your driver's licence and the papers for the car (*Wagenpapiere*) identifying the owner of the car, these should always be carried. If you are fined, it is advisable to pay on-the-spot fines without any debate. Apart from such encounters, you will not normally have anything to do with the police and so will not require identification. In the unfortunate event that you are arrested, you have the right to remain silent. You are also allowed to make a telephone call, and if necessary, have access to a lawyer and an interpreter. The police cannot hold an individual for more than 24 hours without charge, except for terrorist offences.

The Law

The German law code, the Basic Law divides the legal system into Public and Private Law. Private law governs the legal relationships between citizens and takes the form of a civil code, governing such matters as: leasing, loans , purchases and marriage and divorce. It also covers those areas of commercial law relating to tradesmen and labour law with regard to employees. Public Law regulates the relationship of the individual and public authority: central and land government, public corporations, and the relationships of the authorities to each other. Inter-Nationes (Kennedyallee 91-103, D-53175 Bonn) the publishing company produce a very useful English-language booklet explaining German Law and other aspects of German life.

The Judiciary

The judiciary is accorded a powerful position of autonomy in the German legal system. Judges are independent of parliament and government and bound only by the law itself. Judges, public prosecutors and lawyers, as well as civil servants and legal advisers in industry and commerce, are required to receive the same professional training.

The Courts

The court system is divided into five different and independent branches. In addition, there is the Constitutional Court which examines the legality of all practices carried out by the state authorities. Every German citizen has the right to be heard in a court of law and any person who is directly affected by the outcome of legal proceedings is entitled to express his or her view before a judge. The court system operates what is known as Basic Law; formal legislation set up in 1949. This covers all aspects of political and social life and created a system of values within which the protection of individual freedom is deemed to be the highest principle of law.

Regular Courts: A two-tier system of Magistrates' Courts (*Amtsgerichte*) and District Courts (*Landgerichte*) hear both civil and criminal cases. The supreme court for both is the Federal High Court (*Bundesgerichtshof*). Magistrates Courts preside over minor offences and have the power to order up to one year's imprisonment. The higher District Courts are split into two levels and generally hear more serious offences. Minor Criminal Tribunals have one professional judge and decide on crimes punishable by up to three years imprisonment. Major Criminal Tribunals (*Grosse Strafkammer*) handle the most serious crimes and are headed by three professional judges. A separate Court of Assizes (*Schwurgericht*) deals with capital offences. Juvenile Courts decide on crimes committed by youths (aged 14 to 17 at the time of the offence) and adolescents (18- and 19-year-olds).

Trials involving civil cases, such as ownership and damage claims, child maintenance and commercial matters, are settled in Civil Courts. Disputes involving amounts up to 5,000 DM are heard in Magistrates Courts. District Courts handle cases of higher value and appeals from the lower court.

Labour Courts (*Arbeitsgerichte*): These courts settle litigation arising from the breakdown of relationships between employers and employees, disputes between employers and trade unions and matters connected with the Labour Relations Act (*Betriebsverfassungsgesetz*). Appeals can be made to the regional labour courts (*Landesarbeitsgerichte*) and the Federal Labour Court (*Bundesarbeitsgerichte*).

Social Courts (*Sozialgerichte*): Social Courts act as tribunals and settle public law matters, such as those relating to statutory health, old-age and accident insurance schemes, social insurance and unemployment insurance.

The Federal Constitutional Court

The Constitutional Court is located in Karlsruhe and was established to ensure that the laws and rights embodied in the constitution are not violated. It can act only in response to appeals. The court reviews rules of law, international treaties, court sentences and decisions by public authorities, as to their conformity with the constitution. It was instituted in September 1951 and has since dealt with more than 80,000 cases, 95% of which have been complaints. In 3% of proceedings it has been required to amend existing laws. Any court can, and must, appeal to the Federal Constitutional Court (*Bundesverfassungsgericht*) if it considers that a law which it has had to apply is unconstitutional. The Federal Government, the state governments, and the Bundestag (with the support of at least one-third of its members), may appeal to have the constitutionality of a federal or state law reviewed. The Court has two panels, known as senates, each of which has eight judges. Half are appointed by the Bundestag and half by the Bundesrat. The term of office is limited to 12 years and judges cannot be re-elected.

Religion

The German Basic Law guarantees the undisturbed practice of religion. At present more than 55 million Germans are members of a Christian church, divided almost equally between the Protestant and Roman Catholic denominations, with both sides having around 25 million members; this may seem ironic when Germany is seen by many as the home of Protestantism. In addition to this, there are many other Christian denominations represented, almost two million Muslims and in spite of the Holocaust, Germany still retains an active Jewish community. However, of the 15 million or so inhabitants of the new länder, only a quarter are members of any organised religion, even though the democratic revolution in East Germany was hatched in the churches.

There is no State church, the Christian churches have the status of independendent public-law corporations, and are in effect in partnership with the State. The churches levy Church Tax on their members (*Kirchensteur*) to pay the Pastors' stipends, maintain the church fabric and run kindergartens and schools, but the money is collected on behalf of the churches by the State tax apparatus. Hence at present more than a few Germans are renouncing religion so as to save money during this economic downturn. The charitable activities of the churches form a considerable part of the framework of German society. Apart from schools and kindergartens churches administer hospitals, old people's homes, and numerous other social institutions, and of course the parish ministries often provide a safety net for the poor. The churches in Germany address the public in many ways, publishing comments on topical social and moral issues, prompting widespread discussion.

The main churches are the Evangelical Church in Germany (EKD) which is an umbrella organisation for the Protestant community of 24 largely independent Lutheran, Reformed and United regional churches. Although these churches are often linked historically to the länder, only the Bayern Landeskirche follows its länder boundaries. In some areas the map of church boundaries printed by the EKD resembles a work by Jackson Pollock, rather than the patchwork quilt one might expect. The Roman Catholic Church is made up of 27 dioceses, with 70 bishops and archbishops. The Methodists joined forces with the Protestant Community to become the Protestant-Methodist Church (*Evangelisch-methodistische Kirche*) in 1968. There is also the Old-Catholic Church (*Alt-katholische Kirche*) which broke away from Rome in 1870 after the first Vatican Council. The Quakers, Baptists and Salvation Army also have active ministries in Germany.

Anglican churches have existed for a long time in many parts of Germany, the oldest is that of St Thomas à Becket in Hamburg (founded in 1611). Most are part of the Diocese of Europe, some belong to the Convocation of American Episcopal Churches in Europe, but all are part of the Anglican Communion and form the Council of Anglican Episcopal Churches in Germany (*Die Anglikanische Arbeitsgemeinschaft in Deutschland*). Those churches listed as hosting Anglican services below, are part of this council, members of all major Christian denominations are welcome to receive Holy Communion at Anglican services. There are also a few ecumenical and interdenominational services in English across Germany, and Anglicans enjoy a communion relationship with the Old-Catholic Church (*Alt-katholischen Kirche*).

Useful Addresses

Church Office of the Evangelical Church in Germany: *Kirchenamt der Evangelischen Kirche in Deutschland*, Herrenhäuser Strasse 12, D-30419 Hannover; tel 0511-2796460.

Secretariat of the German Bishops Conference: *Sekretariat der Deutschen Bischofskonferenz*, Kaiserstrasse 163, D-53113 Bonn.

Central Council of Jews in Germany *Zentralrat der Juden in Deutschland*, Rüngsdorfer Strasse 6, D-53173 Bonn.

English Language Services in Germany:

Berlin

St George's Church: Rev Christopher Jage-Bowler, Preussenallee 17/19, Charlottenburg D-14052 Berlin; tel 030-3041280; fax 030-9172248. Anglican services at 10 am on Sundays with Roman Catholic services at noon.

Methodist Church: Revd. J. P. Atkinson, tel 030-301 5385 or 030-342 2462. The English speaking congregation meet at Auferstehungskirche, Kaiser-Friedrich-Str. 87, D-10585 Berlin.

Bad Homburg

International Christian Fellowship of the Taunus: Evangelische-Freikirche Gemeinde, Pastor Martin Levey, Sodener Str. 11-18, D-61350 Bad Homburg.

Bochum

International English Church in Bochum: Evangelische Pauluskirche, Rev James Brown, Neustrasse 15, D-44787 Bochum; tel 0234-13365. Worship services in English are held every Sunday at 12.30 pm.

Bonn

St Boniface: Rev. Patrick Curran, Haus Steinbach, Rüdigerstrasse 92-98, D-53179 Bonn; tel 0228-916 7247/384925. Anglican services held at 9.40 am on Sundays. For correspondence please address letters c/o The British Embassy, Friedrich-Ebert-Allee77, D-53113 Bonn.

St Thomas Moore: Stimson Memorial Chapel, Kennedyallee 150, D-53175 Bonn; tel 0228-373526. Catholic Masses held in English at 6 pm Monday to Friday, 5 pm on Saturdays and 9.30 am on Sunday. The chapel building is shared by this Roman Catholic community and the Protestant congregation below.

American Protestant Church: Stimson Memorial Chapel, Kennedyallee 150, D-53175 Bonn; tel 0228-374193/373393. Interdenominational Protestant services are held on Sundays at 11 am with a Sunday School at 9.30 am.

Cologne

All Saints' Church: Rev. Patrick Curran, tel 0228-916 7247. All Saints Church is on Bonner Strasse at the corner with Lindenalle. Anglican services are on Sundays at 11.50 am with Sunday School throughout school terms.

International Baptist Church: Rev Butch Oglesby, Rheinaustr. 9, Cologne; tel 02236-47021; e-mail oglesby@compuserve.com Services are held at 2 pm on Sunday, with Sunday School available.

Darmstadt

Darmstadt International Baptist Church: Pastor G. Garret, Wilhelm-Leuschner-Str. 104, D-64293 Griesheim/Darmstadt.

Dortmund

International English Church in Dortmund: Evangelische-methodistische Kirsche, Rev Manfred Muller, Weiherstrasse 3, D-44135 Dortmund; tel 0231-523955. The Dortmund congregation invites all English-speaking christians to services on the first Sunday of the month at 12.30 pm.

Old-Catholic Church: Weissenburger Strasse, Dortmund, Another interdenominational church which meets on the last Sunday of the month.

Düsseldorf

Christ Church Community: Rev Richard Seed, Rotterdamer Strasse 135, D-40474 Düsseldorf; tel 0211-452759; fax 0211-454 2216. Anglican morning services are held at 11 am every Sunday followed by Holy Communion, on every third Sunday services are at 9 am. Sunday School and a nursery are also available, and social events include meetings and lunches.

St Albertus Magnus: Father Ken McLaughlan PhL BD, Kaiserwerther Str. 211, D-40474 Düsseldorf; tel 0211-459739. Roman Catholic Holy Mass is celebrated at 5 pm on Sundays and weekday services can also be arranged, as Father McLaughlan also works within the German community.

International Baptist Church: Am Bauernhaus 30, D-40472 Düsseldorf-Rath; tel 0211-965 3683. The community meets at 11 am on Sundays, with Children's Church and nursery provided.

Frankfurt am Main

Church of Christ the King: The Ven. David Ratcliffe (Archdeacon), Sebastian-Rinz-Str. 22, D-60323 Frankfurt am Main; tel 069-550184; fax 069-550186; e-mail David.Ratcliff@frankfurt.netsurf.de   website   http://www.dfms.org/europe/FRANKFURT/church.htm The Ven D. W. Ratcliffe is archdeacon for the Anglican community of Scandinavia and Germany. Services in Frankfurt are at 9 and 11 am on Sundays.

St Paul's Gemeinde: Mr Myers, Römerberg 9, D-60311 Frankfurt am Main; tel 069-284235. This church holds services in English during the summer months to cater for English speaking tourists.

St Leonhard's International English Speaking Catholic Parish: Alte Mainzer Gasse 8, D-60311 Frankfurt am Main; tel 069-283177. Roman Catholic Masses are held at 5 pm on Saturday and 10 am on Sunday, with Religous Education classes after Mass on Sunday for children from kindergarten to seventh grade. There is also a youth group for older children.

St Petrus Caneseus: Am Alten Bach, D-61440 Oberursel; tel 06171-25983. Roman Catholic Mass is held at 11 am on Sundays.

Mormon: Church of Jesus Christ of the Latter Day Saints, Eckenheimer Landstr. 264-266, D-60435 Frankfurt am Main; tel 069-747774.

Christian Science Services: First Church of Christ Scientist, Ostparkstrasse 37, D-60385 Frankfurt am Main.

Freiburg-im-Bresigau

Methodist Church: Rev Peter Widdess, Katharinenstrasse 9, D-79098 Freiburg-im-Bresigau; tel 0761-287642; fax 0761-289896. Services are held at 11.30 am 6 pm on the first and third Sundays.

Hamburg

The Church of St Thomas à Becket: Rev John Newsome, Zeughausmarkt 22, D-20459 Hamburg; tel/fax 040-4392334. The oldest Anglican parish in Germany, services are at 10.30 am on Sundays with a concurrent Sunday School. Church of Scotland members and other denominations are welcomed.

The English-Speaking Methodist Church: Kreuzkirche, Röntgenstrasse 1, D-22335 Hamburg; tel 040-523 3373. Services are on Sundays at 11.15 am.

Roman Catholic Church of St Elizabeth: Oberstrasse 65, D-20144 Hamburg; tel 040-454148. Holy Mass is celebrated in English every Sunday at midday.

Heidelberg

Anglican Services are held at the Old-Catholic Church on the corner of Plöck and Schiesstorstrasse, D-69117 Heidelberg.

Karlsruhe

Anglican Episcopal Community: Dr Hanns Englehardt, Bismarckstr. 59, D-76133 Karlsruhe; tel/fax 0721-28379. Services take place in the Old-Catholic Church of the Resurrection of Christ

Christi-Auferstehungs-Kirche on the corner of Südliche Hildapromenade and Helmholtzstrasse, at 5 pm on the first and third Sundays of the month. The congregation often joins others for worship, one example being in December, when the congregation joins in a United Carol Service with the Upper Rhine congregations at Baden Baden, so it is wise to make contact before attending.

Leipzig

Anglican Services: Rev. Martin Reakes-Williams, Andreaskirche, Scharnhorst Strasse 29, D-04275 Leipzig; tel 0341-3027951; fax 0341-3090631; e-mail earwig@t-online.de Services in English every Sunday at 5 pm, with Holy Communion celebrated on the first Sunday and a Family Service on the third Sunday of every month, Sunday school is also available on these days.

Munich

Church of the Ascension: Rev Tom Pellaton, tel 089-648185; fax 089-644428; e-mail 106652.2121@compuserve.com Sunday services are held at the Emmauskirche, Seybothstrasse 4, D-81545 München. Eucharist (rite 1) is celebrated at 9 am in the chapel and at 11.45 am in the Emmauskirche, with Family Eucharist every third Sunday. Sung Evening prayer is held on the first Wednesday of the month at *Skt. Willibrord*, Old-Catholic church, Blumenstrasse 36, München. Morning Prayers and Bible Study take place on Wednesday mornings in the chapel.

Stuttgart

For Anglican services in Stuttgart contact Rev Michael Naidu; tel (Tuesday-Friday) 07454-883136, (Saturday-Monday) 0711-682849; fax 07454-883250. Services are divided between two churches in Stuttgart:

St Catherine's Church: Katharinenplatz 5, D-70182 Stuttgart, at 11 am on the first and third Sundays.

Evangelisches Gemeindezentrum: Im Lauchhau 5, D-70569 Stuttgart, at 11 am on the second and fourth Sundays.

International Baptist Church: Untere Waldplätze 38, D-70569 Stuttgart; tel 0711-687 4365.

Wiesbaden

Church of St Augustine of Canterbury: Rev Karl Bell, Frankfurter Strasse 3, D-65189 Wiesbaden; tel 0611-306674; fax 0611-372270. Anglican services are held at 10 am, with Sunday school. On the first Sunday a Family Service is held with the emphasis on children, so there is no Sunday School.

Immanuel Baptist Church: Pastor C. W. Best, Friedrich-Naumann-Str. 25, D-65195 Wiesbaden; tel 0611-401241.

Social Life

The Germans

The stereotypical image that all Germans are humourless and boring is not borne out by acquaintance. It is true that humour has its time and place, and joking in a formal situation can make a German very uncomfortable. Nevertheless, Germans possess both wit and cheerfulness in abundance. The main difference between British and German humour is the use of sarcasm. In Britain sarcasm is socially acceptable and indeed sarcastic banter makes up a great deal of daily social interaction. Friends think nothing of being each other's targets for mild abuse or of exchanging sarcastic remarks about a third party not present. In Germany, sarcasm is not usually socially acceptable and indeed is liable to cause great offence which is probably why British people often think the Germans humourless. Although Germans rarely make jokes about other people, money or business are two examples of subjects regarded as legitimate targets for jokes. In the same way that jokes about other people are not appreciated, jokes about oneself, particularly of the self-denigrating kind are also puzzling to Germans.

From the ruins of war, the German people have built one of the strongest economies in the world. In general they are very proud of their achievements and as far as they are concerned their way of doing things is best. Germans are competitive, ambitious and do not identify or sympathise with failure. A job well done is something to be proud of. Great store is set on the outward trappings of success, such as the car you drive, the size of your office, and where you take your holidays. They are efficient and conscientious, however, and can sometimes be slow to react to change and appear to be happy to stay set in the old ways. Careful thought and planning pervade almost every aspect of life, from decorating the house to business deals. There is a definite antipathy towards stepping out of line and eccentricity of even the mildest kind will attract open criticism. Policing each other's behaviour is not seen as offensive but as a social duty. There is still a desire to belong and a dislike of non-conformism, which may stem from recent history, but the Germans are becoming more relaxed about life. For instance, passers-by are prone to comment if a motorist parks untidily or a pedestrian crosses at a red light even if there is no traffic in sight.

Manners and Customs

The golden rule to remember when dealing with Germans is that their behaviour in public is often in sharp contrast with the informality and warmth of their private life. An individual may initially strike you as cold, extremely formal and even mistrusting. When addressing a German it is customary to use Frau, Herr or the highest title the person possesses. The attention to manners can seem pedantic in the extreme but this is a sign of respect rather than an avoidance of you.

Other points to bear in mind are that on your birthday you will be expected to provide drink and cakes for your work-mates, or to invite your close friends in for something similar. The 6th of December (*St Nikolaus*) is another such situation, children are traditionally given bags of sweets or small gifts, and bosses are expected to do likewise for their employees. It is also wise to have something for your closest colleagues.

While you may find yourself up against a reserve which can seem almost cool, around Christmas and New Year this all breaks down. Shoppers and staff will merrily wish each other *Frohe Weihnachten* (Merry Christmas), as will anyone you meet on the street, not to reply in kind would be considered as rude as shouting

'Bah ! Humbug !' in Britain. As Christmas passes this will change to *Guten Rutsch ins Neue Jahr* ('Good slide into the New Year').

Making Friends

One of the most rewarding aspects of living in a foreign country is breaking down the barriers and forming lasting friendships. Perseverance is certainly required as making a friend of a German is easier said than done. There is a clear distinction made between an acquaintance (*ein Bekannter*) and a friend (*ein Freund*). This is most apparent when speaking German as the polite plural *Sie* is almost always used in formal and business situations. In the same way as the French use 'vous' and 'tu', *du* is used only between friends and the transition from one to another is a significant event. Using *du* marks the entry into each other's private life and should never be taken lightly. The difference is most marked among the older generations and young people commonly use *du* even to relative strangers. A real friendship requires a lot of work and attention, and is effectively a lifetime commitment — one reason why it is such a lengthy process. However, Germans set great store by *Gemütlichkeit*, a combination of camaraderie and having a good time.

For those of you who need a rest from promoting cross-cultural links, the expatriate population in Germany has established a large number of English-speaking clubs and societies in most major towns. They can often provide a friendly face and guidance on how to settle into your new way of life. A comprehensive list of expatriate social clubs is listed in Chapter Five, *Retirement*.

Entertainment and Culture

German culture has a rich history that has reached far beyond its geographical boundaries and graced virtually every artistic stage. No classical music discussion is complete without mentioning the names of Bach, Beethoven, and Handel while Nietzsche, Hegel and von Humboldt opened new areas of philosophical thought and in literary circles Schiller, Goethe, and Brecht have broadened the reach of the written word. Fine arts, music and theatre have always played an important role in Germany and the state considers it as essential to promote cultural heritage. Among current state-funded restoration projects are those at the cathedrals of Cologne and Aachen, and at Hambach Castle, near Worms. The government also funds the *Deutsche Akademie für Sprache und Dichtung* (German Academy for Language and Poetry), the *Germanische Nationalmuseum* in Nürnberg, and the Goethe Institute, which promotes German language and culture worldwide.

A comprehensive calendar of cultural events and entertainment in Germany is available from The German National Tourist Offices.

Nightlife:

There is no German equivalent to the British pub, although there are a few of these in Germany. Bars are often known as a *Kneipe*, *Bierlokal*, or *Kölschlokale* (in Cologne), beerhalls are known as *Brauereikeller*, *Brauerei* or *Bierkeller* (in Bavaria). In wine growing areas wine bars are called *Weinstuben* and around Frankfurt cider is drunk in an *Apfelweinwirtschaft*. One of the best forms of evening entertainment are beer halls, the majority of which are owned by the major breweries. They are huge and relatively inexpensive. Drinking is often accompanied by bands and food. Most establishments open about 11.30am, and are required to close by 2am, unless a special licence has been granted. The exception to this rule are *Kneipen* in Berlin which only have to close for one hour in every 24 for cleaning. (Some even bypass this rule by cleaning one half of the bar at a time and leaving the other side open.) Drinking toasts are commonly *Zum Wohl, Prost* and *Prosit* which all mean 'Cheers!'.

Germany's hottest night life can be found in the St Pauli, St Georg and Reeperbahn areas of Hamburg. It has been dubbed the world's wickedest mile and lives up to its name. Things start at 10pm and carry on until dawn. Berlin too, has a notorious nightlife and at the last count had 6,000 or so bars, some most definitely of ill-repute. A peculiarity to Stuttgart are Broom Taverns (*Besenwirtschaften*). These literally have a broom hanging over the door and serve up the new wines during winter and early spring. The Altstadt, the heart of Düsseldorf's nightlife, boasts more than 200 bars, discos and nightclubs in one sq km. Frankfurt is not Germany's top night spot and when the wheels of business stop turning it sleeps. But it does have one of the finest selections of wine and beer restaurants in an area that has been dubbed Main-hatten.

The easiest way to find a decent place to drink, dance or just hang-out, according to your tastes is to make friends quickly, either with your co-workers or members of the local expatriate community.

Music:

It has been said that there is no such thing as an unmusical German. This is a pleasant conceit but does possess a grain of truth. Between the 16th and 19th centuries German musical achievements were almost unrivalled. The Germans love their music, and opera is as much a national pastime as it is in Italy. It receives generous government subsidies and every major city has its own operatic company. Nearly all foreign operas are sung in their original language. Every major city has its own philharmonic orchestra; Munich has four orchestras and Stuttgart five. Several states have their own Academies of Music. Singing is also a popular pastime and there are many choral societies across Germany for those of all ages and abilities. Jazz and Blues are also very popular and dozens of clubs host live music most evenings, there are a few Blues Festivals in Germany and bands like The Hamsters tour there regularly. Frankfurt is the jazz capital of the country with hundreds of clubs and the German Jazz festival in the spring. Rock and pop are of course popular, and rap has a definite following. While Britain and America may have musical influences on German pop-culture there is a fine if under publicised (across the world) reservoir of domestic talent. Certainly several major names in rock music like U2 and Julian Cope cite 'krautrock' and bands like Can as influential. While the synth band Kraftwerk have recently reformed to play dance festivals in response to the number of dance and techno outfits who regard their work as ground-breaking.

Cinema:

As in almost every country across the globe Amercian-made films dominate the cinema scene, practically all films are dubbed into German, except in the larger towns, where you may find occasional original language screenings. There are also the 'art-house' cinemas which specialise in original language screenings, but these are rare. The current German film industry is very well established and on the increase; German directors such as Wim Wenders and Werner Herzog have an international reputation for high quality films. There are also several film festivals across Germany the main one being in Berlin where films from around the world compete for the coveted Golden and Silver Bear awards. Several other film festivals are held in Germany, including Würzburg's short film festival in February and Mannheim's international Film Week for young and progressive film-makers in the autumn.

Theatre:
The fact that more than 200 theatres have been built since the war is ample testimony to the popularity of the stage. Germany had 190 theatre companies at the last count and at any one time you will be able to watch almost anything that takes your fancy. Especially popular at the moment are German works which are undergoing something of a revival. Mannheim is home to the 200-year-old Nationaltheater, the oldest municipal theatre in the country. Munich is regarded as one of Germany's main cultural centres, running a close second to the undisputed cultural capital Berlin, which has 18 theatres devoted solely to German works. Stuttgart has a rich year-round theatrical programme and Hamburg has become the ballet centre, holding its Ballet Festival in July. Bonn holds the distinction of having the greatest number of theatres, in proportion to its population, of any German city.

Festivals and Carnivals: Germans love festivals, and innumerable pageants and carnivals make the social calendar a colourful and eventful one. Almost every small town or village has its own summer fair, *Bierfest* or *Weinfest*. One of the most famous is Munich's *Oktoberfest*, starting in late September, which dates from 1810. Four and a half million litres of beer are drunk by six million visitors during the 16-day extravaganza; held every year in a tented village on the Theresien meadow.

The next occurrence of festivities is technically part of the *Carneval* season, as while it is removed from the pre-Lentan festivals it is a forerunner to them. This event is the *Rheinische Karneval* and occurs in the Rhineland towns between Mainz and the Dutch border, and celebrates *Hoppeditz Erwachen* the awakening of Hoppeditz, spirit of Carnival.

The next major feature to appear in the calendar is Christmas, if you are lucky enough to be in the right town then you'll know that December has begun by the appearance of Christmas Market (*Weihnachtsmarkt* or *Christkindelmarkt*) booths in the main market square. The oldest and most famous of which is that of Nürnberg, photographs of which regularly appear in articles about German Christmas celebrations. These markets are usually open from the 1st to 24th of December, and sell a wide range of Christmas gifts, novelties, sweets and of course food and drink for the hungry shopper; including *Gluhwein* a spicy sweet mulled wine, excellent for warding of the chill. Many of the items on sale at these markets are hand-made.

German Christmas itself happens on the 24th of December (*Heiligabend*) rather than the 25th, with presents being given in the evening after or before going to church, as there are three services. Christmas Day is called *Erste Weihnachts-feiertag* and Boxing Day is the *Zweite Weihnachtsfeiertag*. Christmas trees are almost a religion in themselves as the Germans decorate not only their own indoor one, but also any handy tree in their garden, in addition to the efforts of the municipal lighting specialists.

Germany has not had such colourful characters as Guy Fawkes in its political history to give them an excuse for letting off fireworks so they make up for it by driving out evil spirits at the turn of the year. As fireworks are only available to buy just before New Years Day, and their use is limited to New Year's Eve a lot of money and explosives change hands in a very short time, in order to see the New Year in with a bang.

When the Christmas decorations come down on twelfth night the country begins preparations for Carnival. The *Fastnacht* or *Fasching* season peaks around the weekend before Lent. Starting with Women's Day (the Thursday before Shrove Tuesday) when women often cut off men's ties in symbolic revenge for the discrimination they suffer the rest of the year. This is associated mainly with Catholic areas of Germany, but is celebrated to some degree in most regions. People dress up, crack rude jokes, drink and generally buffoon around all day. Munich hosts 200 costume balls and in Düsseldorf the highlight is the 3km long *Rosenmontag* (Rose Monday, the day before Shrove Tuesday) parade of floats through the city streets. The biggest carnival is in Köln where its known as *Karneval*, organisers claim to be able to get every bar and restaurant in the city involved in the celebrations. Everything returns to normal on Ash Wednesday.

Sport

Sports are a major leisure pursuit in Germany, with 85,000 clubs affiliated to the German Sports Federation (*Deutscher Sportbund*), these clubs have a membership of around 26 million, while another 12 million Germans enjoy activities outside of formal associations. Western Germany has a large network of sports facilities, in the eastern Länder facilities are rarer and less well equipped for mass sports. Football, gymnastics, tennis and shooting are by far the most popular activities to take part in; more static games like cricket, darts, and snooker do not seem to interest Germans as much. Football is the number one participation sport, with the national federation (*Deutscher Fussball-Bund*) having twice the membership of the tennis federation (*Deutscher Tennisbund*); which loses out to gymnastics (*Deutscher Turnerbund*) in the membership table (see below). Traditional associations (*Vereine*) play an important role in social life and there are clubs for every kind of hobby. Rifle clubs (*Schützenvereine*), each with its own ceremonies and uniforms, are among the most popular. However, the social nature of the activity is borne out by the fact that members seem to spend more time in the bar than on the range. In addition, adult evening schools (*Volkshochschule*), companies, churches, trade unions, universities and welfare organizations also provide ample opportunity for sports participation.

Membership of the Top Ten Sports Associations

Association	Membership
German Football Federation	5,675,783
German Gymnastics Federation	4,604,485
German Tennis Federation	2,333,326
German Shooting Federation	1,540,929
German Athletics Association	831,618
German Handball Federation	826,757
German Table-Tennis Federation	750,049
German Equestrian Association	680,960
German Ski Federation	680,782
German Swimming Federation	631,744

Sports Facilities

Today nearly every small town has its own swimming pool, athletics track and leisure complex. Responsibility for sport is shared between the Federal authorities, the Länder and the municipalities. The latter are responsible for the construction of sports facilities and promoting local clubs. The Länder support sports associations, which in turn promote sports for the broad masses of the German people. The Federation oversees top international and competitive sports at championship levels. State support is also given to disabled sports, games and activities for older people and the promotion of relations in sport with third world countries

Football: Football in Germany is not just a game, it is an obsession. The national league (*Bundesliga*) comprises 18 teams, the most successful of which was former European Cup winner Bayern Munich. In general, German club sides have not distinguished themselves in Europe in recent years. One of the reasons for this is that many of the leading players have been lured by excessive amounts of lira to Italy. However, flying the German football flag has been left in very capable hands. The national team was widely acclaimed as the best in the world during the 80s and since their recent successes at International level they are widely tipped as favourites in the 1998 World Cup

Tennis: A 17-year-old by the name of Boris Becker changed tennis in Germany from the preserve of the upper classes to the game the whole nation wants to play. In 1985 he succeeded in becoming the youngest player, and first unseeded competitor, to win the men's singles championship at Wimbledon. Becker, and subsequently Steffi Graff and Michael Stich, have won glory to which all young Germans currently appear to be aspiring. The number of tennis facilities has expanded accordingly and every town now seems to have dozens of courts open to the public. A recent survey of German 14 year olds put tennis just behind football and ahead of Formula One in popularity.

Winter Sports: The German winter sports teams always do very well at international competitions and the public are provided with a host of winter sport facilities to emulate their idols. The German Alps are often overlooked, but together with the Harz, Sauerland, Rhön, Fichtel Mountains, Bavarian Forest and the Black Forest offer some fine skiing. Long-distance, cross-country and downhill skiing at medium- or high-altitude are all catered for.

Athletics: Athletics is very popular and excellent facilities exist from school levels upwards. At international level the combination of the east and west German athletics teams has created one of the most potent forces in the world. Recent allegations of drug using, however, have tarnished the image of the German Athletics Association.

Other: Swimming facilities are excellent and an estimated two-thirds of the German population swim regularly. Table tennis is also very popular, as are volleyball and handball. Motor sports are undergoing a revival and the main international venues include Hockenheim (which holds a Formula One Grand Prix every July) and the Nürburgring. For followers of the sport of kings, the horse racing calendar is dominated by Hamburg's Derby week in late June, and the spring and autumn seasons at Iffezheim, near Baden-Baden.

Health and Recreation
The Germans are the world's leading spa-goers, and the country has more than 350 registered spa and health resorts. The majority have ultra-modern amenities to pamper and relax guests. These include treatment centres, sanatoria, sports

facilities, hotels, casinos, restaurants and bars. An estimated six million people attend a spa every year, nearly all of them reimbursed by health insurance. As spouses do not usually accompany each other on a spa *Kur* this can lead to problems and the 'spa romance' (*Kurschatten*) is a common occurrence.

Activity holidays are very popular. The North Sea, Baltic coasts and inland lakes, offer a variety of water sports, including 180 sailing schools. The number of golf courses is rising and horseriding is coming back into fashion.

Useful Addresses

Der Deutsche Alpenverein (German Alpine Club): Praterinsel 5, D-80537 München.

Deutsche Fussball-Bund (German Football Federation): Otto-Fleck-Scheise 6, D-60528 Frankfurt am Main; tel 069-67880; fax 069-678 8266.

Deutscher Baseball und Softball Verband: Feldbergstr. 28, D-55118 Mainz.

Deutscher Basketball Bund: Stresemannstr. 12, D-58905 Hagen.

Deutscher Golfverband (Golf): Friedrichstrasse 12, D-65185 Wiesbaden.

Deutscher Handball-Bund: Westfaldendamm 77, D-44141 Dortmund.

Deutsche Reiterliche Vereinigung (FN) (Equestrian): Postfach 11 02 65, D-48204 Warendorf; tel 02581-63620; fax 02581-62144.

Deutscher Schützenbund (Shooting): Lahnstr. 120, D-65195 Wiesbaden; tel 0611-468070; fax 0611-468 0749.

Deutscher Seglerverband (Sailing): Grüngenstrasse 18, D-22309 Hamburg.

Deutscher Turner-Bund (Gymnastics): Otto-Fleck-Schneise 8, D-60528 Frankfurt am Main; tel 069-678010; fax 069-6780179.

Verband Deutscher Sporttaucher (Scuba Diving): Tannestrasse 25, D-64546 Mörfelden.

Verband Deutscher Sportfischer (Angling): Siemenstrasse 11-13, D-63071 Offenbach.

Shopping

In the 1980s west German households headed the European league table when it came to possessing consumer durables. There was a consistently high level of consumer spending and most households were equipped with tv's, fridges, dishwashers, video recorders etc. Eighteen per cent of families had two cars and three-car households were not uncommon. The Germans appeared to know exactly what they liked, and promptly went out to buy it. Attention was paid more to quality than price, and in fact they preferred more expensive goods. Trends also showed that towards the end of the decade healthier and more environmentally friendly goods were becoming more popular. Many of these attitudes still persist but the money does not, due to the current unemployment situation. The British or American shopper should also be aware that all goods sold in Germany are in metric sizes and weights, including shoe and clothing sizes.

The opening hours of shops can vary considerably, official opening hours tend to apply to large shops, department stores and supermarkets. These hours tend to be 9am to 6.30pm, Monday to Friday; many larger stores stay open until 8.30pm on Thursdays. On Saturdays shop generally close at 2pm, even though a recent experiment moved this back to 4pm, except for the four Saturdays during Advent. Unlike Britain or America there is practically no Sunday trading.

Value Added Tax (*Mehrwertsteuer*) is charged on most goods and services, at the time of writing the rate was 15%, but this is due to rise to 16% in 1998. Some essential items, such as foodstuffs, are charged at the lower rate of 7½%. Düsseldorf is Germany's shopping mecca, thanks to the exclusive and large Königsallee complex, known locally simply as the Kö. Berlin's KaDeWe is the largest department store in Europe. The food department, which alone occupies the entire sixth floor, displays some 25,000 different food products and has 22 lunch bars. Frankfurt's pedestrianised Zeil has the highest turnover of any shopping centre in Germany and Stuttgart's claim to fame is Breuninger, the Harrods of Germany. Almost all cities have a pedestrianised shopping area (*Fussgängerzone*) or at least such an area is traffic calmed (*verkehrsberuhigt*).

For the homesick expat, Marks & Spencer has three shops across Germany and more might be in planning. At least two stores in Frankfurt are run by expats with the needs of the Briton abroad in mind as far as their stock is concerned. There are also a few English-language bookshops across Germany, for the homesick, including one for Australians.

Useful Shops for the Expat

The American Book Centre: Jahnstrasse 36, D-63018 Frankfurt am Main.
The Anglia English Bookshop: Schellingstrasse 3, D-80799 München.
The British Bookshop: Borsenstrasse 17, D-60313 Frankfurt am Main.
Down Under: Ammergasse 21, D-72070 Tübingen.
The English Shop: Schellingstr. 11, D-70174 Stuttgart.
Tom's Bookstore: Rembrandtstr. 184, D-70597 Stuttgart.
Words'Worth: Schellingstrasse 2a, D-80799 München.

Food shopping: Germans prefer to shop at small specialised shops and boutiques (of which there has been a recent resurgence in the face of the supermarket construction boom of the 70s) but there are also many supermarkets, most notable of which are shops like *Aldi* or *Norma*. The goods on sale here being *preiswert* (inexpensive) due to the high volume sales their outlets can generate, which keeps prices down. They tend to have bulk quantities of goods but with a limited choice of brands. Their popularity with shoppers can be seen in the size of the checkout queues, although their till staff are amazingly quick at processing a large number of customers. Outdoor markets are also very popular. Farmers very often bring produce direct, so goods are both fresh and relatively inexpensive. It is important to note however that owing to strict health regulations the touching of fruits and vegetables before purchase is technically prohibited, but that doesn't stop shoppers from assessing quality for themselves. Queueing, in the British sense is not a common practice, German queues tend to be more spread out, and it is up to you to speak up and keep your place.

German Food

Germans have a reputation for liking *gutbürgerlich* food: solid, homely and well-cooked, one example is pork, potatoes, peas, dumplings and gravy. Vegetarians will have a hard time in the face of the amazing range of meat dishes especially the German sausage (*Wurst*). There are hundreds of varieties eaten the world over including Wienerwurst, Milzwurst, Bratwurst, Gelbwurst, Wollwurst, Leberwurst and Weisswurst. The list is seemingly endless in this German *Wurstkultur*. There are even specialized sausage kitchens (*Wurstküchen*). Bread is also something of a

CONVERSION CHART

LENGTH (N.B. 12 inches=1 foot, 10 mm=1 cm, 100 cm=1 metre)

inches	1	2	3	4	5	6	9	12		
cm	2.5	5	7.5	10	12.5	15.2	23	30		
cm	1	2	3	5	10	20	25	50	75	100
inches	0.4	0.8	1.2	2	4	8	10	20	30	39

WEIGHT (N.B. 14 lb=1 stone, 2240 lb=1 ton, 1,000 kg=1 metric tonne)

lb	1	2	3	5	10	14	44	100	2240
kg	0.45	0.9	1.4	2.3	4.5	6.4	20	45	1016
kg	1	2	3	5	10	25	50	100	1000
lb	2.2	4.4	6.6	11	22	55	110	220	2204

DISTANCE

mile	1	5	10	20	30	40	50	75	100	150
km	1.6	8	16	32	48	64	80	120	161	241
km	1	5	10	20	30	40	50	100	150	200
mile	0.6	3.1	6.2	12	19	25	31	62	93	124

VOLUME

gallon (UK)	1	2	3	4	5	10	12	15	20	25
litre	4.5	9	13.6	18	23	45	56	68	91	114
litre	1	2	3	5	10	20	40	50	75	100
gallon (UK)	0.2	0.4	0.7	1.1	2.2	4.4	8.8	11	16.5	22

CLOTHES

UK	8	10	12	14	16	18	20			
Europe	36	38	40	42	44	46	48			

SHOES

UK	3	4	5	6	7	8	9	10	11	12
Europe	36	37	38	39	40	41/42	43	44	45	46

speciality. There are still more than 200 types of bread in production, including the famous *Pumpernickel*, a rich black rye bread.

The pig provides the staple element of most German menus, and virtually every part is eaten in a variety of ways: boiled with Sauerkraut in Frankfurt, roasted with dumplings in Munich and eaten as ham in Westphalia.

Traditionally lunch (*Mittagessen*) is the main meal of the day, when a cooked meal is prepared, the evening meal (*Abendbrot*) is usually made up of bread, sausage, cheese and pickles. Foreign cooking is growing in popularity, which often benefits the Turkish, Greek and other ethnic shopkeepers. Although, old German peasant recipes are also seeing something of a revival. With regard to eating out this means that foreign restaurants are now vying with the more traditional cuisine. Restaurants are clean and efficient, and they are required to display a printed menu, and show that tax and service (*Mehrwertsteuer und Bedienung*) are included, tipping is customary as a thank-you for good service.

Drink

Health concerns and strict drink-driving laws have had a severe effect on the drinking habits of Germans. Contrary to popular belief Germans are not the world's greatest beer drinkers (that distinction goes to the Belgians) and they drink more coffee than beer. The consumption of soft drinks has risen, especially among the young, and mineral water sales have more than trebled since the early 1970s. Spirits are drunk in moderation and by far the most popular is *Schnaps* (which is also deemed to be the principal cause of alcoholism). The regions each have their own brews. These are too numerous to mention individually but include Cologne's *Kölsch*, *Apfelwein* in Frankfurt and Munich's *Weissbier*, brewed from wheat. There are also a few English and Irish style pubs across Germany, mind you there are also a few bars in Berlin which are so full of Irish staff that they may as well be pubs. But the wise expatriate will only repair to the just-like-home when feeling homesick, you can get a lot more from Germany if you mingle.

Beer: Beer lovers will love Germany, and those with an internet connection can find out about it all in advance at http://www.bier.de. Drinking litre mugs full of frothy beer is more than a pastime for Germans, it's an institution. They consume more than 145 litres per head per annum. The country has more than one-third of the world's breweries, with more than half (800) in Bavaria alone. It also has the second and third ranked beer producing cities in the world — namely Dortmund and Munich. Freising boasts the oldest brewery in the world, dating back to the early thirteenth century. Doctors have been known to prescribe it for patients and Augustine monks are reputed to supplement their Lenten diet with Munich's *Augustiner* beer. Bavarian brewers recently gave a nun their highest award for a beer she brews at her convent. Fortunately, the Germans do not keep it all to themselves and brand names such as Hofmeister and Becks are well-known throughout the world.

German beer's good taste and reputation is due in part to a strict purity code laid down five centuries ago by Duke William IV. This code is under threat, however, from EU officials who are trying to standardize beer throughout the Community (very few foreign beers meet the standards, and therefore cannot be imported). The reaction to this has been strong, but the rot appears to have already set in with traditional wooden barrels being replaced by pressurized metal ones.

Alt beers are not old or to be confused with English ale, the term 'alt' means old, as they are brewed to traditional top-fermented methods. *Bock* on the other hand is a bottom fermented brew, bocks come as dark or pale and proliferate around München. *Kölsch* is the local beer of Köln, and is served in tall slim glasses, usually holding 200ml. Another regional speciality is the *Berliner Weisse* a slightly sour tasting cloudy beer, it is often drunk with a shot (*Schuss*) of raspberry syrup or caraway schnapps. In German bars it is not customary to wait at the bar to be served, the standard bar uses a waiter service, so if you want a drink find a free table and wait.

Wine: Germans now annually drink about 26 litres of wine per head — an amount that has more than trebled in the last thirty years. Germany produces seven times less wine than France, but some of what it does produce, usually white, is among the finest in the world. Contrary to what wine merchants in Britain would have us believe, production is not confined to Liebfraumilch; the white wine most drunk in the UK. There are 11 official wine producing regions, all of which are located along rivers or around lakes. The two principal areas are the Rhine (sold in tall brown bottles) and Moselle (in tall green bottles). Throughout the summer and autumn a number of wine festivals (*Weinfeste*) are held. In August the Stuttgart Wine Village has on show more than 350 Baden-Württemberg wines. German wine is divided into two categories: *Tafelwein* (cheap table wine) and *Qualitätswein* (quality wine). The latter is the equivalent to the French *Apellation Controllee*. All *Tafelwein* is either dry (*trocken*) or medium dry (*halb trocken*). *Qualitätswein* can be sub-divided into the better quality *Qualitätswein mit Prädikat*, of which there are six grades, and *Qualitätswein eines bestimmten Anbaugebietes* (usually abbreviated to *Qualitätswein b.A.*). German Champagne-type wines are also available. The two leading brands are Deinhard, from Koblenz, and Henkell, from Wiesbaden.

Recycling

In a country which has had a 'Green' party since the early 1970s, it is hardly surprising that the Germans practise recycling packaging and other materials more than Britain or America. Paper, bottles, cans, plastic wrappings are all recyclable in Germany. In part this has come about from the worrying prospect of running out of places to dump rubbish, but the practical Germans have found a way to make it a sound economic and environmental proposition (see Chapter Six). Apart from the can and bottle banks on street corners or other convenient locations to housing areas, the local rubbish collections usually segregate rubbish by using different coloured or marked bags for each type of waste collected. Part of the cost of all this comes from the householder's nebenkosten, but the bulk of it is paid for by the packaging manufacturers, as they pay licence fees to display the various trademarks on their packaging which indicate that their product can be recycled. It is a legal obligation on the manufacturers and distributors of packaging that they take back anything they put into circulation and forward it for recycling.

Older British readers may fondly remember being able to augment their pocket money by taking back bottles for the deposit on them, a practise discontinued at present. In Germany, however, it is still the case that you can get money back on your empties. The deposit is part of the sale price of the drink to encourage recycling, on bottles of more than 20cl this deposit is 50 pfennigs, this rises to 1 DM on 1.5 litre bottles.

Public Holidays

Germany, like Britain and America has a certain number of days per year which are Public Holidays, these can total between 12 and 15 depending upon where you live. Most are religious in origin but some are wholly secular, especially the third of October which commemorates German Re-Unification. As in Britain expect most shops and travel services to be closed or operating reduced services. Likewise while many of them occur on specific dates Easter and Whitsun are moveable feasts, and others are specific only to certain länder, so it is best to contact the German Tourist Authority for details prior to departure.

Public Holidays across Germany

1 January (New Year's Day; *Neujahrstag*)
March/April (Good Friday; *Karfreitag*)
March/April (Easter Monday; *Ostermontag*)
1 May (Labour Day; *Tag der Arbeit*)
May (Ascension Day; *Christi Himmelfahrt*)
May (Whitsun/Pentecost; *Pfingstsonntag/montag*)
3 October (German Unity Day; *Tag der Deutschen Einheit*)
25 December (Christmas Day; *Erster Weihnachtstag*)
26 December (Boxing Day; *der zweite Weihnachtstag*)

Public Holidays Limited by Region

6 January (Epiphany; *Epiphaniasfest/Erscheinungsfest*) (1)
May/June (Corpus Christi; *Fronleichnam*) (2)
August 15 (Feast of Assumption; *Mariä Himmelfahrt*) (3)
31 October (Reformation Day; *Reformationstag*) (4)
1 November (All Saints; *Alle Heiligen*) (5)
18 November (Repentance Day; *Buss und Betthetag*) (6)

(1) This holiday only applies to Baden-Württemburg, Bayern, and Sachsen-Anhalt.
(2) Corpus Christi is celebrated in Baden-Württemburg, Bayern, Hessen, Nord-Rhein-Westfalen, Rheinland-Pfalz and Saarland, but also in the catholic areas of Sachsen and Thüringen.
(3) Only the Saarland and catholic areas of Bayern.
(4) Only the five new Länder (Brandenburg, Mecklenburg-Vorpommern, Sachsen, Sachsen-Anhalt and Thüringen) celebrate this day to mark Luther's Reformation.
(5) All Saints is celebrated with a public holiday by Baden-Württemburg, Bayern, Nord-Rhein-Westfalen, Rheinland-Pfalz and Saarland.
(6) Saxony is the only land to have this day as a holiday.

Retirement

On average 10,000 British citizens retire from work every week. Many may dream of a cottage by the sea or a villa in Spain, but unless they have some prior link few will contemplate moving to Germany. Anyone considering Germany will do well to take into account the current upheavals of reunification: east and west are still two countries in terms of their standards of living. The cost of reunification is putting a strain on the economy and as a result prices are rising and the value of the German mark fell recently. In less than two years there will also be the problem of European Monetary Union, how this will affect the transfer of sterling pensions to retirees living in Germany is unknown at present.

However, despite these recent upsets there is no reason why retiring to Germany need be anything but a happy and rewarding experience. Provided you take all the necessary precautions before leaving and carry out sufficient background research as to where, when and how you intend to live, there are some real advantages to living in Germany. The climate in the south, and the scenery, compare favourably with anything the UK can offer. The Germans pride themselves on their efficiency and this is apparent in the excellent public services available. They are also a law-abiding and normally polite people. This chapter endeavours to deal with some of the bridges that will have to be crossed to facilitate a successful transition between the two countries.

The Decision to Leave

Germany will never quite be like the UK and anyone contemplating a move must have a clear idea of what they are letting themselves in for. A successful relocation will require not just enthusiasm but a certain degree of adaptability. In addition, the cost of the move could be high. It is unlikely that anyone would decide to uproot themselves and move to a country without having been there before. The majority of individuals settling in Germany are more than likely to have experienced German life while working there. However, living permanently in country, especially on a pension, is not the same as working there on temporary secondment or taking one's holidays there. Before making a commitment to move it is advisable to consider living for a trial period, including the winter, in the area you wish to settle. Alternatively, if you have sufficient funds, you could buy a second home in Germany and should it be a success, sell your UK residence and move permanently.

Entering with Retirement Status:

Since 1 January 1992 pensioners from EU Member States have been able to live wherever they choose in the new boundary-less European Community. As stated above people intending to retire to Germany require a residence permit (*Anmeldebescheinigung*), in compliance with the Foreign Nationals Act (*Ausländergesetz*). It will have to include pension details, proof of adequate medical insurance cover and supply evidence that individuals have 'sufficient' funds to support themselves without working. Under European Union regulations if you work in two or more EU states you will be able to combine state pension contributions paid in each country, for up to date information on this contact the Department of Social Security. UK pensions can be paid directly to individuals resident in Germany, and if your retirement scheme includes health insurance you should have the right to have the same cover as a retired German. To obtain these benefits you should inform your pension authorities of your planned move and obtain a form E121 from your health authority, this should be handed to the relevant authorities in your new homeland.

Choosing and Buying a Retirement Home

The main and obvious point to make regarding buying a retirement home is to choose something which is both within one's scope financially and in an area suitable for year-round living. Large numbers of British expatriates live in the major cities (6,000 in Hamburg alone) and industrial areas. These are not normally the most picturesque regions and the choice of location is often due to work commitments. In general retired people are free to locate wherever they choose. Areas to consider in Germany include the southern sun belt, especially around Lake Constance or in Bavaria, and the north the coast and the Frisian Islands. However, it must be borne in mind that these areas are also amongst the most popular tourist spots in the summer months, and are prone to snow. Proximity to health services and other facilities is also an important consideration for anyone reliant on public transport. Once you have decided on your new home you will need to follow all the procedures regarding property purchase which are explained in Chapter Three, *Setting Up Home*.

Hobbies and Interests

Once you have unpacked and settled into your new home, your thoughts will undoubtedly turn to socializing and the pursuit of interests for which you never quite had the time for in the past. In this department Germany boasts many opportunities. The Germans are keen on sports and recreation and for those looking for an active retirement there are some excellent facilities. Walking and cycling through southern Germany's stunning countryside are especially popular. Virtually every town has a leisure centre, swimming pool and tennis courts. There are also plenty of spectator events on offer, from football to motor racing.

Gardening is a very popular pastime, although in the north gardeners used to the inclement British weather will find a similar hardiness is required. The Germans have spent a lot of time saving and displaying their rich heritage and there are many museums and restored buildings to be explored. Unemployment is rising along with social problems and there is some scope for doing voluntary work, for which both expatriate clubs and the British consulates can be useful sources of information.

English Speaking Clubs & Societies

There is much to be said for forging German friendships and creating an authentic German social life (see the section on Social Life, in Chapter Four *Daily Life*). However, being resident in a country where the language is unfamiliar can make the company of fellow expatriates a welcome relief. Many clubs are run by

Germans as a way of expanding their English vocabulary and this can allow you to rest your vocal cords and mind for a while. Germany has many English-speaking, expatriate social and recreational clubs, so whether you want to indulge a hobby, cultivate a new skill or simply share a drink and a chat your with fellow expatriates there is a range of options. You can even make new friends from your German neighbours. Below is a list of social clubs which should provide a good starting point for any English speaking visitors.

Please bear in mind that the names and addresses of local contacts may change over time.

Baden-Württemburg

Anglo-German Club, Pforzheim: Frau Pat Rouse, Katfenhardter Strasse 14, D-75331 Engelsbrandt; tel 07235-457.

British Baden Club, Rastatt: Mrs Pauline Gebürtig, Lupinenstrasse 9, D-76287 Rheinstetten; tel 07242-1891.

British Business Club: Dr G. O. Smith, c/o Hornbergstr. 41, D-70794 Filderstadt; tel 0711-779310; fax 0711-779 3130.

British International, Villingen-Schwenningen: Cathy & Holga Knorr, Weiherainstr. 9, D-78056 Villingen-Schwennigen; tel 07720-956281.

British Stammtisch, Esslingen: Frau Vivian Beutenmüller, Konigsallee 77,D-73733 Esslingen am Neckar; tel 0711-387956.

Club for English speaking People: Mrs Pat Küstner, Leitzstrasse 15, D-76703 Kraichtal-Goscheim; tel 07258-1439.

Deutsche-Englischer Freundkreis e.V. Karlsruhe: Frau Christa Fuss, Erzbergstr. 49, D-76133 Karlsruhe; tel 0721 74623.

Deutsche-Englische Gesellschaft Arbeitskreis Rhein-Neckar: Prof. M. Liedtke, Pädagogische Hochschule Heidelberg, Im Neuenheimer Feld 561, D-69120 Heidelberg; tel 0621-477436.

The English Round Table, Esslingen: Meets on the first and third Tuesday each month in Zum Schwanen, Blarerplatz, Esslingen, contact Dieter (07711-316 9680) for details.

English-Speaking Group, Tuttlingen: Jeffrey; tel/fax 07461-78119. Informal social meetings on the last Sunday of the month at 8pm in the Alte Wache, 18a Bahnhofstr., Tuttlingen, open to native and non-native English speakers.

Freiburg-Madison Gesellschaft e.V.: Kaiser-Joseph-Str. 266, D-79098 Freiburg.

Heilbronn International Women's Club: Cynthia Teevens; tel 07131-250536.

Bayern

Deutsche-Britische Gesellschaft Wurzburg: Frau Wagner, Wiener Ring 51, D-97084 Wurzburg.

Deutsche-Englische Club Bamberg e.V.: Herr Opelt, Mainstr. 56a, D-96103 Hallstadt.

Deutsche-Englische Gesellschaft: Herr Metzner, Frankenwaldstr. 104, D-95448 Bayreuth.

Deutsche-Englische Gesellschaft Lindau: Herr Auleha, Sonnenbichlerstrasse 9, D-88149 Nonnenhorn.

English Speaking Union: Frau Renate Bruckner, Roseggerstr. 16, D-82229 Seefeld.

Berlin

Berliner Cricket Club: Der Sports und Social Club zu Berlin und Brandenburg e.V., Eichenkamp, Charlottenburg. Contact Tim Sandner (030-852 7654) for more information.

British Berlin Ladies Club: Lynda 030-831 3052 or Jill 030-392 4957. Meets every third Monday evening.

British Business Club: Hugo Haig-Thomas, 2nd Secretary Commercial, British Embassy Berlin Office; tel 030-2018 4249. This is an informal meeting ground for British firms in Germany.

British Freemasons: Newly arrived masons can obtain information by telephone on either 030-361 7567 or 030-462 9612.

Berlin International Women's Club e. V.: BIWC Office, Wolfensteindamm 9, D-12165 Berlin; tel 0844-90650. Founded in 1992 the club is open to women of all nationalities and currently has a membership of around 300.

Deutsch-Englische-Gesellschaft e.V.: Landesgruppe Berlin, c/o Eva Schütz, Postfach 370222, D-14132 Berlin; tel 030-831 6650.

Deutsch-Britischer Yacht Club: Kladower Damm 217, D-14089 Berlin; tel 030-365 4010. The club can be contacted by telephone between 4 pm & 11 pm daily.

Harvard Club of Berlin: c/o Herr T. Baumann, Bismarckstr. 30, D-10625 Berlin.

Royal British Legion: Churchill House 2a, Karolingerplatz, D-14052 Berlin; tel 030-306 2015.

Bielefeld

Deutsche-Englische Gesellschaft e.V.: c/o Prof. Dr. P. Funke, Hufscmiedeweg 8, D-33619 Bielefeld; tel 0521-101657.

Bonn

American Embassy Club: Martin Luther King Strasse 12, Bad Godesberg, Bonn; tel 0228-373093.

American Women's Club: Organises bridge groups, German classes for wives of staff, more information can be obtained from the American Embassy.

Ausländer Club: For members of diplomatic missions in Bonn, contact the American Embassy for details.

Bonn-Oxford Club: Adenauerallee 7, D-53111 Bonn. Pub evenings twice a month to meet and talk in English, contact Karin Watson (0228-621940) for details.

British Embassy Choir: The choir meets on Fridays in the Embassy, contact Andrew Sims (0228-6153517) for details.

British Embassy Players: An amateur dramatic group which holds two major productions per annum plus others. Contact through the Embassy.

The Caledonian Society: Scottish events and weekly country dancing, contact Pat Mackenzie (0228-334141) for information.

Colloquium Humanum e. V.: Am Botanischen Garten 14, D-53115 Bonn; tel 658186. Is an independent association to promote understanding between people of all nations and cultures.

Colloquium Humanum der Damen: as above; tel 0228-659615. The women's group of the above organisation also helps foreign women to settle into Germany.

Deutsch-Englische Gesellschaft e.V.: Beethoven Platz 6, D-53115 Bonn. Promotes Anglo-German friendship.

The Economy Connection: A women's group for those wives who's husbands have been transferred to Germany. Contact Melissa Ferrari (0228-321900) or Jeanne Stahlmann (0228-857009) for more information.

Exiles Motoring Club: The Secretary, c/o British Embassy, Friedrich-Ebert-Allee 77, D-53113 Bonn.

German-American Exchange Students Club: c/o Frau B. Vieser, Adolfstr. 82, D-53111 Bonn.

Gesellschaft zur Förderung der Deutsch-Amerikanischen Freundschaft e.V.: Postfach 12 04 33, D-53046 Bonn.

Braunschweig

The Braunschweig Players e.V.: Frau Grözinger, Händelstrasse 1, D-38106 Braunschweig; tel 0531-339278.

Conversation Club der DEG: c/o Herr Treve Erdmenger; tel 0531-352160. Meets monthly in the Altentagesstäte, Frankfurter Str. 18, Braunschweig.

Deutsch-Englische Gesellschaft e.v., Landesgruppe Braunschweig: Herr Schiff, Am Kleinen Schafkamp 10, D-38126 Braunschweig.

Die Brücke Braunschweig: Herr Bucholz, Steintorwall 3, D-38100 Braunschweig; tel 0531-470 2591. English conversation group.

The Lion Drama Company: Herr Treve Edmenger, Steinhorstwiese 20a, D-38108 Braunschweig; tel 0531-352160.

Öffentliche Bücherei Fremdsprachenbibliothek: Frau Eckert, Hintern Brüdern, D-38100 Braunschweig; tel 0531-470 2181. Holds 12,000 English language books, videos and cassettes, open on Tuesday and Friday afternoons.

Bremen

British-German Association Bremen e.V.: c/o Michael Shelton, Graf-Sponeck-Str. 16, D-28327 Bremen; tel 0421-239993.

Carl-Schurz-Gesellschaft e.V: Hilmannplatz 6, II etage, D-28195 Bremen.

Deutsch-Englische Gesellschaft e.V., Landesgruppe Bremen: c/o Lampe & Schierenbeck, Herrlichkeit 6, Postfach 10 38 60, D-28199 Bremen; tel 0421-590 9102.

The English Club e.V. Bremen: Paul Padgett, Plantage 13, D-28215 Bremen; tel 0421-358355. Meeting place for English speakers open twice a week.

Dortmund

Deutsch-Britische Gesellschaft der Auslandsgesellschaft NW e.V.: Geoff Tranter, Steinstr. 48, D-44147 Dortmund; tel 0231-502 2432.

Düsseldorf

Anglo-German Club e.V.: Peter H, Paumen, Bielefelder Strasse 83, D-40468 Düsseldorf; tel 0211-424113. Meets once a week for dancing, discussions and film shows.

British Businessmen's Club: Open to all business people with UK connections, contact John Rowen (tel 0211-287568; fax 0211-285098) for more details, or surf their website (http://www.british-dgtip.de/BBC).

The Business Network Germany: Garry R. Hurskainen-Green; tel 0211-577 3300. Open to those in business, this information exchange meets in the evening on the first Thursday of each month .

The British Women's Club: PO Box 1106, D-40636 Meersbuch. Open to UK and Commonwealth citizens, this club arranges coffee mornings and and mother and toddlers groups.

Deutsche-Amerikanischer Vereinigung Steuben-Schurz e.V.: Postfach 10 11 00, D-40002 Düsseldorf.

Deutsche-Englische Gesellschaft e.V.: Frau Dr. B. Suchy, Eichenwand 14, D-40627, Düsseldorf; tel 0211-203410.

Die Brücke: Kasernenstr. 6, D-40213 Düsseldorf; tel 0211-899 3448. This international cultural centre has a library with books and videos in English, as well as a range of events.

Düsseldorf Scout Group: Contact Tania White; tel 0211-430 7257.

English Speakers' Circle: Nooren Shah-Preusser, Hochstrasse 16, D-52441 Linnich;

tel 02462-5898. A meeting place for English speakers, holding discussions and social events in the Volkshochschule, Kasernstr. 6, Düsseldorf.

Essen
British Social Club Essen: Peter Caron, Dorotheenstrasse 38, 45130 Essen; tel 0201-776742. Meets once a month on the last Friday of the month.
Deutsch-Englische Gesellschaft e.V.: Arbeitskreis Essen, c/o Frau Lindner, Wolfskuhle 9, D-45529 Hattingen-Niederwenigern; tel 02324-43786.

Frankfurt am Main
American-German Business Club: Brendan McInerney, Beethoven Platz 1-3, D-60325 Frankfurt am Main.
Australian Business in Europe: Bernd Neubauer; tel 069-2739 0923; fax 069-252753.
Business Network Germany e.V.: Contact Axel Stöckmann (069-971 17238) for more information about this English-speaking forum for business people.
Deutsche-Englische Gesellschaft e.V., Landesgruppe Rhein-Main: DEG Geschäftsstelle, c/o Deutsche Bank AG, Taunusanlage 12, A-32, D-60325 Frankfurt am Main.
English Speaking Club Frankfurt: Contact Nigel Assen (069-572610) or Sylvia Klafki (069-737500) for information.
Esperanto Society Frankfurt e.V.: website http://www.esperanto.de/
Exiles Rugby & Hockey Club: c/o Sport-Club Frankfurt 1880 e.V., Feldgerichtstr. 29, D-60320 Frankfurt am Main.
Frankfurt Scottish Country Dance Club: Hannelore Mansky; tel 069-560 1744.
GB Business Network: Contact Janet Hopkins (06196-84009) for details of this social network for business/professional women.
IAF-Verband Binationaler Familien und Partnerschaften: Ludolfusstr. 2-4, D-60487 Frankfurt am Main. A support group for multi-cultural marriages.
International Choir Frankfurt: Metzlerstr. 19, D-60594 Frankfurt am Main; tel 069-629429. Meets Wednesday evenings between 7.30 and 10 pm.
International Women's Club Frankfurt e.V.: Dr (Med) J. Haas; tel 069-471572.
Kontakt Club Frankfurt: Jakob Leisler Str. 7, D-60320 Frankfurt am Main. A German-American friendship club, meetings are on Thursday evenings from 8 pm.
Marketing Club Frankfurt: Eva Moosbrugger, Mainzer Landstr. 251, D-60326 Frankfurt am Main. Professional forum for all those involved in marketing.
Toastmasters International: c/o Felicia Natividad-Grossi, Vice President, Public Relations, PO Box 75-0302, D-60749 Frankfurt am Main. This English speaking club aims to improve its members public speaking skills.
Union International Club e.V.: Villa Merton, Am Leonhardsbrunn, D-60487 Frankfurt am Main.
Working Women's Group of Frankfurt: A divison of the American Women's Group of the Taunus (tel 06171-580835).

Freiburg im Bresigau
Anglo-German Club e.V. Freiburg: Mrs Dorothy Eschlepp MBE, Sonnenbergstr. 3, D-79117 Freiburg im Bresigau; tel 0761-69461.
Deutsche-Englische Gesellschaft Arbeitskreis Südbaden: Mrs A. Foley, Schulungscenter Foley, Poststrasse 3, D-79098 Freiburg im Bresigau; tel 0761-387900.
Network of English Speaking Women: Susan; tel 07665-51332.

Hamburg

Alster Cricket Club: Mark Richardson; tel 040-21947. An amatuer cricket club which welcomes players of all ages and abilities.

American Women's Club of Hamburg e.V.: Kay Franks, Postfach 551066, D-22570 Hamburg; tel 040-75493885; fax 040-5594860. Arranges monthly meetings with a range of activities as well as publishing a useful newsheet for newcomers to the city.

Anglo-German Club e.V.: The Secretary, Harvestehuder Weg 44, D-20149 Hamburg; tel 040-4501550.

The Anglo-German International Women's Association: Postfach 52 02 32, D-22592 Hamburg; tel 040-870 5152; fax 040-873595. Monthly discussion meetings or outings with conversation groups in English, German, French or Spanish.

Anglo-Hanseatic Lodge: Mr D.J. Cochrane, Am Royberg 11, 21226 Jesterburg; tel 04183-2433. Constituent lodge of the Grand Lodge, British Freemasons in Germany.

The British Club Hamburg: Linda Struck, Süllbergstreppe 6, D-22587 Hamburg; tel 040 864062. For English-speaking residents or Germans with strong British connections, the club organises a wide range of activities including a croquet team.

The British and Commonwealth Ladies Luncheon Club: Karen Melia, Hoisdorfer Landstr. 38, D-22927 Groshansdorf; tel 04102-65320. Monthly lunch meetings and other activities for Commonwealth citizens or their wives.

The British Decorative & Fine Arts Society of Hamburg e.V.: Diana Westermann, Grotiusweg 7, D-22587 Hamburg; tel 040-863798. Lectures on Fine Arts.

The British Women's Guild: Erica-Nanette Butler, Uhlenhorster Weg 4, D-22085 Hamburg; tel 040-227 9394.

The Caledonian Society: Mrs Gwen Cochrane-Jorswieck; tel 040-448032 (office). Celebrates the main Scottish festivals (e.g. Burns Night) see also Scottish Country Dancing.

The Cambridge Society (Germany): Dr Ekkehard Kretschmar, RA, Kl. Johannisstr. 2-4, Rathausmarkt Hof, D-20457 Hamburg; tel 040-362353. Entry eligible to all those who have studied or taught at Cambridge University.

Club for English Speaking Children: Meets on Wednesday afternoons in the Elternschule, Doormannsweg, Eimsbüttel. Contact Elaine (040 439 6433) for details.

Deutsche-Englische Gesellschaft e.V., Landgruppe Hamburg: Geschäftsstelle, Kampchaussee 8-32, D-21027 Hamburg.

English Kindergarten: Verein zur Förderung der Englischen Sprache e.V.: Haus d. Jugend, Bebelallee 22, D-22299 Hamburg; tel 040-511 4256. This operates two playgroups; for children aged 3 and over, weekday mornings and on Wednesday afternoons for children aged from $4\frac{1}{2}$ to 7-8.

The English Library: Staats-und-Universitäts-bibliothek, Von-Melle-Park 3, D-20146 Hamburg; tel 040-4123/5537. The library contains approximately 21,000 English language texts.

English-Speaking Union: Postfach 10 39 01, D-20027 Hamburg. Aims to promote international understanding through the use of English.

The English Theatre Hamburg: Frau Heike Koch, Lerchenfeld 14, D-22081 Hamburg; tel 040-225543. A professional full-time English Language Theatre.

The Exiles Rugby Club: John Holway, Imbekstieg 70, D-22527 Hamburg; tel 040-540 1690.

Hamburg English Language Teaching Association e.V.: Elbie Picker, Hanssensweg 1, D-22303 Hamburg; tel 040-279 4010. Professional and social events for TEFL teachers.

The Hamburg Players: Dawn Craig, Neubertstr. 43, D-22087 Hamburg; tel 040-258627.

Hamburg Cricket-Verein e.V. & Norddeutscher Cricket Verband: Mr Jamal Mirza, Haller Str. 1, D-20146 Hamburg; tel 040-422 1917.

Harvard Club of Hamburg: c/o Herr Dr Dieter Ahrens, Deutsche-Shell AG, Überseering 35, D-22297 Hamburg.

International Women's Club of Hamburg e.V.: Postfach 52 02 20, D-22592 Hamburg.

Leyton-Wandsbek Freundschaftsbund: Rolf Mäkel, Grasnelkenweg 21, D-22391 Hamburg; 040-328826 (office). Oldest town twinning scheme in Hamburg between the Wandsbek district and the London Borough of Waltham Forest.

New Zealand Club: John Piggin, Gottschedstr. 26, D-22301 Hamburg; tel 040-270 0662.

The Oxford Society (Germany): Ernst-August-Str. 17, D-22605 Hamburg. Open to all those who have studied or taught at Oxford University.

Professional Women's Forum e.V.: Pat Pledger MIPD, Görresring 1, D-22609 Hamburg; tel 040-821858; facx 040-820676. Professional networking group for businesswomen, arranges seminars and lectures in English and German.

The Royal British Legion: Mr P. Bigglestone MBE, Jahnstr. 9, D-21435 Stelle; 04171-50153.

Royal-Overseas-League: Mr M. Sairally, Eichelhäherkamp 62, D-22397 Hamburg; tel 040-608 3861; fax 040-608 2562. Membership open to all British and Commonwealth citizens.

Scottish Country Dancing: Mrs Valerie Puschmann, Freesienweg 40, D-22395 Hamburg; tel 040-600 7710. Dancers meet every Thursday at 8pm (except in school holidays) at the Wolfgang-Bochert-Schule in Eppendorf.

Der Übersee-Club e.V.: Herr K.D. dettweiler, Neuer Jungfernstieg 19, D-20354 Hamburg; tel 040-355290. Concentrates on International relations between Hamburg, Europe and overseas.

The University Players: Theatre Workshop des Seminars für Englische Sprache und Kultur, Von-Melle-Park 6, D-20146 Hamburg. Plays performed by students of english twice a year.

Young Mother's Club: Hans-Salb-Str. 24, D-22851 Norderstedt; tel 040-524 1796.

Hannover

Bridge Club Hannover DBV: Podbielskistr. 14, D-30163 Hannover; tel 0511-873567.

Bridge Club Hannover von 1955: Frau Uecker, Appelstr. 24, D-30167 Hannover; tel 0511-804941 or 0511-717621.

The English Conversation Club e.V.: Carl Duisburg Gesellschaft e.V., Theaterstr. 16, D-30159 Hannover; tel 0511-363466. Informal monthly meetings.

Hannover-Bristol Gesellschaft e.V.: Gesellschäftsstelle, c/o Arbeit u. Leben, Entenfangweg 2, D-30419 Hannover; tel 0511-979 9150.

Hannoverische-Britische Gesellschaft e.V.: Mr Robin Burford, Heiligengeiststr. 13, D-30173 Hannover; tel 0511-851034.

Hannover English Language School: Wallmodenstrasse 45, D-30625 Hannover; tel 0511-537077.

International Women's Association: Susan Aurich, Zweibrückener Str. 28, D-30559 Hannover; tel 0511-522238.

Hessen

64 Business Club: Ian Percy; tel 06172-983220; fax 06172-983221.

The American Women's Group of the Taunus: tel 06171-580835; fax 06171-57371.

The Anglo-Deutsch Club (Ober-Ramstadt): William Kean; tel 06154-3554.

The Anglo-German Club Kassel .V.: Marion Blumenstein; tel 05608-3906.

The British Club of the Taunus: Membership Secretary, Postfach 2222, D-65804 Bad Soden.

Cricket Club Hanau e.V.: Simon Wedgbury; tel 069-603 1760.

Deutsche-Englische Gesellschaft Giessen e.V.: Juliane Kemmer, Eichendorffring 9, D-35394 Giessen; tel 0641-43600.

Deutsche-Englische Gesellschaft Wetzlar e.V.: Frau von Falkenhausen; tel 06441-422286.

English -American Club Offenbach: Ulrich Biermann; tel 069-831769.

The English Club Darmstadt: Chris Weaver, Schützenstr. 20, D-64283 Darmstadt; tel 06150-4470.

The Erbach English Language Club: Christel Loeb, Heuberweg 10, D-64720 Michelstadt-Weitengesäss; tel 06061-2082.

Exiles Rugby Club: Contact Walter Jones (06150-3897) or Paul Denby (069-210 7436) for details.

German-English Friendship Society Kulturkreis Sulzbach e.V.: Jeanne Riemenschneider, Postfach 1141, D-65843 Sulzbach/Ts.

Interessengemeinschaft mehrsrachiger Familien e.V.: c/o Marina Zvetina, Van-Gogh-Str. 16, D-64546 Mörfelden; tel 06105-277827.

Permanent Parents Rhein-Main: Contact Astrid Meffert (06142-955555) for information about this support group for English and German-speaking families living permanently in the Rhein-Main region.

The Picadilly Club (Kelkheim): Jutta & Dennis Miller; tel 06195-74755.

Pickwick's English Club: Contact Hugh Kennedy (069-9139 7020 (work) or e-mail 70042.170@compuserve.com) for details of the clubs outings and parties.

Rhein-Main Deutsch-Amerikanische C/Klub: Postfach 15 74, D-63205 Langen.

Schottland Vereinigung (Odenwald): Elfriede Kissinger; tel 06163-2113.

Verband der Deutscher-Amerikanischen Clubs e.V.: c/o Frau Frank, Am Steinwerth 4, D-47269 Duisburg-Rahm.

Köln

Deutsche-Britische Gesellschaft e.V.: c/o The British Council, Hahnenstr. 6, D-50667 Köln; tel 0221-206440. Organises talks, slide shows and outings.

Deutsche Tolkien Gesellschaft e.V.: c/o Marcel Bülles, Thomas-Dehler-Weg 11, D51109 Köln.

Overseas Club (Anglo-German Social Club) Köln: Heidi and Anthony Gray, Weyerstrasse 84, D-50676 Köln; tel 0221-212416 (evenings). This informal social club meets twice a week and has over 100 members.

Leipzig

Deutsch-Englische Gesellschaft e.V., Arbeitskreis Leipzig: Geschäftsführung: Christel Friedlin, J-R-Becher-Str. 10/402, D-04279 Leipzig; tel 0341-338 2418.

Mecklenburg-Vorpommern

Deutsch-Englische Gesellschaft e.V., Landesgruppe, Sitz Schwerin: Roland Gutte, Hamburger Allee 9-6/5, D10963 Schwerin; tel 0385-455134.

München

Anglo-Bavarian Club: David Scrimgeour, c/o Locate in Scotland, Arnultsr. 27, D-80335 München; tel 089-5904 7130.

Deutsche-Englische Gesellschaft München e.V.: c/o Magritta Caroli, Postfach 34 01 47, D-80098 München; tel 089-2302 3042; fax 089-2302 2749.

Deutsch mit Freunden: c/o Sue Bollans, Keferstrasse 24a, D-80802 München.
German-English Association: Ms Sue Turner; tel 089-141 3660.
Munich Scottish Association: Ms Sue Bollans, Keferstrasse 24,b D-80802 München.
Munich Caledonians: Christine Vavra, Greinerberg 14, D-81371 München.
Verein zur Forderung von Wilton Park: Dr Paul Fischer, Bayerische Staatskanzlei, Referat A III 3, Franz-Josef-Strauss-Ring 1, D-80539 München.

Münster
Deutsch-Englische Gesellschaft e.V.: Frau Ingeborg Webb; tel 0251-624190.
English Club International Münster: Wendy Lynch, Coesfeldweg 32, D-48161 Münster; tel 0251-862079. Friendly informal clubs for English speakers. There is a branch of this club in the Greven area, contact Dave Roberts (Ludigeristr. 30, D-48734 Reken; tel 02864-5864) for details of their meetings and bowling parties.
English Club Münster-Nord: Colin Wagstaff, Sprickmannstrasse 39, D-48159 Münster; tel 0251-214303. Social club for English and German speakers, involving discussions and literary groups.

Niedersachsen
Anglo-German Club: Brian Ledger, Summerland 12, D-49090 Osnabrück; tel 0541-682065 (eves).
Bradford-Gesellschaft Norden e.V.: Karl-Heinz Lücke, Hooge Sand 5, D-26506 Norden; tel 04931-6082. Town-twinning association for Norden and Bradford-on-Avon.
Brücke der Nationen Oldenburg: c/o Frau Dr Rippel-Mauss, Peterstr. 1, D-26122 Oldenburg.
Deutsche-Englische Gesellschaft e.V., Landesgruppe Oldenburg: Frau Dr. Thompson-Meyer-Bohlen, DEG Oldenburg, Lindenallee 65, D-26122 Oldenburg; tel 0441-776552; fax 0441-77471.
Deutsche-Englische Gesellschaft e.V., Landesgruppe Salzgitter: Volker Franke, Amtsvogtweg 32, D-38228 Salzgitter.

Nord-Rhein-Westfalen
Anglo-German Club Gütersloh: Frau Almuth Wessel, Kirchstrasse 21, Gütersloh; tel 05241-26771.
Deutsch-Britische Gesellschaft Bocholt: Herr Karl-Gerd Gessner, Dingdener Strasse 59, D-46395 Bocholt; tel 02871-12881. Regular social events and contacts with Bocholt's twin town Rossendale.
Friends of Sheffield e.V.: Monika Wulfhorst, c/o Werner Gabelsberger Str. 10, D-44789 Bochum; tel 0234-337057.
Internationaler Club Hamm: Herr Lothar Wentker, Albert-Struck-Strasse 34, D-59075 Hamm; tel 02381-73068.
Freundeskreis Yorkshire-Hamm e.V.: Herr Kahlke, Ziehrerstr. 11, D-59069 Hamm; tel 02385-8224.
Deutsch-Britische Gesellschaft Harsewinkel e.V.: Dr Hans Strake, Hesselteicher-strasse 12, D33428 Harsewinkel; tel 05247-2393. Meets twice a month on the first and third Tuesday.
Deutsch-Britischer Club Holzwickede e.V.: Frau Marie-Luise Wehlack, Massener Str. 111, D59439 Holzwicede; tel 02301-5201. As well as promoting contact between the local British and German communities the club aims to develop the twinning arrangement with Weymouth.

Deutsch-Britische Gesellschaft Lippe: Herr H. Lotz, Rosenstr. 14, D-32756 Detmold; tel 05321-24538.

Die Brücke: Frau Monika Hegemann-Lischer, Willy-Brandt-Park 1, D-45655 Recklinghausen; tel 02361-502012.

Nürnberg

Deutsch-Britische Gesellschaft Nürnberg: c/o Herr Martin, Deutsche Bank, Karolinenstrasse 30, D-90402 Nürnberg; fax 0911-201 4100.

German-American Men's Club of Middle Franconia: Herr H. Bader, Steubenstr. 31, D-90763 Fürth.

Rheinland-Pfalz:

Deutsch-Amerikanische Freundschaftsgruppe Siegelbach e.V.: Am Wäldchen 3, D-67661 Kaiserlautern.

German-American Press Club: Auf der Rott 4, D-67661 Kaiserlautern.

Saxony-Anhalt

Deutsche-Englische Gesellschaft e.V., Magdeburg & Halle: Geschäftsstelle, c/o Vereins und Westbank, Otto-von-Guericke-Str. 27/28, D-39104 Magdeburg.

Schleswig-Holstein

Arbeitskreis Niebüll-Malmesbury: Frau Diana Kluger, Klockries 48, D-25920 Risum-Lindholm; tel 04661-2193. Town-twinning association since 1976.

Deutsche-Englische Gesellschaft e.V., Landesgruppe: Dr L. Homrich, Barstenkamp 35, D-24113 Molfsee; tel 0431-650790.

Stuttgart

Anglo-Stuttgart Society e.V.: Jane Hayward, Uhlbacher Str. 83, D-70329 Stuttgart; tel 0711-326269.

British Business Club Round Table: Holds informal evening meetings on wednesdays in the George & Dragon English Pub, c/o the Hotel Inter-continental, Willy-Brandtstr. 30 (Neckarstr.), D-70173 Stuttgart. Contact Nick (07152-929800) for more information.

British Club Stuttgart: Mrs A. Seyerle, Hagebuttenweg 4a, D-70599 Stuttgart; tel 0711-455464.

Deutsche-Englische Gesellschaft Arbeitskreis Württemburg: Dr R. Stephan, Postfach 10 60 13, D-70049 Stuttgart; tel 0711-125 3717.

English Language Teachers' Association Stuttgart e.V.: Ulrike Banhardt, Im Greut 43/2, D-73770 Denkendorf; fax 0711-174 1999.

The Vegemite Club (Australian-German): Meets at the George & Dragon English Pub (address above) on the first Wednesday of the month at 8 pm.

Thüringen

Deutsche-Englische Gesellschaft e.V., Jena & Erfurt: Frau Dr. A. Degott, Institut für Anglistik, Friedrich-Schiller-Universität Jena, Uhh/23OG, D-07740 Jena.

Wiesbaden

British Women's Association: Mrs Bertha Müller, Alexandrastr. 19, D-65187 Wiesbaden; tel 0611-844894.

German-American Women's Club of Wiesbaden: Contact Anna-Marita Leibbraud; tel 0611-957 0000.

Internationaler Freundschaftskreis Wiesbaden: Hildegaard Lorentzen; tel 0611-808425.

Wiesbaden British Women: Wendy Rathgeber, Biebricher Allee 26, D-65187 Wiesbaden; tel 0611-86270.

Pensions

If you became entitled to a UK state pension before moving to Germany there is no reason why it cannot be paid to you in Germany. The one important point to note is that a UK pension is paid in sterling and therefore index linked with UK levels. This did at one time pose a problem due to the strength of the German mark against sterling. How it will fare against the Euro is harder to fathom, and the best advice given recent events is to wait and see.

People who move to Germany and work for an EU Employer before reaching pension age are usually insured under the social security laws of Germany. You will not usually have to pay UK National Insurance contributions but paragraphs 2-11 in the leaflet SA29 *Your Social Security, Health Care and Pension rights in the European Community*, explain when you have to or decide to, pay UK National Insurance Contributions.

Each EU country where you have paid insurance towards a pension, will look at your insurance under its own scheme and work out how much pension you can have. Each EU country will also take into account any insurance you have paid in any other EU State to make sure you are paid the highest possible pension entitlement. Paragraph 20 of the leaflet SA29 explains how these calculations are made.

You can claim any of your pensions direct from any EU country that you have been insured in. If you have been insured in the UK and providing you have kept the DSS informed (address below) of any change in your address, you will usually be sent a claim form 4 months before you reach pension age in the UK.

German pension schemes are administered by the *Land* Insurance Agencies (*Landesversicherungsanstalten*) and the Federal Insurance Agency (*Bundesversicherungsanstalt für Angestellte*). To be eligible to receive a German pension an individual must have paid a minimum of 60 months German insurance contributions. German pensions are only awarded if applied for, by the individual, to the German pension authorities.

Useful Addresses:

Department of Social Security: Pensions and Overseas Benefits Directorate, Overseas Benefits (Awards), Longbenton, Newcastle upon Tyne, NE98 1BA; tel 0191-218 7777; fax 0191-218 7293.
Landesversicherungsanstalt Freie und Hansesstadt Hamburg: Postfach 60 15 60, D-22215 Hamburg.
Bundesversicherungsanstalt fur Angestellte: Ruhrstrasse 2, D-10704 Berlin.

Finance

Anyone considering retiring abroad should take specialist advice regarding their financial situation. The majority of people coming to retirement age have some capital to invest, or will have after selling their UK property. It is worth remembering that any nest egg must last you the rest of your life so resist the temptation to splash out on the first opportunity that comes your way. Those intending to maintain connections with both the UK and Germany will need advice on how their taxation affairs can best be arranged.

Taxation

The DSS will not deduct tax from your UK state pension providing you can prove that you are resident in Germany. In this case payments must be transferred into a German bank account and will subsequently be liable for German income tax. A more complex situation arises if one spends time in both Germany and the UK and for this it is essential to get professional advice.

Offshore Banking

For a retired British citizen not resident in the UK, a number of high street banks, building societies and merchant banks offer attractive, long-term accounts through offices in Gibraltar, the Channel Islands and the Isle of Man. The minimum amount of money required to open a deposit account ranges from £500 to £10,000. The interest rate is proportional to the inaccessibility of one's money. Interest can be paid monthly or annually and although the investor will receive much the same amount of gross interest either way, the monthly payments, which bring with them a steady flow of income, are more popular with retired account holders.

Health

Germans enjoy notionally free health care, with the system entirely funded by compulsory contributions. State health insurance covers German pensioners and pension claimants who have provided proof of having completed the prescribed insurance periods, including periods completed in other EU States. Pensioners are required to continue paying health insurance contributions from their pension. It is therefore worth contacting the local health insurance office (*Allgemeine Ortskrankenkasse, AOK*) soon after arrival, and the Contributions Agency of the DSS (Contributions Agency, International Services, Department of Social Security, Longbenton, Newcastle Upon Tyne, NE98 1YX) prior to departure to confirm your eligibility. If eligible you will be issued with a sickness insurance card (*Krankenversicherungskarte*) which you must present on any visit to a medical practitioner.

An alternative is to have private health insurance. It will be necessary to prove you have or are entitled to medical insurance not only to receive treatment but also to be issued with a residence permit (*Aufenthaltserlaubnis*). It is also a wise precaution to make arrangements with friends or neighbours in Germany to inform your family in the case of illness or accident.

Wills

Making a will can seem only one step removed from pre-arranging one's own funeral; although both are arrangements that need to be dealt with at some point. However, should you die intestate — without having made a will — in a foreign country the question of inheritance can become extremely complicated. Assets in the UK and Germany (and elsewhere) will be treated differently. This will mean a minefield of inheritance laws for relatives to sort out and the legal costs will almost certainly mount up.

If you have not made a will then take the advice of a UK solicitor with experience of both the German and British legal systems. If a UK will has already been drawn up it may be necessary to have it reviewed. A new will automatically renders all previous wills void under international law, although a new will can still incorporate parts of an old will if you wish. If you have assets in both countries it is necessary to draw up a will for each.

Certainly the wisest course is to make these arrangements in the country where you plan to retire, and to make it clear to your family what these arrangements are, or how they differ from the accepted rules in your homeland.

Death

Dying abroad can complicate matters in that one's relatives are not always on the spot to deal with the necessary formalities. It is therefore advisable to make your funeral wishes known in advance and preferably written down in a will. The costs of repatriating a body to the UK for burial are very high, so it might be worth considering making arrangements in Germany itself. A death must be certified by a doctor and registered within 24 hours at the town hall, with a valid death certificate and identity papers. The British Embassy and General Consulates can help with the arrangements.

SECTION II

Working in Germany

Employment

Temporary Work

Permanent Work

Business and Industry Report

Directory of Major Employers

Starting a Business

Employment

The Employment Scene

The employment scene in Germany has been complicated by the unification and redevelopment of the former East Germany. At present the economic situation has seen unemployment statistics leap to record levels, yet the view of the leading firms is that an economic upswing is coming; lead by high export figures on the back of the mark's exchange rate troubles of 1997. So while the unemployment figures may look grim, Germany is still a country to look at when seeking wok in another country. The climate may not have the allure of Italy or Spain, but the with right skills and some careful planning you can find a very rewarding position. Especially as at present the opportunities and concomitant benefits of working in another country are not being exploited by many Europeans.

In a country with one of the best trained workforces in Europe, if not the world, competition for jobs is understandably high. Foreigners therefore have to offer skills or services which are in demand and which cannot be provided, or which have not yet been exploited by Germans themselves. The Common Market has created a demand for top flight executives with a knowledge of foreign markets and experts in fields like taxation and business law and for services which will facilitate commercial dealings between different Member States, all of which are expanding areas for investment. In theory, the principle of free movement of labour within the EU, gives nationals of all EU countries the right to work in the Member State of their choice and to move around freely in search of work.

Foreigners who do get jobs, particularly those at management level or in high demand areas like Information Technology, will find their salaries are higher than in the UK, but this may be offset by more expensive living costs and higher taxes and health and social security contributions. On the plus side, greater employee benefits, better healthcare and the shortest working week in Europe are amongst the attractions of working in Germany, and it is possible to 'shop around' to get yourself the best deal on accommodation.

Unemployment

Unemployment in Germany is currently high at 4,520,000 or 11.8% of the workforce. In part this record figure, the highest since the thirties, has come from the laying off of workers from the old overmanned East German industries. Added to this are the problems for German business caused by the recession of the early nineties. The depressed mark has improved exports and hence manufacturing, though recent troubles in the Asian economies are a worry. Nonetheless, Germany is still looking for skilled workers especially in the IT industry.

Residence and Work Regulations

Foreigners coming from another EU Member State to live and work in Germany will have the minimum of residence formalities and work permits are not required at all. EU nationals are required only to register with the *Einwohnermeldeamt* (local registration office) with the *Stadtverwaltung* (City Council) or *Gemeinde-verwaltung* (Community Council) depending on whether they live in a city or in one of the rural communes to gain their *Aufenthaltserlaubnis* (residence permit). This should be obtained within three months of arrival or as soon as you obtain a job whichever is earlier.

Non-EU nationals will have to obtain a visa and residence permit before entering Germany, the exceptions to this are Americans and nationals of the European Free Trade Area (EFTA) states (Iceland, Liechtenstein, Norway and Switzerland).

Anyone applying for employment which involves the handling or serving of food is obliged to obtain a health certificate (*Gesundheitszeugnis*) from the local health department (*Gesundheitsamt*). A fee is charged for the compulsory medical examination involved.

The *Bundesverwaltungsamt* (Federal Office of Administration) publishes a free information booklet (Information Booklet 119) for *Aliens Working in the Federal Republic* obtainable from Bundesverwaltungsamt, D-50728 Köln. Although the last edition of this was dated 1992, the *Cost of Living Appendix*, which is a separate booklet, was dated 1995 so an updated edition may be available soon. Further details on residence and entry regulations for non-EU nationals are in Chapter Two, *Residence and Entry*.

EU Professional Qualifications Directives

Each country in the EU has its own educational system and standards, which means that in spite of the single European market, professional and vocational qualifications are gained in different fashions. However, in order that qualified workers in one state can work freely in another state various commissions and professional bodies have worked to ensure that qualifications gained in one country are recognised by the competent authorities for that trade or profession in all countries of the EU. The work of these bodies is covered by the EC directives 89/48EEC and 92/51 EEC, the former concerns qualifications gained through higher education while the latter covers vocational qualifications. If you gained your qualification by a route other than university, but it confers the same right to practise as that of a university qualification then your qualification is just as valid under the directive. The directives also mean that National and Scottish Vocational Qualifications (NVQs/SVQs) are recognised by the EU states.

However, where there are significant differences in the training for a qualification; the EU directives do allow for the authorities of your new location to ask you to pass an aptitude test or undertake a period of supervised practice.

In the UK the organisation responsible for providing information on the comparability of qualifications is the National Academic Recognition Information Centre (NARIC, c/o ECCTIS 2000 Ltd, Oriel House, Oriel Road, Cheltenham, GL50 1XP; tel 01242-260010; fax 01242-258600; e-mail 106736.2043@compuserve.com).

Certificates of Experience: In Britain, those craftsmen wishing to practise their trade or profession in another EU state can obtain a *European Community Certificate of Experience*. These can be obtained from the British Chambers of Commerce, who issue them on behalf of the Department of Trade and Industry. You should contact them requesting an application form for a European Community Certificate of Experience (form EC2/GN). This form will be accompanied by a copy of the relevant Directive (see above) applicable to the job.

The applicant should check whether he or she meets the terms of the Directive before completing the application form. The certificates cost £80 to process, so it is worth checking your position before applying, there is an enquiry line on 01203-695688 or you can write to: Certification Unit, British Chambers of Commerce, 4 Westwood House, Westwood Business Park, Coventry, CV4 8HS; fax 01203-695844; e-mail 101473.3705@compuserve.com website http://www.brainstorm.co.uk

Sources of Jobs

EURES and the UK Employment Service

EURES (European Employment Service) is a computerised network which exchanges information about living and working conditions and job vacancies between the employment services of the EU/EEA countries. Launched in 1994 to replace the SEDOC system, it is administered by specially trained Euroadivsers.

The central point of contact in the UK for EURES is the Overseas Placing Unit (OPU) of the Employment Service (Rockingham House, 123 West Street, Sheffield, S1 4ER; tel 0114-259 6086/6089). However there are Euroadvisers across the UK, contact your local Job Centre for more information. All local Employment Service Job Centres have computer access to the vacancy details held by the OPU and can supply clients with a print-out and application form for such posts. The spectrum of jobs available varies from those for highly skilled craftsmen and women to seasonal work. EURES also has its own website (http://www.europa.eu.int/en/comm/dg05/elm/eures/job.htm) with links to the government employment agency sites of eleven EU countries. Not all of them have databases that can be 'surfed', however, Germany is one of the ones which you can search online.

A selection of vacancies is published in the fortnightly subscription newspaper *Overseas Jobs Express* (PO Box 22, Brighton BN1 6HX) and on the Central Television Jobfinder.

The Employment Service also publishes factsheets entitled 'Working in..', these are available from Job Centres and Employment Service offices. These cover all the EU/EEA states and give basic information on issues such as Accommodation, Education, Health Issues with contact names and addresses for more detailed help.

The European Union also operates a website where you can find information about living and working in any EU state, and where you can either read up on specific issues, order an information booklet or even download the booklets in PDF format.

Employment Organisations

Many employment agencies specialise in recruiting staff for foreign positions, others are such highly regarded recruiters that foreign companies come to them with the recruitment requirements. Some useful contacts are:

Federation of Recruitment and Employment Services Ltd: 36-38 Mortimer Street, London SW1X 8PH; tel 071-323 4300. Details of employment agency members of this national organization can be obtained direct from this address. Those interested should ask for the Overseas Agency List and enclose an A4, self-addressed envelope and a fee of £3. The agencies listed deal mainly with specific sectors, e.g. electronics, secretarial, accountancy etc. and will only handle qualified and experienced staff.

CEPEC Recruitment Guide: 13 Hanover Square, London, W1R 9HD; tel 0171-629 2266. Is available in reference libraries or directly from the Centre for Professional Employment Counselling, and lists 400 recruitment agencies and search consultants; the guide costs £37 including postage and packing.

CLC Language Services: Buckingham House, Buckingham Street, London, WC2 6BU; tel 0171-499 3365. Offer employment opportunities for Americans with appropriate visas in EU countries at all levels, from secretarial to executive.

The German National Employment Service
The Federal Employment Institute or *Bundesanstalt für Arbeit* (D-90327, Nürnberg) has a nationwide network of hundreds of offices, *Arbeitsämter* (Employment Offices) which are very important for job-finding since private agencies are relatively rare in Germany (see below). It is possible to use the Bundesanstalt's services from outside the country as they have a Central Placement Office (*Zentralstelle fr Arbeitsvermittlung:* Feuerbachstr. 42-46, D-60325 Frankfurt am Main; tel 069-71110; website http://www.arbeitsamt.de fax 069-711 1540). All applications addressed to the National Employment Service from abroad are processed centrally at this address; even if they are sent to the regional Arbeitsämter they will automatically be forwarded to the Zentralstelle. Although nationals of any country can apply through the Zentralstelle, only EU nationals can expect the same treatment as German nationals. Other nationalities will generally need some trade in demand in order to be considered. There is no obligation to use the National Employment Service; many people bypass it by writing to employers direct (see *Temporary Employment* below).

Anyone who goes to Germany to look for work can find the address of the nearest Arbeitsamt (Employment Service) by consulting the local German telephone book.

The one exception to the rule of preferential treatment for EU and German nationals is the Zentralstelle's Student Employment Department which will accept students of any nationality for summer work lasting 2-4 months.

There are also the *Raphaels-Werk* (*Raphaels-Werk e.V.:* Vilbeler Str. 36, D-60313 Frankfurt am Main.) employment advice agencies across Germany, which deal with employment issues and often have a EURES adviser on the staff, although they were set up to advise Germans looking for work abroad.

German Employment Agencies:
The Federal Employment Institute is at present reviewing its policy of discouraging the setting up of private employment agencies (*Zeitarbeitsbüros, Stellenvermittlungsbüros*) in Germany and the number of these is likely to increase in the future. The international chains dealing in temporary work including Manpower (with 75 offices), Adecco, and Randstad (with around 630 offices), have had branches in large cities for some years. At the time of writing, a German law prevents such agencies offering contracts for longer than 12 months at a time.

Useful Addresses
Manpower: Head Office (Germany), Stiftstrasse 30, D-60313 Frankfurt am Main; tel 069-299 80 50; fax 069-289474.

The Internet

In addition to the vast store of knowledge accessible from your computer the internet has recently started to make life easier for the prospective expatriate worker. Not only can you uncover a wealth of information about your intended location and companies operating there, but you can also look for jobs. More than a few employment agencies now have websites through which you can not only read about vacancies, but often apply for them too. If the agency sites do not have the type of job or country that you are looking for then there are also websites of international newspapers, such as the *International Herald Tribune* (see below) which have classified sections on-line including situations vacant. Below is a list of useful websites including that of the German Employment Agency, however, due to the nature of the internet some of these addresses may change over time and there is no guarantee that there will be jobs in Germany listed every day. We should also point out that most German based websites (.de) do not have an English version of the site, and in some cases you will need a web-browser which can read 'frames'.

Arbeit-Online: http:www//www.arbeit-online.de/index.htm
Arbeitsmarkt Online: http://mamas.de/index.htm
Dv-job: http://www.dv-job.de (Specialises in IT jobs and has an English version)
Euroleaders: http://www.euroleaders.com (Graduate recruitment for business and engineering)
Jobnet: http://www.jobnet.de
Jobsite: http://www.jobsite.co.uk   (IT,   accounting,   sales,   &   management recruitment)
Net Com Jobs: http://netcomjobs.com (English version available)
Netjobs: http://www.netjobs.com (Canadian website with 500 opportunites per week)
Only For Me: http://members.aol.com/aupaironly/aupair.htm
Overseas Jobs Express: http://www.overseasjobs.com
Track International: http://www.trackint.com (IT specialists)

Newspapers

UK Newspapers and Directories

The combined effects of the Single Market and the implementation of the EU Professional Qualifications Directives (see above) are likely to trigger a spate of trans-continental job advertising and it is probable that UK newspapers will run an increasing number of recruitment advertisements from other Member States including Germany. Most British newspapers including, *The Times, The Financial Times, The Guardian* and *The European* carry regular job adverts from European countries. The *Times Educational Supplement* (published Fridays) and the Education pages of the Tuesday edition of the *Guardian*, carry prolific advertisements for teaching English abroad. The *Guardian* also has a Europe supplement on Fridays, which includes a job section. A specialist fortnightly newspaper *Overseas Jobs Express* (available only on subscription from PO Box 22, Brighton BN1 6HX) contains articles from a range of working travellers and a substantial jobs section under headings including: Education/TEFL, Hotel and Catering, Information Technology and Trade. Jobs advertised recently included Automated Systems Engineers, Personnel Recruitment Managers, Internet Consulants, Applications Developers, Java and C++ Programmers, PC Support Specialists and Quality Surveyors.

Alternatively, a wide range of casual jobs, including secretarial, agricultural, tourism and domestic work, are advertised in some of the other publications available from Vacation Work such as *Summer Jobs Abroad* (updated annually), or *Teaching English Abroad* which lists those schools and agencies worldwide which employ English language teachers; both are available from 9 Park End Street, Oxford OX1 1HJ; tel 01865-241978; fax 01865-790885.

International and European Newspapers
International newspapers circulate editions across several national boundaries and usually carry a modest amount of job advertising. Presently, the newspapers to consult include the *Wall Street Journal, Financial Times, The International Herald Tribune* and *The European*. As well as employers advertising in these papers, individuals can place their own adverts for any kind of job, although bilingual secretaries and assistants, marketing managers and other professionally qualified people seeking to relocate abroad are in the greatest demand. Obviously advertising rates vary, but anyone interested should contact the advertising department at the addresses listed below.

Useful Addresses

The Financial Times: 1 Southwark Bridge, London SE1 9HL; tel 071-8373 300; fax 0171-873 3922 and Nibelungen Platz 3, D-60318 Frankfurt am Main. International appointments appear in the UK and German editions on Thursday.
The European: Classified Advertising Department, 200 Grays Inn Road, London, WC1X 8NE; tel 0171-418 7777; fax 0171-713 1840.
International Herald Tribune: Barbican City Gate, 1-3 Dufferin Street, London, EC1Y 8NA; tel 0171-628511; fax 0171-628 5533; and Friedrichstrasse 15, D-60323 Frankfurt am Main; tel 069-726755; fax 069-727310 website http://www.paris-anglo.com/iht.
Wall Street Journal: The International Press Centre, 76 Shoe Lane, London EU4; tel 071-334 0008.

Advertising in Newspapers
Axel Springer Group, (2 Princeton Court, 53-55 Felsham Road, London, SW15 1BY; tel 0181-789 4929; fax 0181-780 5519.) represents *Die Welt, Welt am Sonntag, Auto-Bild, Computer Bild, Hamburger Abendblatt, Medical Tribune*, and many others.
International Graphic Press Ltd, (4 Wimpole Street, London, W1M 7AB; tel 0171-436 1199; fax 0171-436 9900) represents *Der Spiegel, Architektur & Wohnen, Manager Magazin*, and *Harvard Business Magazine*.
Anyone wishing to advertise in the widely read *Frankfurter Allgemeine Zeitung* should contact their London office (2nd Floor, West, Bedford Chambers, Covent Garden piazza, London, WC2E 8HA; tel 0171-836 5540). Situations wanted usually appear in the Wednesday edition.
It is also possible to advertise in the British Chamber of Commerce journal further details can be obtained from the Secretary, BCCG, Severinstrasse 60, D-50678 Köln; tel 0221-314458.

Professional and Trade Publications

Professional journals and magazines are another possible source of job vacancies abroad, from British companies wishing to set up offices elsewhere in Europe and foreign firms advertising for staff e.g. *The Architects' Journal, The Architectural*

Review, Accountancy, Administrator, Brewing & Distilling International and *The Bookseller* to name but a few. Anyone in the air transport industry should consult *Flight International* while those employed in the catering trade could try *Caterer and Hotel Keeper* and agricultural workers *Farmers Weekly*. Although published in the UK, some of these magazines are considered world authorities in their field and have a correspondingly wide international readership.

An exhaustive list of trade magazines can be found in media directories, for example *Benn's Media* and *Writers' and Artists' Yearbook* both of which are available in UK reference libraries.

Professional Associations

Those readers who hold professional qualifications are probably already aware of the benefits of membership in a professional association. They may not know though, that during the negotiations involved in the mutual recognition of qualifications, many professional associations negotiated with their counterparts in other Member States and can therefore be helpful in providing contacts.

For British readers details of all professional associations may be found in the directory *Trade Associations and Professional Bodies of the UK*, available at most UK reference libraries. It is also worth trying to contact the German equivalent of UK professional associations: the UK body should be able to provide the address, if not then you can contact them through the German-British Chamber of Commerce, or the information department of the German Embassy. Non UK readers should contact the German Chamber of Commerce and Embassy in their own country. Alternatively you can consult your trade union for information, as they may have links with their counterpart organization in Germany. Below is a list of addresses of the main British professional organizations.

Useful Addresses

Architects Registration Council for the United Kingdom: 73 Hallam Street, London, W1N 6EE: tel 0171-580 5861.

Association of Professional Music Therapists: D. Ashbridge, 38 Pierce Lane, Fulbourn, CB1 5DL.

Biochemical Society: 7 Warwick Court, Holborn, London, WC1R 5DP.

British Computer Society: 1 Sandford Street, Swindon, Wilts, SN1 1HJ; tel 01793-417417.

British Medical Association: BMA House, Tavistock square, London, WC1H 9JP; tel 0171-387 4499; fax (International Department) 0171-383 6644. The International Department offers extensive help and advice to members wishing to work in Europe.

British Dietetic Association: 7th Floor, Elizabeth House, 22 Suffolk Street, Queensway, Birmingham, B1 1LS; tel 0121-643 5483.

Chartered Institute of Bankers: 10 Lombard Street, London EU3Y 9AS.

Chartered Institute of Building: Englemere Kings Ride, Ascot, Berks SL5 8BJ; tel 01344-23355; fax 01344-875346.

Chartered Institute of Building Services Engineers: Delta House, 222 Balham High Road, London, SW12 9BS; tel 0181-675 5211; fax 0181-675 5449.

Chartered Institute of Housing: Octavia House, Westwood Business Park, Westwood Way, Coventry CV4 8JP.

Chartered Institute of Marketing: Moor Hall, Cookham, Maidenhead, Berks SL6 9QH; tel 01628-427500; fax 01628-427499; e-mail marketing@cim.co.uk website http://www.cim.co.uk

College of Radiographers: 2 Carriage Row, 183 Eversholt Street, London NW1 1BU; tel 0171-391 4500.

College of Speech Therapists: Harold Poster House, 6 Lechmee Road, London NW2 5BU; tel 0181-459 8521.

Department of Education and Science: Elizabeth House, York Road, London SE1 7PH.

Faculty of Advocates: Parliament House, 11 Parliament Square, Edinburgh EH1 1RF; tel 0131-226 5071.

General Council of the Bar: 11 South Square, Gray's Inn, London WC1R 5EL.

General Dental Council: 37 Wimpole Street, London W1M 8DQ; tel 0171-486 2171; fax 0171-224 3294.

General Optical Council: 41 Harley Street, London W1N 2DJ; tel 0171-580 3898; fax 0171-436 3525; e-mail optical@global.net.com.uk

Institute of Actuaries: Napier House, 4 Worcester Street, Gloucester Green, Oxford OX1 2AW; 01865-794144; fax 01865-794094.

Institute of Biology: 20-22 Queensberry Place, London SW7 2DZ; tel 0171-581 8333; fax 0171-823 9409.

Institute of British Foundrymen: Bordersley Hall, Alvchurch, Birmingham B48 7QA; tel 01527-596100; fax 01527-596102.

Institute of Chartered Accountants in England & Wales: Chartered Accounts' Hall, PO Box 433, Moorgate Place, London EU2P 2BJ; tel 0171-920 8100; fax 0171-920 0547. The institute can offer advice to members wishing to work within the EU, and maintains an office in Brussels with a charge free line (0500-893369).

Institute of Chartered Foresters: 7a Colne Street, Edinburgh EH3 6AA; tel 0131-225 2705.

Institute of Chartered Secretaries and Administrators: 16 Park Crescent, London W1N 4AH; tel 0171-580 4741; fax 0171-323 1132.

Institute of Chartered Shipbrokers: 24 St Mary Axe, London EU3A 8DE.

Institute of Civil Engineers: 1-7 Great Ceorge Street, London SW1P 3AA; tel 0171-222 7722; website http://www.ice.org.uk

Institute of Marine Engineers: The Memorial Building, 76 Mark Lane, London EU3R 7JN; tel 0171-481 8493; fax 0171-488 1854; website http://www.engc. org.uk/imare

Institute of Mining and Metallurgy: 44 Portland Place, London W1N 4BR.

Institution of Electrical Engineers: Michael Faraday House, Six Hills Way, Stevenage, Herts SG1 2AY; tel (International Department) 01438-767272; fax 01438-742856.

Institution of Gas Engineers: 17 Grosvenor Crescent, London SW1X 7ES.

Library Association: 7 Ridgmount Street, London WC1E 7AE; tel 0171-636 7543; fax 0171-436 7128.

Pharmaceutical Society of Northern Ireland: 73 University Street, Belfast BT7 1HL.

Royal Aeronautical Society: 4 Hamilton Place, London W1V OBQ.

Royal College of Veterinary Surgeons: Belgravia House, 62-64 Horseferry Road, London SW1P 2AF; tel 0171-2222 2001; fax 0171-222 2004.

Royal Pharmaceutical Society of Great Britain: 1 Lambeth High Street, London SE1 7JN; tel 0171-735 9141; fax 0171-735 7629.

Royal Town Planning Institute: 26 Portland Place, London W1N 4BE; 0171-636 9107; fax 0171-323 1582.

The Registrar and Chief Executive, United Kingdom Central Council for Nursing, Midwifery and Health Visiting: 23 Portland Place, London W1N 3AF; tel 0171-637 7181.

Chambers of Commerce

The main function of the German chambers of commerce (Industrie-und Handelskammer) is not to provide assistance with finding jobs, but rather to promote the business interests of their members. However, they are an important source of potentially useful information and can provide lists of their member companies, (both British and German), which could be utilized for speculative job applications. In some cases, chambers of commerce may also be useful sources of job demands in their area. A list of chambers of commerce can be found on pages 220-223 of Chapter Seven, *Setting up a Business.*

The Speculative Application

If you are not using one of the professional recruiting agencies but intend to apply speculatively, direct to potential employers, it is as well to accept that you may have to fire off a good many letters of application before even one positive response is received. It is therefore advisable to target applications where they have the best chance of falling on fertile ground. This means that your preparations should include thorough research into the types of companies likely to have positions for which you are qualified. Such research can often be carried out at Trade Fairs.

The most important constituents of the speculative application after research, are the CV and the letter of application. The CV should contain concise information and should if possible be no more than one page (two pages maximum), and the information should create the best possible impression. For this reason, many people entrust the preparation and presentation of their CV to a company that specializes in this type of service.

The covering letter with a CV, should be tailored to the company/type of job for which you are applying and if possible should appear as if individually prepared. The temptation to pour out reams of personal history should be resisted as the full dynamism and drive of your personality should be unfolded at an interview and not at the application stage. Make sure that you indicate clearly the job(s) in which you are interested. If possible, you should find out the name of the person to whom the letter should be addressed. One telephone call is usually sufficient to obtain this information. If you feel that the letter would be more effective in German (i.e. understood) then the Institute of Translating and Interpreting (ITI: 377 City Road, London, EC1V 1NA; tel 0171-713 7600; e-mail iti@compuserve.com fax 0171-713 7650) provides a good service, putting callers in touch with translators who will provide a fluent translation.

Note that speculative applications need not be confined to employers, they can also be sent to recruitment agencies and search consultants a list of which may be found in the CEPEC Recruitment Guide mentioned above.

If you are offered an interview, remember that first impressions and appearances are very important, and this is especially so in Germany. Dress smartly, but conservatively for interviews (a tie is a must for men), and address all adult women as Frau whether they are married or not, and adult men as Herr. If you do not know someone's name it is correct to address her or him by their title: Frau Doktor, Herr Direktor etc. Handshaking both on arrival and departure is customary. Reserve, formality and strict punctuality are still key factors in business relationships, far more so than in the UK or America. As with a job interview in any country, it is recommended that you find out as much background information as possible about the company in advance of the interview. An interest based on a thorough knowledge and hard facts is bound to impress a potential employer.

Studying in Germany

At present there are around 135,000 foreign students studying at German universities, with courses ranging from mining, media studies and applied cultural studies to the typical courses offered by universities. In order to study in Germany you will have to prove that you are sufficiently competent in the language to make study there worthwhile, and have carried out sufficient research on the course you wish to study and where it is available. The easiest way to do this is to contact an educational exchange organisation, either one of those run by your own national authorities eg the British Council's Central Bureau, the German Academic Exchange Service, the Fulbright Student Programme or a multi-national enterprise like the EU's Socrates/Erasmus scheme. Within the EU, the encouragement of student mobility means that periods of study at a foreign university are fully recognised as modules towards your final degree and you may well be eligible for a grant.

The German Academic Exchange Service (*Deutscher Akademischer Austauschdienst*) publishes a very useful guide for students as well as lists of scholarships and sources of funding. The addresses of the DAAD are given at the end of this section. In addition to their offices in other countries, the DAAD can also be contacted through the offices of the Goethe Institute. Any place offered will only be open for the duration of one semester rather than an academic year as German universities, unlike those in Britain, work on the semester system, although you can apply to extend your study. The semesters run from September-February and March-August. The main universities have their own Foreign Student Offices (*Akademisches Auslandsamt*), which you should contact at least 6 months, preferably a year, in advance of your planned start date for studying. These offices in conjunction with the DAAD will be able to advise you on all aspects of entering Germany to study.

While entering Germany to study is easier for EU and American nationals the basic requirements for entry are: that you have documentary proof of your place at a German university; a passport which will remain valid for the entire period of your stay; proof that you have sufficient funds to support you during your studies and if necessary the correct visa. The DAAD recommend that you arrive with at least 300 DM on you to cover the various expenses of the first few weeks of term, they also recommend that you should allow between 1,000-1,300 DM a month for living expenses. On registering at the Aliens Registration Office with your various documents and passport photos you will be issued with a Student Residence Permit (*Aufentsbewelligung*), this is only valid for study and does not permit the holder to take up any temporary work between semesters.

The EU operates a series of study programmes, aimed at developing educational and cultural links across Europe. The SOCRATES/ERASMUS schemes enable students to study at universities abroad, and grants funding to universities to develop joint courses across EU borders. Candidates for a SOCRATES-ERASMUS placement and bursary must have a sufficient knowledge of the language of the country they wish to study in, that they can communicate with fellow students. However, many universities offer language study programmes for those wishing to take part in the exchange programme. The deadline for applications is the 31st October of the year preceding the academic year you wish to spend abroad. The schemes are administered by the Erasmus Bureau in Belgium (70 rue de Montoyer, 1040 Brussels, Belgium; tel 2-233 0111; fax 2-233 0150) and in Britain by either the Central Bureau for Educational Visits and

Exchanges (10 Spring Gardens, London, SW1A 2BN; tel 0171-389 4004; fax 0171-389 4426; website http://www.britcoun.org/cbeve/) or the UK SOCRATES-ERASMUS Students Grants Council (R & D Centre, The University, Canterbury, CT2 7PD; tel 01227-762712; fax 01227-762711).

Citizens of the USA can apply for grants to assist studying in Germany by applying to the USIA Fulbright Program (809 UN Plaza, New York, NY 10017-3580; tel 212-984 5330; fax 212-984 5325; website http://www.iee.org/fulbright). These study programmes and grants are designed to give American graduates opportunities for personal development and to gain international experience, based on cross-cultural interaction. The full grant covers travel and maintenance costs, health and medical insurance, book grants and if necessary language orientation, while the travel grant speaks for itself. Most university campuses will have a Fulbright Adviser, but applicants no longer enrolled in an establishment can contact the address given above for application details. Candidates are selected on their academic record, language preparation and the extent to which their project will promote mutual understanding. For those wishing to study in Germany there are 91 full grants available and 10 travel grants, the full grant is given for a ten month period beginning in September. Applications for awards should be submitted by October of the year prior to the year you wish to spend overseas.

Addresses of the German Academic Exchange Service

Head Office: Deutscher Akademischer Austauschdienst (DAAD): Kennedyallee 50, D-53175 Bonn; tel 0228-8820; fax 0228-882444; e-mail postmaster@daad.de website http://www.daad.de

London Office: German Academic Exchange Service, 17 Bloomsbury Square, London, SW1X 8QB; tel 0171-404 4065; fax 0171-430 2634; e-mail address daad@intonet.co.uk website http://www.daad.org.uk

New York Office: German Academic Exchange Service, 950 Third Avenue 19th Floor, New York, NY 10022, USA; tel 212-758 3223; fax 212-755 5780; e-mail daadny@daad.org website http://www.daad.org

Temporary Work

Teaching English

It seems that in whichever foreign country you are thinking of living and working, teaching English is one of the main employment possibilities. However, it is true to say that in some countries, notably Spain and Italy, the demand is considerably greater than in others. Germany has an excellent state education system which ensures that a very high proportion of Germans have a good grounding in English. The result is that there is less demand for beginners' courses at language schools and evening classes. The greatest demand is from business people taking courses at language schools, or ones organised by their firms. Even so, many German business people tend to prefer a summer language course in Britain to one taken at home. Unification has thrown up increased opportunities for English teachers in that eastern Germans, many of whom never had the chance to learn English under the communists, suddenly want to learn commercial English at *Volkshochschulen* (People's High School), where various adult education courses are run free of charge. An additional possibility for teaching English is in secondary schools throughout Germany which often employ native English-speakers as assistant

English teachers (*Helfer*). Such posts are normally reserved for students of German and can be arranged through the Central Bureau for Educational Visits and Exchanges (see below).

Prospects for Teachers
The best prospects for teachers are to be found teaching the business and professional community. There are government incentives for companies to provide training to their employees and one of the most popular options is the in-company language course. From the teacher's point of view this means plenty of highly paid positions for EFL teachers, as well as a number of agencies and consultancies which supply teachers to their clients. The only advantage of working for a language school is that initially it may be a useful source of contacts for company English teaching, translation and private tuition jobs. The worldwide chain of language schools Inlingua, has schools in Germany which can be approached individually or through their Birmingham address (see below).

Qualifications
Perhaps not surprisingly, a business or economics background is pretty essential when chasing one of the company jobs above. This is often more important than the type of degree held, or previous teaching experience gained. For instance it is much less important to know what a participle is, than to have an in-depth knowledge of international banking. Many schools offer *Oberstufe*, advanced or specialist courses dealing with a particular sector of business or banking, or for bilingual secretaries etc., where even an RSA Diploma would not be of much relevance. Another fairly essential qualification is a reasonable knowledge of German. Very few schools would be willing to consider you without this. Even though the most utilized teaching method is the one-to-one, total immersion system, teachers are still expected to offer explanations in German. If the school prepares its clients for the Chamber of Commerce Exams (called LCCI), the teacher will be expected not only to understand the syllabus, but to interpret and teach it with confidence. One other qualification usually required is a driving licence so that teachers can hurtle from one assignment to another. Anyone with the above accomplishments should have little difficulty finding a job in a German city.

Training:
Despite not being the most important qualification for teaching English in Germany, English as a Foreign Language (EFL), qualifications can be useful in building up confidence. There is a bewildering array of courses available, the best known of which are probably the RSA courses. A comprehensive guide to all the courses on offer in Britain and abroad can be found in the *ELT Guide* available in bookshops or from the same address as the *EL Gazette* listed below. Alternatively, a free information leaflet of about courses *Academic Courses in TEFL* can be obtained from the English Information Centre of the British Council (Medlock Street, Manchester, M15 4PR; tel 0161-957 7755).

Sources of Teaching Jobs
Some jobs are advertised in the British press, although there are currently more advertisements for TEFL courses than vacancies. The best, if not the only places to look are the *Education* section of the *Guardian* printed on Tuesdays and the *Times Educational Supplement* which comes out on Fridays. The monthly trade paper *EL Gazette* is an excellent source of news and developments in the TEFL industry, the recruitment section *Prospects* carries adverts for posts worldwide, although many

are for senior positions. Nevertheless it is worth consulting regularly, and has recently been updated with the introduction of a job grid, which carries more than 100 jobs each month. Single issues cost £2.10, or £25.50 for a year's subscription (£30 in Europe, £34.50 Worldwide) and is available from Dilke House, 1 Malet Street, London, WC1E 7JA; tel 0171-255 1969.

The best source of job ads for American TEFL teachers is the *TESOL Placement Bulletin* (TESOL, 1600 Cameron Street, Suite 300, Alexandria, VA 22314-2751). This eight page listing of English teaching jobs appears every two months and is sent to TESOL members who register for the Placement Service and pay an extra fee of $21 in North America ($31 abroad) in addition to the membership fee.

The Central Bureau for Educational Visits and Exchanges (10 Spring Gardens, London, SW1A 2BN; tel 0171-389 4764; fax 0171-389 4594; website http://www.britcoun.org/cbeve) can direct you to short and mid term placements in Germany. For more details of these see their entry in the section on *Permanent Work* on pp. XX. One scheme which they operate is the Language Assistant Scheme which enables modern language students from Britain and 30 other countries to spend a year working in a school or college where their target language is spoken. Places as Junior Language Assistants are available in Germany for young people with 'A' Level German who are opting for a Gap Year.

Another option is to contact the individual *Volkshochschulen* directly, the addresses of the nearest to where you plan to go of the 1,400 such establishments across Germany can be obtained from the *Deutscher Volkhochschul-Verband e.V.:* Obere Wilhelmstrasse 32, D-53225 Bonn; tel 0228-975690; fax 0228-9756930; e-mail buero@dvv-vhs.de website http://www.dvv-vhs.de

TEFL Language Schools in Germany:
American Language Academy: Charlottenstr. 65, 10117 Berlin; tel 030-2039 7810; fax 030-2039 7813. Hires part-time TEFL teachers for this and three other schools in Saxony. A minimum of six months Business English is required by client companies.
Die Neue Schule: Sprachen und Mehr, Gieselerstrasse 30a, D-10173 Berlin.
Englisches Institut Köln: Gertrudenstr. 24-28 D-50667 Köln; tel 0221-257 8274.
English Language Centre: Biebererstr. 205, D-63071 Offenbach am Main; tel 069-858787.
Euro-Schulen Nürnberg: Am Plärrer 6, D-90429 Nürnberg; tel 0911-264363.
Euro Sprachen-Institut: Donaustr. 11, D-85049 Ingolstadt; tel 0841-17001.
Heliwell Institute of English: Burgstr. 21, D-50321 Brühl.
International House: LGS Sprachkurse, Werderring 18, D-79078 Freiburg; tel 0761-34751; fax 0761-382476; e-mail ihfreiburg@ihfreiburg.toplink.de
International House: Poststrasse 51, D-20354 Hamburg; tel 040-352041; fax 040-352265.
Inlingua Sprachschule: Königstr. 61, D-47051 Duisburg; tel 0203-305340.
Inlingua Sprachschule: Kaiserstr 37, D-60329 Frankfurt am Main; tel 069-242900.
Linguarama Sprachinstitut: Kant Strasse 150, D-10623 Berlin; tel 030-621 8148.
Linguarama Sprachinstitut GmbH: Karl-Liebknecht-Strasse 38, D04107 Leipzig; tel 0341-213 1464.
Sprachschule-Centrum Dreieich: Frankfurtstr. 114, D-63268 Dreieich; tel 06103 34113.

TEFL Recruitment Agencies/Language Schools in the UK:
Inlingua Teacher Service: Rodney Lodge, Rodney Road, Cheltenham, GL50 1XY; tel 01242-253171; fax 01242-253181; website http://www.inlingua.com
International House: 106 Piccadilly, London W1V 9FL: 0171-491 2598; fax 0171-491 0959.
Linguarama: Oceanic House, 89 High Street, Alton, Hampshire GU34 1LG; 01420-80899.

Opportunities for US Citizens

A number of short-term working exchanges are open to young Americans, *CDS International* (330 Seventh Avenue, New york, NY 10001-5010, USA; tel 212-497 3503; fax 212-497 3535; website http://www.cdsintl.org) are specialists in arranging career training, fellowships and internships in Germany. While the *Council on International Educational Exchange (CIEE)* (205 East 42nd Street, New York, NY 10071-5706, USA; tel 212-822 2695; fax 212-822 2689; website http:///www.ciee.org) sponsors 2-4 week volunteer work placements in 600 projects around the world.

Au Pair and Domestic Work

If you want to try out life in a specific city in Germany, au-pairing can be a useful way to do this. It can also be a stepping-stone, which gives you time to learn or improve your German while gradually acclimatising to the country and providing an opportunity to build up potentially useful contacts. In Germany, as anywhere, au-pairing is a case of free board and some pocket money, however as it is a vocation rather than a gold-mine this should not really be surprising. Pocket money varies but averages at around 400 DM per month, but it has the advantage of being open to both young men and women and providing them with an initially secure base in a strange country. Be warned that standards of cleanliness are high in Germany, and idleness is not appreciated so the workload of household chores can be rather demanding, and may turn out to be more than you were told to expect. Au pairs have the opportunity to attend free evening classes in German at the local *Volkshochschulen* which in some cities can resemble a meeting of the United Nations. Alternatively, advanced and serious students can enrol for German courses at most German universities. The cost of everyday travel is usually provided by the family, in the form of an integrated season ticket, valid on most forms of local transport.

Sources of Jobs:
Zentralstelle für Arbeitsvermittlung: Feuerbachstr. 42-46, D-60325 Frankfurt am Main; tel 069-71110; fax 069-711 1540.
In Via or the *Katholischer Mädchensozialarbeit, Deutscher Verband e.V.:* Ludwigstrasse 36, Postfach 420, D-79004 Freiburg. Has its headquarters in Freiburg and branches around Germany. The UK representative is the German Catholic Social Centre (40 Exeter Road, London NW2 4SB; tel 0181-452 8566; fax 0181-454 4114.).
Verein für Internationale Jugendarbeit: Wesselstr. 8, D-53113 Bonn. Allied to the YWCA, with a central office in Bonn and 25 branches across Germany. Its London office is at 39 Craven Road, London W2 3BX; tel 0171-723 0216.
   Many of the UK-based au pair and domestic agencies can find placements in Germany. A useful source of agency addresses is *The Au Pair and Nanny's Guide to Working Abroad* (£9.99), available from bookshops, or Vacation Work Publications (9 Park End Street, Oxford OX1 1HJ; tel 01865-241978).

Addresses of UK agencies for au pair work in Germany:

Anglo-Continental Au Pairs Placement Agency: 21 Amesbury Crescent, Hove, BN3 5RD; tel 01273-705959. Recruits Au Pairs for Germany, pocket money can be between £35-£50 per week, plus board and lodging in your own room, for around 5-6 hours work per day. Length of stay from 2-3 months (summer only) to 2 years. Summer and long term stays also arranged for overseas applicants. Apply to Sharon Wolfe at the above address.

Solihull Au Pair & Nanny Agency: 1565 Stratford Road, Hall Green, Birmingham, B28 9JA; tel 0121-733 6444; fax 0121-733 6555. Place Au Pairs aged 18-27 across Germany. Their placement fee is £47 including VAT and Au Pairs in Germany usually receive 100 DM per week, placements can be between 2-12 months duration. Au Pairs usually have their own room but eat with the family.

If you are already in Germany, you can consult the regional offices of In Via, the VIJ or the local *Arbeitsamt* which can be located through the telephone directory. It is also possible to find a job by advertising in the jobs wanted section of regional newspapers. Another possibility is to use one's contacts to put up notices on school and hospital notice boards.

Domestic Work:

For those who are not daunted by German standards of hygiene there is plenty of cleaning work available. Use the Yellow Pages for the names and addresses of cleaning firms to ask for work or, put up notices on supermarket notice boards where they are likely to catch the eye of German housewives. Cleaning and other casual jobs such as working on supermarket checkouts, on factory lines, gardening etc. can be obtained through the student employment departments at Universities.

Agricultural Work

Unlike France and other European countries, farming in Germany accounts for a very small part of German GNP and only about 3.2 of the working population are engaged on the land. Farming is a declining business in Germany. Some farms are highly mechanised, but the majority are smallholdings (the average size is 42 acres). Either way, they do not normally require a large number of itinerant workers, except possibly during harvest time at fruit-growing farms. In such cases, the work is often done by the same local people every year, but farmers do take on occasional foreigners as well. The most important area for fruit picking is the Altes Land, which lies between Stade and Hamburg to the south of the Elbe and includes the towns of Steinkirchen, Jork and Horneburg. The main crops are cherries, which are picked in July and August, and apples in September and October. Apples and other fruit are grown in an area between Heidelberg and Darmstadt called the Bergstrasse, and also in the far south, around Friedrichshafen and Ravensburg near Lake Konstanz. The Bodensee area is also recommended for apple picking. The other work for which casual labour is traditionally used, is the grape gathering which takes place in autumn along the banks of the Rhine and Mosel rivers. There are reports however that over recent years, hordes of hard drinking, hard working Poles have monopolized such vacancies, particularly along the Mosel valley. This has made it virtually impossible for other foreigners to get a look in. If you are willing to have a try, such work is best obtained on the spot. Although the harvest does not begin until October, farmers have often recruited their workers by August.

If you want to arrange agricultural work in Germany from the UK, the International Farm Experience Programme is worth noting. Based at the YFC Centre (National Agricultural Centre, Stoneleigh Park, Kenilworth, CV8 2LG; tel 01203-696544; fax 01203-696559). The IFEP arranges courses comprising language tuition and work-experience on farms all over Germany, for periods of three to twelve months. The scheme can arrange time at a language school before departure, applications for European placements can be made throughout the year. Free board and lodging are provided while on the language course and wages at local rates while on the farm. Applicants should be aged 18-28 with at least two years agricultural experience, one of which can be at college. A registration fee of £125 for European Placements is required as a sign of commitment before your application will be processed.

Tourism and Catering

The German hotel industry relies heavily on immigrants and students during the summer months, and has the advantage of not necessarily requiring a knowledge of German as a condition of acceptance (e.g. for washing up or kitchen portering). Pubs and restaurants, (including MacDonalds) are a fruitful source of casual jobs. Owing to a series of punitive regulations, the hygiene standard required of German catering establishments has health department inspectors making routine monthly visits to catering premises. Jobs in catering establishments are advertised in local newspapers and through notices pinned on the doors of the establishments themselves, e.g. for: *Küchenhilfe* (kitchen assistant), *Spüler* (dishwasher), *Kellner/ Bedienung* (bar/waiting staff), *Büfettier* (bartender), *Büfettkräfte* (fast-food server). Jobs of this kind are likely to be easily available in all large cities, university towns and tourist areas. For hotel jobs, the best prospects are likely to be in the Bavarian Alps (along the border with Austria), the Bohmerwald (along the south-east border), the Schwarzwald (in the south-west), the Rhine and Mosel tourist routes, and the seaside resorts along the Baltic and North Seas.

The wages for hotel work are usually reasonable, around £400 per month net including board and lodging. Other possibilities for catering and hotel work for those who do not have a command of German exist on the American and British army bases However, since the end of the Cold War these have been reduced drastically and casual jobs have likewise decreased. Recruitment for American bases takes place through Civilian Personnel Offices (CPO's). Applicants' details are computerized and fed into the Civilian Automated Referral System (CARS) which is a centralized clearing house for vacancies on American bases in Germany. For some bases a base pass is needed to gain entry to the on-site CPO and this is best obtained through local contacts with G.I.'s. In some areas the local Arbeitsamt will carry vacancies on both American and British bases. The American army also has several recreation centres for army personnel of which the ones at Chiemsee (near Munich) and Garmisch-Partenkirchen (near the Austrian border) are two of the best known, and these are also worth trying for catering jobs.

In addition to hotel work, jobs connected with tourism can include working for coastal campsite/caravan park operators, either British or German. The hours are long and spoken German is essential. The German operators pay better than the British ones. Applications should be submitted in the spring.

Useful Addresses and Publications:
Alpotels (Employment Agency): 17 High Street, Gretton, NN17 3DE. Recruits and carries out aptitude tests for employers looking for seasonal hotel staff.

Camping Wulfener Hals: Wulfener Hals, D-23769 Wulfen-Fehmarn; tel 04371-86280. Employs general assistants, catering and kitchen staff and childrens entertainers.

The Directory of Summer Jobs Abroad: Annual publication containing list of German hotels requiring seasonal staff. Available from bookshops and Vacation Work, 9 Park End Street, Oxford OX1 1HJ; tel 01865-241978.

Canvas Holidays: 12, Abbey Park Place, Dunfermline, Fife KY12 7PD; tel 01383-644018.

Zentral und International Fachvermittlung für Hotel und Gaststätpersonal: (International Catering Employment Information Bureau), Feuerbachstrasse 42-46, D-60325 Frankfurt am Main; tel 069-7111460.

Voluntary Work

For those considering a short stay in Germany there are a number of organisations which arrange a variety of unpaid work schemes including: helping handicapped or disabled children and adults, ecological surveying, archaeology and environmental conservation work. The volunteer usually has to pay their own travel costs and a registration fee, but in return for the 30-35 hours work a week you receive free board and lodging. The bonus of such work is that you get to see Germany, practise your German and make contacts, all of which may prove useful should you wish to work or study in Germany later. Volunteers are usually accepted between the ages of 18 and 30. For further details contact:

International Begegnung in Gemeinschaftsdiensten e.V.: Schlosserstrasse 28, D-70180 Stuttgart; tel 0711-649 1128; fax 0711-640 9867; e-mail address IBG-workcamps@t-online.de website http://www.workcamps.com

International Jugendgemeinschaftsdienste e.V.: Kaiserstrasse 43, D-53113 Bonn; tel 0228-228 0011; fax 0228-228 0024.

Vereinigung Junger Freiwilliger: Hans-Otto-strasse 7, D-10407 Berlin; tel 030-4285 0603; fax 030-4285 0604.

Permanent Work

Building and Construction Work

The unification of 1990, set off a long-term construction boom in Germany, although the bulk of the work lay in Berlin and the new eastern Länder where multifarious construction projects are underway. However, with the economic downturn suffered by Germany recently, the construction industry has entered a slump, although this is only a relative term given the number of construction projects underway. These range from new office buildings and accommodation in Berlin, the rebuilding of Dresden's Frauenkirche, and the upgrading of several autobahns. British companies already involved in building projects in Germany include Balfour Beatty, The Carroll Group, Ove Arup, Nicholas Grimshaw and Partners, and Sir Norman Foster's architectural practice. The construction industry should pick up again as the economic upswing of the industrial and service sectors of the eastern länder pulls more investment into the region from foreign investors and developers. Part of the problem was that the downturn forced public agencies to curb spending plans in line with the outlines for economic union. The knock-on effect of this was falling output and a rise in insolvencies, however, financial aid for the region from 1999-2004 has been agreed, and this should generate confidence among investors. These financial problems effect the whole of the German building industry but are more noticeable in the new länder, where there are less reserves to keep building projects going during hard times.

One of the unpleasant side effects of the slump in the building industry and the general downward trend of the German economy was that the inferiority the easterners feel towards the west was exacerbated thus increasing xenophobia. In many cases, this is brought on by the perception that foreigners are taking their jobs, which is in many cases true, as it is easier to pay someone cash in hand at half the official rate than to pay the official rate and the employer's share of benefits contributions. The problem for British building workers is that very often they are being employed legitimately, but German workers consider them to be on the same level as the various Poles, Turks and other Eastern Europeans, who are effectively cheating them out of jobs. The German Building, Agricultural and Environmental union (*Industriegewerkschaft Bauen-Agrar-Umwelt*) has, together with the GMB in Britain, put together an explanatory bilingual booklet on the terms and conditions which apply to building and construction workers, including details of the minimum wages due to building site workers (at present these are 16 DM per hour in west Germany and 15 DM per hour in the east following a reduction negotiated with the intention of boosting the employment of German building workers). The booklet *Fellow Worker, Do You Know Your Rights ?*, is available from the GMB, and can be ordered by calling freephone 0800-834690.

Unfortunately another pitfall awaiting those seeking building work in Germany, is the risk of being exploited by the system of contracting. This works as follows: labourers are lured to Germany by middlemen who promise high wages. Many of the middlemen operate from Dutch border towns, or advertise in British publications giving Dutch telephone numbers (beginning 0031). This has to be done outside Germany because the contracting system is illegal within Germany. When the workers begin their jobs, they discover that they are earning less than the going rate for such work to which they are bound by contract.

However, while the danger to foreigners from right-wing extremists is very real, it is not endemic to the whole of Germany and should not deter anyone who takes reasonable precautions to avoid the trouble. If possible, talk to people who have already been to Germany and can recommend both an agency and an area. If possible try to find out who the middlemen are contracting for in Germany and contact the Germans direct. Failing this, it is worth going out to Germany to try to find work on the spot. The main cities are likely to prove fruitful and some useful research can be carried out in the favoured watering holes of the of expat construction workers. It won't be worth it, even with the EU's generous labour regulations if you don't know some German before you go and continue to brush it up at the evening classes available at the local Volkshochschule when you are in Germany.

Useful Addresses:

GMB: St Georges Lodge, 79 The Burrows, Hendon, London, NW4 4AY.

AMEC Plc: Sandiway House, Hartford, Northwich, CW8 2YA; tel 01606-883885.

The Carvill Group Ltd: 75 Derriaghy Industrial Park, Dunmurry, Belfast, BT17 9HU.

Alfred McAlpine International Ltd: Hooton Road, South Wirral, LL66 7ND.

Mike Stacey Ltd: Station Road, Wiveliscombe, Taunton, TA4 2LX.

Secretarial and Administrative Work

Opportunities are both widely available and lucrative for bilingual secretaries and administrators in Germany. For anyone thinking of doing this kind of work there are a number of UK-based agencies that specialise in placing polyglots with secretarial and office management skills. Such agencies only handle applicants who are genuinely bilingual, have recognized secretarial qualifications/administrative experience, and are interested in permanent positions lasting for a minimum of one year, but preferably longer. Salaries vary according to age, experience and area.

Useful Addresses:
Bilingual People Ltd: 18 Hanover Street, London, W1R 9HG; tel 0171-491 2400; fax 0171-491 1900. Providers of permanent, contract and temporary staff in all fields such as Secretarial, PA, Translation, Interpretation, Sales & Marketing, Banking, Legal, Customer Services & Administration. They have many years experience of providing staff, both in the UK and abroad who are fluent in two or more languages.
Institute of Linguists: Saxon House, 48 Southwark Street, London, SE21 1UN; tel 0171-940 3100; fax 0171-940 3101. The Institute cannot find employment but does offer general advice on careers with languages, how to make use of qualifications already held, and details of qualifications required for specific jobs connected with languages.
Institute of Translating and Interpreting (ITI): 377 City Road, London, EC1V 1NA; tel 0171-713 7600; fax 0171-713 7650; e-mail iti@compuserve.com ITI is a professional association of translators and interpreters aiming to promote the highest standards in translating and interpreting. It has strong corporate membership and runs professional development courses and conferences. Membership is open to those with a proven involvement in translation and interpreting (including students). ITI's Directory of Members, its bi-monthly bulletin and other publications are available from the Secretariat. The Secretariat also offers a referral service whereby enquirers can be given, free of charge, the names of suitable members for any interpreting/translating assignment.
Multilingual Services: 56 Haymarket, London, SW1Y 4RN; tel 0171-930 4886. Specializes in bilingual secretaries and personal assistants, occasional posts in Germany for administrators and secretarial staff.

Teaching

Teaching in German State Schools

About twenty-five years ago, the Germans had a big recruitment drive for English teachers to teach in German state schools, but over the years the shortage eased as German teachers became increasingly proficient at teaching English. Following the implementation in Germany of 1992 EU directives on the mutual acceptance of qualifications within the EU (including teaching qualifications), British teachers can compete freely for positions in German schools and should reasonably expect that their applications will be favourably scrutinised. As educational policy is organized on a Länder basis, any teacher interested in working in the state system should contact the *Kultursministerium* (Education Ministry) of whichever of the sixteen Länder they wish to work in. However one crucial difference will remain between the status of German nationals and foreigners employed as teachers in state schools. Teachers who are German nationals are *Beamte* (civil servants) and as such are entitled to job security for life and perks such as reduced national insurance contributions. This status difference between German and non-German nationals will remain, even under the EU Directives.

As well as trying to find positions in Germany through agencies, one can always scan the recruitment sections of publications such as *The Guardian*'s *Education Supplement*, *The Times Educational Supplement*, and the *EL Gazette* (see page 160 in the section on *Temporary Work*). Suitably qualified Americans can browse the *TESOL Placement Bulletin*, while most of the jobs advertised in these publications are likely to be for short-term work, some may be of a more permanent nature.

As an alternative to applying direct to Germany, or shuffling through piles of newspapers, teachers can apply to The Central Bureau for Educational Visits and Exchanges (10 Spring Gardens, London SW1A 2BN; tel 0171-389 4764; fax 0171-389 4594; website http://www.britcoun.org/cbeve) which arranges placements in German schools. Placements can be for a few weeks, a term, a year or longer depending on the scheme involved:

1. Posts as Helpers (*Helfer*) in Germany can be arranged for 18-20 year olds with 'A level German'. Posts are for a half or full academic year. Helpers receive free board and lodging, normally within the school and a monthly allowance of not less than 250 DM. However travel arrangements to Germany are at the helper's expense. Most schools are located in small towns or isolated districts and applicants will be appointed according to suitability for the post rather than area of preference. Helpers teach English under the guidance of the permanent staff for 12-14 hours per week. It should be possible to attend other classes at the school which are of personal interest. It is essential to apply early. The closing date for applications is 31st March.
2. Posts as English Language Assistants in Germany is a senior version of the above. Applicants should normally be aged 20-30 years (up to 40 is possible), and have completed at least two years of a degree or diploma course. For positions in the new Länder where conditions are difficult, graduates with previous experience of the assistant scheme, or with some teaching experience are preferred. Posts are for a minimum of one academic year and the monthly allowance is 1,000 DM. Applicants have to pay their own travel expenses and for board and lodging. As the scheme is expensive for the participant it is advisable to obtain sponsorship e.g. from their institute of higher education.
3. Post to post teacher exchange programmes are for qualified teachers of modern languages or related subjects with more than two years' experience. Exchanges are for four weeks, one term or one year. Further details may be obtained from the In-Service Education Department of the Central Bureau.

In America budding teachers of German can obtain help from the USIA Fulbright Program (809 UN Plaza, New York, NY 10017-3580, USA) which places 50 teaching assistants (*Pedagogischer Austauschdienst*) in German schools. Candidates are paid a monthly stipend of 1,150 DM in addition to free flights and insurance.

Teaching in International Schools
The definition of an international school covers primary and secondary schools which either follow the British curriculum or a US-style curriculum or a combination of the two, plus elements from other sources. An increasing number of schools are also offering the International Baccalaureate which is recognised worldwide as a university entrance qualification. The main language of instruction is usually English and the clientele is largely the offspring of the expatriate

population. There are international schools in most of the large cities in Germany i.e. where there are expatriate communities (see Chapter 4 *Daily Life* for details). Most of the schools are members of the European Council of International Schools which handles staff applications for their member schools in Germany. Vacancies are advertised on the ECIS website (http://www.ecis.org) which also hosts their On-line Directory of International Schools. This allows the interested surfer to browse information about 800 international schools; a newsletter and the International Schools Journal, an academic journal concerned with international education issues. Applications are welcome from teachers who are suitably qualified and who have a minimum of two year's recent full-time experience within the age range 3-18. Registered candidates' applications are matched to current vacancies and they may be invited to the twice yearly London Recruitment Centres which are attended by school representatives from all over the world. As well as the UK office there are offices in the US, Australia and Spain.

In addition to the publications mentioned above American teachers can consult *The International Educator* (PO Box 513 Cummaquid, MA 02637, USA.) a quarterly publication, also available in Britain, which focuses on jobs in international English-medium schools, such as the International or European Schools found in Germany, and thus follow either American curriculum or International Baccalaureate. The schools which advertise in *TIE* are looking for state-certified teachers in all subjects including ESL/EFL, although they are normally for educators used to dealing with children not adults. The journal comes out in January, April, September and November, with an additional Jobs Only Supplement in May/June. A one year subscription to the journal costs £22, while membership costs £35 including a free *Guide to Finding a Job Abroad* booklet.

Teaching in the European Schools
The other possibilities for teaching jobs are the European Schools, which in Germany are in Karlsruhe and Munich. There are around nine European schools in the European Community, which cater primarily for the children of officials employed in EU institutions. The schools are divided up into mother tongue language groups and the UK and Irish governments recruit staff for the English language sections. The Department for Education and Employment directly recruits and employs some 200 UK teachers for these schools. The Department's main recruitment for vacancies arising in September usually takes place in the preceding January or February. Posts are advertised in the national press at this time and, less frequently at other times throughout the year as and when occasional vacancies arise. Applications are only accepted in response to these advertisements.

Useful Addresses

Deutscher Volkhochschule-Verband e.V.: Obere Wilhelmstrasse 32, D-53225 Bonn; tel 0228-975690; fax 0228-9756930; e-mail buero@dvv-vhs.de website http://www.dvv-vhs.de At present the association of Volkhochschulen does not have an overall list of vacancies in the 1004 schools across Germany, so interested applicants should contact their local VHS through the yellow pages. However, in response to the many enquiries they recieve a job fair will be added to their website early in 1998. This will allow schools to post up adverts for positions while allowing applicants to post their resumés.

*The Department for Education and Employment:*European Schools Team, Department for Education and Employment, Caxton House, Tothill Street, London, SW1H 9NF; tel 0171-273 5713; fax 0171-273 5813.

European Council of International Schools: 21 Lavant Street, Petersfield, Hampshire GU32 3EL; telephone 01730-268244; fax 01730-267914; e-mail address staffingservices@ecis.org website http://www.ecis.org

ECIS Office of the Americas: 105 Tuxford Terrace, Basking Ridge, New Jersey 07920, USA; tel 908-903 0552; fax 908- 580 9381; e-mail malyccisna@aol.com

*ECIS Office Australia:*Cumburri I.E.C., PO Box 367, Kilmore 3764, Victoria, Australia.

The International Educator: PO Box 513, Cummaquid, MA 02637 USA and 102a Pope's Lane, London, W5 4NS; tel 0181-840 2587.

International Schools Recruitment Centres in the US

International Schools Services: (ISS), PO Box 5910, Princeton, NJ 08543-5910, USA; tel 609-452 0990; fax 609-452 2690; e-mail iss@iss.edu webswite http://www.iss.edu

University of Northern Iowa, Overseas Placement Service for Educators: UNI, Cedar Falls, Iowa 50614-0390, USA.

Service Children's Education:

As mentioned earlier in Chapter 4 *Daily Life* an independent agency, The *Service Children's Education Service* operates schools on the remaining military bases in Germany. These primary, middle and secondary level schools are primarily for the children of service personnel and other entitled personnel serving abroad. Occasionally vacancies for teachers occur. To apply for a teaching post with the SCE you must repond to an advertisement placed in the Times Educational Supplement (Overseas Appointment section). Unfortunately speculative letters of application and CVs can not be kept on file.

Other Teaching Possibilities

One year contracts in Language schools in Freiburg, Hamburg and Munich are sometimes available through International House (Staffing Unit, 106 Piccadilly, London W1V 9FL; tel 0171-491 2410; e-mail 100645.1547@compuserve.com fax 0171-491 2679). Contracts are usually for one year and applicants must have the Cambridge/RSA CELTA (formerly CTEFLA) and experience. Those without relevant qualifications can apply for UCLES/RSA courses; further details from the Teacher Training Department of International House (tel; 071-491 2598). For other details of TEFL teaching in Germany, see *Temporary Work*.

Information Technology

In recent years the demand for IT professionals has increased enormously, with employers crying out for skilled staff. However, the skills required by employers have changed over the years, in 1992 having COBOL and fluent German was enough. Now having a mixture of skills such as SAP, C++ and Java on your CV is what will help you get the job you want. That said at present it is still an employee's market, with some staff commanding 180 DM per hour, a situation that is unlikely to change until 2002. Although the jobs on offer vary, if you are looking for a permanent post you will be asked to show certficates for any qualifications which you have. On the other hand contracted staff are taken on trust and so will be expected to do what they claim and if they don't have the skills to back up their claims, then they will be back out on the street in a few hours.

Useful Addresses

Computer Futures Group: 2 Foubert's Place, Regent Street, London, W1V 2AD; tel 0171-446 6644; fax 0171-446 0099; e-mail permanent@compfutures.co.uk website http://www.compfutures.co.uk The UK's largest independent international recruitment consultancy offering both permanent and contract Information Technology recruitment services for clients and candidates.

Easysoft Applications Ltd: The Old Forge, St. Nicholas, South Elmham, Harleston, Norfolk IP20 OPS; tel 01986-782231; fax 01986-782404; e-mail easysoft@Delphi.com

Track International Ltd: PO Box 1, Perranporth, Cornwall, TR6 0YG; tel 01872-573937; fax 01872-571282; e-mail gt@trackint.com website http://www.trackint.com Run by Gertie Thiemann, Track International Ltd is an employment agency specialising in the placement of IT Professionals in Permanent or Contract positions throughout Europe. Their website has regularly updated listings of places available, and they can advise on the life in Germany.

Nursing

There are regular vacancies for British qualified nurses in Germany, as well as vacancies for laboratory technicians and MLSOs. Attractive packages are usually offered including subsidised accommodation, free flights, 38 hour week, free language tuition and an average nurse to patient ratio of 1:3. More information for health professionals seeking work abroad can be found in Vacation Work's book *Health Professionals Abroad*.

Jenrick Nursing: 145-147 Frimley Road, Camberley, Surrey, GU15 2PS. Can place nurses with a minimum of one year's post-registration experience in positions throughout Germany.

German Nursing Association (Deutscher Berufsverband für Pflegeberufe e.V.): Hauptstrasse 392, D-65760 Eschborn; fax 06137-61644; e-mail 101333.576@compuserve.com

Managers and Executives

There is always a demand amongst international companies in Germany for British and American managers and other top-level executives. The typical sought-after candidate is someone who has a background in the industrial or financial sectors, or perhaps less obviously, skills acquired in the armed services, accountancy or the law which can be utilised by international companies. Other vital requirements are that candidates should speak fluent German and have a knowledge of foreign markets and mentalities. Of particular interest to many German companies are those with experience in dealing with the Japanese. Also in demand are export managers which Germany needs to combat the increasing threat from far eastern markets.

Those who have the requisite background and skills for executive jobs can contact multi-nationals and German international firms directly. Alternatively speculative letters to agencies that specialise in executive search and selection in Germany and the UK will almost certainly not be wasted. Below are the details of some management recruiters with experience of recruiting for Germany:

Butler Service Group UK Ltd: Kings Mill, Kings Mill Lane, South Nutfield, Redhill, Surrey, RH1 5NE; tel 01737-822000; fax 01737-823031. Is one of the leading providers of managers and technical specialists for all areas of industry.

Butler Sevice Group Inc (110 Summit Avenue, Po Box 460, Montvale, NJ 07645 USA) has 50 offices throught North America.

Miller, Brand & Co Ltd: 36 Spital Square, London, E1 6DY; tel 0171-377 5661; fax 0171-377 5437; e-mail MillerBrand@eurorecr.demon.co.uk Recruit middle and senior managers and other professionals for posts across the EU, Eastern Europe and Hong Kong. They have associated offices in Belgium, Denmark, France, Finland, Germany, the Netherlands, Italy, Norway, Spain and Sweden.

Fischer & Partner GmbH: Altheimer Eck 3, D-80063 München; tel 089-264014; fax 089-260 7314. German partner firm of Miller, Brand & Co Ltd.

Opta Resources: Cockayne House, 126-128 Crockhamwell Road, Woodley, RG5 3JH; tel 01189-695600; fax 01189-691412. Is primarily a management consultancy specialising in the telecommunications industry. Experienced personnel with technical or business backgrounds in this area are required for work on a sub-contractor basis.

Aspects of Employment

Salaries

German salaries, are probably the highest in the world averaging the equivalent of £21 per hour. However, after taxes and social security deductions, a salary will be reduced by around half to produce the net pay, an example is the mechanic who earns 32.91 DM per hour and takes home 11.61 DM. On top of their standard salary most German workers receive Christmas bonuses and extra pay towards their holidays. While there are no official minimum wages set by the German government, strong unions and the activities of workers councils have ensured that there are widely perceived minimum figures for most types of employment, even if wage negotiations tend to occur on a case by case basis. The exception to this is the construction industry which has negotiated a minimum wage for building site workers, although there is a lower rate for eastern Germany.

Income Tax

Income tax (*Lohnsteuer*) in Germany is graduated, according to how much you earn; for married people the income liable for taxation is the whole income of the couple, although the income limits appear to be simply duplicated. When you begin working for a German employer you should give them the tax card (*Lohnsteuerkarte*) that you obtained when registering at the Einwohnermeldeamt. The German tax-year is the calendar year. If you earn more than 27,000 DM annually then you will be required to complete an income tax declaration (*Einkommensteuer-Erklärung*), these are available at local tax offices (*Finanzbehörde/Finanzamt*) and should be completed by May of the year following the tax year declared (ie the tax year 1997 should be declared by May 1998). If you are expecting a tax rebate then it is wise to complete your declaration as soon as possible, conversely if you submit your declaration late then you may be fined up to 10% of your total tax, and if you pay your taxes late you may also be penalised by an additional 6%. Various expenses including occupational ones, are deductible from income tax and your local tax office can advise on these.

The personal allowance (in 1997), below which income tax cannot be levied is 12, 095 DM for single people and 23,191 DM for married people. Single workers who earn between 12,096 DM and 55,727 DM will be taxed at 25.9%, while for married people the income allowed for this level of taxation is 111,455 DM. Over these limits tax is deducted at geometrically progressive rates up to a maximum tax deduction of 53% of income, which applies to those earning over 120,042 DM or 240,083 DM. However, at these levels of taxation there is a slight rebate; while as a single person you may be liable for taxes at 53% of your 120,042 DM per annum, you will actually pay that percentage less 22,842 DM, for married people this reduction is 45,684 DM. Although German income tax is not the highest in the EC, social security deductions are amongst the steepest (see below).

The following is only a simplified explanation of the UK tax system as it affects expatriate workers, and we recommend that you confirm your tax situation prior to arranging any work abroad. Simply put if you are working on a long term basis abroad your UK tax liability depends on several factors, the principal one being whether, or not, you are classed as resident in the UK for that tax year.

In the simplest case, a UK citizen who works abroad for an entire tax year is not normally liable for UK tax. The tax year in the UK runs from 6th April 199x to 5th April 199y, so if at all possible it is always easiest to move at the end of a tax year. Especially as at present if you are non-resident for a tax year you are not liable for tax on any savings or investments in the UK, and will in effect be treated as a new taxpayer on your return to work in Britain. Being non-resident allows you to return to the UK for a maximum of 91 days in that tax year without forfeiting your status. So be careful to keep track of your trips home and that you return to the UK to work at the right time of year.

The next slightly more complex situation is that of the worker who works abroad for 365 days, but outside of the tax year dates e.g. 1st May 1997 - 30th April 1998, they are only allowed to spend 62 days in the UK within this 365. This Foreign Income Deduction means that as they have started the tax year in the UK they are liable for UK taxes, but only on any income from savings or investments, not the wages earned in Germany which are only liable for German taxation.

The third situation is the most financially awkward. Should the expatriate for whatever reason have to return to work in Britain part way through a tax year or stay longer than the allowed 91 or 62 days they will be taxed on all forms of income, both wages and investments. However the taxes paid on the wages earned abroad (ie German wages and subsequent tax) will be taken into account, in calculating their UK tax bill. So its not as bad as it first seems, so long as you keep your wage slips and tax documentation from Germany.

In order to help people understand the situation the Inland Revenue produces some leaflets: IR20 *Resident and Non-Residents:Liability to Tax in the UK*, IR139 *Income from Abroad ? A Guide to UK Tax on Overseas Income*, IR58 *Going to Work Abroad ? A Guide to the Tax Position of UK Residents Working Abroad* and IR146 *Double Taxation Relief*. General tax enquiries may be addressed to the Inland Revenue Financial Intermediaries and Claims Office (non-Residents), St. John's House, Merton Road, Bootle, Merseyside L69 9BB (0151-472 6214). The Inland Revenue also has an EC Unit: G17 Strand Bridge House, 138-142 Strand, London WC2R 1HH (0171-438 6051). General enquiries are dealt with in Somerset House, Room G1, West Wing, Strand, London WC2R 1LB (0171-438 6240/5).

Non-UK Taxpayers Working in Germany

For those nationals of countries such as the USA, Canada, and Australia the arrangements for paying tax are broadly similar; allowing for the differences in national systems. As we do not have sufficient space to cover these details in full we recommend that the reader consults his or her local tax office for exact details of double-taxation agreements, and their position with regard to the tax laws of their homeland.

Working Conditions

German blue collar workers work fewer hours than their British, French or American counterparts, but as their productivity statistics show, they work more productively and more efficiently. Only 14% of the German workforce works a 40 hour week, compared to 47% in Britain; at present the weekly average is 35 hours (in some cases this is shift work) but in some industries unions have negotiated a 29 hour week in a bid to stave off redundancies. In order to be off sick from work, a doctor's note is required only after three days illness and employees receive full pay for the first six weeks of their illness after which sickness benefit is paid. Employees in Germany are entitled to an average of 42 days holiday a year (including public holidays) compared with 36 days in France and 25 days in Japan. Although Germans once had the reputation of taking work too seriously, it seems that now they have achieved the standard of living to which most aspire, the famous work ethic is in decline. However, although the signs of this are everywhere: in the office workers who stream home at 3pm on Fridays for the weekend, it should not tempt the unwary into considering Germany a soft billet. When they are working, Germans are still perfectionists.

Health and Social Security Deductions

In both France and Germany, unemployment benefits and pensions are directly related to the amount of money being paid into the system by those in work. It can be said however, that workers in Germany get better value for money from their taxes and deductions than some of their EU neighbours, through the generous social security system (see below). As a worker in Germany, unless registered as self-employed and retained in the UK tax scheme, you will have to pay contributions for sickness (and maternity), unemployment, invalidity, old age and survivor's insurance. The amount of your contributions is determined as a percentage of your wages in each tax/calendar year, which will be deducted by your employer for forwarding to the relevant authorities, as a rule the contributions are borne half and half by employer and employee. Contributions for insurance against accidents at work are paid for solely by the employer.

The contribution for sickness insurance is currently around 14%, with an added 1.7% for long-term care. Pension contributions amount to 19.2% and unemployment insurance is another 6.5%

Benefits

The following is a brief introduction and breakdown of the main benefits available to those living and working in Germany. Further details with explanatory notes can be obtained from the Federal Ministry for Labour and Social Affairs (*Bundesministerium für Arbeit und Sozialordnung:* Postfach 14 02 80, D-53107 Bonn) which also publishes an English-language version of these benefits in a booklet entitled *Social Security At The Glance.*

Unemployment Benefit (*Arbeitslosengeld*): In order to qualify for unemployment benefit, a person must have worked more than 18 hours a week for not less than 360 days in the previous three years. Those working for fewer than 18 hours a week can also claim unemployment benefit in certain circumstances. Trainees, who have become unemployed on finishing their training are also eligible for unemployment benefit. The level of unemployment benefit is 67% of previous net wages if you have at least one child and 60% if not. Generally, anyone unemployed will also have their accommodation paid for and in addition the State will also provide for continuing health and pension contributions. To claim benefit you must register as unemployed with the local Arbeitsamt, be available for work and willing to accept any suitable employment offered to you. The length of time over which benefits will be paid to you depends upon the length of time that you were in work. It begins at 156 days for workers under 42 who have worked the minimum of 360 days in the last three years and rises to a maximum of 832 days for those over 54 who have worked for 1,920 days in the last seven years.

Benefit will not be awarded for a period of 12 weeks (*Sperrzeit*) if you terminated your employment, you refuse work offered by the Arbeitsamt, or you refuse to take part in reasonable activities aimed at providing you with a vocational reward.

Unemployment Assistance (*Arbeitslosenhilfe*): Is paid to those who are still unemployed at the end of their entitlement to unemployment benefit, but is means tested. Assistance is paid out at 57% and 53% of previous earnings according to whether or not you have children. Also eligible are general school and university graduates and those who have completed vocational training provided they have been employed for at least 26 weeks before taking up schooling.

If you become unemployed in Germany, you should register with the local Arbeitsamt and ask for information on benefits. Unemployment benefit or assistance will be paid into your bank account fortnightly so it is advisable to open a German account in advance of claiming.

Claiming UK Benefit in Germany: UK citizens who are unemployed in the UK can go to Germany to look for work and claim UK unemployment benefit for up to three months, provided they have been available for work and claiming benefits for four weeks before leaving the UK. In order to claim UK benefit in Germany a certificate of authorisation from the UK Department of Employment must be presented to the Arbeitsamt on arrival in Germany. The procedure is to inform the office where you are claiming unemployment benefit in the UK of your intention to seek work in Germany and request form E303. You can only obtain benefits in Germany if you register with an Arbeitsamt within seven days of leaving the UK, and as there may be a delay in your receiving the money, you should take sufficient funds with you to survive on.

Shortened Working-Week Allowance (*Kurzarbeitergeld*):
If a company is forced to put its workforce on reduced working week for justifiable economic reasons, an allowance covering 60% (67% if you have children) of the net wages lost will be paid for six months. This allowance is applied for at the Arbeitsamt, by the company or works council.

Winter Allowance:
To promote year-round employment in the building trade, building workers receive a winter allowance, of 2 DM per hour, for hours worked between the 1st of December and the 31st of March, excluding the period of 25th December-1st January.

Children's Allowances (*Bundeskindergeldgesetz*): Children's allowances are granted to those whose permanent or ordinary residence is in Germany. The rates are graduated according to the number of children: DM 70 (per month) for the first child; DM 130 for the second; DM 220 for the third and DM 240 for each additional child. These benefits are reduced for those earning more than 37,880 DM if single, or 45,480 DM if married.

All dependent children are covered including step, illegitimate and children by a previous relationship and grandchildren if they live in the same household or are primarily maintained by the claimant. The same is also true for foster children where a care and custody relationship no longer exists with their natural parents. Generally the allowance is paid for children up to the age of 16.

However, if a child remains in the education system or takes up vocational training they are eligible up to the age of 27. Those in vocational training are only eligible if they earn less than 750 DM (gross) per month or are entitled to wage replacement benefits not exceeding 610 DM per month. Benefits also remain payable to over 16s who: are disabled, undertake a year of voluntary work, or who interrupt their training to look after a child of their own.

There is, in addition to the Child Benefit, an income tax allowance for those with children of 4,104 DM per annum for each child.

Savings Benefits

The German government promotes the creation of capital by employees by offering savings allowances or tax concessions for equity participation in a company. All employees in Germany including foreigners may invest in a government savings scheme under the *Vermögensbildungsgesetz* (Asset Accumulation Acts), provided their taxable income is not more than DM 27,000 for unmarried people and DM 54,000 for married couples. At the employee's request, if they are eligible for capital forming payments in addition to their wages, or if they ask for a portion of their wages to be deposited instead, the employer is obliged to deposit payments into one of the state-promoted investment schemes. The government will then top up the savings with a tax-free savings benefit which the employer pays out together with the employee's wages. The savings allowance is 10% of the payments deposited up to a limit of 936 DM per year. For those taking part in investment in their employer's company the tax concession allows your employer to offer you a discount on the amount to be invested. This benefits the saver as they are exempt from taxes on the saving, if the discount is 300 DM or less. In order that capital is built up there are 'blocking periods' so that capital can only be disposed of after 6 or 7 years.

It is quite common in Germany for collective agreements between unions and employers to contain provisions for additional assets accumulation benefits which can be used to take out a life assurance policy. There is a similar scheme for those who are not employed, Home Savings Benefits, whereby annual savings up to certain ceilings receive government assistance.

Pensions

The State Pension Scheme

As stated earlier in Chapter Five *Retirement*, people who move to Germany and work for an EU Employer before reaching pension age are usually insured under the social security laws of Germany, due to the contributions paid from their wages. If you have worked in other EU states prior to working and retiring in Germany, then under EU law, any pension contributions already paid will also count towards a pension payable to you in Germany.   Each EU country where you have paid insurance towards a pension, will look at your insurance under its own scheme and work out how much pension you can have. Each EU country will also take into account any insurance you have paid in any other EU State to make sure you are paid the highest possible pension entitlement.

You can claim any of your pensions direct from any EU country that you have been insured in. If you have been insured in the UK and providing you have kept the DSS informed of any change in your address, you will usually be sent a claim form 4 months before you reach pension age in the UK.

In order to receive any pension due to you in Germany, you must apply to either the *Land* Insurance Agencies (*Landesversicherungsanstalten*) or the Federal Insurance Agency (*Bundesversicherungsanstalt für Angestellte*). To be eligible to receive a German pension an individual must have paid a minimum of 60 months German insurance contributions.

Company Pension Funds

Company pension funds, are popular and protected in Germany. The practice of self-investment (pension funds investing in their own companies) is perfectly acceptable in Germany and the pension fund is not kept separate from the company's assets. The balance sheet of a German company will show the pension funds and provision for future payments. If the company goes bankrupt, the pension fund is liable to disappear with it. However, pensioners in Germany are protected by the compulsory state insurance scheme, underpinned by a statutory levy imposed on the rest of industry. The levy ensures that a collapsed company's pension fund liabilities will be covered by industry as a whole. Together these measures make German pensioners some of the most secure in the EU.

At the time of writing a directive to safeguard the company pension rights of individuals moving between EU countries was under consideration by the European Commission. The proposal would ensure that employees paying into one company scheme in one state, who then move to another company in another country, would have the same rights as if they had changed jobs while staying in the one country. This would also guarantee cross-border pension rights and allow employees on secondment to another country to continue paying into their scheme. Further details of this proposed directive can be obtained from The European Commission (8 Storey's Gate, London, SW1P 3AT; tel 0171-973-1992) or read on their website (http://www.cec.org.uk) Anyone wishing to transfer their UK company pension to one run by a new employer in Germany should contact the Inland Revenue in the UK.

Women in Work

As in much of the western world German women achieved suffrage rather late in the political history of their nation, only gaining the right to vote in 1918. Having won the opportunity to attend university towards the end of the nineteenth century women finally began to make headway in the professions, this increased during the Weimar Republic of the 1920s. A reversal of fortune came under the Nazis when women were firmly relegated back to *Kinder, Kirche, Kuche* (children, church and hearth). After the outbreak of the Second World War, as more and more men were called to fight, the Nazi regime was forced to allow women back into higher education to keep the country running and the schools functioning. After the war, women were able to continue developing their potential in the professions and the workplace. The Basic Law enshrined equality of the sexes in the constitution, however, for many years this was still more a wish than reality.

Germany, in spite of a high proportion of university-educated women (41% of all students), still has a machismo problem when it comes to women at the top. While there are 2 million more women than men in Germany they only hold 21%

of the seats in the Bundestag, although the President, and one of the Vice-Presidents, of the Bundestag are women. In 1991 the Federal Ministry for Family Affairs, Senior Citizens, Women and Youth was founded (initially as the Ministry for Women and Youth), now all state governments have ministers or commissions for women's affairs and equality. There is also a powerful 'women's lobby' the German Women's Council (*Deutscher Frauenrat:* Simrockstrasse 5, D-53113 Bonn), which represents 50 women's associations and has a membership of over 11 million.

Although Germany has women (Protestant) priests, there are no women in the armed forces except medical staff. Although women in Germany frequently carve out names for themselves as freelances in the media, few are selected for executive positions. The same applies to senior positions in industry, banking and business where a minute 2% of women are to be found at the top. This has very little to do with talent and much to do with the fact that their way is barred by men determined to hang on to the senior positions. The one obvious course of action open to women and one which they are increasingly taking up, is to start their own businesses. In western Germany, over three-quarters of all new businesses are being founded by women, a handful of whom have been outstandingly successful. This is also a trend in Europe generally, where the number of female-owned companies has doubled in the past ten years.

Women wanting to further their careers in Germany will either have to enter a partnership with Germans or choose to start their own business in a sphere where they are most likely to succeed, e.g. legal and financial services, a language school, translating or relocation agency. A check of the relocation agency listings will show that this has been a very successful area for female entrepreneurs.

Legislation aimed at creating equal pay in Germany has been enacted but seems difficult to enforce as statistics show that in practice women earn less than men, mostly through the way that work is assigned. The differential is argued away by the claim that men do more overtime or night work and the heavier jobs. However, if a women is doing the same or substantially similar work as a man she can take her employer to court if she is paid less. As mentioned in Chapter Seven, *Starting a Business*, employment costs are high in Germany and one way of reducing them is to avoid the generous paid maternity leave (see below), by choosing men.

Maternity Benefits, Parental Leave and Employment Rights

Maternity benefits: As soon as a working woman obtains a certificate of pregnancy from her doctor she will receive a maternity care certificate from her health insurance agency which entitles her to free maternity care before and after delivery. She is also entitled to fully paid maternity leave for a period of six weeks before delivery and eight weeks after (12 for multiple births). The expectant mother can work in the pre-natal six week rest period but only if she expressly wishes to, but all work is prohibited in the eight week rest period. The employee's health insurance agency makes tax free payments of up to DM 25 per day (DM 600 per month), and employers are required to make up the balance if you were paid more than that. The employee is also allowed time off work for breast feeding.

Parental Leave: The parental leave system was introduced so that children will be in parental care up to the age of 3 years. The system allows the parents to decide who will look after their child, should both of them be in gainful employment, or if one is unemployed or in training the other can take parental leave. During Child-raising leave the employee is protected against dismissal, although if you wish to take up this leave you should approach your employer at least 4 weeks in advance and state how long you intend to take off work. During the first six months of parental leave all parents are entitled to the same allowance of DM 600 per month. After this period the payment is dependent on income and benefit is reduced. In the case of children born since the 1st of January 1994 the child-raising allowance is cancelled for married couples earning 100,000 DM (nett) annually or 75,000 DM for single parents.

Either parent is also entitled to take five days paid leave to care for a sick child under eight years old.

In the private sector parental leave arrangements may be more flexible depending on the needs of the employer. For instance, sometimes career breaks can be arranged where an employee, by arrangement with the employer, takes a period of full-time leave which is normally unpaid but with a job guarantee. There may also be scope for part-time and flexible working hours made by arrangement with individual employers.

Childcare Provision Relevant to Working Women
Women in most EC countries rightly complain that childcare provision is insufficient to allow them to continue working full-time following a period of maternity leave. Belgium and Denmark are the only two countries with an outstanding record in this respect and, surprisingly perhaps, Germany does not compete with them, especially in the realm of pre-kindergarten (ages 1-3) care.

Around 3% of children under three are cared for in publicly funded nurseries (*Krippen*), or mixed-age centres which take children from 0-6 years. Occasionally, children of two years are accepted in kindergartens but this is in defiance of official regulations. Also, in some instances child-minders' (*Tagesmutter*) fees may be subsidized from public funds.

For children from three to six years childcare is readily available in the form of kindergartens, the majority of which are provided by national private organizations with public funding. Around 70% of children in this age-band attend kindergarten. Only around 12% of kindergartens are open for eight hours. The usual pattern is for them to open for four hours in the morning with a two-hour break for lunch when children have to go home before returning for a two-hour session in the afternoon. Since January 1996, children have had a legal right to attend kindergarten, and by now enough kindergartens and child-care establishments should have been built to allow any parent in Germany to send their children to one. However, attendance is voluntary and these places are funded by parental contributions, graded according to income.

At primary school level, only a few schools are open all day. The majority operate for four or five hours in the morning and many have hours that vary from day to day; children cannot eat lunch at school. Such short and irregular school hours, plus the expectation that mothers will devote a considerable time to helping their children with homework, mean that it is unrealistic for the majority of women to work full-time.

Trade Unions

The origin of German trade unionism goes back to the 1880's and Bismarck's precocious industrial reforms, which included the setting up of workers' councils in factories. Today, such councils constitute an integral part of German labour management. Up to the Nazi era, German trade unions had a membership of around 6.5 million and, in common with other European countries, this was splintered into hundreds of different bodies representing variants of different ideologies as well as religious differences. Once the Nazis seized power, trade unions were abolished and their leaders imprisoned. After the War the unions were reorganised under the guidance of British union leaders, who helped the Germans set up a rational grouping of seventeen trade unions that continues today. Around 9 million German workers are members of trade unions, at present, marking a drop of 17% in union membership since 1985.

In Germany, annual wage increases are decided by means of collective bargaining (agreement between the employers' associations with the appropriate trade unions). Once agreement has been reached, it is legally binding on both parties thus making strikes illegal except under certain conditions. A strike can only be called as a last resort and only if there is a 75% majority in favour of such action.

The German Federation of Trade Unions (*Deutscher Gewerkschaftsbund (DGB):* Hans-Böckler-Strasse 39, D-40476 Düsseldorf; tel 0211-430 1221; fax 0211-430 1408) is organized so that within one works, all employees belong to the same union, irrespective of their speciality. Trade unions are independent of government, political parties, religious interests, the works administration and employers. The main unions belonging to the DGB are:

IndustrieGewerkschaft Metall: Postfach 71 04 18, D-60519 Frankfurt; tel 069-66930. IG Metall, German's biggest union with 2.9 million members represents the steel and metal workers. IG Metall's members last went on strike in 1996 to protest against the hostile takeover of Krupp by Thyssen which was backed by a banking cartel.

Gewerkschaft Öffentliche Dienste, Transport und Verkehr (ÖTV): Postfach 10 36 62, D-70031 Stuttgart; tel 0711-20970. ÖTV is the main public-service union with 1.83 million members who are employees in public services, transport and communications.

IndustrieGewerkschaft Chemie, Papier, Keramik: Postfach 30 47, D-30030 Hannover; tel 0511-76310. ICPK has a membership of approximately 742,367 members in the chemical, paper and ceramics industries.

IndustrieGewerkschaft Bauen-Agrar-Umwelt: Postfach 10 11 44 is the union for construction workers with approximately 652,964 members.

Other Unions Belonging to the DGB are:

Deutsche PostGewerkschaft: Rhonestrasse 2, D-60528 Frankfurt am Main; tel 069-66950. Is the postal workers union representing half a million post office staff.

Gewerkschaft Handel Banken und Versicherungen: Postfach 33 02 11, D-40435 Düsseldorf; tel 0211-77030. Represents the commerce, banking and insurance sector.

The German Railwaymen's Union. **Gewerkschaft der Eisenbahner Deutschlands:** Postfach 17 03 31, D-60077 Frankfurt am Main; tel 069-75360.

Mining and Energy. **IndustrieGewerkschaft Bergbau und Energie:** Postfach 10 12 29, D-44712 Bochum; tel 0234-3190.

Education and Science. **Gewerkschaft Erziehung und Wissenschaft:** Postfach 90 04 09, D-60444 Frankfurt am Main; tel 069-789730.

Media Workers. **IndustrieGewerkschaft Medien:** Postfach 10 24 51, D-70020 Stuttgart; tel 0711-20180.

Police. **Gewerkschaft der Polizei:** Postfach 309, D-40703 Hilden; tel 0211-71040.

Food, Beverages and Catering. **Gewerkschaft Nahrung-Genuss-Gaststätten:** Postfach 50 11 80, D-22711 Hamburg; tel 040-380130.

Textile and Garment Industry. **Gewerkschaften Textil-Bekleidung:** Postfach 32 04 60, D-40419 Düsseldorf; tel 0211-43090.

Agriculture, Horticulture and Forestry. **Gewerkschaft Gartenbau, Land und Forstwirtschaft:** Postfach 41 01 58, D-34063 Kassel; tel 0561-93790.

As stated, the unions protect their members' economic interests through the collective bargaining process. However, their role extends over a wider range of workers' affairs: in the social sphere it embraces social and cultural policy as well as working conditions. Union membership is not compulsory but if taken out, dues based on a percentage of gross earnings have to be paid annually by the employee. In the event of a strike, or other dispute with the company, such as litigation arising from a dispute in an employment relationship, the union will provide financial assistance. For example, for every day of a strike, workers' organisations in the public services pay three times the member's contributions, plus five Deutsche Marks for every child.

Etiquette at Work

The formality of German business etiquette can come as a surprise to those accustomed to the more informal working atmospheres found in other European countries or the USA. In German offices it is usual to shake hands with everyone on arrival at work and before leaving. Calling associates by their first names is uncommon; even people who have been working together for years still call each other Herr or Frau followed by the surname. Even more approachable employees such as secretaries and receptionists are traditionally accorded the same respectful form of address; in fact it would be considered patronising to call them by their first names. In Germany, if a man puts his arm round his secretary or calls her by her first name, it will be automatically assumed that they are romantically involved. The same formality surrounds the polite form of address *Sie* (you), which should always be used, unless one is invited to use the informal version, *du*. Amongst younger people, working relationships are much less formal, probably because in most schools, pupils invariably address their teachers by the familiar second person and this habit has now entered the workplace with them. However, it is always wisest to wait for your colleagues to initiate any changes in how you address each other.

Using professional titles is another point of etiquette. It is also indicative of the fact that in continental Europe generally, status tends to be linked to profession. On the whole, use of titles is however declining, so making a mistake in this respect is not considered unpardonable, especially on the part of a non-German. On the other hand, over use of titles can easily make you look ridiculous. The best policy, if you are unsure is simply to ask people how they wish to be addressed. As a foreigner, you can easily get away with this. Academic doctorates are not commonly used in Britain as part of forms of address, but in Germany both medical and academic doctors can be addressed as Herr or Frau Doktor. Other titles which may be used are *Herr/Frau Professor, Herr Pfarrer* (for a vicar), and occasionally, *Herr Ingenieur* (engineer). If the German concerned has more than one degree, e.g. *Professor Doktor*, both may be used in addressing him or her, however in such a case most people would consider *Herr/Frau Professor* sufficient.

Regional Business and Industry Report

The following breakdown of industry and business interests region by region indicates the types of skills likely to be in demand:

BADEN-WÜRTTEMBERG

With the third largest länder population and borders with Switzerland and France, Baden-Württemberg has access to a market of 200 million people. The capital, Stuttgart is highly industrial, largely as a result of being the home of Daimler-Benz, the car manufacturer. The states 1994 GDP of 484 billion DM, exceeds those of Belgium, Switzerland or Sweden. World famous names such as Mercedes-Benz, Bosch, Porsche, Dornier and Zeiss all have locations in the state. Half of Germany's net inward investment flows into Baden-Württemberg with companies such as Hewlett-Packard, IBM, Minolta, Sony, Nokia, Kodak and Michelin establishing presences in the region.

Germany leads the world in environmental technology and Baden-Württemberg produces a quarter of its environmental products and services. Technology is one of the keys to this prosperity, microelectronics, precision engineering, telecommunications and biotechnology all play major roles in the state's economic framework. 62 million DM have been spent on a multi-media 'data-highway' project to link various firms, universities and research centres. This is being constructed as a joint venture by Deutsche Telekom, IBM, Hewlett-Packard, Alcatel and Bosch-ANT.

Technological expertise is largely focused on Karlsruhe which is one of the leading *Technologieregionen* and is backed financially by the Fridericiana University, which has a renowned computer science faculty, and around 100 other scientific and technological institutes. In the Karlsruhe region, there is now a ratio of 32 scientists to 1,000 workers. Many companies are attracted to the area because of the availability of highly trained staff, the result of one of Europe's most highly-concentrated and mature Research and Development infrastructures. The state has 9 universities, 39 polytechnics, and 38 research institutes, the results of their labours are translated into practical applications by the 269 technology transfer centres.

BAYERN (Bavaria)

Once Germany's largest agricultural economy, Bayern has swapped its ploughs for lathes. Agriculture now only accounts for less than 2% of the state's production figures, manufacturing and the engineering processes have taken over with an expanding IT market making Bayern Germany's 'Silicon Valley'. Over a third of companies in the region are involved in technology information and data processing. The automobile sector is also present in force not least because Bavaria is the birthplace of Bayerische Motoren-Werke (BMW), which has several plants in this, its home territory. Other sectors with a flourishing presence include electrical and mechanical engineering, railway vehicle construction, textiles, fashion, publishing and finance. The state capital München has become the focus of an expanding industrial area, with automotive, aerospace, electrical and electronics firms setting up there. Other centres are Nürnberg-Furth with companies like Siemens, Grundig and Playmobil having production sites there, Regensburg, with electrical engineering and a BMW factory, Schweinfurt is the hub of Europe's ballbearing manufacture, Würzburg is a major centre for printing machinery and Augsburg which has engineering and textiles firms. In 1994 Bayern economically out-performed 9 of the 15 EU member states, its per capita income is the highest in Germany. Currently 700,000 enterprises are operating in the state, a potent supply of investment and partnership opportunities.

Bayern has two international airports at München and Nürnberg, and the Main-Danube Canal runs through the state linking the Black Sea with the North Sea via the Rhine. It is also at the intersection of rail lines stretching form Lisbon to Prague and Naples to Stockholm.

The area around Munich is home to a quarter of the state's population, amongst them many foreign residents. Munich is a technology centre with several universities and technical colleges specializing in scientific disciplines including bio-technology, experimental physics and engineering automation. With its various universities and scientific research institutes Bayern offers a wide intellectual base for businesses investing in applied technology. Fields of study cover microsystems, bio-sensors, bio-technology and medicines, and in 1994 the state government invested 3 billion DM in supporting applied research.

BERLIN

Berlin is a city state facing many changes, from the collapse of its infamous wall and the inherent problems of reintegrating two disparate halves of a city into one; to the need to prepare for its forthcoming role as the new Federal Capital. With unification Berlin has resumed its role as an industrial and commercial hub for Eastern and Central Europe. Great efforts are being made to modernise the city's infrastructure of roads, underground and regional railways, and its external links. The autobahn route to Nürnberg and Bavaria is one of many modernisation schemes planned by the Federal transport authority; as is the high sped train link to Hamburg. In addition to these links Berlin has three airports, although to allow space for development, the inner city one at Templehof is to be redeveloped as the new site at Schönefeld takes over as the main airport.

Germany's largest industrial centre, concentrating on engineering, pharmaceuticals, electrical goods and textiles, Berlin was the birthplace of firms such as Siemens and AEG. It is likely to remain one of central Europe's largest industrial centres, as the Berlin Senate has plans for 21 contiguous industrial sites totalling 3,300 hectares of manufacturing area. However, there is also a large supply of business locations available throughout the city, and it is likely that while Berlin will become a focus for business activity, much of its economy will be determined by private services.

Berlin is an excellent location for innovative enterprises, with its highly qualified workforce, expanding service sector and improved transport links, at present it has the highest figures in Germany for newly created firms. In part this is due to the interplay between the three universities, 14 technical colleges and 250 research institutes, and the new business centres.

BRANDENBURG

With a GNP growth rate of 5-6% the region is set to become one of the most dynamic economic regions in Europe. Surrounding the city-state of Berlin means that the region sits astride the London-Moscow and Stockholm-Budapest axes, and can therefore take advantage of developing trade routes. Close co-operation with neighbouring Poland already offers opportunities from procuring raw materials to processing and sales activities. In addition to being close enough to make use of Berlin's universities, Brandenburg has three universities and five technical colleges of its own.

Manufacturing and development businesses in the region have expertise in traffic control, microsystems, energy and construction technology, electronics optics, synthetic chemistry and bio-technology. The länder investment council has developed a 'one-stop-shop' system to help investors with reduced red-tape and generous grants. Tax-deductions and deprecation allowances allow the retrieval of up to 50% of costs. These favourable conditions have already attracted firms such as BMW/Rolls-Royce (aero-engine development), Readymix (cement plant), BASF, Bosch-Siemens Appliances (synthetic chemicals) and MAN (heavy-duty machinery). In addition, opportunities in media related business are likely to grow as the German Film industry returns to its cradle at Potsdam-Babelsberg.

New transport links will have fringe benefits for the region; the new airport development at Berlin-Schönefeld Brandenburg, and the magnetic rail system between Hamburg and Berlin are examples. The region's many canals and rail lines are being renewed or redeveloped with the Federal Government's commitment to upgrading the infrastructure of the eastern länder.

HANSESTADT BREMEN

Of the three German city-states, Bremen, with its satellite port Bremerhaven, is the smallest and also a two-city, city-state. Both ports are free ports, and have one of the world's largest covered container terminals. As well as freight handling the city can arrange Europe wide distribution, with its road/rail terminals and storage facilities. The city has autobahn and high speed rail links with all the main European towns and cities.

Not only a cargo port, Bremen has a history of food processing stemming from a productive fishing fleet; long established industries include fish processing, and the production of cigarettes, coffee, chocolate, and beer. Naturally the city has a shipbuilding industry, but apart from constructing and refitting cargo carriers the yards also produce luxury yachts, ferries, cruise liners and research vessels. Arising from this the city is a centre for the development and production of marine electronics including radars, sonars and other navigational aids. With an international airport nearby Bremen is also the headquarters of MBB/Erno, one of the powerhouses behind the European space rocket, Ariane and the highly successful Airbus project. Components for Ariane, the Eureca space research platform and the A320 Airbus are manufactured and assembled in Bremen.

The presence of the aerospace industries has attracted many research centres and institutions which are research leaders into physics, telecommunications, magnetic waves, superconductor research and software development. The city can also boast the 146m high drop tower of the Centre for Applied Aerospace Technology and Microgravitation, which is used by scientists across the globe to research gravity, anti-gravity and weightlessness. Other research institutes include the Max Planck Institute for Marine Microbiology, the Alfred Wegener Institute for Polar and Maritime Research and the Frauenhofer Institute for Applied Material Research. Bremen's Innovation and Technology Centre (BITZ) provides accommodation, know-how and contacts between researchers and technology minded businesses.

The automobile industry has been in Bremen since 1978, in the form of a 5 billion DM investment by Mercedes Benz in plant for the manufacture of its latest models.

HANSESTADT HAMBURG

Germany's second largest city, Hamburg has a long tradition of being a great trading city dating from the 13th century when it was part of the Hanseatic League. These days modern Hamburg is working with its neighbours Lower Saxony and Schleswig-Holstein to outline a development plan for this area of Germany. Hamburg is Germany's largest seaport and Europe's second largest container port, with some 70 docks for inland canal and sea-going cargo vessels. The port's nucleus is the *Freihafen*, one of the world's largest freeports. Hamburg is currently building on its success as an important distribution centre. Already the headquarters of several of the world's main shipping lines, Hamburg is also attracting an increasing number of industries from Asia, the United States and Europe. In addition to the 1,800 firms based here, which are engaged in foreign trade, there are now over 30 trade centres in Hamburg including the China United Trade Corporation whose headquarters in Hamburg is the commercial conduit for Chinese trade relations with the whole of Europe. Hamburg is also Germany's most Anglophile city and therefore very welcoming to British enterprises.

Hamburg is an important transport hub for northern Europe, as well as the sea trade, rail traffic and a large portion of the road traffic to and from Scandinavia, passes over the Elbe bridges or through tunnels. The city's airport (Germany's fourth largest) is linked to the network of regional airports across Germany, and has flights to the European capitals and the main American cities.

The reunificaton of Germany has tripled its cargo traffic with the return of access to its traditional hinterland. The city's GNP has grown since 1990, as has its population, as new firms have set up in the area in addition to the traditional port industries, of shipbuilding, engineering and refining. Industries in Hamburg now include aviation, aerospace, precision and optical engineering and of the workforce of 780,000, 145,000 are employed in manufacturing. The port activity of refining and processing chemicals means a ready supply of raw materials for the new Boots factory based near Hamburg.

For a long time Hamburg has had a large service sector to meet the needs of the city's merchants, since the war this has included the media as the main newspaper publishers set up home here. These have been followed by the leading German television and film companies. Within the service industry Hamburg is Germany's largest insurance centre, second largest banking centre and has one of the world's oldest stock exchanges.

HESSEN (Hesse)

Hessen is dominated by the world financial centre of Frankfurt am Main. Around 370 banks are based in Frankfurt and between them employ over 45,000 people. In addition to the banks, there are many insurance and advertising companies. Commerzbank, one of the large German banks is investing in a £200 million global investment bank to be based in Frankfurt, which will soon be home to the European Central Bank, which will oversee the Euro, at present it is home to the European Monetary Institute which is controlling the Single Currency convergence.

The centre of Frankfurt, is dominated by a cluster of skyscrapers including the 55-floor Messe Turm which purports to be the highest office tower in Europe and is undoubtedly home to some of the larger and more important trade fairs, especially the famous Frankfurt Book Fair each year. The city's airport is the busiest in continental Europe with around 30 million passengers a year and Europe's largest air-freight facility. Hesse is also home to some of Germany's major industrial companies amongst them, Opel (part of General Motors),

Hoechst (chemicals) and the international companies AEG, Metallgesellschaft and Degussa.

Apart from financial services, international trade is very important to Hessen, every third job depends on exports, and these account for 30% of annual turnover. Exported goods total up to 47 billion DM annually. Trade with Britain is healthy, especially from a British viewpoint, Hessian firms sent 3.8 billion DM worth of exports to Britain, while importing 6.8 billion.

As a place in which to live and work, Frankfurt may not be the most beautiful German city, but a recent survey put it into fifth place in a business magazines study of enterprise-friendly cities; a place which was won on so called 'soft-location factors' as well as those which suited good business.

MECKLENBURG-VORPOMMERN (Mecklenburg-West Pomerania)
Sparsely populated the region has plenty of room for agriculture and related processing industries. Its clean, almost unsullied environment makes it an ideal location for producing foodstuffs and one global manufacturer who has noticed this potential is Nestlé, which has a large baby-food production facility here. Youth is another point in the region's favour as 42% of the available workforce is under 35.

Geographically Mecklenburg-Vorpommern can be seen as Germany's northern gateway through its Baltic ports which give access to 25 million Scandinavian consumers. This also makes the region an excellent base for firms interested in importing goods and raw materials from Sweden and Finland. With the fall of communism the old Hanseatic trade routes to the Baltic states are being revived, which should help the port industries of Rostock.

The most up to date transport and logistics technologies facilitate short and efficient travel or shipment by road, rail, sea or air, which means that producers of perishable goods benefit accordingly, and thus are at the root of the state's economy. However, shipbuilding and marine technology continue to hold a large share, in the face of competition from new technologies such as micro-electronics and microsystems. These new industries are benefiting from the state having two of the oldest universities in Europe, and a network of technology transfer agencies, which arrange for good ideas to be converted into practical applications.

NIEDERSACHSEN (Lower Saxony)
Formerly dependent on heavy industry, agriculture and shipbuilding, Niedersachsen has been transformed by unification into a transport and communications nexus. Its dense network of canals and navigable waterways allow the easy transport of goods and materials from central and eastern Europe to the ports of Hamburg and Bremen for onward shipment worldwide. The state capital Hannover is a hub for the major trans-European motor routes (E3 Denmark-Portugal, E4 Helsinki-Lisbon, and E8 London-Moscow). The state has a co-ordinated network of ISDN and fibre-optic cables for high-speed data communications, and Hannover's trade fair often hosts CeBIT the world's largest information and communication technology exhibitions. The city is currently preparing for the 2000 World Fair 'Expo 2000' which is expected to attract millions of visitors.

Industry still has a home here and the state's industrial workforce accounts for 9.5% of total German turnover. Business incentives in the region include remarkably low prices for property; developed property, undeveloped land, and development plots for industrial use are respectively 46%, 30% and 20% below the national average. Among the major foreign and domestic firms with their headquarters in Niedersachsen are companies like Volkswagen (automobiles), Bahlsen (foods), Siemens (electronics), Blaupunkt (electronics), BEB Erdgas (energy), Alcan and WABCO Westinghouse. Other firms with sites in the state are Dow Chemical, ICI, Matsushita, Konica, Minolta and Citibank. Siemens employ some 10,000 workers in the region and Daimler-Benz have recently set up a new vehicle test track.

Niedersachsen's economic policy is geared towards flexibility and support for investment and expansion, with institutes promoting technology transfer and energy conservation. Other service agencies have been created to advise businesses with scientific expertise, and provide assistance in setting up in the region.

NORD-RHEIN-WESTFALEN (North-Rhine-Westphalia)

The most densely populated German state, with a population of 18 million, is also Germany's economic powerhouse; in 1993 it generated a quarter of Germany's GDP. The state capital, Düsseldorf is host to many foreign companies and several thousand foreign residents including Japanese, Americans, British and Scandinavians. Nord-Rhein-Westfalen (NRW) is the home of Germany's famous industrial heart the Ruhr, although the heavy industries which once dominated the area have declined in size. Where once the iron, steel and coal industry employed almost half of the state's workers this figure is now closer to one tenth. The main industrial strengths of the region are in the chemical, plant, and engineering sectors, with service oriented firms accounting for half of the state's turnover. More than a third of Germany's top 500 companies have their headquarters in NRW, including Bertelsmann, one of the world's largest media companies. Düsseldorf, the state capital, is one of Germany's largest banking and international finance centres, with its stock exchange being the fourth largest in Europe. After London Düsseldorf is the second largest Japanese business centre in Europe. Nearly half of Germany's trade fairs are held in the region attracting 5 million visitors from 150 nations.

NRW has six new freight centres for road/rail transport, and Aachen is Germany's leading border crossing for goods transport. Overall NRW is responsible for almost half of Germany's wholesale foreign trade turnover, and with a 23% share of total exports, its the largest exporter. Of the three international airports in the state, Düsseldorf is the second largest in Germany, handling over 7 million passengers a year. Added to these are the five regional airports and eight airfields used for chartered and private business flights. The main transport link however, is the Rhine, this connects Europe's largest port at Rotterdam with the Black Sea, via Duisburg and the Rhine-Main-Danube canal. Duisburg is not just a freeport on the Rhine but is the world's largest inland-waterway port.

Intellectually, the state is a leader in research and development for industry with the largest percentage of any workforce employed in this sector. Half a million students are enrolled at the 50 colleges and universities, six out of ten of Germany's largest institutions are in NRW. There are three national research centres and ten Max Planck Institutes here, not to mention several Frauenhofer Society facilities. The state has set up 48 technology centres to interface with industry, resulting in the setting up of 850 companies. the change from heavy industry to services has lead to a 'greening' of the region and a third of Germany's environmental technology research occurs here.

Other industrial companies located there include: Ford, Toyota, Mazda, Renault, Sony and Henkel. Although the state is dominated by industry, Düsseldorf and the other important city of Köln are also centres for the advertising and fashion industries. More than 800 foreign firms are located in Köln and the surrounding area. As a major German media centre, Köln has resident broadcasting companies, publishing houses, record companies, advertising agencies, film and video production companies and others dealing with telematic and computer technology. In addition, Köln is the site of Europe's first Media Park, a centre for information and technology companies, which will facilitate co-operation and developments in different media: information technology and audiovisual. Köln is the site of Marks & Spencer's first German store, opened in 1996, and plans are in hand to create three more stores across NRW.

RHEINLAND-PFALZ (Rhineland-Palatinate)

Rheinland-Pfalz lies at the heart of a consumer market with a population of 40 million, and borders the economic centres of the Rhine-Ruhr, Rhine-Main, Belgium and the mega region Saar-Lor-Lux. Primarily known for its high quality wines, the region's vineyards produce two thirds of Germany's wine.

Apart from the wine trade, the region's forests and spas attract over seven million tourists a year, either to relax or to seek a cure. Rheinland-Pfalz is also the location of the 'German-Wine Route', a tourist trail around the various vineyards and historical towns of the area.

The state is also home to the headquarters of BASF, the giant chemical concern, at Ludwigshafen and 900 million DM has been invested in economic infrastructure over the last few years as the state seeks to develop its business base. At present the majority of firms in the region are small enterprises and only 2% of manufacturing firms here employ more than 500 staff.

SAARLAND

Saarland's historically close links with France have led in recent years to its participation in the Saar-Lor-Lux European Mega-region (a cross-border association of Saarland, Luxembourg and the Lorraine province of France). In this interface between regional markets, there is a great deal of cross border trade and employment, and as Britain's main trading partners are France and Germany, this is are is an excellent investment and expansion opportunity for British firms. In recent years five major US companies have invested in the Saarland as a business base for Germany and Europe.

In 1995 Bundy set up a manufacturing plant, and Adaptaflex built a warehouse and distribution plant, in Neuenkirchen. The Saarland has recently-founded research centres for artificial intelligence, microsystems and medically-oriented technology, including the Max Planck Institute for Computer Science. Already, Siemens, Wang, IBM and over a dozen smaller computer software companies have set up operations there. The highly trained workforce with skills in CAD/CAM and CASE has attracted the American company Litton Industries, while the Ford plant at Saarlouis employs 7,000 staff and produces 1,400 cars a day. Plastics processing, electronics, computers and IT are all major employment areas, with companies like Bosch, ABB and SKF. According to the British-German Chamber of Commerce the region has lower than average labour costs and low prices for industrial or commercial property.

SACHSEN (Saxony)

Once the industrial heartland of former East Germany, Saxony accounted for a third of the entire East German production and was home to the nationally celebrated Trabant motor car. Now with its borders with Poland and the Czech Republic it is an economic gateway to Central and South Eastern Europe. An industrial region before the birth of the Ruhr region, Saxony is building on its past. GDP Growth in 1995 stood at 7.4%, the highest of all the German states, with a predicted continuation at 7% until at least 2010. While mechanical engineering takes the lion's share of the states productivity; the electronics, electrical engineering, environmental technology, automotive, chemical, glass and ceramics industries, all play a noticeable part.

Since 1990 around 8,800 industrial projects worth 43 billion DM have been subsidised with around 7 billion DM from the state. This investment means the region is now home to a brand new Volkswagen factory, as well as inducing Siemens Advanced Micro Devices and Canon to set up production facilities in Saxony. Leipzig recently became home to Europe's biggest mail order warehouse with Quelle making Germany's largest logistics investment in German history. While in April 1996 part of the old airport was reopened as a new trade fair centre, with design work by a firm of British architects. Saxony currently has 400 industrial estates of which 288 are supported by the länder government.

Six out of ten Saxons have specialised skills training and one in five is a graduate. With its four universities, thirteen colleges or other higher education establishments and 40 research companies the state has an excellent Research and Development infrastructure.

In addition to this immense sums are being invested in upgrading the Elbe ports and the inter-connections between road, rail and canal. Dresden and Leipzig/Halle are to be connected to the high speed rail network (ICE) and their airports are being modernised. At present until the development of Berlin-Schönefeld Leipzig /Halle is eastern Germany's second largest airport. New motorway routes to Prague and Wroclaw are under construction, and Poland has plans in development for a motorway which will run between Görlitz in Saxony and the Ukraine.

SACHSEN-ANHALT (Saxony-Anhalt)

The state's geographic location means that economically it benefits from its proximity to Berlin, and the Rhine-Ruhr. The state also straddles the routes between Hamburg, Bremen and south-east Europe, and by extension its links with the Ruhr also bring it into contact with the Rhine-Main area. Most of the top priority, post-reunification, transport projects directly affected the state and its economic/industrial potential. These include the high-speed Hannover-Berlin rail link, the six-lane trunk routes Berlin-Hannover and Berlin-Nürnberg, as well as the Halle-Magdeburg motorway. A motorway linking Halle and Göttingen is also being planned at present. Magdeburg's harbour on the Elbe has been improved and the telecommunications network of Sachsen-Anhalt extended, giving the region a sound modern infrastructure for businesses to grow in.

Government retraining means the workforce that ran East Germany's chemical industry is highly qualified and adaptable, coupled with EU and regional funding programmes this makes the state a good candidate for industrial investment. Since 1990 over 300 new industrial and commercial estates have been constructed, with lower than average prices for floorspace. Over the last six years the state's economic ministry has supported 4,423 investment projects worth 37 billion DM, around 9 billion DM were available to support the manufacturing industry, with a third of this available for infrastructure improvements. The construction of new power plants and the upgrading of the chemical industry throughout the eastern länder will probably mean that the region will attract investment worth roughly 40 billion into the state's control instruments industry.

SCHLESWIG-HOLSTEIN

According to a recent report from the German Institute for Urban Studies in 1995, Schleswig-Holstein has the second-best economic climate in Germany. While 54 new businesses were set up in 1991 this figure grew to 138 for 1995. The state's GDP has grown consistently over the years improving by 21% over the period

1990-1995. As a small state with little in the way of raw materials or industrial heritage Schleswig-Holstein is reinventing itself as a home for modern technology. New investment in the region includes the founding of a microchip production site by a subsidiary of Daimler-Benz and the expansion of their facility at Flensburg by Motorola. The state is also home to a number of research institutes with links to industry, the most famous of which is the Frauenhofer Institute for Silicon Technology at Itzehoe.

Recent improvements in communications have been the construction of new motorways and a fourth tunnel under the Elbe as well as a new crossing west of Hamburg. While the state has a history of sea-borne links with Scandinavia, airports are an expanding line of communication as the airport at Hamburg-Fuhlsbüttel is just over the state border in addition to the number of regional airports with flights to Cologne/Bonn or Frankfurt.

Although micro-electronics are not likely to overtake sea trade as the region's main industry for a while yet, a more likely contender, given the shorter German working week, is the tourism and leisure industry. Given the picturesque and varied coast, its historic Hanseatic ports (Lübeck was recently made a World Heritage Site) and its many lakes and nature reserves (see Chapter One) the state is becoming a leading tourist destination.

THÜRINGEN (Thüringia)

As part of the Federal drive to rebuild the transport system of the eastern länder, Thüringen will benefit from new motorway links with Berlin, Bayern, Leipzig and the Ruhr. By the year 2000 it is planned to link the state into the high-speed rail network, with a new freight and container terminal under construction at Erfurt. The international airport at Leipzig is a short distance across the state border and Erfurt's own airport is being expanded to form part of a chain of regional airports. Already 20 billion DM has been invested in upgrading the telecommunications network, with a further 3 billion spent on the energy supply systems.

In the first four years after unification over 200,000 jobs were created or safeguarded by over 20 billion DM worth of investment by private firms, although these did benefit from 5 billion DM worth of state subsidies.

Thüringen's main industrial strengths are in the automotive, engineering, electronics and ceramics industries. The well known pre-war optical firm of Carl Zeiss is still going strong and with Jenoptik exports opto-electronic precision tools around the world. General Motors has a site at Eisenach employing 2,000 people in the production of 16,000 Opel cars annually, and ICL-Fujitsu has a computer production facility with an annual capacity to turn out 300,000 PCs. Other investors in the region are Coca-Cola (soft drinks), Cresson (foods), AMS (semi-conductors) and Langenscheidt (publishers). Tourism is also a major source of income as the state has 1,400 castles, one of which the Wartburg is the start of the 'Classical Route' a tour through Germany's cultural and intellectual history.

Directory of Major Employers

British Firms in Germany

This list hs been compiled with the help of the British-German Chamber of Commerce and lists major British firms with offices, subsidiaries or partners in Germany, it includes some firms who have offices in Britain which may recruit for posts in Germany.

Banking & Insurance Brokers

Albion Insurance Co. Ltd: Niederlassung für Deutschland, Schlachte 2, D-28195 Bremen.

Albright & Wilson Plc: Albright & Wilson GmbH, Frankfurter Strasse 181, D-63263 Neu-Isenberg.

Aspen Tech (UK) Ltd: Aspentech Europe S.A.-N.V., Niederlassung Düsseldorf, Am Seestern 24, Düsseldorf.

W S Atkins International Ltd: Dachsberg 36, D-85665 Moosach.

AXA Equity & Law: AXA Fondsmanagement, Gesellschaft für Kapitalanlagen mbH, Hans-Bredlow-Str. 1, D-65189 Wiesbaden.

AXA Equity & Law (Life Assurance): AXA Leben Versicherung, Hans-Bredlow-Str. 1, D-65189 Wiesbaden.

Barclays Bank Plc: BZW Deutschland GmbH, Branch of Barclays Bank Plc, Bockenheimer Landstr. 38-40, D-60323 Frankfurt am Main.

Barclays Bank Plc: Merck Finck & Co, Privatbankiers, Pacellistrasse 16, D-80333 München.

Barclays Bank Plc: OPTIMUS, Bank für Finanz-Service GmbH, Flughafenstrasse 21 D-63263 Neu-Isenberg.

Barclays de Zoete Wedd Ltd: Barclays de Zoete Wedd Deutschland GmbH, Bockenheimer Landstr. 38-40, D-60323 Frankfurt am Main.

Baring Brothers International Ltd: Baring Brothers GmbH, Friedrichstrasse 2-6, D-60323 Frankfurt am Main.

Beninvestments (KPMG Peat Markwick): Benedict & Dannheisser GmbH, Welsertstrasse 88, D-90489 Nürnberg.

BPP Holdings Plc: BPP Bank Training, Goetheplatz 2, D-60311 Frankfurt am Main.

Brown Financial Advisers Ltd: BFA Ltd, Tucholskystrasse 18, D-60598 Frankfurt am Main.

Brushes International Plc: Osborn International GmbH, Ringstrasse 10, D-35099 Burgwald.

CCN Systems Ltd: CCN Deutschland Verwaltungs-GmbH, Schlüterstrasse 3, D-40235 Düsseldorf.

CCN International Ltd: CFS Card Finanz Systeme AG, Albert-Einstein-Ring 3, D-22761 Hamburg.

Commercial Union Assurance Co Plc: The Northern Assurance Co Ltd, London Direktion für Deutschalnd, c/o Gothaer Versicherungsbank VvaG, Gothaer Allee 1, D-50969 Köln.

The Equitable Life Assurance Society: Equitable Life Deutschland, Oberländer Ufer 180-182, D-50968 Köln.

Ford Credit Europe Plc: Ford Bank AG, Postfach 10 13 41, D-50453 Köln.

Gartmore Investment Management Plc: Gartmore Investment Services GmbH, Friedrichstr. 47, D-60323 Frankfurt am Main.

General Accident Fire & Life Assurance Corporation Plc.: Otto-Volger-Strasse 19, D-65843 Sulzbach/Taunus.

Guardian Royal Exchange Plc: Albingia Versicherungs-AG, Ballindamm 39, D-20095 Hamburg.

Hiscox Holdings Ltd: Hiscox Versicherungs-Services GmbH, Richterstrasse 31, D-80339 München.

ICI Plc: Kloeckner Pentatec GmbH, Strasse der Einheit 22, D-04808 Thallwitz-Nischwitz.

Kleinwort Benson Ltd: Kleinwort Benson Deutschland GmbH, Wilhelm-Leuschner-Str. 41, D-60329 Frankfurt am Main.

LGT Asset Management Plc: GT Global Fondsservice GmbH, Herzog-Wilhelm-Strasse 19, D-80331 München.

Lloyd's of London: Lloyd's Versicherer London, Bockenheimer Anlage 4, D-60322 Frankfurt am Main.

Lloyd's Register of Shipping: Lloyd's Register of Shipping Germany, Mönckebergstr. 27, D-20095 Hamburg.

Lloyds TSB Group Plc: Schröder, Münchmeyer, Hengst & Co, Friedenstrasse 6-10, D-60311 Frankfurt am Main.

Lombard North Central Plc: Lombard Leasing GmbH, Werner-von-Braun-Str. 10a, D-85640 Putzbrunn.

Lowndes Lambert Group Plc: Lowndes Lambert Deutschland AG, Mozartstrasse 1, D-04107 Leipzig.

Merrill Lynch International Bank Ltd: Nürnberger Strasse 67, D-10787 Berlin.

Midland Bank Plc: Trinkaus & Burkhardt KGaA, Königsallee 21-23, D-40212 Düsseldorf.

Midland Bank Plc, International Financial Services Ltd: Midland Holdings Germany GmbH, Konigsallee 21/23, D-40212 Düsseldorf.

National Westminster Bank Plc: National Westminster Bank AG, Postfach 11 10 51, D-60045 Frankfurt am Main.

Norwich Union Fire Insurance Society Ltd: Direktion fr Deutschland, c/o Gothaer Versicherungsbank VvaG, Gothaer Allee 1, D-50969 Köln.

Robert Fleming Holdings Ltd: Robert Fleming (Deutschland) GmbH, Im Trutz Frankfurt 55, D-60322 Frankfurt am Main.

Rothmans International Plc: Bremer Assekuranz-Kontor-GmbH, Dötlinger Strasse 4, D-28197 Bremen.

NM Rothschild & Sons: Rothschild GmbH, Ulmenstrasse 22, D-60325 Frankfurt am Main.

Sedgwick Group Plc: Interassekuranz Sitt., Overlack & Co GmbH, Konrad-Adenauer-Str. 13, D-50996 Köln.

SG Warburg Group Plc: SG Warburg & Co GmbH, Taunusanlage 11, D-60329 Frankfurt am Main.

SmithKline Beecham Plc: Abtei Pharma, Vertriebsgesellschaft mbH, Mühlenstrasse 31, D-33607 Bielefeld.

Standard Life Assurance Co: c/o MLP Finanzdienstleistungen, Forum 7, D-69126 Heidelberg.

Sturge Lloyd's Agencies Ltd: Sturge Insurance Agencies GmbH: Ballindamm 37, D-20095 Hamburg.

also Sturge Lloyd's Agencies Holdings GmbH, Karl-Rudolf-Strasse 178, D-40215 Düsseldorf.

Sun Alliance Group Plc: Deutsche Versicherungs Gesellschaft in Bremen AG, Am Wall 121, D-28195 Bremen.

West Merchant Bank Ltd: Niederlassung Düsseldorf, Königsallee 33, D-40212 Düsseldorf.

Lawyers, Accountants, Consultants and Surveyors

3i International Holdings: 3i Deutschland Gesellschaft für Industriebeteiligungen mbH, Bockenheimer Landstr. 55, D-60325 Frankfurt am Main.

Bucknall Group Plc: Bucknall, Day & Belconsult GmbH, Danckelmannstrasse 20, D-14059 Berlin.

Cambridge Consultants Ltd: Gustav-Stresemann-Ring 1, D-65189 Wiesbaden.

CIA Medianetwork: CIA Medianetwork Deutschland GmbH, Berliner Allee 25, D-40212 Düsseldorf.

CMG Plc: CMG Deutschland GmbH, Kölner Strasse 10, D-65760 Eschborn.

Control Risks Group Ltd: Control Risks Deutschland GmbH, Am Herrengarten 1, D-53721 Siegburg.

Coutts Career Consultants Ltd: Saalburgstrasse 157, D-61350 Bad Homburg v. d. H.

Data Sciences Ltd: Data Sciences GmbH, Sittarder Strasse 31, D-52078 Aachen.

Ernst & Young: Ernst &Young GmbH, Wirtschaftsprüfungsgesellschaft, Eschersheimer Landstr. 14, D-60322 Frankfurt am Main.

Freshfields: Messe Turm, Box-Nr 61, Friedrich-Abert-Anlage 49, D-60327 Frankfurt am Main.

Graham Consulting Group: O'Sullivan & Graham GmbH, Grimmaische Strasse 29, D-04109 Leipzig.

Herring Baker Harris Group Plc: Herring Baker Harris Deutschland GmbH, Wallstrasse 23-24, D-10179 Berlin.

Thomas Howell Group: Thomas Howell Group (Deutschland) GmbH, Hohenstaufenstrasse 2, D-40547 Düsseldorf.

JBA Holding Plc: JBA International Ratioplan GmbH, Max-Planck-Strasse 11, D-78052 Villingen-Schwenningen.

J D Kingsfield Ltd: Königsallee 60f, D-40212 Düsseldorf.

Michael Knox & Associates: Michael Knox FCMA, Management Consultant, Griechische Allee 24, D-12459 Berlin.

KPMG: KPMG Deutsche Treuhand-Gesellschaft AG, Kurze Mühren 1, D-20095 Hamburg.

LEK: LEK Unternehmensberatung GmbH, Possartstrasse 22, D-81679 München.

Management Selection Group Ltd: MSL Deutschland GmbH, Berliner Allee 55, D-40212 Düsseldorf.

PA Consulting Group: PA Consulting Services GmbH, Wiesenau 27-29, D-60323 Frankfurt am Main.

Michael Page Group Plc: Michael Page International (Deutschland) GmbH, Steinstrasse 13, D-40212 Düsseldorf.

Panell Kerr Forster: Ball, Baker, Leake, Weber Wirtschaftsprüfungsgesellschaft mbH, Kölner Landstr. 115, D-40591 Düsseldorf.

Parkinson Group Plc: Anderson, Squires (Deutschland) GmbH, Niedenau 41, D-60325 Frankfurt am Main.

Price Waterhouse: Price Waterhouse GmbH, ABC-Strasse 45, D-20354 Hamburg.

Powergen: CUI Consultinggesellschaft für Umwelt und Infrastruktur, Eisenbahnstr. 10, D-06132 Halle/Salle.

PRICOA Capital group: Melemstrasse 2, D-60322 Frankfurt am Main.

Pritchard Englefield: Wiesenau 51, D-60323 Frankfurt am Main.

Purcell, Miller, Tritton & Partners: Büro Straslund, Mönchstrasse 53, D-18439 Straslund.

Spencer Stuart & Associates: Lyoner Strasse 14, D-60528 Frankfurt am Main.

Stewart & Clark Associates Ltd: Rotkäppchenstrasse 81a, D-81739 München.

TTP Group Plc: The Technology Partnership GmbH, Offenbacher Strasse 5, D-63303 Dreireich.

Construction Companies, Estate Agents, Architects, Inspectors, Engineers and Suppliers:

Acanthus Associated Architectural Practices Ltd: Acanthus Architects and Town Planners bei ASK, Reichstrasse 108, D-14052 Berlin.

Allot & Lomax (Holdings) Ltd: INKOPLAN- Gesellschaft für Industrie und Kommunalplanung mbH, Hendrik-Witte-Strasse 6, D-45128 Essen.

AMEC Plc: AMEC Ingenieurbau GmbH, Von-Miller-Strasse 13, D-67661 Kaiserlautern.
   also Gebr. Kittelberger GmbH & Co KG, Von-Miller-Strasse 13, D-67661 Kaiserlautern.
Aukett Ltd: Aukett + Heese GmbH, Budapesterstrasse 43, D-10787 Berlin.
Peter Brett Associates: PBA Ingenieurbüro, Behlertstrasse 26, D-14469 Potsdam.
Brixton Estate Plc: Brixton Estate Deutschland GmbH, Albert-Einstein-Strasse 7, D-40699 Erkrath.
   also ELY Grundstückverwaltung GmbH at the same address.
Building Design Partnership: BDR Rohling GmbH, Alt Moabit 73, D-10555 Berlin.
The Carvill Group Ltd: Carvill Group (Deutschland) GmbH, Chausseestrasse 11, D-10115 Berlin.
Davis, Langdon & Everest: Davis, Langdon & Weiss, Kostenberatung + Projektmanagement GmbH, Kantstrasse 72, D-10627 Berlin.
DGI International Plc: DGI Bauwerk Architekturbüro GmbH, Schillstr. 9-10, D-10785 Berlin.
Drivers Jonas: Rankestrasse 3, D-10879 Berlin.
DTZ Debenham Thorpe: DTZ Zadelhof GmbH, Robert-Bosch-Str. 32, D-63303 Dreieich.
Entec Europe Ltd: Hydrogeologie GmbH, Rothenburgstrasse 10-11, D-99734 Nordhausen.
Foster and Partners: Giesebrechtstrasse 10, D-10629 Berlin.
Sir Alexander Gibb Ltd: IHT Rosser Gibb GmbH, Postfach 3843, D-39013 Magdeburg.
Nicholas Grimshaw & Partners Ltd: Hardenbergstrasse 19, D-10623 Berlin.
E C Harris International Ltd: E C Harris GmbH & Co KG, Birkbuchstrasse 10, D-12167 Berlin.
Healey & Baker: Rossmarkt 11, D-63011 Frankfurt am Main.
Heery International Ltd: Heery International c/o Balfour Beatty GmbH, Friedrichstrasse 130 b, D-10117 Berlin.
Hepworth Building Products Ltd: EuroCeramic GmbH, Hormesfeld 9 b, D-41478 Viersen.
Housham Henderson Architects: Rheinstrasse 45, D-12161 Berlin.
JCB Sales Ltd: JCB Baumaschinen und Industriemaschinen GmbH, Graf-Zeppelin-Strasse 16, D-51147 Köln.
Jung & Partner Consultants: Jung & Partner Landschaftsarchitekten und Diplomingenieure BDLA ALI, Beermannstrasse 6, D-12435 Berlin.
Lloyd's Register of Shipping: Lloyd's Register Quality Assurance Ltd, Bonner Strasse 172-176, D-50968 Köln.
Alfred McAlpine International Ltd: Bau Borna GmbH, Abtsdorfer Strasse 36, D-04552 Borna.
MDA Overseas Ltd: MDA Bysh GmbH: Schloss Lembeck, D-46286 Dorsten.
Mott MacDonald: Mott Ipro Planungsgesellschaft, Grimmaische Str. 26, D-04109 Leipzig.
John Mowlem & Co Plc: Mowlem BauTec GmbH, Hönower Weg, d-15366 Dahlwitz-Hoppegarten.
OVE Arup Partnership: Arup GmbH, Malkastenstrasse 2, D-40211 Düsseldorf.
Redac Systems Ltd: Zuken-Redac-Design-System GmbH, Muthmannstrasse 4, D-80939 München.
RMC Group Plc: Ready Mixed Concrete Europe Management Services GmbH, Alt-Niederkassel 56, D-40547 Düsseldorf.

also Readymix Beton Berlin Brandenburg GmbH, Sophienwerdungweg 40-50, D-13597 Berlin.

also Readymix AG für Beteiligungen, Daniel-Goldbach-Str. 25, D-40880 Ratingen.

also Rüdersdorfer Zement GmbH, Postfach13/14, D-15562 Rüdersdorf.

also Seyd & Heinrichs Transportkontor GmbH, Sophienwerder Weg 40-50, D-13597 Berlin.

The Salvage Association: Kleine Rosenstrasse 8, D-20095 Hamburg.

Siegel & Gale Ltd: Steinhöft 9, D-20459 Hamburg.

Slough Estates Plc: Slough Commercial Properties GmbH, Elisabethstrasse 40, D-40217 Düsseldorf.

Smiths Industries Plc: Benzing Ventilatoren GmbH, Werastrasse 62, D-78056 VS-Schwenningen.

Soltkahn Ltd: Brandenburgische Strasse 43, D-10707 Berlin.

Mike Stacey Ltd: Stacey Bau GmbH, Stallupöner Allee 51, D-14055 Berlin.

Kyle Stewart Ltd: Kyle Stewart ARGE Berlin, Eichborndamm 167-175, D-13403 Berlin.

Tarmac Professional Services: Schal International GmbH, Nürnberger Strasse 8, D-10787 Berlin.

TSL Group Plc: TQS Thermal Quarz-Schmelze gmbH, Hüttenstrasse 10, D-65201 Wiesbaden.

Weatherall Green & Smith: Weatherall Green & Smith GmbH, Untermainkai 30, D-60329 Frankfurt am Main.

Wintersgill, Faulkner: Duane Phillips Architects & City Planners, Kluckstrasse 31, D-10875 Berlin.

James Lang Wooten: Platz der Einheit 2, D-60327 Frankfurt am Main.

Transport, Travel & Tourism

Aviareps Ltd: Stresemann Allee 41, D-60596 Frankfurt am Main.

Avis Europe Plc: AVIS Autovermietung GmbH & Co KG, Zimmersmühlenweg 21, D-61437 Oberursel.

British Aerospace (Military Aircraft) Ltd: PANAVIA Aircraft GmbH, Am Söldermoos 17, D-85399 Halbergmoos.

British Airways Plc: Postfach 75 01 63, D-60531 Frankfurt am Main.

British Midland Airways Ltd: British Midland Deutschland, Frankfurt Airport Center, Briefkasten 7, Hugo-Eckener-Ring, D-60549 Frankfurt am Main.

British Railways Board: British Rail International- Britische Eisenbahn, Düsseldorfer Str. 15-17, D-60329 Frankfurt am Main.

British Tourist Authority: BTA-Britische zentrale für Fremdenverkehr, Taunusstr. 52-60, D-60329 Frankfurt am Main.

Castle Transport UK Ltd: Max-Planck-Strasse 20b, D-33428 Harsewinkel.

Chapman Freeborn Airmarketing Ltd: Chapman Freeborn Airmarketing GmbH, Im Taubengrund 27, D-65451 Kelsterbach.

Thomas Cook Group Ltd: Thomas Cook Reisebüro GmbH, Direktion, Hahnstrasse 68, D-60528 Frankfurt am Main.

Cunard Line Ltd: Neue Rabenstrasse 3, D-20354 Hamburg.

Europa European Express Ltd: Europa Spedition AGA GmbH, Freiburger Strasse 9, D-74379 Ingersheim.

European EconomicCouriers Ltd: European Express Couriers, Kleiner Kornweg 32a, D-65451 Kelsterbach.

Holyman Sally Ltd: Münchener Strasse 48, D-60329 Frankfurt am Main.

Imperial Chemical Industries Plc: PRO-LOG Gesellschaft für logistische Dienstleistungen mbH, Inhausersieler Strasse 25, D-26388 Wilhelmshaven.

Inchcape Shipping Services (Europe) Ltd: Gellatly, Hanky & Co. GmbH, Ehrenbergstrasse 59, D-22767 Hamburg.
  also H & M Freight Services GmbH, Pelzerstrasse 8, D-28195 Bremen.
LEP International Worldwide Ltd: LEP International GmbH: Curienstrasse 2, D-20095 Hamburg.
Marken Worldwide Express: Jülicherstrasse 67, D-41464 Neuss.
MSAS Cargo International Ltd: MSAS Cargo International GmbH, Heilbronner Strasse 3, D-70771 Leinfelden-Echterdingen.
Norfolk Line Ltd: Norfolk Line GmbH, Schirmerstrasse 6, D-40211 Düsseldorf.
Ocean Group Plc: McGregor Cory Cargo Service GmbH, Langer Kornweg 34d, D-65451 Kelsterbach.
  also Oceangate Distribution GmbH, Dradenauer Hauptdeich 3, D-21129 Hamburg.
P & O Containers Ltd: P & O Containers Europe GmbH, Am Sandtorkai 37, D-20457 Hamburg.
P & O European Ferries Ltd: P & O European Ferries (Dover) Ltd, Graf-Adolf-Strasse 41, D-40210 Düsseldorf.
Peninsular and Oriental Steam Navigation Company: P & O Trans European Management GmbH, Antwerpener Strasse 23, D-68219 Mannheim-Rheinau.
Plane Trucking Ltd: Plane Trucking GmbH, Theodor-Storm-Strasse 1, D-40699 Erkrath.
Powerline Services Ltd: Powerline Services GmbH, Internationale Spedition, Rudolf-Diesel-Strasse 12, D-46446 Emmerich.
Reed Telepublishing Group Plc: Reed Travel Group Germany GmbH, Heerdter Landstr. 191, D-40549 Düsseldorf.
Christian Salvesen Plc: Christian Salvesen GmbH, Rondenbarg 25, D-22525 Hamburg.
Sea Containers Ltd: Sea Containers GmbH, Deichstr. 11, D-204589 Hamburg.
United Transport Container Holdings Ltd: Seawheel GmbH, Schiess Str.44, D-40549 Düsseldorf.
Venice-Simplon-Orient-Express Ltd: Venice-Simplon-Orient-Express Deutschland GmbH, Oststrasse 122, D-40210 Düsseldorf.
Andrew Weir & Company Ltd: United Baltic Corporation GmbH, Maklerstrasse 1, D-24159 Kiel.

Hotels, Catering, Conferences and Trade Fairs
Amstrad Plc: Amstrad GmbH, Dreieichstrasse 8, D-64546 Mörfelden-Walldorf.
AOKI Corporation: Hotel 'Vier Jahreszeiten' von Friedrich Haerlin GmbH, Neuer Jungfernsteig 9-14, D-20354 Hamburg.
Bass Plc: Holiday Inns Germany Inc, Adolfstrasse 16, D-65185 Wiesbaden.
Blenheim Group Plc: Blenheim International (Deutschland) GmbH, Neusse Strasse 111, D-40219 Düsseldorf.
CCA Galleries Ltd: Braugasse 6, D-50859 Köln.
Christie, Manson & Woods Ltd: Christie's (Deutschland) GmbH, Inselstrasse 15, D-40479 Düsseldorf.
Europa Acquisition Capital : ADS Anker GmbH, Am Stadtholz 39, D-33609 Bielefeld.
Four Seasons Hotel: Four Seasons Regent Hotels and Resorts, Oeder Weg 15, D-60318 Frankfurt am Main.
Forte (UK) Ltd: Forte Hotels Deutschland GmbH, Neue Mainzer Str. 22, D-60311 Frankfurt am Main.
Hilton International: Berlin Hilton, Mohrenstrasse 30, D 10117 Berlin.

Marler Hayley ExpoSystems Ltd: Meissener Exposysteme GmbH, Lemsahler Weg 23, D-22851 Norderstedt.

Millenium & Copthorne Hotels: Copthorne Hotel Stuttgart International Freizeit und Erlebnicentrum Sl, Plieninger Strasse 100, D-70561 Stuttgart.

Miller Freeman Exhibitions Ltd: Miller Freeman Deutschland GmbH, Nerotal 3, D-65193 Wiesbaden.

Queens Moat Houses Plc: Queens Gruppe Deutschland, Isenburger Schneise 40, D-60528 Frankfurt am Main.

　also Queens Moat Houses (Deutschland) GmbH, Frankenring 31-33, D-30855 Langenhagen.

　also　Queens Moat Houses (Germany) Holding GmbH, Mailänderstrasse 1, D-60598 Frankfurt am Main.

Reed Exhibition CompaniesLtd : Reed Exhibitions Germany GmbH, Heerdter Sandberg 32, D-40549 Düsseldorf.

Sotheby's: Sotheby's-Berliner Dependance Palais am Festungensgraben, Unter den Linden/Neue Wache, D-10117 Berlin.

Thiste Hotels: Abraham-Lincoln-Strasse 7, D-65189 Wiesbaden.

Whitbread Plc: Whitbread Restaurants Holding GmbH, Elisabethstrasse 22, D-40217 Düsseldorf.

Communications: Language Services, Printing, Publishing & Advertising

3i International Holdings: Schlott Tiefdruck GmbH, Wittensweilerstrasse 3, D-72250 Freundstadt.

Alan Pane Plc: Essanelle Holding GmbH, Friedrich-Ebert-Strasse 54, D-40210 Düsseldorf.

Ascott Marketing Communications: ede-Elmar Distelhoff Communications, Postfach 4265, D-40655 Meerbusch.

BBA Group Plc: BBA Group Beteiligungsgesellschaft mbH, Mülheimerstrasse 65, D-51375 Leverkusen.

Blackwell Science Ltd: Blackwell Wissenschaftsverlag, Kurfürstendamm 57, D-10707 Berlin.

Boosey & Hawkes Plc: Justus-von-Liebig-Strasse 22, D-53121 Bonn.

　also: Jakob Winter GmbH, Graslitzer Strassse 10, D-64569 Nauheim.

　also Bote & Bock GmbH & Co KG, Hardenbergstrasse 9a, D-10623 Berlin.

Bowthorpe Plc: Bowthorpe GmbH, Siemensstr. 5, D-25421 Pinneberg.

British Telecommunications Plc: British Telecom (Deutschland) GmbH, Godesberger Allee 73, D-53175 Bonn.

Bunzl Plc: Bunzl international GmbH, In Der Fleute 53, D-42389 Wuppertal.

Cable & Wireless Plc: Cable & Wireless GmbH, Saonestrasse 3a, D-60528 Frankfurt am Main.

Cape Ltd: Cape Entsorgungstechnik GmbH, Auf dem Bürgel 26, D-34821 Gudensberg.

Clifford Thames (Holdings) Ltd: Moeker Merkur Druck GmbH, Niehler Gürtel 102, D-50733 Köln.

Cookson Group Plc: Cookson Overseas Verwaltungs GmbH, Am Bonneshof 5, D-40474 Düsseldorf.

J R Crompton Ltd: Bahnhofstrasse 41, D-65185 Wiesbaden.

D + B Europe Ltd: Dun & Bradstreet Deutschland GmbH, Hahnstrasse 31, D-60528 Frankfurt am Main.

Economist Intelligence Unit: Bettinastrasse, D-60325 Frankfurt.

EMAP Business Communication Ltd: Cermic Forum International Berichte der DKG, Bauverlag GmbH, Am Klingenweg 4, D-65396 Walluf.

The EMI Group: EMI Electrola GmbH, Maarweg 149, D-50825 Köln.
also EMI Music Publishing Germany GmbH, Alsterufer 1, D-20354 Hamburg.

The Financial Times Ltd: The Financial Times (Europe) GmbH, Nibelungenplatz 3, D-63018 Frankfurt am Main.

Fine Art Developments Plc: IVORY Glückwunchkarten GmbH, Mettmanner Strasse 15, D-40699 Erkrath.

GKN Plc: Chep Deutschland GmbH, Konrad-Adenauer-Strasse 13, D-50996 Köln.

Imagine Transfers Ltd: Imagine International Trade GmbH, Brückenstrasse 17, D-60594 Frankfurt am Main.

Lawson-Marden Bristol: Lawson Marden Hanse-Druck GmbH & Co, Hüttenkamp 12, D-24536 Neumünster.

Linguarama International Group Plc: Linguarama Spracheninstitut GmbH, Goetheplatz 2, D-60311 Frankfurt am Main.

Lopex Plc: Gültig & Hoffmeister Alliance Werbeagentur GmbH, Eschersheimer Landstrasse 8, D-60322 Frankfurt am Main.

Mark-o-Print Ltd: Mark-o-Print Druck und Signiergeräte für Verpackungen GmbH, Reepschlägerstrasse 11a, D-23556 Lübeck.

Meyer International Plc: Meyer International Deutschland GmbH, Rombacher Hütte 5, D-44795 Bochum.

Music Sales Ltd: Edition Wilhelm Hansen GmbH, Gerresheimer Landstrasse 71, D-40627 Düsseldorf.

NOP Information Group: MIL Marktfgorschung GmbH, Theodor-Heuss-Ring 36, D-50668 Köln.

The Open University: The Open University Co-Ordinator Louise Henrichsen, Postfach 10 13 60, D-40833 Ratingen.

Oxford Intensive School of English: OISE-Sprachtraining (Deutschland) GmbH, Kaiser Friedrich Promenade 59, D-61348 Bad Homburg.

Oxford University Press: Cornelsen & Oxford University Press, Johannisberger Strasse 74, D-14197 Berlin.

Penguin Books Ltd: Penguin Books Deutschland GmbH, Metzlerstrasse 26, D-60594 Frankfurt am Main.

Reed Telepublishing Ltd: Kompass Deutschland Verlags-und-Vertriebsges. MbH, Jechtinger Strasse 13, D-79111 Freiburg im Bresigau.

Reuters Holdings Plc: Reuters AG, Friedrich-Ebert-Anlage 49, D-60327 Frankfurt am Main.

Rexam Plc: Wickrather Bauelemente AG, Olefant 14a, D-51427 Bergisch-Gladbach.
also McCorquodale GmbH, Robert-Bosch-Breite 1, D-37079 Göttingen.

Rothmans International Plc: Montblanc-Simplo GmbH, Hellgrundweg 100, D-2525 Hamburg.

Saatchi & Saatchi Co Plc: BSB Baumgartner-Spalek-Bayer, Mühlhöle Hs Nr 2, D-65202 Wiesbaden.

Sappi Europe Ltd: Hannoversche Papierfabriken, Mühlenmasch 1, D-31061 Alfeld.

Sony Music Entertainment: Sony Music holdings GmbH, Berner Strasse 81-83, D-60437 Frankfurt am Main.

Virgin Voyager Ltd: Virgin schallplatten GmbH, Herzogstrasse 64, D-80803 München.

WPP Group Plc: Ogilvy & Mather GmbH, Hainer Weg 44, D-60599 Frankfurt am Main.

also Saatchi & Saatchi Advertising GmbH, Wiesenau 38, D-60323 Frankfurt am Main.

Food & Drink Producers

B A T Industries Plc: BATIG Gesellschaft für Beteiligungen mbH, Alsterufer 4, D-20354 Hamburg.

also British-American Tobacco (Germany) GmbH, Postfach 30 06 60, D-20347 Hamburg.

Cadbury Schweppes Plc: Apollinaris & Schweppes GmbH & Co, Fischertweite 1 Chile Haus A, D-20095 Hamburg.

also Basset Confectionery Deutschland GmbH & Co, Gutenbergring 60, D-22848 Norderstedt.

also Cadbury Schweppes GmbH, Fischertwiete 1, Chile-Haus A, D-20095 Hamburg.

CPL Aromas Plc: CPL Group (Deutschland) GmbH, Rudolf-Diesel-Str. 5, D-46446 Emmerich.

Dalgety Plc: Deutsche PIG Improvement GmbH, Ratsteich 31, D-24837 Schleswig.

The Albert Fisher Group Plc: Alber Fisher Deutschland GmbH, Kesslerweg 10, D-48155 Münster.

Grand Metropolitan Plc: Aries Getränkevetrieb GmbH, Bahnstrasse 10, D-65025 Wiesbaden.

also Hofmann Menü GmbH & Co oHG, Industriestr. 6, D-97949 Boxberg.

also Jokisch Schnellgerichte GmbH & Co oHG, Am Schülenplatz 19, D-24211 Preetz.

also Pillsbury Vetreibs GmbH, Geniner Strasse 88-100, D-23560 Lübeck.

Guiness Brewing Worldwide Ltd: Guiness GmbH, Ruhrallee 54, D-45138 Essen.

E J Harrison & Sons Ltd: Harrison Sorrell & Co GmbH, Hohnzollernstrasse 44, D-53173 Bonn.

Hillsdown Holdings Plc: Nadler Feinkost GmbH, Käfertaler Strasse 190, D-68167 Mannheim.

Howegarden: Bördegarden Frischmüse GmbH, Wittenberger Strasse 4, D-06917 Rehain/Jessen.

Lyons Seafoods Ltd: Lyons Seefods GmbH, Almsstrasse 20, D-31134 Hildesheim.

Meat Corpoation of Namibia (UK) Ltd: Meat Corporation of Namibia (Deutschland) GmbH, Emscherstrasse 43, D-45891 Gelsenkirchen.

Milk Product Holdings (Europe) Ltd: New Zealand Milk Products (Europe) GmbH, Siemensstrasse 6-14, D-25462 Rellingen.

Newsham Hybrid Pigs Ltd: Newsham Hybrid Schwein GmbH, Oststrasse 12, D-48341 Altenberge.

Rothmans International Plc: Brinkmann Tabakfabriken GmbH, Hermann-Ritter-Str. 112, D-28197 Bremen.

also Rothmans Cigaretten GmbH, Bleichenbrücke 10, D-20354 Hamburg.

Tate & Lyle Plc: Biolinol Futterfette-Produktions-GmbH, Ausschläger Elbdeich 62, D-20539 Hamburg.

also Prignitz Stärke GmbH, Hauptstrasse 96, D-19357 Dallmin.

GW Thoman Ltd: Rheinallee 5-7, D-65375 Oestrich-Winkel.

Towers & Co Ltd: Towers & Co Hamburg GmbH, c/o BPU GmbH, Wirtschaftsprüfungsges , Mundsburger Damm 45, D-22087 Hamburg.

Unilever Plc: Deutsche Unilever GmbH, Dammtorwall 15, D-20355 Hamburg.

The Union International Plc: Weddel & Co GmbH, Frauenthal 6, D-20149 Hamburg.

The Hiram Walker Group Ltd: Langenbach & Co GmbH, Wilhelm-Rauten-strauch-Str. 3, D-54290 Trier.

Computers, Software, IT & Services:
Dataserv Group Ltd: Dataserv GmbH, Immermannstrasse 65b, D-40210 Düsseldorf.

Eurosoft (UK) Ltd: Eurosoft Deutschland GmbH, Friedrichstrasse 10-12, D-60323 Frankfurt am Main.

Husky Computers Ltd: Husky Computers GmbH, Auelsweg 18, D-53797 Lohmar.

ICL International Computer Ltd: ICL Service GmbH, Vogelsanger Weg 91, D-40470 Düsseldorf.

ICL Plc: ECRC European Computer Industry Research Center GmbH (Internet Provider), Arabellastrasse 17, D-81925 München.

   also ICL technology GmbH, Vogelsanger Weg 91, D-40470 Düsseldorf.

Kalamazoo Computer Group Plc: Kalamazoo Computer Group GmbH, Martin-Behaim-Strasse 12, D-63263 Neu-Isenberg.

Microgen Holdings Plc: Eurocom-Depora Informationssysteme GmbH, Mör-felder Landstrasse 6, D-60598 Frankfurt am Main.

MOSS Systems Ltd: MSL Engineering Software GmbH, Eberstädter Strasse 38, D-64319 Pfungstadt.

PAFEC Ltd: PAFEC CAE (Deutschland) GmbH, Zum Fürstenmoor 11, D-21079 Hamburg.

The Sage Group Plc: KHK Software GmbH & Co KG, Berner Strasse 23, D-60437 Frankfurt am Main.

Sema Group Plc: Sema Group GmbH, Kaltenbornweg 3, D-50679 Köln.

Smallworld Plc: Smallworld Systems GmbH, Europaring 60, D-40878 Ratingen.

Tenhill Computer Systems Ltd: Tenhill Computer Systeme GmbH, Theodor-Heuss-Allee 80, D060486 Frankfurt am Main.

Trintech Group: Trintech GmbH, Siemensstrasse 20, D-63263 Neu-Isenberg.

Mineral, Chemical, Petro-Chemical, Pharmaceutical & Energy Producers:
Advance Tapes International Ltd: Advance Tapes Dutschland GmbH, Enzstrasse 9, D-70806 Kornwestheim.

Akcros Chemicals Ltd: Akcros Chemicals GmbH & Co KG, Phillipstrasse 27, D-52301 Düren.

Allied Colloids Plc: Allied Colloids Manufacturing GmbH, Tarpenring 23, D-22149 Hamburg.

Amersham International Plc: Amersham Buchler GmbH & Co KG, Gieselweg 1, D-38110 Braunschweig.

Anglian Water Plc: Purac Leuna GmbH, Weissenfelser Strasse 46, D-06217 Merseburg.

Anzon Ltd: S. Goldmann GmbH & Co KG, Schillerstrasse 79, D-33609 Bielefeld.

Avon Polymer Products Ltd: Avon Industrial Polymers (Deutschland) GmbH, Vahrenwalder Platz 3, D-30165 Hannover.

Avon Rubber Plc: AVON Reifen (Deutschland) GmbH, Rossstrasse 8, D-40476 Düsseldorf.

Barrow Hepburn International Ltd: Mydrin ags GmbH, Kalkarer Strasse 81, D-47533 Kleve.

B G Plc: British Gas Deutschland GmbH, Kurfürstendamm 207-208, D-10719 Berlin.

Boots Contract Manufacturing: BCM Kosmetik GmbH, Messenhäuser Strasse 22, D-63128 Dietzenbach.

Borax Europe Ltd: Deutsche Borax GmbH, Otto-Volger-Str. 19, D-65843 Sulzbach/Taunus.

Bowater Plc: DYNA Fenster und Türen GmbH, Hugo-Wagener-Strasse, Industriegebeit, D-55481 Kirchberg.

BP Europe Holdings: Deutsche BP Holding AG, Postfach 60 03 40, D-22291 Hamburg.

BPB Industries Plc: Börgardts GmbH, D-37445 Walkenreid-Kutzhütte.

Brent Chemicals International Plc: Brent GmbH, Rostockstrasse 40, D-4119 Mönchengladbach.

Burmah Castrol: Deutsche Castrol Vertriebsgesellschaft mbH, Esplanade 39, D-20354 Hamburg.

Burmah Castrol Plc: Burmah Oil (Deutschland) GmbH, Esplanade 39, D-20354 Hamburg.

　　also: FOSECO GmbH, Gelsenkircherstrasse 10, D-46325 Borken.

　　also: Optimol Ölwerke Industrie GmbH, Friedenstr. 10, D-81671 München.

　　also: Tribol GmbH, Postfach 50 02 10, D-41172 Mönchengladbach.

Bush Boake Allen Holdings (UK) Ltd: Bush Boake Allen Deutschland GmbH, Burholz 17, D-52372 Krefeld.

British Vita Plc: Metzeler Schaum GmbH, Postfach 16 53, D-87686 Memmingen.

W. Canning Materials Ltd: W. Canning GmbH, Mündelheimer Weg 55a, D-40472 Düsseldorf.

Carbo Plc; Carborundum, Schleifmittelwerke GmbH, Kappeler Strasse 105, D-40597 Düsseldorf.

Castrol Ltd: Deutsche Veedol GmbH, Esplanade 39, D-20354 Hamburg.

Cookson Group Plc: Otawi Minen AG, Mergenthaler Allee 19-21, D-65670 Eschborn.

Courtaulds Coatings (Holdings) Ltd: Courtaulds Coatings GmbH, Postfach 80 04 49, D-21004 Hamburg.

　　also International Farbenwerke GmbH, Lauenberger Landstrasse 11, D-21039 Börnsen.

Courtaulds Plc: Courtaulds GmbH, Schiessstr. 64, D-40549 Düsseldorf.

Croda International Plc: Croda GmbH, Herenpfad Süd 33, D-41334 Nettetal.

　　also Croda Kosmetik Deutschland GmbH, Postfach 11 40, D-6311 Dietzenbach.

Darian Trading Ltd: Südufer 30, D-59519 Möhnesee.

James Durrans & Sons Ltd: James Durrans GmbH, Wilhelm-Hörmes-Str. 48, D-47877 Willich.

Ethyl-Petroleum Additives Ltd: Ethyl Mineralöl-Additive GmbH, Oberstrasse 14b, D-20144 Hamburg.

Ethyone- OMI Holdings (UK) Ltd: LPW-Chemie GmbH, Heerdterbuschstrasse 1-3, D-41460 Neuss.

Fisons Plc: Fisons Deutschland GmbH, Horbeller Strasse 15, D-50858 Köln.

Glaxo Holdings Plc: Glaxo Wellcome GmbH & Co, Alsterufer 1, D-20354 Hamburg.

Glaxo Wellcome Plc: Cascan GmbH & Co KG, Hohenstaufenstr. 7, D-65189 Wiesbaden.

Goodwin Plc: Goodwin GmbH, Aderstrasse 24, D-40215 Düsseldorf.

Grampian Holdings Plc: Meca Tierarzneimittel und Wirkstoffe GmbH & Co KG, Boschstrasse 27, D-47574 Goch.

Hepworth Minerals & Chemicals Ltd: Benzstrasse 12, D-46395 Bocholt.

Holt Lloyd International Plc: Holt Lloyd GmbH, Ringofenstrasse 3, D-53424 Remagen.

Imperial Chemical Industries Plc: Deutsche ICI GmbH, Emil-von-Behring-Strasse 2, D-60439 Frankfurt am Main.

   also: ICI Acrylics GmbH, Industriegebiet 'Heiterer Blick', D-04808 Nischwitz.

   also: ICI Wilhelmshaven GmbH, Inhausersieler Strasse 25, D-26388 Wilhelmshaven.

ICI Paints: ICI Lacke Farben GmbH, Düsseldorfer Strasse 102, D-40721 Hilden.

Ilford Ltd: Ilford Photo GmbH, Postfach 10 11 68, D-63265 Dreieich.

Industrial Acoustics Company Ltd: Sohlweg 17, D-41372 Niederkrüchten.

Jeyes Group Plc: Jeyes Deutschalnd GmbH, Anna-von-Phillip-Strasse B 33, D-86633 Neuberg.

Johnson Matthey Investments Ltd: Johnson Matthey GmbH, Otto-Volger-Strasse 9b, D-65843 Sulzbach.

Kelco International Ltd: Kelco International GmbH, Neuer Wall 63, D-20354 Hamburg.

KS Paul Products Ltd: KS Paul GmbH, Spezialschmierstoffe, Ronsdorfer Strasse 53, D-40233 Dsseldorf.

Laird Group Plc: Draftex GmbH & Co KG, Am Schluff 18-20, D-41748 Viersen.

Lancaster Synthesis Ltd: Lancaster Synthesis GmbH, Lämmerspeiler Str. 100a, D-63165 Mühlheim.

Laporte Industries Ltd: Deutsche HeyDi Chemische Baustoffe GmbH, Pollerstrasse 161-169, D-26639 Wiesmoor.

Laporte Plc: Peroxid-Chemie GmbH, Dr Gustav-Adolph-Strasse 3, D-82049 Pullach.

Linpac Materials Handling: Bahnhofstrasse, D-53533 Antweiler.

Linpac Plastics International Ltd: Linpac Plastics GmbH & Co KG, Deltastrasse, D-27721 Ritterhude.

Marley Plc: Marley European Holdings GmbH, Eichride, D-31515 Wunstorf.

Mast Laboratories Ltd: 'Mast Diagnostica' Laboratoriumspräparate GmbH, Feldstrasse 20, D-23854 Reinfeld.

McKechnie Plc: Homelux GmbH, Heim und Badausstattung, Landwehr 25, D-46325 Borken.

Melton Medes Ltd: Bolta Werke GmbH, Industriestrasse 22, D-91227 Leinburg-Diepersdorf.

   also: Bolta Industrie und Bauprofile GmbH, Postfach 40, D-94509 Schönberg.

Pharmacia Upjohn Inc: Pharmacia GmbH, Munzinger Strasse 9, D-79111 Freiburg.

PowerGen Plc: Mitteldeutsche Braunkohlengesellschaft mbH (MIBRAG), Wiesenstrasse 20, D-06727 Theissen.

Reckitt & Colman Plc: Dr Günter Becher, Fabrik für Chemische Spezial-Erzeugnisse GmbH, Vor Den Sprecken 3, D-30926 Seelze.

Reynolds Medical Ltd: Reynolds Medizinische Elektronik GmbH, Schwabache Strasse 34, D-90537 Feucht.

Rocol Ltd: Rocol GmbH, Ungelsheimer Weg 7, D-40472 Düsseldorf.

SCM Chemicals Ltd: c/o Zweigniederlassung Haan, Neuer Markt 1, D-42781 Haan.

Sericol Ltd: SERICOL (Deutschland) GmbH, Leimkugelstrasse 1, D-45141 Essen.

Shell International Petroleum Co Ltd: Deutsche Shell AG, Überseering 35, D-22297 Hamburg.

The Shell Petroleum Co: BEB Erdgas and Erdöl GmbH, Riethorst 12, D-30659 Hannover.

David S. Smith (Holdings) Plc: David S. Smith Liquid-Packaging GmbH, Willi-Bleicher-Strasse 9, D-52353 Düren.

Smith & Nephew Plc: Smith & Nephew GmbH, Medical Division, Max-Planck-Strasse 1-3, D-34253 Lohfelden.

Smiths Industries Aerospace & Defence Systems Ltd: Medic-Eschmann Handelsgesellschaft für Medizinische Instrumente mbH, Schnackenburgallee 116, D-22525 Hamburg.

SmithKline Beecham Plc: Sächsisches Serumwerk Dresden, Zirkusstrasse 40, D-01257 Dresden.

also Lingner-Fissan Produktion GmbH, Am Trippelsberg 100, D-40589 Düsseldorf.

Stamford Group Ltd: OPTO System GmbH, Christian-Schäfer-Strasse 26, D-53881 Euskirchen.

Sterling-Winthrop Group Ltd: Winthrop GmbH, Augustenstrasse 10, D-80333 München.

The Steetley Company Plc: Bentone-Chemie GmbH, Peschstrasse 5, D-51373 Leverkeusen.

Thor Chemical Holdings Ltd: Thor Chemie GmbH, Landwehrstrasse 1, D-67346 Speyer.

Unichem Plc: PAG Pharma-Holding AG, Platz der Republik, D-60325 Frankfurt am Main.

Unicorn Abrasives Ltd: Unicorn Abrasives (Deutschland) GmbH & Co KG, Postfach 13 80, D-22941 Bargteheide.

Unilever Plc: Elida Gibbs GmbH, Hamburger Strasse 23, D-22083 Hamburg.

also: Quest International (Deutschland) GmbH, Bonner Ring 43, D-50374 Erfstadt-Lechenich.

Urenco Ltd: Urenco Deutschland GmbH, Postfach 14 11, D-52409 Jülich.

Vitalograph Ltd: Vitalograph Medical Instruments GmbH, Jacobsenweg 12, D-22525 Hamburg.

Watts, Blake, Bearne & Co Plc: Fuchs'sche Tongruben GmbH & Co KG, Postfach 347, D-56223 Ransbach-Baumbach.

also: Kaolin und Tonwerke Seitlitz-Löthain GmbH, Mehren 11, D-01655 Mehren.

also: WBB Mineral Trading GmbH & Co KG, Postfach 347, D-56235 Ransbach-Baumbach.

Wellington Holding Plc: Dichtelemente Hallite GmbH, Billwerder Ring 17, D-21035 Hamburg.

Williams Holdings Plc: MOLTO GmbH, Postfach 11 20, D-35790 Löhnberg.

Rudolf Wolff & Co Ltd: Rudolf Wolff & Co GmbH, Dornbusch 4, D-20095 Hamburg.

Yorkshire Chemicals Plc: Yorkshire Farben GmbH, Mevissenstrasse 72, D-47803 Krefeld.

Yule Catto & Co Plc: Synthomer Chemie GmbH, Reuterweg 51-53, D-60323 Frankfurt am Main.

Zeneca Plc: Zeneca GmbH, Otto-Hahn-Strasse, D-68723 Plankstadt.

Electrical & Precision Engineering:

ABB Kent Plc: ABB Kent GmbH, Otto-Hahn-Strasse 25, D-68623 Lampertheim.

also: ABB Kent Messtechnik GmbH, Otto-Han-Strasse 25, D-68623 Lampertheim.

Adam & Harvey Group Plc: Anglo Saxon Maschinen, Maschinen Vertrieb GmbH, Ziegelstrasse1, D-01844 Langburkersdorf.

Adaptaflex Ltd: Adaptaflex GmbH, Irrgartenstrasse 17, D-66538 Neunkirchen.

Advance Power Ltd: Advance Power Electronic GmbH, Dieselstrasse 21, D-63533 Mainhausen-Mainflingen.

Alba Plc: Hinari Consumer Electronics GmbH, Kaiserwerther Strasse 85, D-40882 Ratingen.

APV Corporation Ltd: APV Rose Foregrove GmbH, Herstellungs und Verpack-sungsanlagen, Herder-Strasse 85, D-40721 Hilden.

APV Plc: APV Homogeniser GmbH, Postfach 16 01 64, D-23519 Lübeck.
  also: APV Rosista GmbH, Zechenstrasse 49, D-59425 Unna-Königsborn.

Asea Brown Bovari Ltd: Aqua Messtechnik GmbH, Pahlkestrasse 46d, D-42115 Wuppertal.

Automated Security (Holdings) Plc: Sensormartic GmbH, Am Schimmersfeld 7, D-40880 Ratingen.

BBA Group Plc: Textar GmbH, Jägerstrasse 1-25, D-51375 Leverkusen.

BICC Cables Ltd: BICC KWO Kabel GmbH, Wilhelminenhofstrasse 76-77, D-12459 Berlin.

Bodycote International Plc: Eurobrass GmbH, Holzener Strasse 39, D-58708 Menden.
  also Mahler Dienstleistungs-GmbH, Fritz-Müller-Strasse 95, D-73730 Esslingen.
  also Schmetz GmbH, Holzener Strasse 39, D-58708 Menden.

EJ Bowman Ltd: Apparatetechnik Harald Schoenstein GmbH, Ingenieurbüro Cranachstrasse 49, D-22607 Hamburg.

Bowthorpe Plc: Hellermann Engineering GmbH, Postfach, D-25405 Pinneberg.
  also Wago-Kontakttechnik GmbH, Hansasstrasse 27, D-32423 Minden.

BPB Industries Plc: BPB Instruments Ltd und Co GmbH, Oberbecker Strasse 13, D-44329 Dortmund.

Brite Voice Systems Ltd: Brite Voice Systems Group GmbH, Bleichstrasse 1-3, D-65183 Wiesbaden.

David Brown Holdings Ltd: David Brown Radicon Antriebstechnik GmbH, Postfach 10 09 64, D-34009 Kassel.

David Brown Hydraulics Ltd: David Brown Hydraulics Deutschland GmbH, Christinenstrasse 4, D-40880 Ratingen.

B.S.G. International Plc: Britax Autozubehör GmbH, Blaubeurer Strasse 71, D-89077 Ulm.

BTR Industries Ltd: Hawker Batterien GmbH, Kurt-Fischer-Str. 23g, D-22926 Ahrensburg.

BTR Plc: Argus GmbH, Rudolph Plank Strasse 2, D-54568 Gerolstein.
  also: Deutsche Audco GmbH, Peiner Hag, D-25497 Prisdorf.

Bundy Europe: Technoflow Tube Systems GmbH, Industriestrasse 3, D-34277 Fuldabrück.

Bunzl Plc: 'Filtrona' Filter gmbH, Gutenbergstrasse 5-9, D-21465 Reinbek.

Burgess Micro Switch Company Ltd: Burgess GmbH, Am Kreyenhof 10-12, D-26127 Oldenburg.

Caradon Plc: Caradon Esser GmbH, Dieselstrasse 2, D-41469 Neuss.

Caradon Friedland Ltd: Caradon Friedland GmbH, Kirschbaumweg 20a, D-50996 Köln.

Chloride Group Plc: Chloride Power Electronics GmbH, Talhofstrasse 30, D-82205 Gilching.

Chronos Richardson Ltd: Chronos Richardson GmbH, Reuther Strasse 3, D-53773 Hennef.

Cimex International Ltd: Cimex GmbH, Mündelheimer Weg 54, D-40472 Düsseldorf.

Cobble Blackburn Ltd: Cobble Deutschland GmbH i.L., Windscheidstrasse 19, D-40239 Düsseldorf.

Coin Controls Ltd: Coin Controls GmbH, Friedensallee 35, D-22765 Hamburg.

Colt International Ltd: c/o Briener Strasse 186, D-47533 Kleve.

Control Techniques Plc: Dr Henschen GmbH & Co KG, Mahdentalstrasse 44, D-71065 Sindelfingen.

Cooper Roller Bearings Co Ltd: Copper Geteilte Rollenlager GmbH, Oberbenrader Strasse 407, D-47804 Krefeld.

John Crane (UK) Ltd: John Crane GmbhH, Werner-von-Siemens-Strasse 6, D-36041 Fulda.

Cristie Electronics Ltd: Cristie Electronics GmbH, Riemekestrasse 160, D-33106 Paderborn.

Crompton Instruments Ltd: Crompton Meissinstrumente GmbH, Harkort Strasse 35, D-40880 Ratingen.

Datapoint International Ltd: Datapoint Deutschland GmbH, Martin-Behaim-Strasse 12, D-63263 Neu-Isenburg.

Delta Circuit Protection & Controls Ltd: Schoeller & Co Elektrotechnische Fabrik GmbH & Co, Mörfelder Landstrasse 115-119, D-60598 Frankfurt am Main.

DEK Printing Machines Ltd: DEK Printing Machines GmbH, Im Rosengarten 25c, D-61118 Bad Vilbel.

De La Rue Plc: De La Rue Garny GmbH, Hellersdorf Weg 33, D-12689 Berlin.

Delta Circuit Protection & Controls Ltd: DELTA MEM Elektrotechniksvertiebs GmbH, Mörfelder Landstrasse 115-119, D-60598 Frankfurt am Main.

Dexion Group Plc: Dexion Holding GmbH, Dexionstrasse 1-5, D-35321 Laubach.

Domino Printing Sciences Plc: Chromos Maschinen Bereich DOMINO, Ober der Roeth 4, D-65824 Schwalbach.

EA Technology Ltd: EA Technology, Hildesheimer Strasse 53, D-30169 Hannover.

EIMCO GB: EIMCO Zweigniederlassung der Baker Hughes (Deutschland) GmbH, Gothaer Strasse 4, D-40880 Ratingen.

Electrosonic Ltd: Electrosonic GmbH, Hans-Böckler-Strasse 60, D-40764 Langenfeld.

Erskine House Group Plc: Copytex Kopier und Bürosysteme GmbH, Siemensstrasse 46, D-04229 Leipzig.

   also S.KOP Kopier und Bürosysteme GmbH, Zimmermannstrasse 11/13, D-30453 Hannover.

Eurotherm Drives Ltd: Eurotherm Antriebstechnik GmbH, Birkenweg 8, D-64665 Alsbach-Hähnlein.

Eurotherm Plc: Eurotherm Messdatentechnik GmbH, Im Wiegenfeld 4, D-85570 Markt Schwaben.

   also: Eurotherm Regler GmbH, Postfach 14 53, D-65534 Limburg an der Lahn.

Farnell Electronics Plc: Advanced Electronics GmbH, Ges. für Mikroelektronik, Stefan-George-Ring 19, D-81929 München.

Farnell Premier Plc: Farnell Electronic Components GmbH, Grünwalderweg 30, D-82041, Deisenhofen.

Fenner Plc: Fenner GmbH, Ritzbruch39, D-41334 Nettetal.

Ferranti International Ltd: Ferranti GmbH, Peter-Sander-Strasse 41, D-55252 Mainz.

Fort Fibre Optics Research & Technology Ltd: Fort GmbH Fiber Optik Research & Technology, Postfach 12 49, D-21249 Tostedt.

Forward Technology Industries Plc: KLN Ultraschall GmbH, Siegfriedstrasse 124, D-64646 Heppenheim.

RJ Fullwood & Bland Ltd: Lemmer-Fullwood GmbH, Oberste Höhe, D-53797 Lohmar.

GEC Alsthom Ltd: GEC Alsthom T & D GmbH, Köpenicker Chaussee 15, D-10317 Berlin.

   also Kesselbau EVT-Neumark GmbH, Am Bahnhof 11, D-08496 Neumark/ Sachsen.

General Electric Company: Walther & Cie, Waltherstrasse 51, D-51069 Köln.

Geoquip Ltd: Vodecke Strasse 21, D-58642 Iserlohn.

Gestetner Group Holdings Plc: NRG Office System GmbH, Postfach 21 47, D-30021 Hannover.

GKN Plc: GKN Automotive International GmbH, Hauptstrasse 150, D-53797 Lohmar.

   also GKN Gelelnkwellenwerk Mosel GmbH, Glaucher Strasse 38, D-08129 Mosel.

   also GKN Walterscheid Presswerk GmbH, Hafenstrasse, D-54293 Trier.

   also Löhr & Bromkamp GmbH, Carl-Liegen-Strasse 10, D-63073 Offenbach.

   also Mabeg Gesellschaft für Abfallwirtschaft und Entwicklungstechnik mbH, Am Fischkai 23, D-27572 Bremerhaven.

   also Westland-SITEC GmbH, Schopfgraben 1, D-83714 Miesbach,

   also Emitec Gesellschaft für Emissionstechnologie mbH, Hauptstrasse 150, D-53797 Lohmar.

The Glacier Metal Co Ltd: Glacier GmbH, Schulstrasse 20, D-35260 Stadtallendorf.

Goldman Sachs International Ltd: Empe Holding GmbH, Dieselweg 10, D-82538 Geretsried.

Granada Group Plc: Granada Computer Sevices GmbH, Pallaswiesenstrasse 174-182, D-64293 Darmstadt.

GTS Flexible Materials Ltd: GTS Flexible Verbundwerkstoffe Vetriebs GmbH, Hagener Strasse 113, D-57072 Siegen.

Hadland Photonics Ltd: Hadland Photonics GmbH, Postfach 12 60, D-50329 Hürth.

Hale Hamilton (Valves) Ltd: Vorburgstrasse 11, D-22946 Trittau.

Adam Hall Supplies Ltd: Adam Hall GmbH, Siemensstrasse 20, D-61267 Neu Anspach.

Hanson Plc: Krupp Mobikrane GmbH, Industriestrasse, D-26389 Wilhelshaven.

Herga Electric Ltd: Herga Schaltsysteme Vetriebs GmbH, Rohrbergstrasse 23, D-65343 Eltville.

Holstet Engineering Co Ltd: Holstet Engineering Co Ltd Technisches Informationsbüro, Oldenwaldstrasse 23, D-64521 Gross-Gerau.

   also Holstet Kompressorenbau, Windbergstrasse 45, D-01728 Bannewitz.

Howden Group Plc: Howden Deutschland GmbH, Kölner Strasse 71-78, D-41812 Erkelenz.

   also Wirth Maschinen und Bohrgeräte Fabrik GmbH, Kölner Strasse 71-78, D-41812 Erkelenz.

Dominick Hunter Ltd: Kimplerstrasse 282, D047807 Krefeld.

Dominick Hunter Group Plc: Zander Aufbereitungstechnik GmbH, Im Teelbruch 118, D-45219 Essen.

IMI Plc: Theodor Heimeier Metallwerk KG, Völlinghauser Weg, D-59597 Erwitte.

also IMI Cornelius Deutschland GmbH, Carl-Leverkeus-Strasse 15, D-40764 Langenfeld.

IMI Yorkshire Fittings Ltd: R Woeste & Co 'Yorkshire' GmbH, Suitbertusstrasse 123, D-40223 Düsseldorf.

Imperial Machine Company (Peelers) Ltd: IMC Maschinen Vertiebsgesellschaft mbH, Grossfeld 4, D-42929 Wermelskirchen.

Inchape Plc: Autohaus Fernstrasse GmbH, Fernstrasse, D-66538 Neunkirchen.

also: Autohaus Feyock Pirmasens GmbH, Zweibrücker Strasse 173, D-66954 Pirmasens.

also Inchape Automobile GmbH, Nortkirchenstrasse 111, D-44263 Dortmund.

also Schmoldt & Axmann Fahrzeug GmbH, Holzkappelweg 1, D-24118 Kiel.

International Automotive Design Plc/Mayflower Vehicle Systems Plc: IAD Deutschland GmbH, Hans-Sachs-Strasse 35, D-65428 Rüsselsheim.

Jaguar Cars Ltd: Jaguar Deutschland GmbH, Frankfurter Strasse, D-61476 Kronberg.

Krone (UK) Technique Ltd: Krone Aktiengesellschaft, Beeskowdamm 3-11, D-14167 Berlin.

Lucas Automotive Ltd: Lucas Kfz-Ausrüstung GmbH, Rudolf-Diesel-Strasse 7, D-56566 Neuweid.

Lucas Industries Plc: Lucas Automotive GmbH, Carl-Spaeter-Strasse 8, D-56070 Koblenz.

M4 Data Ltd: M4 Data GmbH, Ludwig-Wagner-Strasse 41a, D-69168 Wiesloch.

Marconi Instruments Ltd: Marconi Messtechnik GmbH, Landsberger Strasse 65, D-82110 Germering.

Matra-Marconi Space UK: Intospace GmbH, Sophienstrasse 6, D-30159 Hannover.

Meggit Plc: Bestobell Mobrey GmbH, Nürnberger Strasse 22/24, D-40599 Düsseldorf.

Microlights Ltd: Microlights GmbH, Auf dem Hüls 1, D-40822 Mettman.

Microvitec Plc: Microvitec (Deutschland) GmbH, Heinrich-Hertz-Strasse 4, D-40699 Erkrath.

ML Holdings Plc: Schopf Maschinenbau GmbH, Parkstrasse 21, D-73760 Ostfinden.

The Morgan Crucible Company Plc: Morgan GmbH, Ringofenstrasse 3, D-53424 Remagen.

Morse Controls Ltd: Teleflex Gesellschaft mit beschränkter Haftung, Hüsselerstrasse 40, D-42579 Heiligenhaus.

Multitone Electronics Plc: Multiton Elektronik GmbH, Rossstrasse 11, D-40476 Düsseldorf.

Neotronics Ltd: Bahnhofstrasse 43, D-40764 Langenfeld.

Newage International Ltd: Newage engineers GmbH, Rotenbrückweg 14, D-22113 Hamburg.

Norgren Martonair Ltd: Norgren Martonair GmbH, Bruckstrasse 93, D-46519 Alpen.

Nowitext Europe: Nowitext Europe ServiceLtd, Betriebsstätte, Schne Aussicht 20, D-65527 Niedernhausen.

The Oxford Instruments Group Plc: Oxford Instruments GmbH, Kreuzberger Ring 38, D-65205 Wiesbaden.

P & S Filtration Ltd: Zur Finkenkuhle 42, D-38259 Salzgitter.

*PCS Portable Cold Storage Ltd:*Thermobil Mobile Kühlager GmbH, Jacobistrasse 18, D-40211 Düsseldorf.

Perkins Engines Ltd: Perkins Motoren GmbH, Postfach 1180, D-63797 Kleinhostheim.

Photo-Me International Plc: Fotofix-Schnellphotoautomaten GmbH, Viersenerstrasse 47, D-47805 Krefeld.

Plessey Semiconductors Ltd: Plessey GmbH, Ungerer Strasse 129, D-80805 München.

Prab Robots International Ltd: Zweigniederlassung Deutschland, Schreberstrasse 28, D-63069 Offenbach.

Prudential Nominees Ltd: VEMAG Maschinen und Anlagenbau GmbH, Weserstrasse 32, D-27283 Verden.

Psion Plc: Psion GmbH, Saalburgstrasse 157, D-63150 Bad Homburg-Dornolzhausen.

Pulsafe Safety Products Ltd: OPMA Arbeitsschutz GmbH, Fabrikweg 3, D-91448 Emskirchen.

Pyrotek Engineering Materials Ltd: Im Taubental 9, D-41468 Neuss.

Raab Karcher (UK) Plc: Metronik GmbH, Leonhardsweg 2, D-82008 Unterhaching.

Racal Electronics Plc: Racal Elektronik System GmbH, Frankenforster Strasse 211, D-51427 Bergisch Gladbach.

Racal Health & Safety Ltd: Racal Arbeitssichererheit GmbH, Waldstrasse76a, D-63128 Dietzenbach.

Rack Engineering Ltd: Postfach 67, D-26387 Osthauderfehn.

Radiodetection Ltd: Radidetection GmbH, Reeser Strasse 83, D-46446 Emmerich.

Rank Xerox Ltd: Rank Xerox GmbH, Emanuel-Leutze-Strasse 20, D-40547 Düsseldorf.

Ransomes Plc: Ransomes GmbH, Borkstrasse 4, D-48163 Münster.

Redland Plc: Braas GmbH, Frankfurter Landstrasse 2-4, D-61440 Oberursel.

Renold Plc: Arnold & Stolzenberg GmbH, Antriebstechnik, Postfach 1635, D-37557 Einbeck.

Reometric Scientific: Schwanheimer Strasse 144a, D-64625 Bensheim.

Robert Hudson Raletrux (Midlands) Ltd: Becker-Prünte GmbH, August-Becker-Strasse 10, D-45711 Datteln.

The Roditi International Corporation Ltd: Bergdorfer Strasse 142, D-21029 Hamburg.

Rolls-Royce Plc: BMW-Rolls-Royce GmbH, Hohemakstrasse 60-70, D-61440 Oberursel.

Rotork Plc: Rotork Controls (Deutschland) GmbH, Niedenstrasse 111, D-40721 Hilden.

Rover Group Ltd: Rover Deutschland GmbH, Forumstrasse 22, D-41468 Neuss.

Royal Ordnance Plc: Heckler & Koch Maschinen und Anlagenbau GmbH, Seedorfer Strasse 91, D-78713 Schramberg (Waldmössingen).

Senior Engineering Group Plc: Polenz GmbH, Langenharmer Weg 219, D-22844 Norderstedt.

   also Senior Flexonics GmbH, Nordring 17, D-25474 Bönningstedt.

Siebe Plc: EBERLE Controls GmbH, Oedenberger Strasse 55-65, D-90491 Nürnberg.

   also GESTRA AG, Hemmstrasse 130, D-28215 Bremen.

   also CompAir Mahle GmbH, Schaflandstrasse 10/1, D-70736 Fellbach.

   also Deutsche Tecalemit GmbH, Am Metallwerk 11, D-33659 Bielefeld.

Silvermines Group Plc: ISC Computerautomation GmbH, Guericke Weg 7, D-64291 Darmstadt-Ahreiligen.

Spirax Sarco Engineering Ltd: Spirax Sarco GmbH, Postfach 10 20 42, D-78420 Konstanz.

Spirax Sarco Ltd: Hygromatik Luftechnischer Apparatebau GmbH, Oststrasse 55, D-22844 Norderstedt.

Strand Lighting Ltd: Salzbergstrasse 2, D-38302 Wolfenbüttel.

Streamline Holdings Ltd: Wolff GmbH, Dieselstrase 19, D-71665 Vaihingen/Enz.

Telemetrix Plc: Trend Communications GmbH, Joseph-Dollinger-Bogen 18, D-80807 München.

TI Group Plc: Bundy GmbH, Dischingerstrasse 11, D-69123 Heidelberg.
    also: Dowty Seals GmbH, Cappeler Strasse 147, D-59368 Werne.

The Tintometer Plc: Tintometer GmbH, Schleefstrasse 8a, D-44287 Dortmund.

TLG Plc: Thorn Licht GmbH, Möhnestrasse 55, D-59755 Arnsberg.

T & N Plc; AE Motorenteile GmbH, Frankfurter Strasse 10, D-71732 Tamm.
    also: AE Goetze GmbH, Bürgermeister-Schmidt-Strasse 17, D-51399 Burscheid.
    also: Ferodo Beral GmbH, Klosterstrasse 16, D-51709 Marienheide.
    also T &N Holdings GmbH, Bürgemeister-Schmidt-Strasse 17, D-51399 Burscheid.
    also Weyburn-Bartel GmbH, Adlerstrasse 53-67, D-25462 Rellingen.

TT Group Plc: AB Elektronik GmbH, Klöcknerstrasse 4, D-59368 Werne.

Tunstall Group Plc: Tunstall ComSystem GmbH, Orkotten 66, D-48291 Telgte.

Unbrako: Unbrako Schrauben GmbH, Ernst-Sachs-Str. 11, D-56070 Koblenz.

Utell International Ltd: Noredstrasse 2, D-40477 Düsseldorf.

Vaccumatic Pelcombe Ltd: Vauumatic Maschinen GmbH, Kaiserring 6-8, D-46483 Wesel.

Vax Appliances Ltd: Vax Elektro-Geräte GmbH, Kränkelsweg 2, D-41478 Viersen.

Vero Electronics Ltd: Carsten-Dressler-Strasse 10, D-28279 Bremen.

Vickers Plc: Vickers Systems GmbH, Frölingstrasse 41, D-61348 Bad Homburg.

Vision Engineering Ltd: Centraleurope, Anton-Pendele-Str. 3, D-82275 Emmering.

Vitec Group Plc: Vinten GmbH, An der Fahrt 8, D-55124 Mainz.

Wagon Industrial Holdings Plc: Forkardt GmbH, Heinrich-Hertz-Strasse 7, D-40699 Erkrath.

Whitecroft Lighting Divison: Whitecroft Beleuchtung GmbH, Niederlassung Brand-Erbisdorf Industriegebeit Nord, D-09618 Brand-Erbisdorf.

Willet International Ltd: Willet GmbH, Kleberstrasse 11, D-40822 Mettman.

Williams Holdings Plc: Kidde-Deugra Brandschutzsysteme GmbH, Halskestrasse 30, D-40880 Ratingen.

F G Wilson Engineering Ltd: F G Wilson Engineering Vetriebs-GmbH, Mombach-strasse 84, D-34127 Kassel.

Woods of Colchester Ltd: Woods Ventilatoren GmbH, Siemensstrasse 16, D-40885 Ratingen.

Zetex Plc: Zetex Neuhaus GmbH, Thomas-Mann-Strasse 2, D-98724 Neuhaus am Rennweg.

Foundries and Toolmakers:

Avdel Plc: Avdel Verbindungselemente GmbH, Klusreide 24, D-308351 Langenhagen.

Avesta Sheffield Ltd: Hans-Böckler-Strasse 36, D-47877 Willich.

BICC Plc: Aluminium Oxid Stade GmbH, Bütziflerther Sand, D-21683 Stade.
    also BICC Bran-Rex GmbH, Im Taubental 58, D-41468 Neuss.

Bridon Plc: Rhein-Ruhr-Fabrikations Und Handelsgesellschaft mbH, Rethel-strasse 147, D-40237 Düsseldorf.

also Schalkeseil GmbH, Kurt-Schumacher-Str. 100, D-45881 Gelsenkirchen.

British Steel Plc: British Steel Deutschland GmbH, Postfach 32 01 67, D-40416 Düsseldorf.

also British Steel, Walter Blume Handels GmbH, Postfach 10 06 42, D-70005 Stuttgart.

Bromsgrove Industries Plc: Mestra GmbH Metall und Stranggushandel, Postfach 31 02 21, D-57045 Siegen.

James Burn Bindings Ltd: James Burn International GmbH, Försterweg 65, D-22525 Hamburg.

Chubb Security Plc: Chubb Sicherheitstechnik GmbH, Augustinusstrasse 37, D-50226 Frechen.

J & P Coats Ltd: Dynacast Deutschland GmbH, Postfach 12 63, D-78196 Bräunlingen.

DSRM Group Plc: DSRM International Stahlhandel GmbH, Postfach 13 03, D-40638 Meersbusch.

Dzus Fastener Europe Ltd: Dzus Fastener GmbH, Paul-Ehrlich-Str. 16-20, D-63322 Rödermark.

Ellison Holding plc: Niederlassung Deutschland, Postfach 13 02 63, D-47754 Krefeld.

Fastbolt (UK) Ltd: Fastbolt Schraubengrosshansdels GmbH, Am Königsweg 4, D-48599 Gronau.

Ferraris Group Plc: Jenaer Gewindetechnik GmbH, Göschwitzer Strasse 39, D-07745 Jena.

Glynwed Metal Sevices Ltd: Jera Metall Nürnberg ZN der Amari GmbH, Hahenbalz 35, D-90411 Nürnberg.

also LCK Metall Castens & Krohn Zweigniederlassung der Glynwed Metall GmbH, Lise-Meitner-Strasse 2-4, D-24558 Henstedt-Ulzburg.

Inco Alloys Ltd: Inco Alloys International Ltd, Postfach 20 04 09, D-40102 Düsseldorf.

Kee Klamps Ltd: Voltenseestr 22, D-60385 Frankfurt amMain.

N V Tools Ltd: Wittener Strasse 162, D-42279 Wuppertal.

Primary Industries Trading Ltd: Königsallee 1, D-40212 Düsseldorf.

RMC Group Plc: Aluminium Oxid Stade GmbH, Bütziflerther Sand, D-21683 Stade.

Rubicon Group Plc: Röhr + Stohlberg GmbH, Bruchfeld 52, D-47809 Krefeld.

The Rugby Group Plc: Atlas Hallen, Atlas Bausysteme GmbH, Am Schornacker 2, D-46485 Wesel.

Sheffield Forgemasters Ltd: Euro SFM Edelsthl GmbH, Schumannstrasse 55, D-40237 Düsseldorf.

Siebe Plc: Deutsche CompAir GmbH, Edsel-Ford-Strasse 21, D-50769 Köln.

also Industrie-Schutz-Produkte GmbH, Bessemerstr. 12, D-212339 Lüneburg.

also Rieth 7 Co GmbH, Stuttgarter strasse 128, d-73230 Kirchheim-Ötlingen.

T & N Plc: Flexitalic GmbH, Dichtungsfabrik Industriestrasse 8-10, D-51399 Burscheid.

Titman Tip Tools Ltd: Titman Tools GmbH, Münsterstr. 52a, d-48167 Münster.

Welding Alloys Ltd: WA Schweisslegierungs GmbH, Ostring 52, D-47669 Wachtendonk.

Wilsons Plc: Hamburger Rohrbogenwerk GmbH, Brückenstrasse 2, D-22926 Ahrensburg.

Manufactured Goods

Alexon Group Plc: Elangol Freizeitkleidung Vetriebs GmbH, Rosstrasse 130, D-40476 Düsseldorf. (Clothing)

Allied Textiles Companies Plc: Hugh Mackay & Co GmbH, Flotowstrasse 41-43, D-22083 Hamburg.

Laura Ashley Holdings Plc: Laura Ashley GmbH, Hunsrückenstrasse 43, D-40213 Düsseldorf. (Clothing)

J Barbour & Sons Ltd: Barbour (Europe) Ltd, Niederlassung Deutschland, Kränkelsweg 12, D-41748 Viersen.

Berghaus Ltd: Berghaus Sportartikel Vetriebs-GmbH, Conradtystrasse 2, D-83059 Kolbermoor. (Clothing)

BPB Industries Plc: Rigips GmbH, Rühler Strasse, d-37619 Bodenwerder.

Burberrys Ltd: Burberrys (Deutschland) GmbH, Perusastrasse 1, D-80333 München. (Clothing)

Caldwell Plc: Nissel Textilien GmbH, Mathias-Brüggen-Str. 18, D-50827 Köln. (Textiles)

Campari International Plc: 'Campri' Sport-Handels-GmbH, Dieselstrasse 22, D-85748 Garching. (Clothing)

Camtex Fabrics Ltd: Avitex Armand Vissers, Postfach 30 02 06, D-63089 Rodgau. (Textiles)

C & J Clark Ltd: Clarks Shoes Vetriebs GmbH, Friedrich-Ebert-Str. 8, D-55411 Bingen. (Footwear)

Coates Viyella Plc: Coats Opti GmbH, 1. Südwieke 180, D-26817 Rhauderfehn.
   also Schachenmayr Mann & Cie GmbH, Postfach 1254, D-73081 Salach.

Coutaulds Clothing Brands Ltd: Coutaulds Textile Holding GmbH, Bahnhofstrasse 32, D-72406 Bisingen.(Clothing)

Courtaulds Textiles Investments Ltd: Penn Elastic GmbH, An der talle 20, D-33102 Paderborn. (Textiles)

Crowson Fabrics Ltd: Oliver Heal Textil GmbH, Postfach 10 22 28, D-70018 Stuttgart. (Textiles)

Daks Simpson Ltd: Elite Fashion-Vetriebs GmBh, Generalvertretung Daks, Maximilianstrasse 34, D-80539 München. (Clothing)

Dawson International Plc: Pringle of Scotland Strickwarenhandelsgesellschaft mbH, Königsallee 30, D-40212 Düsseldorf.

Alfred Dunhill Ltd: Hellgrundweg 100, D-22525 Hamburg.

Gillette UK Ltd: Gillette Deutschland GmbH & Co, Oberlandstrasse 75-84, D-14052 Berlin.

Hadrian Internatioanl Ltd: Hadrian Crystalglass GmbH, Rheinstrasse 187a, D56235 Ransbach-Baumbach.

High & Mighty Ltd: High & Mighty Outsize manshops GmbH, Bahnstrasse 40, D-40210 Düsseldorf.

IKON Office Solutions Europe Plc: Julius-Vosseler-Str. 100-102, D-22527 Hamburg.
   also Berner Strasse 34, D-60347 Frankfurt am Main.

McKechnie Plc: Spur-Regal-Systeme SRS GmbH, Landwehr 25, D-46325 Borken.

Mediscus Products Ltd: KCT-Mediscus Produkte GmbH, Lappacherweg 30, D-91315 Höchstadt. (Furniture)

Alain Paine Ltd: Diesseme Bruch 114f, D-47805 Krefeld. (Clothing)

Parker Pen Ltd: Parker Pen GmbH, Postfach 2160, D-76491 Baden-Baden.

Pentland Group Plc: Karl Reusch Handschufabrik GmbH & Co KG, Metzinger Strasse 75, D-72555 Metzingen-Neuhausen.

Pilkington Plc: Flachglass AG, Otto-Seeling-Promenade 10, D-90762 Fürth. (Glassware)
   also Glaszentrum Rhein-Main GmbH, Daimlerstrasse 9, D-63741 Aschaffenburg.
   also Pilkington Deutschland GmbH, Ernestinenstrasse 60, D-45141 Essen. ·
Portakin Ltd: Siemensring 24, D-47877 Willich.
Potters-Ballotini Ltd: Postfach 1226, D-67285 Kirchheimbolanden.
The Readicut International Plc: The Readicut Wool gmbH, Charlottenplatz 6, D-70173 Stuttgart.
RMC Group Plc: Hans Baltus GmbH & Co, Beim Industriehafen 149, D-28237 Bremen. (Ceramics)
   also Mixbeton Berlin GmbH & Co KG, Sophienwerder Weg, D-13597 Berlin.
Speedo (Europe) Ltd: Speedo Deutschland GmbH, Wahlerstrasse 20, D-40472 Düsseldorf. (Sportswear)
Sunlight Textile Services Ltd: Spring Grove Services GmbH, Otto-Hahn-Strasse 4, D-21509 Glinde.
Tie Rack Plc: Tie rack (Deutschland) GmbH, Fliederweg 4, D-65527 Niedernhausen.
Tootal Group Plc: Rhenanaia-Unigarn AG, Schricksweg 2, D-41751 Viersen. (Clothing)
Transport Development Group Plc: Albatross Speditionsges MbH, Max-Planck-Str. 2, D-77694 Kehl-Auenheim. (Ceramics)
Waterford Wedgewood UK Plc: Rosenthal AG, Wittelsbacher Str. 43, D-95100 Selb. (Glassware)
Josiah Wedgewood & Sons Ltd: Wedgewood GmbH, Frankfurter Strasse 63-69, D-65760 Eschborn. (Ceramics)
Whitecroft Plc: DOX International ETS Bogaerts GmbH, Braunstrasse 13, D-63741 Aschaffenburg.

Miscellaneous Firms
Acal Plc: Acal GmbH, Fischeräcker 2, D-74223 Flein.
The Dr Edward Bach Centre: 'Dr Bach' Blüten-Essenzen Handelsgesellschaft mbH, Lippmannstrasse 53, D-22769 Hamburg.
Barrow, Hepburn, Sala Ltd: Barrow Hepburn Sala GmbH, Kalkarer Strasse 81, D-47533 Kleve.
Blenheim Group Plc: Equitana Team Verwaltungs und Beteilgungsgesellschaft mbH, Nuesser Strasse 111, D-40219 Düsseldorf.
Bodycote European Holdings Ltd: Bodycote VTN GmbH, Klingenhfstrasse 14, D-90411 Nürnberg.
Braitrim Plc: Braitrim (Deutschland) GmbH, Lagesche Str. 32, D-32657 Lemgo.
Caradon Plc: Weru AG, Zurnhofer Strasse 25, D-73635 Rudesberg.
Cash Bases GB Ltd: Cash Bases Deutschland GmbH, Werftstrasse 26, D-40549 Düsseldorf.
Chelsfield Plc: CIP Deutschland GmbH, August-Bebel-Str. 26-53, D-14482 Potsdam.
Circle Industries (UK) Plc: Circle Industries Deutschland, Kreuzstrasse 1, D-14552 Saarmund.
CNT-Commision for the New Towns: CNT Frankfurt Office, Kleiner Hirschgraben 10-12, D-60311 Frankfurt am Main.
Cookson Group Plc: Alpha Grillo Lötsysteme GmbH, Busch Strasse 95, D-47166 Duisburg. (Wholesalers)
Coutaulds Plc: Mehnert & Veeck GmbH & Co KG, Lochnerstrasse 12, D-90441 Nürnberg.

Sir Rowland Hill (Stamps) Ltd: Buchorstblick 7a, D-38162 Weddel.
Industrial Development Board for Northern Ireland: Oststrasse 152, D-40210 Düsseldorf.
Link Analytical Ltd: Frangenheimstrasse 9, D-50931 Köln.
Locate in Scotland: Arnulfstrasse 27, D-80335 München.
Maghraby moody International Ltd: MMI-BMIQA GmbH, Postfach 30 01 54, D-41191 Mönchengladbach.
Marks & Spencer Plc: Marks & Spencer Deutschland GmbH, Antoniterstrasse 17, D-50667 Köln.
Mocap Ltd: Mocap (Deutschland), Auf Dem Blick 18, D-44289 Dortmund.
Narden Habaford Ltd: Hessenstrasse 25a, D-65618 Selters.
Prestige Group Plc: Prestige-Haushaltswaren GmbH, Burger Landstrasse 27, D-42659 Solingen.
Reckit & Colman Plc: Reckitt & Colman Deutschland AG, Heidenkampsweg 51-57, D-20097 Hamburg.
Rubery Owen Holdings Ltd: Rubery Owen-Rockwell GmbH, Hagener Strasse 20, D-58285 Gevelsberg.
Saville & Holdsworth Ltd: SHL Saville & Holdsworth Deutschland GmbH, Hofweg 58, D-22085 Hamburg.
Securicor Security Services Ltd: Securicor Deutschland GmbH, Wahler Strasse 14, D-40472 Düsseldorf.
Serco Europe Ltd: Serco services GmbH, Wilhelm-Leuschner-Str. 6, D-64347 Griesheim.
Severn Trent Plc: Severn Trent Wasser und Abwasser GmbH (STREWA), Friedrichstrasse 95 IHZ, D-10117 Berlin.
Sitex Security Products Ltd: SITEX Sicherheitsanlagen GmbH, Alexanderplatz 6, D-10178 Berlin.
Smiths Industries Plc: Icore International GmbH, Friedberger Strasse 2, D-63150 Bad Homburg.
Steelite International Plc: Sandwiesenstrasse 11, d-64665 Alsbach-Hähnlein.
Taylor Hobson Ltd: Kreuzberger Ring 6, D-65205 Wiesbaden.
Trafalgar House Offshore Holding Ltd: Brown GmbH, Hansaallee 158, D-60320 Frankfurt am Main.
Watts of Lydney Group Ltd: Watts Industrie-reifen GmbH, Am Bandsbusch 52, D-40723 Hilden.

Starting a Business

In Germany, the effect of the Single Market is less of a novelty than in some other EU countries as Germany has for some decades imposed no extra restrictions on foreign investors other than those in force against German nationals themselves. Foreign enterprises have long been welcomed in Germany, particularly if they provide new employment opportunities. There are no regulations prohibiting foreign corporations from buying up the total capital stock of a German company, neither are there any restrictions on the transfer of profits to foreign investors or the repatriation of capital, all of which provide an encouraging climate for foreign entrepreneurs.

At the time of writing, Germany is facing immense economic, social and industrial challenges arising from the unification of 1990 and the following recession. The German economy, which until the early 1990's showed remarkable resilience is now showing a slight decline. On the positive side, the German economy has built up a reputation for stability, especially in the corporate sector.

In eastern Germany, the inefficient pre-unification economy is in the throes of transition to a market economy. There are modest signs that the huge investment programme which has led to half a million new firms being created in the east is beginning to show minor returns.

In order to set up a business in Germany, you would need to have experience of running a successful business and be looking to Germany for greater opportunities for business expansion, or self-employment as a career advancement. Opportunities for practising a profession, e.g. law, would be extremely limited without a thorough knowledge of German. Those most likely to succeed are entrepreneurs with a track record, who speak German and can integrate into German business life and those interested in partnerships with German individuals and firms. This chapter outlines the main ways of approaching these objectives.

The German Context for Small Businesses

Unlike other EU countries such as Spain and Portugal where the majority of businesses have always been on a small scale, Germany was dominated before the Second World War by mega-companies, the so-called cartels, with worldwide operations. The concept of small business promotion is entirely a post-war one designed as an antidote to the pre-war cartels. Despite the traditional dominance of large-scale industries, the German government has shown itself extremely keen to encourage the starting up of small businesses and offers a large amount of additional support in the form of various incentives including the provision of capital at below market rates. The development of small businesses in Germany has been phenomenally successful so that around 70% of exports are generated by companies employing fewer than 25 staff.

There is no single definition for a small business as it varies from country to country. A small business in Germany usually means one with up to nine employees and a turnover of around one million DM. The term SME (Small and Medium Enterprises) is currently used by the European Commission to refer to enterprises with fewer than 500 employees and fixed assets net of depreciation of less than 75 million ECU and with capital no more than one third owned by a larger concern. The German term, *Mittelstand* eludes precise translation but embraces independent professionals and small and medium sized enterprises.

SME policy has been an integral part of German economic policy since 1960 when the first small business legislation was passed. Anyone used to the UK attitude to small businesses in which their worth is evaluated almost solely on their financial contribution to the economy, should note that the German approach is philosophical as well as material. In Germany, as in the rest of continental Europe, small businesses are viewed as a social as well as an economic asset. The German credo is that the value of small businesses should not just be measured in terms of their contribution to the GNP, but also to their direct and indirect stimulation of the productive efficiency of larger companies through competition and sub-contracting which in turn contribute to the overall efficiency of the economy. The added social dimension is in the widely held belief that small businesses are needed to prevent an imbalance in the sources of power and wealth as happened between the wars.

The other main difference between Britain and Germany is that unlike Britain where the promotion of SMEs has been vested in central agencies and voluntary bodies in the private sector, the Germans have evolved a more locally based system of implementation. The decentralized German system works through the Länder governments, a network of trade associations and the public law chambers of Trade Craft and Industry. Under the law in Germany all businesses must belong to and are monitored by their local chamber of commerce.

The Environmental Factor

Anyone contemplating starting a manufacturing business in Germany should be aware that Germany puts enormous emphasis on environmental issues and this is reflected in the extensive anti-pollution, anti-noise regulations. These include the following initial requirements:

1. Preventative measures must be instituted before the installation of new machinery or operation of existing machinery.
2. Distances between industrial sites and residential areas are subject to specific regulations.
3. Statistical documentation is required for proper waste disposal, anti-pollution investments and water use.

German Packaging Law & The Dual System

German Packaging Law: In pursuance of the above, the German waste recovery system as laid down in the German packaging/recycling law (*Verordnung über die Vermeidung von Verpackungsabfällen Verpackungs-Verordnung vom 12 Juni 1991*) is a measure aimed at the reduction and ultimately avoidance of packaging waste, this was based on estimates that showed German landfill capacity for waste disposal would be full by 2000. The Verpackungs-Verordnung obliges manu-facturers to take back sales packaging or arrange for its collection and recycling by a third party. The object of the Verpackungs-Verordnung is to make all industrial producers responsible for the collection, disposal or recycling of the packaging of

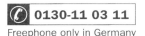

their products. The law also forbids the incineration of any items. The ambitious aim of the Verpackungs-Verordnung, is that it will embrace everything from a yoghurt carton to an automobile. Between 1990 and 1993 the total tonnage of municipal waste collected in Germany dropped by 10% while the amount of material recycled rose by 17%. As for household waste the amount recycled rose from 13% in 1990 to over 30% in 1993.

The Dual System *(Duales System Deutschland):*
Manufacturers and distributors of packaging materials may use third parties to fulfil their obligations under the above ordinance. These third parties are the Dual System with its Green Dot (*Grüne Punkt*) marking on packaging or the RESY company with its triple arrow logo. The Duales System was set up in 1990 as a non profit organisation (*Duales System Deutschland GmbH, Gesellschaft für Abfallvermeidung und Sekundärrohstoffgewinnung mbH*) by companies from the retail trade, consumer goods and packaging industries. The system has set up a nationwide collection system for sales packaging, thus exempting retailers and others from their obligation to take back packaging materials for recycling. In 1996 5.32 million tonnes of recyclable packaging material were sorted out for recycling, equivalent to 84% of all packaging used in households and businesses.

The DSD is also obliged to collect packaging from homes or collection points (see below), sort it, and forward the recyclable parts for recycling. This collection and sorting is financed by the licensing of the Green Dot trademark. This indicates that the packaging in question is participating in the system and meets its requirements for recyclability (the same is roughly true of the RESY symbol, see entry below). The symbol may only be marked on materials if the licence fee has been paid, companies using the Green Dot without a valid licence contract will be prosecuted for violation of the trade mark law. The amount to be paid is based on the material and weight and includes an item fee based on volume or area, fees in general being based on the overall costs for sorting and recycling. The DSD documents the fulfilment of collection quotas set in the 1991 ordinance in an annual mass flow verification. This documentation lists the quantities and types of materials collected, sorted and recycled, with a certificate compiled annually for each state. At present the system costs about 4 Billion DM to run.

In addition to this, as part of its mandate to organise the nationwide collection of recyclable material the DSD has harmonised its collection of waste with the systems operated by local authorities. In principal it offers two systems the 'kerbside collection' and the 'bring' system. In the former the lightweight packaging fraction (cardboard, plastic, aluminium, tin) is normally collected in yellow bags or bins from consumers houses by waste management companies. In the latter system people deposit used containers at collection points near their homes; these are not just bottle banks divided by colour but include card and paper banks. In 1996 the collection of recyclable household waste amounted to 5.8 million tonnes, or a per capita figure of 72 kilogrammes. All in all, 14.4 million tonnes of used bags, bottles, jars and tins were forwarded for recycling by the Dual System between 1991 and 1995. With the added awareness of the need to recycle brought about by the new law and the DSD, the consumption of sales packaging in homes and small businesses across Germany in the same period fell from 7.6 to 6.7 million tonnes. The recycling of plastics has risen from a meagre 10,000 tonnes in 1989 to 500,000 tonnes in 1995, with some plastics being used instead of other natural resources in industrial processes, such as the purification of iron ore in the steel industry. In 1996 the DSD managed to surpass the recycling quotas by around 10% in each category.

In addition to these changes German packaging materials have gradually become lighter as manufacturers realise that there is a cost saving to be made with regard to the Green Dot licence fee, the current trend is towards refill packs and minimal packaging.

Packaging or industrial firms seeking to relocate to Germany may also wish to note that the Duales System has an annual Innovation Prize for Packaging (*Innovationspreis Verpackung*), with four categories covering various types of packing material and usage, and a prize fund of 112,000 DM.

Useful Addresses

Duales System Deutschland: Gesellschaft für Abfallvermeidung und Sekundärroh-stoffgewinnung mbH, Frankfurter Strasse 720-726, D-51145 Köln; tel 02203-9370; fax 02203-937190. The DSD is the main organization responsible for recycling sales packaging.

RESY GmbH: Hilpertstr. 22, D-64295 Darmstadt; tel 06151-92950; fax 06151-929540. Is a firm created by the VfW (*Vereiningung für Wertstoffrecycling GmbH* see below), VDW (*Verband der Wellpappen-Industrie e.V.*) and the Paper Industry, to ensure the recycling of packaging made of paper or cardboard. Packaging firms can mark their cartons with the 'RESY' symbol under contract with the firm, the fee being based upon the total tonnage of shipping containers and packaging which contracting parties deliver for disposal each year. Packaging bearing the 'RESY' symbol is guaranteed to be collected and recycled by the German paper industry and VfW member companies.

Frankfurt Chamber of Commerce: Industrie und Handelskammer, Postanschrift 60284, Frankfurt am Main; fax 069-219 71424. The Frankfurt Chamber has prepared an English translation of the German Packaging Law which is available free of charge.

Department of Trade and Industry, German Desk: Overseas Trade Services, Kingsgate House, 66-74 Victoria Street, London SW1E 6SW; tel 0171-215 4285; fax 0171-215 4870. The DTI Germany Desk distributes a free translation of the German Packaging Law and details of the Duales System Deutschland including the application forms for the Green Dot. A list of recycling companies for different types of packaging is also included.

ISD Intersroh GmbH: Stollwerckstr. 9a, D-51149 Köln (Porz); tel 02203-91470; fax 02203-9147394. Has 75,000 pick up points throughout Germany and in 1996 had a turnover of 120 Million DM for industrial packaging recycling. Intersroh's agreement with the DSD means that the firm recycles paper, cardboard, tin, steel, aluminium, and other materials for 3,200 companies through its pick up points to 300 raw materials companies.

Vereiningung für Wertstoffrecycling GmbH: Postfach 400644, D-50836 Köln; tel 02234-95870; fax 02234-9587200. The VfW is an association of 450 medium sized materials recycling firms and has 18 regional offices servicing 800 collection sites nationwide. This association accounts for the collection prior to recycling of 65% of the total amount of used paper in Germany. VfW firms can also ensure the recycling of pharmaceutical industry waste, sensitive industrial data and provide documentary proof of recycling should it be required.

Procedures Involved in Starting a New Business

Licences and Certificates of Experience

Under the Treaty of Rome, the national of any EU country is free to set up business in another EU member country on equal terms with nationals of that country. Despite EU measures towards harmonising laws and taxes across the EU, there remain some laws which differ from country to country. In Germany certain industries are subject to strict regulations in order to safeguard health and restrict unqualified persons. Enterprises that deal with food, pharmaceuticals, medicine, banking, insurance, hotels and restaurants, handicrafts and transport all require a special licence.

Proof of professional qualification and in some cases a Certificate of Experience are also needed by those wishing to open a business in Germany. In the UK, Certificates of Experience for Germany can be issued by the British Chambers of Commerce on behalf of the Department of Trade and Industry. For further details of the trades and professions covered by the EU directive on professional qualifications, see Chapter Six, *Employment*, page 149.

Government Incentives

The procedures for starting a business in Germany have become extremely well-organised since the introduction of small business legislation over thirty years ago. There are various government incentives aimed at both Germans and foreigners, for specific territories and industries. These include investment grants and subsidies, tax incentives and financial assistance through long-term soft loans. In addition some Municipal and Länder governments provide land at low prices or reduced rents, infrastructure improvements and low utility costs. Grants are also provided to small firms to promote new businesses, research and development, vocational training, management consultancy and foreign trade.

In the new länder there are a number of financial incentives for the new business to encourage enterprises to set up there. These range from grants and loans, through capital equity loans to company reinforcement programmes to help finance expansion. Details of these can be obtained from the Foreign Investor Information Centre at the Federal Ministry of Economics (see below and *Useful Publications* on p230.)

As already mentioned implementation of incentives is dealt with at local level and applications and enquiries about incentives should therefore be addressed to the different agencies in the various Länder. The following is a list of such agencies:

Foreign Investor Information Centre, Federal Ministry of Economics: Scharn-horststr. 36, D-10115 Berlin; tel 030-20149; fax 030-2014 7010.
Reconstruction Loan Corporation (Kreditanstallt für Wiederaufbau): PO Box 11 11 41, D-60046 Frankfurt am Main; tel 069-74310; fax 069-7431 2944.
German Equalisation Bank (Deutsche Ausgleichsbank): Wielandstr 4, D-53170 Bonn; tel 0228-8311; fax 0228-831255.
Gesellschaft für Internationale Wirtschaftliche Zusammenarbeit Baden-Württemberg mbH: Willi-Bleicher-Str 19, D-70174 Stuttgart; tel 0711-227870; fax 0711-227 8722.

Bayerische Gesellschaft für Internationale Wirtschaftsbeziehungen mbH: PO Box 21 01 27, D-80030 München; tel 089-5003 4445; fax 089-5003 4426.

Wirtschaftsförderung Berlin GmbH: Hallerstrasse 6, D-10587 Berlin; tel 030-399800; fax 030-3998 0239.

Berlin and Brandenburg Representative in the UK: c/o Eversheds, Senator House, 85 Queen Victoria Street, London, EC4V 4JL.

Wirtschaftsförderung Brandenburg GmbH: Am Lehnitzsee, D-14476 Neu Fahrland; tel 033208-550; fax 033208-55100.

Wirtschaftsförderungsgesellschaft der Freien Hansestadt Bremen: Hanseatonhof 8, D-28195 Bremen; tel 0421-308850; fax 0421-308 8544.

Hamburgische Gesellschaft für Wirtschaftsförderung GmbH: Hamburger Strasse 11, D22083 Hamburg; tel 040-2270190; fax 040-2270 1929.

UK Representative of Hamburg Business Development Corporation: Mr J. Dumbrell, Riverholme, The Towpath, Shepperton, TW17 9LL; tel 01932-267272; e-mail john@infogermany.co.uk

HLT Wirschaftförderung Hessen Investitionsbank AG: PO Box 31 07, D-65021 Wiesbaden; tel 0611-7740; fax 0611-774265.

Gesellschaft für Wirschaftförderung Mecklenburg-Vorpommern mbH: Schlossgartenallee 15, D-19061 Schwerin; tel 0385-592250; fax 0385-592 2522.

IPA Investment Promotion Agency Niedersachsen: Hamburger Allee 4, D-30161 Hannover; tel 0511-343466; fax 0511-31 5909.

Gesellschaft für Wirschaftförderung Nordrhein-Westfalen mbH: PO Box 20 03 09, D-40101 Düsseldorf; tel 0211-83702; fax 0211-837 2200.

Investitions und Strukturbank Rheinland-Pfalz (ISB) GmbH: Wilhelm-Theodor-Röheld-Str. 22, D-55130 Mainz; tel 06131-985200; fax 06131-985299.

Gesellschaft für Wirschaftförderung Saar mbH: Trierer Str. 8, D-66111 Saarbrücken; tel 0681-948550; fax 0681-9485511.

Wirschaftförderung Sachsen GmbH: Bertolt-Brecht-Alle 22, D-01309 Dresden; tel 0351-31991000; fax 0351-31991099.

Wirschaftförderungsgesesllschaft für das Land Sachsen-Anhalt mbH: Schleinufer 16, D-39104 Magdeburg; tel 0391-568990; fax 0391-568 9950.

Wirschaftförderung Schleswig-Holstein GmbH: Lorentzendamm 43, D-24103 Kiel; tel 0431-593390; fax 0431-5933930.

Landesentwicklungsgesellschaft Thüringen mbH: Mainzerhofstr. 12, D-99084 Erfurt; tel 0361-56030; fax 0361-348 4381.

Information and Advice in Germany

Other information and advice in Germany is provided by chambers of commerce and professional trade associations. In Germany all such bodies are state subsidised and have public law status. The chambers of commerce can provide information on government regulations, market opportunities, exports and premises as well as accountancy and payroll management. Other sources of information for potential investors include their nearest consulate/ Embassy all of which have Commercial Sections and the German banks.

The British Chamber of Commerce in Germany.
Formed in 1960 by British and German businessmen, the chamber provides a forum for the exchange of information and the sharing of experience to benefit the development of trade between Britain and Germany. The BCCG also arranges trade fairs and 'British Days' which help to raise the profile of British firms in Germany. At the time of writing the membership included around 800 businesses,

including Thomas Cook, Siemens, & Deutsche Bank, which are engaged in a variety of activities servicing bi-directional trade and investment.

As well as providing its own services the BCCG also represents the Confederation of British Industry in Germany and has access to all the services provided by both the Council of British Chambers of Commerce in Continental Europe and the Association of British Chambers of Commerce. With its own regional groups ranging across Germany from Berlin to Munich (including one in London), it can provide up to date local and national help for the business seeking to establish a presence in Germany. In addition to a monthly bilingual newsletter, the BCCG produces an annual directory of members (including regional trade reports) which with a round of meetings and discussions creates a networking environment for the modern manager. Full membership details can be arranged by contacting the Chamber at the above address.

Useful Addresses

American Chamber of Commerce in Germany: Rossmarkt 12, D-60311 Frankfurt am Main; tel 069-929 1040.

British Chamber of Commerce in Germany: General Office, Severinstrasse 60, D-50678 Köln, tel 0221-314458; fax 0221-315335.

German-British Chamber of Industry & Commerce (Deutsche Industrie und Handelskammer): Mecklenburg House, 16 Buckingham Gate, London SW1E 6LB; tel 0171-976 4100; fax 0171-976 4101.

Robert Hanslip: 19 Ashley Close, Earley, Reading Berks. RG6 2QY; tel 0118-986 1496. International Business Consultant with many years experience as the UK representative for the Hamburg Business Development Corporation.

In addition to the Commercial Sections at the British Embassy and Consular Offices there are also:

Directorte General for Trade & Investment Promotion in Germany: Yorckstrasse 19, D-40476 Düsseldorf; tel 0211-94480; fax 0211-486359.

British Trade Office Leipzig: Gohliser Strasse 7, D-04105 Leipzig: tel 0341-564 9672; fax 0341-564 9673.

Chambers of Commerce (Industrie und Handelskammern) in Germany:

AACHEN: Theaterstrasse 6-10, D-52062 Aachen; tel 0241-44600; fax 0241-446 0259; e-mail info@aachen.ihk.de website http://www.aachen.ihk.de

ARNSBERG: Königstrasse 18-20, D-59821 Arnsberg; tel 02931-8780; fax 02931-878100.

ASCHAFFENBURG: Kerschensteinerstrasse 9, D-63741 Aschaffenburg; tel 06021-8800; fax 06021-87981.

AUGSBURG: Stettenstrasse 1 u. 3, D-86150 Augsburg; tel 0821-31620; fax 0821-3162323; e-mail info@augsburg.ihk.de website http://www.augsburg.ihk.de

BAYREUTH: Bahnhofstrasse 25-27, D-95444 Bayreuth; tel 0921-8860; fax 0921-12778; e-mail ihk.bt@bayreuth.ihk.de website http://www.bayreuth.ihk.de

BERLIN: Hardenbergstrasse 16-18, D-10623 Berlin; tel 030-315100; fax 030-31510278; website http://www.berlin.ihk.de

BIELEFELD: Elsa-Brändströ-Strasse 1-3, D-33602 Bielefeld; tel 0512-5540; fax 0521-554219; e-mail bielef@kilian.ihk.de website http://www.ihk.de/bielefeld/

BOCHUM: Ostring 30-32, D-44787 Bochum; tel 0234-91130; fax 0234-911 3110; website http://www.bochum.ihk.de

BONN: Bonner Talweg 17, D-53113 Bonn; tel 0228-22840; fax 0228-228 4170; website http://www.ihk-bonn.de

BRAUNSCHWEIG: Brabandtstrasse 11, D-38100 Braunschweig; tel 0531-47150; fax 0531-4715299; e-mail postmaster@braunschweig.ihk.de website http:/ /www.man-bs.de/ihk/index.html

BREMEN: Am Markt 13, Haus Schütting, D-28195 Bremen; tel 0421-36370; fax 0421-363 7299; website http://www.bremen.de

BREMERHAVEN: Friedrich-Ebert-Strasse 6, D-27570 Bremerhaven; tel 0471-924600; fax 0471-924 6090.

CHEMNITZ: Strasse der Nationen 25, D-09111 Chemnitz; tel 0371-69000; fax 0371-643018; e-mail chemnitz@chemnitz.ihk.de website http:/ /www.chemnitz.ihk.de

COBURG: Schlossplatz 5, Palais Edinburg, D-96450 Coburg; tel 09561-74260; fax 09561-742650; website http://www.coburg.ihk.de

COTTBUS: Goethestrasse 1, D-03046 Cottbus; tel 0355-3650; fax 0355-365266; website http://www.ihk.de/ihk/ihkn/cottbus.htm

DARMSTADT: Rheinstrasse 89, D-64295 Darmstadt; tel 06151-8710; fax 06151-871281; website http://ihk.darmstadt.de

DETMOLD: Willi-Hoffman-Strasse 5, D-32756 Detmold; tel 05231-76010; fax 05231-760157; e-mail ihk@detmold.ihk.de

DILLENBURG: Wilhelmstrasse 10, D-35683 Dillenburg; tel 02771-9050; fax 02771-90528; e-mail info@ihk-dillenburg.de website http://www.ihk-dillenburg.de

DORTMUND: Märkische Strasse 120, D-44141 Dortmund; tel 0231-54170; fax 0231-541 7109; website http://www.ihk.de/dortmund

DRESDEN: Niedersedlitzer Strasse 63, D-01257 Dresden; tel 0351-28020; fax 0351-280 2280; website http://www.dresden.ihk.de

DÜSSELDORF: Ernst-Schneider-Platz 1, D-40212 Düsseldorf; tel 0211-35570; fax 0211-355 7400; e-mail ihkdus@duesseldorf.ihk.de websitehttp:/ /www.duesseldorf.ihk.de

DUISBURG: Mercatorstrasse 22/24, D-47051 Duisburg; tel 0203-28210; fax 0203-26533; website http://www.ihk.duisburg.de

EMDEN: Ringstrasse 4, D-26721 Emden; tel 04921-89010; fax 04921-890133; e-mail ihk@emden.ihk.de website http://homepages.emsnet.de/-ihk

ERFURT: Weimarische Strasse 45, D-99099 Erfurt; tel 0361-34840; fax 0361-348 4299.

ESSEN: Am Waldthausenpark 2, D-45127 Essen; tel 0201-18920; fax 0201-207866; website http://www.ihk.de/essen

FLENSBURG: Heinrichstrasse 28-34, D-24937 Flensburg; tel 0461-8060; fax 0461-806171; e-mail ihk@flensburg.ihk.de

FRANKFURT/MAIN: Börsenplatz, D-60313 Frankfurt am Main; tel 069-21970; fax 069-2197 1424; website http://www.ihk.de.frankfurt-main/

FRANKFURT/ODER: Humboldtstrasse 3, D-15230 Frankfurt/Oder; tel 0335-56210; fax 0335-325492; website http://www.ihk.de.ffo

FREIBURG: Sitz und Hauptstelle, Schnewlinstrasse 11-13, D-79098 Freiburg; tel 0761-38580; fax 0761-3858222.

FRIEDBERG: Goetheplatz 3, D-61169 Friedburg; tel 06031-6090; fax 06031-609180.

FULDA: Heinrichstrasse 8, D-36037 Fulda; tel 0661-2840; fax 0661-28444; e-mail ihk@fulda.net website http://www.ihk.fulda.net

GERA: Humboldtstrasse 14, D-07545 Gera; tel 0365-85530; fax 0365-855 3290; website http://www.ihk.de/gera

GIESSEN: Lonystrasse 7, D-35390 Giessen; tel 0641-79540; fax 0641-75914.

HAGEN: Bahnhofstrasse 18, D-58095 Hagen; tel 02331-3900; fax 02331-13586; e-mail sihk@hagen.ihk.de website http://www.ihk.de/hagen

HALLE: Franckestrasse 5, D-06110 Halle; tel 0345-21260; fax 0345-202 9649.

HAMBURG: Adolphsplatz 1, D-20457 Hamburg; tel 040-361380; fax 040-361 38401; e-mail service@hamburg.handelskammer.de website http://www.handelskammer.de/hamburg

HANAU: Am-Pedro-Jung-Park 14, D-63450 Hanau; tel 06181-92900; fax 06181-929077; e-mail info@hanau.ihk.de website http://ihk.hanau.main-kinzig.net

HANNOVER: Sitz Hannover, Schiffgraben 49, D-30175 Hannover; tel 0511-31070; fax 0511-310 7333; website http://www.hannover.ihk.de

HEIDENHEIM: Ludwig-Erhard-Strasse 1, D-89520 Heidenheim; tel 07321-3240; fax 07321-324169; e-mail zentrale@heidenheim.ihk.de

HEILBRONN: Rosenbergstrasse 8, D-74072 Heilbronn; tel 07131-96770; fax 07131-967 7199; website http://www.ihk.de/heilbronn

KARLSRUHE: Lammstrasse 13-17, D-76133 Karlsruhe; tel 0721-1740; fax 0721-174290; e-mail info@karlsruhe.ihk.de website http://www.karlsruhe.ihk.de

KASSEL: Kurfürstenstrasse 9, D-34117 Kassel; tel 0561-78910; fax 0561-891290; e-mail ihkkassel@ad.com website http://www.ihk-kassel.de

KIEL: Lorentzdamm 24, D-24103 Kiel; tel 0431-51940; fax 0431-519 4234; e-mail ihk@kiel.ihk.de website http://www.ihk.de/kiel

KOBLENZ: Schlossstrasse 2, D-56068 Koblenz; tel 0261-1060; fax 0261-106234; e-mail service@koblenz.ihk.de website http://www.ihk-koblenz.de

KÖLN: Unter Sachsenhausen 10-26, D-50667 Köln; tel 0221-16400; fax 0221-164 0123; website http://www.ihk-koeln.de

KONSTANZ: Sitz Konstanz, Schützenstrasse 8, D-78462 Konstanz; tel 07531-28600; fax 07531-286070; website http://www.konstanz.ihk.de

KREFELD: Nordwall 39, D-47798 Krefeld; tel 02151-6350; fax 02151-635138.

LEIPZIG: Goerdelerring 5, D-04109 Leipzig; tel 0341-12670; fax 0341-126 7421.

LIMBURG: Walderdorffstrasse 7, D-65549 Limburg; tel 06431-8091; fax 06431-25190.

LINDAU: Maximilianstrasse 1, D-88131 Lindau; tel 08382-93830; fax 08382-938373; e-mail ihklindau@t-online.de

LUDWIGSHAFEN: Ludwigsplatz 2/4, D-67059 Ludwigshafen; tel 0621-59040; fax 0621-590 4166; website http://www.ihk.de/ludwigshafen

LÜBECK: Breite Strasse 6-8, D-23552 Lübeck; tel 0451-708501; fax 0451-708 5284; website http://www.tzl.de/ihkl

LÜNEBURG: Am Sande 1, D-21335 Lüneburg; tel 04131-7420; fax 04131-742180; website http@://www.ihk.de/lueneburg

MAGDEBURG: Alter Markt 8, D-39104 Magdeburg; tel 0391-569309; fax 0391-569 3105.

MAINZ: Schillerplatz 7, D-55116 Mainz; tel 06131-2620; fax 06131-262169.

MANNHEIM: Postfach 10 16 61, D-68016 Mannheim; tel 0621-17090; fax 0621-170 9100; website http://www.mannheim.ihk.de

MÜNCHEN: Max-Joseph-Strasse 2, D-80333 München; tel 089-51160; fax 089-511 6360; website http://www.muenchen.ihk.de

MÜNSTER: Sentmaringer Weg 61, D-48151 Münster; tel 0251-7070; fax 0251-707325; e-mail ihkisz@muenster.ihk.de website http://www.ihk.de/muenster

NEUBRANDENBURG: Katharinenstrasse 48, D-17033 Neubrandenburg; tel 0395-55970; fax 0395-59 7510; e-mail ihk@neubrandenburg.ihk.de

NÜRNBERG: Hauptmarkt 25-27, D-90403 Nürnberg; tel 0911-13350; fax

0911-133 5200; e-mail info@ihk-nuernberg.de website http://www.ihk-nuernberg.de

OFFENBACH: Frankfurter Strasse 90, D-63067 Offenbach am Main; tel 069-82070; fax 069-820 7199.

OLDENBURG: Moslestrasse 6, D-26122 Oldenburg; tel 0441-22200; fax 0441-222 0111; website http://www.ihk-oldenburg.de

OSNABRÜCK: Neuer Graben 38, D-49074 Osnabrück; tel 0541-3530; fax 0541-353171; e-mail ihk@osnabrueck.ihk.de

PASSAU: Nibelungenstrasse 15, D-94032 Passau; tel 0851-5070; fax 0851-507280; e-mail ihk@passau.ihk.de

PFORZHEIM: Dr-Brandenburg-Strasse 6, D-75173 Pforzheim; tel 07231-2010; fax 07231-201158; website http://www.nordschwarzwald.ihk.de

POTSDAM: Grosse Weinmeisterstrasse 59, D-14469 Potsdam; tel 0331-27860; fax 0331-278 6111; website http://www.ihk.de/potsdam

REGENSBURG: D.-Martin-Luther-Strasse 12, D-93047 Regensburg; tel 0941-56940; fax 0941-569 4279.

REUTLINGEN: Hindenbürgstrasse 54, D-727762 Reutlingen; tel 07121-2010; fax 07121-201181; website http://www. reutlingen.ihk.de

ROSTOCK: Ernst-Barlach-Strasse 1-3, D-18055 Rostock; tel 0381-3380; fax 0381-459 1156; website http://www.rostock.ihk.de or http://www.ihk.de/rostock

SAARBRÜCKEN: Franz-Josef-Röder-Strasse 9 D-66119 Saarbrücken; tel 0681-95200; fax 0681-952 0888; website http://www.saarland.ihk.de

SCHWERIN: Schlossstrasse 17, D-19053 Schwerin; tel 0385-51030; fax 0385-510 3136; e-mail info@schwerin.ihk.de website http://www.ihk.de/schwerin

SIEGEN: Koblenzer Strasse 121, D-57072 Siegen; tel 0271-33020; fax 0271-330 2400; e-mail si@siegen.ihk.de website http://www.ihk.de/siegen

STADE: Am Schäferstieg 2, D-21680 Stade; tel 04141-5240; fax 04141-524111.

STUTTGART: Jägerstrasse 30, D-70174 Stuttgart; tel 0711-20050; fax 0711-200 5354; website http://www.stuttgart.ihk.de

SUHL: Hauptstrasse 33, D-98529 Suhl; tel 03681-3620; fax 03681-362100; website http://www.ihk.de/suhl

TRIER: Kornmarkt 6, D-54290 Trier; tel 0651-97770; fax 0651-977 7153; e-mail info@trier.ihk.de

ULM: Olgastrasse 101, D-89073 Ulm (Donau); tel 0731-1730; fax 0731-173173; website http://www.ulm.ihk.de

VILLINGEN-SCHWENNIGEN: Romäusring 4, D-78050 Villingen-Schwenningen; tel 07721-9220; fax 07721-922166; e-mail info@villingen-schwenningen.ihk.de website http://www.schwarzwald-baar-heuberg.ihk.de

WEINGARTEN: Lindenstrasse 2, D-88250 Weingarten; tel 0751-4090; fax 0751-409159; e-mail weingarten@weingarten.ihk.de website http://www.weingarten.ihk.de

WETZLAR: Friedenstrasse 2, D-35578 Wetzlar; tel 06441-94480; fax 06441-944833; e-mail ihk-wz@t-online.de

WIESBADEN: Wilhelmstrasse 24-26, D-65183 Wiesbaden; tel 0611-15000; fax 0611-377271.

WÜRZBURG: Mainaustrasse 33, D-97082 Würzburg; tel 0931-41940; fax 0931-419 4100; e-mail info@wuerzburg.ihk.de website http://www.wuerzburg.ihk.de

WUPPERTAL: Heinrich-Kamp-Platz 2, D-42103 Wuppertal; tel 0202-24900; fax 0202-249 0999.

SME Policy and Euro-Info Centres

The main EC initiative on small and medium-sized businesses (SMEs) was outlined in the 1985 meeting of the European Council. The Commission adopted a policy that was aimed at creating a favourable climate for small businesses. The aims of the policy included provision of capital, promoting the spirit of enterprise through education and training and simplifying the administrative burden for SME's. The EU promotes cross-border co-operation between SMEs through a network of Euro-Info Centres (EICs), BRE and BC-Net. The former provide SMEs at local level in the UK with a service to enable them to enter the markets of other EU member countries and also updated data on markets, standards, sources of finance from the EU etc. It is also important for SME's to be aware of their rights under Community law and of the means of ensuring their enforcement. Advice can be sought through the Euro-Info Centre network (see below). Of the latter the BRE or *Bureau de Rapprochment des Enterprises* is a non-confidential information exchange service designed to help companies find trading partners across the EU. Companies submit a profile of their business and the partnerships they are seeking to their local BRE correspondent. This is then sent off to BRE correspondents in the target country, each co-operation request is then circulated, publicised or entered onto a database. Co-operation requests have a lifetime of six months, although they can be renewed. BC-Net operates in a similar fashion to the BRE but operates through a confidential central database.

Useful Addresses:

The European Commission: Jean Monnet House, 8 Storey's Gate, London SW1P 3AT; tel 0171-973 1992; fax 0171-973 1900. The Commission can supply a range of information on setting up business links with Germany as well as EC background information.

London Chamber of Commerce: 33 Queen Street, London EC4R 1AP; tel 0171-489 1992.

Bureau de Rapprochment des Enterprises: 200 rue de la Loi, AN80/670, B-1049 Brussels, Belgium; tel +32-22959117; fax +32-22964271; e-mail bre-helpdesk@dg23.cec.be

BC-Net: Rue de la Loi 200 (ARLN 80-6/20), B-1049 Brussels; fax +32-22962572; e-mail bcnet-helpdesk@dg23.cec.be

Euro-Information Centres in the UK:

BELFAST: Euro Info Centre, Local Enterprise Development Unit, LEDU House, Upper Galwally, Belfast, BT8 4TB; 01232-491031; fax 01232-691432.

BIRMINGHAM: Euro Info Centre, Birmingham Chamber of Industry and Commerce, 75 Harborne Road, Birmingham, B15 3DH; tel 0121-454 6171; 0121-455 8670.

BRADFORD: Euro Info Centre, West Yorkshire Business Information Centre, 4 Manchester Road, Bradford, BD5 0Gl; tel 01274-754262; fax 01274-393226.

BRISTOL: Euro Info Centre, Bristol Chamber of Commerce and Business Link, 16 Clifton Park, Bristol, BS8 3BY; tel 0117-973 7373; fax 0117-974 5365.

BURGESS HILL: Euro Info Centre, Sussex Chamber of Commerce Training and Enterprise, Greenacre Court, Station Road, Burgess Hill, RH15 9DS; tel 01444-259200; fax 01444-259255; e-mail SCCTE@pawilicn.com

CARDIFF: Wales Euro Info Centre, Welsh Development Agency, UWCC, Guest Building, PO Box 430, Cardiff CF1 3XT; tel 01222-229525; fax 01222-229740; website http://www.cityscape.co.uk/users/fd13

EXETER: Euro Info Centre South-West, Exeter Enterprises Ltd., Reed Hall, University of Exeter, Exeter EX4 4QR; tel 01392-214085; fax 01392-264375; e-mail c.young@exeter.ac.uk

GLASGOW: Scottish Enterprise, Euro Info Centre Ltd, 21 Bothwell Street, Glasgow G2 6NL; tel 0141-221 0999; fax 0141-221 6539; e-mail lesley.magaire@scotnet.co.uk

HULL: Euro Info Centre, Humberside Brynmor Jones Library, The University of Hull, Cottingham Road, Hull, HU6 7RX; tel 01482-465940; fax 01482-466488.

INVERNESS: Euro Info Centre, Business Information Source, Highland Opportunity Ltd, 20 Bridge Street, Inverness IV1 1QR; tel 01463-715400; fax 01463-715600; e-mail eic@sprite.co.uk.

LEICESTER: Euro Info Centre, The Business Centre, 10 New Road, Leicester, LE1 5TS; 0116-255 59944; fax 0116-255 3470.

LIVERPOOL: Euro Info Centre North West, Liverpool City Libraries, William Brown Street, Liverpool, L3 8EW; tel 0151-298 1928; fax 0151-207 1342; e-mail info@eicnw.u-net.com.uk.

LONDON: London Chamber of Commerce and Industry, 33 Queen Street, London, EC4R 1AP; tel 0171-489 1992; fax 0171-489 0391.

MAIDSTONE: Euro Info Centre, Kent County Council Economic Development Dept, Springfield, Maidstone, ME14 2LL; tel 01622-694109; fax 01622-691418; e-mail ecdido@tcns.co.uk website http://spectrum.tcns.co.uk/uk/kent-euro/welcome.ht

MANCHESTER: Euro Info Centre, Business Link Manchester, 56 Oxford Street, Manchester, M60 7BL; tel 0161-237 4020; fax 0161-236 9945.

NEWCASTLE: Euro Info Centre, Northern Development Company, Great North House, Sandyford Road, Newcastle upon Tyne, NE1 8ND; 0191-261 0026; fax 0191-222 1774; e-mail gb-newcastle@vans.infonet.com

NORWICH: Euro Info Centre, East Anglia and Norfolk Chamber of Commerce and Industry, 112 Barrack Street, Norwich, NR3 1UB; tel 01603-625977; fax 01603-633032; e-mail euro-info@netcom.co.uk

NOTTINGHAM: Euro Info Centre, The Nottingham Chamber of Commerce and Industry, 309 Haydn Road, Nottingham, NG5 1DG; tel 0115-962424; fax 0115-985 6612.

SLOUGH: Euro Info Centre, Thames Valley Chamber of Commerce and Industry, Commerce House, 2-6 Bath Road, Slough, SL1 3SB; tel 01753-577877; fax 01753-524644.

SOUTHAMPTON: Euro Info Centre, Southern Area EIC Consortium, Civic Centre, Southampton S014 7LW; tel 01703-832866; fax 01703-231714.

STAFFORD: Euro Info Centre, Staffordshire Business Centre, Staffordshire Technology Park, Beaconside, Stafford, ST18 4AR; tel 01785-222300; fax 01785-253207.

TELFORD: Euro Info Centre, Shropshire and Staffordshire, Trevithick House, 4 Stafford Park, Telford, TF3 3BA; tel 01952-208213; fax 01952-208208.

Relocation Agencies and Consultants

As already mentioned, general relocation agencies that can help you relocate everything from your business to your family possessions from the UK or USA to Germany are an expanding field of business, with some very experienced and helpful staff. The following organizations and individuals offer business advice and/or practical help with the procedures involved in setting up a business:

Business & Relocation Services: Nanda Leick, Rosenstrasse 7, D-80331 München; tel 089-231 1380; fax 089-2311 3811. In business since 1990 and helping companies such as Motorola and Coca Cola relocate executives and premises to Germany, this Bavarian based company has a multilingual staff (English, French, Italian and Japanese are spoken) to help you move in. Their services include support with moving, registering, settling in and moving home again after your stay in Germany.

Entrepreneurial Management Services International (EMSI): Breitscheider Weg 115, D-40885 Ratingen; tel 02102-731066; fax 02102-39657. Will tailor an individual information package according to your needs. The basic information package costs around 300 DM for individuals and 880 DM for businesses.

Erding Relocation: Gabrielle Schmid, Freisinger Str.45, D-85435 Erding; tel 08122-84393; fax 08122 84315; e-mail RELOCATION@t-online.de Based at the München's new airport, this company offers start-up, housing and ongoing services for those moving to Bavaria. These services range from meeting you on arrival, (eg registering you, obtaining residence permits and tax cards) to helping out with school meetings and finding a good plumber.

Regus: Instant Offices Worldwide: Lindencorso, Unter den Linden 21, D-10117 Berlin; tel 030-2092 4111; fax 030-2092 4200; Freephone (Germany only) 0130-110311; website http://www.regus.com With 20 business centres across Germany Regus has the ideal solution for businesses wishing to relocate, or set up 'instant offices' in Germany. These immediately available, staffed, equipped and furnished offices are in over 140 locations across the world now, thus allowing your business to act flexibly and without the constraints of building maintenance or purchase. Multi-lingual support staff, conference rooms and video conferencing are available and leases are flexible from one day to three years.

RSB Deutschland GmbH: Dreieichstrasse 59, D-60594 Frankfurt am Main; tel 069-6109470; fax 069-611759. In business since 1987 RSB can assist clients to settle in more than 40 German cities, and offers relocation services for transfers of staff: to Germany, within Germany, from Germany elsewhere and from one country to another.

Ulf Glattkowski-International Cooperations: Postfach 1268, D-23740 Grömitz; tel 04562-222026; fax 04562-222027; e-mail glattkowski@compuserve.com Consortium of professionals providing range of market access services for companies that want to enter the German market. Specializes in on-the-spot active assistance (i.e. does the legwork) involved in initial market studies right through to helping find staff and domicile for their branch office in Germany.

UBI-Bischof: Franz-Georg Bischof, Aubinger Str 86, D-81243 München; tel 089-871 3624; fax 089-874083. Enterprise consultant and press agency. Acts as a facilitator for those wishing to enter the German market. Has excellent connections with almost all industries, especially high tech. Can assist with all aspects of business including finding offices, preparing business foundations and handling advertising. Willing to act as partner, distributor, agency for UK companies or those interested in Global player strategies.

Business Structures

In order to operate commercially in Germany, an individual or company must choose one of the various legal business forms from sole proprietorship to corporation. The tax burden for companies is notoriously high in Germany, and for this reason it is advisable to contact as many experts as possible with a view to choosing the most advantageous locality and legal form. The two main limited liability structures are the *Aktiengesellschaft (AG)* a joint stock corporation, and the *Gesellschaft mit beschränkter Haftung, GmbH* a limited liability company.

Other structures include Partnerships, Co-operatives, branches of foreign companies and Limited Stock Partnerships. More detailed information on founding businesses, and business types in Germany, can be obtained from the Federal Office of Trade Information *Bundesstelle für Aussenhandelsinformation (BfAI)*, Postfach 10 05 22, D-50445 Köln.

Aktiengesellschaft (AG): Is the legal form of business used when funds are to be raised from the general public, shareholders are not personally liable for company debts. Five members are required to form an AG either private individuals or corporate bodies. On founding the company the contract and statutes must be signed in the presence of a notary. The formation documents must contain details of the founders' nominal value (in the case of corporations), the value of shares issued to each founder, the objects of the enterprise, the share capital and domicile (which must be in Germany) of the company. To found an AG a minimum share capital of 100,000 DM is required, this must be fully subscribed and 25% paid up at the time of formation, shares must have a minimum value of 50 DM, with higher values divisible by 100. A management board legally represents the joint stock corporation.

Gesellschaft mit beschränkter Haftung (GmbH): The GmbH is the most usual form adopted by foreign companies' subsidiary operations in Germany and for German family-run businesses. The legal format is simpler than for an AG and shareholders can control and instruct management directly .

The management structure and the method of operation of a large GmbH and an AG are broadly similar. However there are some differences in the start up procedure. A GmbH may be formed by a single shareholder and the minimum share capital requirement is DM 50,000, this capital must be expressed in Deutsche Marks and be evenly divisible by 100 and at least half of this capital must be paid up when forming the company. A GmbH does not normally issue share certificates, but should it choose to do so, these must be registered and are not freely transferable. Share transfers may only be effected by notarized deed and can be made the subject of other restrictions similar to an AG. A GmbH can also issue different classes of shares and can take up loans. However, such loans are agreed by contract with the lender and therefore do not have the characteristics of debentures etc. which are capable of being traded on the money markets. As for an AG company statutes must be notarized.

In the case of a GmbH, the board of management is replaced by one or more directors (usually called *Geschäftsführer*). Unlike an AG there is no legal requirement for registered managers' meetings. A supervisory board (*Aufsichtsrat*) is not required if the regular complement of employees is fewer than 500 people.

Partnerships: As in other countries partnerships can take various forms:
offene Handelsgesellschaft, OHG: A general partnership in which all general partners have unlimited liability for partnership debts. The firm name must include the family name of one of the partners with the addendum '& Co'.

Kommanditgesellschaft, KG: A limited partnership in which one or more of the active partners is liable without limit for the debts of the partnership and one or more limited partners is liable up to the amount of their capital input to the partnership as specified in the document drawing up the partnership. Authority to manage the partnership on a day-to-day basis is vested in the partner(s) with unlimited liability.

GmbH & Co Kommanditgesellschaft (GmbH & Co KG): This is a limited partnership with the GmbH as the general partner and individuals as limited partners. In such a structure the limited liability partners put up the whole share capital and form a GmbH to hold the general partnership and exercise managerial rights. In this way the company obtains overall limited liability which is worthless to a would-be creditor as its assets are restricted to a share in the partnership's capital which may be zero.

Gesellschaft des bürgerlichen Rechtes (GbR or BGB-Gesellschaft): This is a Civil Law Partnership and as such is not a legal structure, nor is it self accounting. Members of a civil law partnership agree to share the cost of running office premises but retain their own fees from their separate business pursuits. This structure is often used by groups of professionals, e.g. lawyers. It is not normally suitable for international corporations.

Stille Gesellschaft: This is a silent partnership of the usual kind where an unregistered person, in return for a share of company profits, participates in the business of another partner solely by making a capital contribution which becomes part of the business assets of the active partner. The active partner(ship) has sole responsibility for the running of the business. There is also an atypical silent partnership (*atypische stille Gesellschaft*) in which a contract is made with the silent partner to the effect that he or she has a stake in the net assets (including reserves) of the business and can influence managerial decisions.

Genossenschaft (Co-operative): A co-operative is a legal entity which may be limited, with the members' liability limited to the amount of capital stated in the articles of association needed for registration. Co-operatives can also be unlimited. This form is particularly suitable for where a large number of individuals need to benefit from financial support provided by a jointly-financed association. It is particularly useful for agriculturalists.

Einzelkaufmann: Sole trader or sole proprietor. This status is excluded from the legislation pertaining to the control of limited liability and partnerships and typically has unlimited liability.

Niederlassung einer susländisch Gesellschaft: A branch of a foreign company which has to be registered in the commercial register in order to carry out the full range of business activities. This is known as an independent branch. If the branch is dependent (i.e. a representation office) it cannot be registered with the commercial register. In either case, the foreign organization is fully liable for the debts of the branch. In the market place, the branch is sometimes seen as not carrying the same weight as a GmbH. Its chief advantage for the foreign company can be reduced taxation depending on the fiscal laws of the country of origin. Expert financial advice is therefore essential before establishing a branch.

Costs of Business Formation

Start up costs include notary and lawyers' fees, registration charges, and press gazetting; obviously the charges will vary, depending on the size and type of business.

Ideas for New Businesses

No budding Euro-entrepreneur can afford to overlook Germany, not least because, with a population of over 78 million, it constitutes the largest consumer market in the EC. In addition Germany (notably through Hamburg and Berlin) is rapidly becoming a springboard for access to the markets of Eastern Europe. Small businesses however should not try to cover too much ground at the beginning; by far the most challenging step is to establish yourself in the German market. The main problem here for foreign businesses is that the Germans are spoilt for choice: they are more widely accustomed than any other Europeans to high-quality goods and excellent services. The foreigner therefore has to offer a product at least as good and preferably better, or a service with better incentives and benefits. Various agencies in the UK including the DTI, the chambers of commerce in Germany and various EU organizations mentioned earlier in this chapter can help prepare you for starting business in Germany and carry out the necessary fact finding on your behalf for any of the suggested areas mentioned below. Thorough research is a prerequisite to entering the German market and you should also be prepared to make exploratory trips to Germany to make contacts and assess the competition and visit trade fairs. In some cases your research may involve buying the opposition's products and learning from them. There are a number of opportunities open to foreign entrepreneurs to provide goods and services to the Germans.

On the material side, Germans are interested in many types of quality wares and so businesses selling an exclusive range of products, particularly crafts from exotic countries are almost certain to find a market. In the services market there is an insatiable demand in Germany for translation services and this is one area in which British entrepreneurs have been exploiting their potential.

Whatever the aspirations of the Single Market to harmonise taxes and laws in individual member states, the existing bevy of variations belies the hope that this will actually happen in either the short or medium term. As far as business opportunities are concerned this is a possible goldmine for British enterprises providing consultancy services to Germans wishing to break into the UK market. Such services could be provided by lawyers and accountants with the relevant expertise, perhaps working with German partners. Other areas that offer scope are computer technology and language schools for teaching business English.

One of the main aims of the Commission is to see the establishment of a common market for services, even those which are traditionally government regulated like banking, transport and insurance. It is therefore envisaged that these will continue to be regulated by national authorities who will enforce certain rules of commercial operation whilst opening them up to companies from around the Community on an equal basis. Much of the legislation needed to make the financial services sector accessible to foreign companies has already been passed and in the case of banking is already well exploited.

Telecommunications: On the 1st of January 1998 the European telecommunications markets were opened up to outside competition. While some states have already allowed competition within their domestic markets, these companies can now compete with the domestic provider in other EU states. At present the German telecoms market is worth around 70 billion DM, and while Deutsche Telekom is allegedly a private company open to competition they have effectively operated in a monopoly, but this can now be challenged. This is especially the case in the mobile phone market.

The Internet: Whether the cabling you use to provide connections to users is supplied by Deutsche Telekom or not this is still an area ripe for exploration as the Germans are keen investors in modern technology and 'das Net' is no exception, either at work or in the home.

Shopping: Modern technology and fast transport methods now means that canny shop owners can set up shop in Germany. Good research on German shopping trends and customer requirements will pay dividends; as will having the right format, committed staff at all levels, a well identified target market and something new to offer shoppers. Examples of this can be seen in the spread of the Dutch retail chain C & A across Germany and the recent advance of Marks & Spencer into Germany.

Useful Publications

The following is a list of useful publications for those wishing to set up in business in Germany:

German Tax & Business Law Guide: In collaboration with the German law firm Boesebeck Droste, this is a one volume loose-leaf reporting service providing a concise yet comprehensive overview of Germany's business law and tax systems. The guide is a practical reference source for investors and company managers involved in doing business in and with Germany, and also for their legal, tax and financial advisers. Available from CCH Editions Ltd (Telford Road, Bicester, OX6 0XD; tel 01869-253300) for an annual subscription of £440 which includes six reporter updates and ten newsletters.

Mergers & Acquisitions in Germany: Written in 1995 by the German law firm Droste, this book offers information on the legal situation with an emphasis on the viewpoint of purchasers, and highlights the differences between German contract law and that of other jurisdictions. Available from CCH Editions Ltd (Telford Road, Bicester, OX6 0XD; tel 01869-253300) for £110.

Transactions in Real Property in Germany: Also written by the Droste law firm, this book is a practical guide, including bilingual sample agreements, to the legal and tax aspects of buying property in Germany. Also available from CCH Editions Ltd (Telford Road, Bicester, OX6 0XD; tel 01869-253300) for £110.

Germany Brief: Frankfurter Allgemeine Zeitung Information Services, D-60267 Frankfurt am Main; tel 069-75910; fax 069-7591 2178. This fortnightly publication provides an economic and business breakdown of current trends in Germany. It is available on subscription from the above address.

Department of Trade & Industry Publications: The DTI in Britain publishes a range of booklets which are constantly being updated. For more information contact the Germany Desk, DTI Overseas Trade Services, Rm 964, Kingsgate House, 66-74 Victoria Street, London, SW1E 6SW; tel 0171-215 4796/4995.

The Single Market: Making It Work For You: This DTI booklet highlights the benefits provided by the Single Market, and advises on how the DTI can help British business fight illegal trade barriers.

Germany: Market Menu: Another DTI booklet, this lists the help available to businesses from the DTI, giving details of the advice and information, technical services, and free information booklets available from the German Helpdesk. These include digests in English of German packaging law, opportunities for new businesses, listings of the major retail groups, reports on different industries, and translations of German Standards.

Working for the German Construction Industry: Is a book published by the British Chamber of Commerce (tel 0171-976 4100) priced £28.

Germany Your Business Partner: Published by the Federal Office of Foreign Trade Information (*Bundesstelle für Aussenhandels-information*, Agrippastr. 87-93, D-50676 Köln; tel 0221-20570; fax 0221-205 7212; website http://www.bfai.com) this book summarises major trade and investment figures as well as providing an overview of German business types, taxes, incentives and the practical aspects of doing business in Germany. It also has a handy address list of all the major ministries and overseas offices related to trading with Germany, and a list of the ministries publications and reports including those published in English.

Economic Incentives in Germany's New Federal States: Published by the Foreign Investor Information Centre of the Federal Ministry of Economics (*Bundesministerium für Wirtschaft*, Scharnhorststrasse 36, D-10115 Berlin; tel 030-20147755/7751; fax 030-2014 7036; website http://www.bmwi.de) this lists all the tax allowances, loan and grant assistance programmes available to investors in eastern Germany. There is also a similar booklet for western Germany entitled *Economic Assistance for Small and Medium-Sized Enterprises In Western Germany.*

Taxes in the Federal Republic of Germany: Available from the Foreign Investor Information Centre and published by them in conjunction with Price Waterhouse GmbH. This English language booklet gives a breakdown of the taxation system in Germany for the foreign investor or business.

Kontaktadressen In Deutschland (Contacts for Firms Wishing to Do Business in Germany): Another of the Foreign Investor Information Centre's publications this is a partially bilingual address listing which essentially reproduces the address list in *Germany Your Business Partner.*

Doing Business In Germany: Also produced by the Foreign Investor Information Centre this booklet is aimed at American firms as it lists all the addresses of Germany's diplomatic and trade organisations across Germany and those of the USA in Germany.

Major Investment Incentives In Germany: Is an English-language breakdown of the major tax breaks and grants available, including tips on securing financial assistance for new enterprises. Available from the Foreign Investor Information Centre. The Foreign Investor Information Centre of the Ministry of Economics also publishes a wide range of industrial and business reports, examples are *Foreigners and the German Economy: Ten Propositions*, and *Rebuilding Eastern Germany: Opportunities and Risks*, details of their availability can be obtained from the above address.

How to Do Business in Germany: Put together by the German American Chamber of Commerce of the Midwest (104 South Michigan Avenue, Suite 600, Chicago Illinois 60603-5978, USA), this booklet details the permits and regulations regarding businesses in Germany, as well as offering a breakdown of business types.

Running a Business

Employing Staff

Germany has some of the strongest labour laws in the world which many employers complain are too restrictive and work too much in favour of their workers. Amongst the battery of German legislation is the obligation for employers to have worker delegations participating in the decision-making in larger firms, and others that oblige managements to seek consultation with their staff (through workers' councils) and obtain their approval before implementing a whole range of matters. Another set of laws fixes job security, welfare and fringe benefits, working conditions, and the procedures for collective wage bargaining. Whilst the spectrum of matters covered by labour legislation is not in itself unique to Germany, the precision and exactness with which the laws are set out, is.

The high level of skills and training amongst the German labour force is the object of envy throughout Europe. Over 70% of the workforce in western Germany is occupationally qualified compared with 30% in the UK. The availability of staff: managerial, skilled and unskilled, is generally good. However there is a shortage of specific skills in some areas (e.g. Information Technology). In eastern Germany there is high unemployment but the workforce there is retraining and willing to work.

Unskilled and to a lesser extent, skilled workers can be recruited through the local *Arbeitsamt* (employment office). In common with other EU countries except the UK, private employment agencies, except for temporary work, are illegal. Employers wishing to recruit staff at white collar and middle management level can advertise in newspapers and use the services of management consultants.

When employing staff the general considerations for the foreign employer are:

1. Wage settlements are usually negotiated through agreement with trade unions.
2. Annual wage increases have tended to be above inflation rates.
3. Unit wage costs, which relate wages and productivity, are rising faster in Germany than in either France or the UK.
4. Hourly wages in Germany are now the highest amongst the world's leading economies including Switzerland.
5. Worker Councils have a powerful voice in staff matters.

The Current Direction of German Labour Legislation

German labour legislation sets out the basis for union negotiations over wages and other conditions of employment. The Government's thrust in labour legislation is towards supporting the rights of workers and spreading the available work over as many full-time employees as is practicable while maintaining competitiveness, efficiency and productivity. The overall aim in both western and eastern Germany is to reduce or minimize unemployment.

Workers Councils

The management of every business employing five or more staff over 18, must agree to the setting up of a *Betriebsrat* (Works Council) at the request of the staff. There is no legal obligation on the staff to have a Council if they do not wish to, but in practice they nearly always do. The Betriebsrat is elected by secret ballot and candidates may be either independent and/or union sponsored. However, the Betriebsrat can function entirely separately from the trade unions and many small companies whose staff are not unionized will still have a Betriebsrat. Depending on the size of the company, the Betriebsrat has an on-site office and one or more senior members who are occupied full-time in the execution of their Council duties whilst being fully salaried by the company. The Betriebsrat expects to be consulted by the management on a wide field of matters. For instance, legislation obliges the management to inform the Council regularly of any investment projects and financial plans for the company though it is not obligated to act on any suggestions put forward by the Council. In matters which concern the daily life of the staff, the boot is firmly on the Council's foot: safety regulations, installation of new equipment, catering facilities, working hours and holiday schedules all come within the Council's jurisdiction and the management is legally bound to seek the approval of the council before making any changes in these areas. The Betriebsrat can object and if no agreement can be reached with the management, the matter is taken before a labour court.

From the employer's point of view the works council system generally operates smoothly. However, over the past few years there has been a growth in friction particularly in the area of recruitment and dismissals, the introduction of flexible working hours and new technology. The works councils are inherently on the side of the employee and it can make dismissal for incompetence or indiscipline very difficult for the employer to accomplish. As Germany has relatively high unemployment, the frictions between Councils and management generally are bound to be exacerbated. However, in smaller firms the system should continue to work smoothly and, as the majority of foreigners starting up businesses in Germany will be running SME's or tiny companies, the system should not prove a hindrance.

Co-Determination

An extension of the principal behind works councils, that everything a company does affects its employees, co-determination gives employees representatives on a supervisory board which oversees the company's activities. Companies not engaged in mining, or iron and steel production and which employ more than 2,000 staff fall within the scope of the 1976 Co-Determination Act. This specifies that companies should have supervisory boards made up of workers' and shareholders' representatives, at ratios of 6:6, 8:8 and 10:10 for companies employing up to 10,000, between 10,000-20,000 and over 20,000 staff respectively. Employees of joint stock company, a private limited company, a partnership limited by shares, a co-operative or a mutual insurance company can influence policy through the supervisory boards; including dismissing members of the management board (except in partnerships limited by shares).

Collective Bargaining

Wage settlements are agreed by the employers with the trade unions. Each employer is a member of the employers' federation for his or her particular industry. There is a branch of every type of employers' association in each of the Lander and collective bargaining therefore takes place on a regional basis. Generally, each employer comes within the ambit of a single trade union and the legally-binding wage agreements apply to all the employees in a given place of work, regardless of whether or not they are union members.

Employee Training

Germany is a byword for youth vocational training (*berufliche Ausbildung*). The advantages of an overall vocational training system, whereby every employer from the Siemens corporation to the village baker pays for the apprentice scheme have been plain to see in Germany's abundance of highly-trained employees. The system is regulated at federal (*Bund*) level, but administration is handled at local level. Positions as trainees (*Auszubildende*) are provided annually for the majority of school leavers; usually around one and a half million take them up.

Trainees, known colloquially as *Azubis*, are given contracts for two or three-year courses on a dual training basis which means they spend two days a week at the *Berufsschule* (vocational school) and the remainder at the *Betrieb* (firm) learning a specific job. A formal training system covers a range of over 300 jobs and occupations ranging from bank clerk, to hairdressing or car mechanics. Employers pay the apprentice a small allowance of around 700 DM monthly. The Azubi takes examinations to continue as a journeyman (*Geselle*), assistant (*Gehilfe*) or Skilled Worker (*Facharbeiter*) and has his or her salary increased accordingly. The highest qualification is master craftsman (*Meister*) for which an exam must be taken after several years of practical professional experience. Another possibility after successful completion of basic trade training, is access to a specific *Fachschule* offering further training programmes and attendance at *Abendgymnasium* (Evening Grammar School) or *Kolleg* (special courses).

Almost all employers in industry provide training schemes for their employees. Training contracts are supervised by the local chambers of commerce in conjunction with local educational establishments. Many employers also encourage qualified employees to attend outside courses in order to ensure that their work keeps professionally up to date. Employees have a legal right to claim one week's paid training time a year in order to attend such courses, many of which are subsidized by the Government or trade unions.

Social Security Contributions

The German social security system is comprehensive and together with fringe benefits constitutes a considerable expense for employers. Social security consists of three main payment areas: old age pension insurance, unemployment insurance and health insurance. The contributions in each case are compulsory and are divided equally between employer and employee. Although some forms of social insurance are provided solely at the employers expense, such as the statutory occupational accident insurance. Exemption from German social security payments may be claimed by foreigners from countries (including the United States and Australia) with which Germany has a social security treaty; under this agreement they may work in Germany but still be registered with the social security system in their own country. More details on the responsibilities, exemptions and payments towards the social security system can be obtained from local chambers of commerce or the Federal Ministry for Labour and Social Affairs (*Bundesministirium für Arbeit und Sozialordnung:* Postfach 14 02 80, D-53107 Bonn).

Pension Contributions: The national pension scheme requires contributions for practically all employees regardless of their salary level. The only exceptions are temporary staff from other countries (see above). For further information on pensions, see Chapter Six, *Employment.*

Unemployment Insurance: This covers all wage and salary earners. In 1997 the contributions were 6.5% of income up to the same ceiling as pension contributions.

Health Insurance: This covers all employees and their families, with monthly earnings up to 6,150 DM. The amount of the contribution is fixed by the respective sickness fund of which the employee is a member and is liable to variation between funds. The current rate for contributions is around 14% of gross wages.

Employees being paid above the 6,150 DM ceiling can elect to pay voluntary contributions to the state system or to take out private health insurance. In either case they are still entitled to a tax-free contribution from their employer of 50% of the cost.

Occupational Accident Insurance *(Unfallversicherung)***:** The cost of this is borne by the employer through their payments to the employer's liability insurance funds. These premiums are based on the sum of wages paid each year and the risks to employees. The benefits provided by this are indefinite medical treatment, injury benefit (80% of lost wages) payable after six weeks, occupational assistance (for re-training), injury pension (if your capacity to earn is reduced by 20% or more), and funeral allowance and survivors pension (payable to dependents).

Other Employee Benefits

Quite apart from the contributions mentioned above, employers are also liable for other employee benefits which can add considerably to labour costs:

Sickness benefit: A sick employee is entitled to receive a full salary for up to six weeks during his or her absence. For longer periods, the employee is paid out of the sickness fund.

Maternity leave: Working women are entitled to a fully paid maternity leave of six weeks before and eight weeks after childbirth. The health insurance fund pays a daily, tax-free allowance of up to DM 25 and the employer must pay the difference up to the employee's net salary of the last three months.

Parental leave: In addition to maternity leave, either parent may claim parental leave of up to three years following the birth. For six months the parent is paid 600 DM per month after which the allowance may be decreased depending on the level of other income. The employer is obliged to resume the parent's previous employment after this period.

Bonuses: In common with several other European countries, companies in Germany pay their employees two extra months salary, one around mid-year and the other at Christmas.

Holidays: Although the minimum amount of paid holiday allowed per year is 24 days, many German employees are actually entitled (though binding agreements with trade unions) to as much as six weeks paid holiday a year.

Taxation

Once a company has been registered notice has to be given to the tax authorities (*Finanzamt*) who will then allocate a tax number. Businesses in Germany bear one of the heaviest tax burdens in the EU and the total of all the taxes for which businesses may be liable can be as high as 60%. The main taxes are as follows:

Municipal Trade Tax: Every business enterprise in Germany is liable for municipal trade tax at rates that vary between the municipalities. Trade tax is made up of two components, income and capital, the tax is calculated by applying a base rate of tax (5% of income and 0.2% of capital) and a local assessment rate (between 300 and 500%) to trade income and trading capital. There are allowances in the cases of individual traders and partnerships of up to 48,000 DM.

Corporation Tax *(Körperschaftssteuer)***:** The tax rate is 45% on undistributed profits and is reduced to 30% if profits are distributed to shareholders.

VAT *(Mehrwertsteuer)***:** In Germany VAT is levied as in the rest of Europe on delivery of domestic goods and services and on the importation of goods. The standard rate is 15%, at present but this is set to rise to 16% in 1998. On some goods such as groceries and books, VAT is at a reduced rate of 7%, this includes banking, insurance and medical services. From a business perspective, VAT is not an element of production cost as it is relayed on to the customer. Similarly, VAT paid by a company for goods and services received is reclaimable from the tax authorities.

Taxation of Partnerships

Partnerships tend to be treated differently from AGs or GmbHs for tax purposes. They are subject to transaction taxes including VAT and trade tax, but not to income, corporation or net assets taxes. The nature of the partnership arrangement ensures that taxable income and net assets are shared amongst the partners who then become subject to corporation tax or if acting individually, to income tax (*Einkommensteuer*) and net assets tax in their own name.

Personal Case Histories

Sarah Foster

Sarah is a 24 year old student, studying Fine Art and German at Oxford Brookes University. She recently spent eight months in Regensburg at the university there, on an ERASMUS exchange, studying German. We asked her:

How awful was German red-tape in practice?
Registering at the various places such as the Einwohnermeldeamt, the university and the DAK did not present too much of a problem as I and the other foreign students were given a lot of useful information from our home universities, and Regensburg has an induction programme designed for foreign students which was extremely helpful. I would describe the process as time-consuming rather than a nightmare. What I did find annoying was the fact that many offices closed at 11.30 am, and twice I found myself waiting in a queue for two hours only to be handed a form; which made getting all the red-tape over and done with in one day impossible.

Was it difficult to find work?
Although studying at university, I did do some part-time work (please note that this is not an option open to students from outside the EU, due to the nature of the visa *Aufenthaltsbewilligung* which you will be issued with in order to study in Germany), as it happened upon arrival. I managed to get a job at 'Toys R Us', the application was a case of walking in and talking to the a manager, who was suitably impressed by the fact that I had worked for the company in England, and being offered a job. However, my advice to anyone seeking work in Germany would be to avoid shop work; the pay is quite low in comparison with average wages (which are a lot higher than in the UK), and shop staff seem to have no concept of customer service. Many of my friends (the other 'foreign students') managed to find work in bars and restaurants during the summer, often by simply going in and asking for work as I had. English-speaking people seemed to be quite well accepted, although I would strongly advise people not to attempt work that involves dealing with the public or being under a lot of pressure without being at least 'A'-level standard in German. (As an example of the language problem even students can have at first, Sarah comments that) I found the atmosphere quite depressing and often got treated as if I was stupid because of not always understanding what people were saying to me, although I found out later that nobody realised that I'd only been in the country for a week.

Is the working environment pleasant?
One thing that was noticeable was that our German colleagues never seemed to socialise together after work, or even chat very much during breaks. All in all, I would say that working in a foreign country can be an enjoyable and challenging

experience, and being from within the EU, there were no problems with visas. However, anyone intending to work with food in Germany has to pass a health test; the results of which can take three weeks to arrive.

How do you find the social life and the Germans?
I found socialising in Germany really enjoyable, for one thing the pubs stay open a lot later than in the UK; till 2 am, and on some occasions such as *Fasching* many stayed open all night. The atmosphere in pubs was generally relaxed — you could sit there as long as you liked with one beer without feeling pressured to buy another. It took some getting used to the fact that drinks are ordered from waiters rather than by queuing at the bar.

Initially I found making friends quite difficult, as the Germans tend to take friendship very seriously and do not have time for casual chit-chat. but with a little perseverance, I gradually found myself being invited out. One thing I liked about the Germans was that they often organised small events in their own homes such as video evenings, parties and barbecues, which were enjoyable and a good way to get to know people. I found the Germans I met very helpful and trustworthy: at the beginning of my time in Regensburg I could hardly string a sentence together, yet they listened to me politely and gave me lots of encouragement.

What is German public transport like ?
Travelling in Germany is easy, due to the extremely efficient bus and train services. Prices on buses are fairly reasonable and although trains can be quite expensive, there are various offers to be taken advantage of, a 'Bahnkarte' is the equivalent of a railcard, and worth buying if you intend to travel a lot. The 'Wochenendkarte', which can only be purchased at the weekends is great, for 35 DM up to five people can travel anywhere in Germany. It does not allow you to travel on some trains, so long journeys can take hours due to your having to keep changing trains, but when you consider how cheap it is you can not complain.

Were you given accommodation or did you rent a flat ?
As an exchange student I was given a place in a university hall of residence, which was brilliant. My room, a reasonable size with ensuite shower and a balcony cost only 235 DM per month, including heating and electricity. The kitchen was separate and shared with 10 other students. Regensburg university lets its unoccupied rooms out during the summer, as I imagine other universities do. So for anyone wishing to work in Germany over the summer it may be possible to arrange accommodation through the local university.

Have you any advice for anyone thinking of taking the plunge?
My advice to anyone intending to live or work in Germany would be to be prepared — find out as much as possible before you go, make sure that you have all the relevant documents, such as the E111 form, passport etc, and where possible arrange a job and accommodation before arriving in Germany. Do not get depressed about problems with the language, it gets easier as you go along. many regions have their own dialects — most notably *Bayerisch* and *Swäbisch* which are impossible for Germans to understand, never mind foreigners. I found that if I explained to people that I was English and did not understand what they were saying, then they were generally sympathetic and quite pleased that I was attempting to speak German at all. Making friends can be a slow process, as even the Germans themselves admit; they are not the most forthcoming or spontaneous people. But, if you persevere and show that you are serious about friendship then you will generally be treated very well. The cost of living is not a great deal higher

than in Britain, in fact with the high pound many things are actually cheaper. Shops are generally similar to Britain but some of the supermarkets are awful.

Ted Wheeler

Ted Wheeler is 56 years old and since 1988 he has been working for the research department of the chartered surveyors Jones Lang Wootton in Frankfurt. For ten years prior to 1988 he was working in Saudi Arabia and before that he spent two years in Germany. He has a two-roomed flat in central Frankfurt which he rents. We asked him:

Was it difficult to find work
On the contrary, it was easier for me to find work in Germany than in the UK, largely because I can speak German. There are lots of opportunities in Germany for anyone with a thorough knowledge of the German language. If you don't speak German you have to be prepared to go down a grade or three. I know an Australian architect here in Frankfurt who speaks no German and is working at MacDonalds. There are around two to three thousands Brits here and of course there are Americans and Japanese. If you don't speak German, you can apply to work on the American compounds where they need nurses, cooks etc. However, now that the foreign forces are pulling out of Germany, there will be fewer of these jobs.

How difficult was it to find accommodation?
It is difficult. I spent my first eighteen months in Frankfurt in a furnished room which I found through an estate agent. I had to pay the estate agent two months rent for their services. I got my present flat when a colleague of mine who was leaving offered it to me. The main problem for British people coming to work here, even if they have a pre-arranged job, is that there are no company flats. Therefore everyone has to find their own accommodation. Most British people here live in the suburbs of Frankfurt in the Taunus area which tends to be cheaper and more spacious. There is quite an expatriate community there which many people like to join.

Have you any advice for those thinking of taking the plunge?
It is advisable to learn some German before you come here. If you don't speak German you are likely to find life twice as difficult. For instance Germans when they feel are not being understood are liable to start shouting, which can be an awesome experience. Anyone who is thinking of coming here to live and work for the money, but who does not speak fluent German will probably have to live quite modestly. I have met a number of Brits who are earning as little as £1,000 monthly. After paying £40 per week for rent, you can still feed yourself quite reasonably on the remainder. However, I would strongly advise anyone considering taking the plunge to get a job before they go, even if it's not the job you are intending to keep. The reason is that you will save yourself two or three weeks of walking the streets looking for work and accommodation. As soon as you arrive you can then concentrate on meeting the other expats here as quickly as possible. You can do this through the English-speaking churches and expatriate clubs. They will give you the low-down on the current situation regarding accommodation and you may be offered a room to rent on a temporary basis until you find your own place. This

way you get a foot in the door immediately, plus and invaluable briefing session on what to expect, which can do a lot to reduce the inevitable culture shock.

Mark Creamon

Mark is a thirty-one year old freelance researcher who spent much of the last year in Germany on an assignment with an agency. He lived in Nuremburg, with occasional trips across country to other cities as part of his research work.

How awful was German red-tape in practice?
Luckily for me I have a friend from an earlier period of working abroad in Belgium who had recently moved back to Bavaria, so he very kindly did some of the preliminary footwork for me having had to go through the rigmarole of registering with the local authorities himself. So rather than have to look for the relevant offices myself he showed me where to go, which saved a lot of time, as I would have automatically headed for the town-hall or *Rathuas*, when the offices I wanted were in a completely separate building half a kilometre away. My German is not too brilliant, having only the remnants of my 'O-level' classes and a short 'Conversational German' course to back it up, but I got by, although I suspect things might have gone quicker, but I had to ask the staff to slow down every so often, so that I could keep up. The offices themselves are similar to most council or social security offices the world over. The *Einwhoneramt* in Nürnberg had several other offices in the building including one large hall with various desks for the different authorities, anyone wishing to register, de-register or obtain proof that they had no criminal record would take a numbered ticket and wait their turn. This actually worked a lot more quickly than I was used to in DSS offices or supermarkets in Britain.

Was it difficult to find work?
I had a job before I went out there as a freelance researcher for an agency, however, they are only a small company so I could not get any help with relocating until I had spent a fair amount of money, and not having too much spare cash I really had to trust to luck and the help of my friends in Germany. If I'd been working for a larger concern I probably would have had a fair amount of the organisation taken out of my hands by a relocation agency, or by the personnel staff at the German offices. I should point out though, that some of the expatriate workers did have a few choice words to say about the amount of help that their employers did not give them. It seems that some companies do not really look very hard at the housing situation in Germany, and a newcomer moving to Germany suddenly finds his or herself having to shell out a lot of money for *Makler* fees. So it is wise to make sure that your employer covers your costs for arranging accommodation in addition to getting you there.

Is the working environment pleasant?
I can not comment personally, as I mostly worked by myself in libraries, public archives and such like, but certainly from the changes in the attitudes of quite a few public servants (council staff, post office counter staff etc) and bank staff compared to those prevalent in the 1980s, I would say that Germany is in some respects getting more relaxed. Those friends I mentioned earlier certainly commented that while it had taken a few weeks or even months to be accepted in the workplace,

once you became a name rather than 'Herr..' then you really became aware of how friendly the Germans can be once you get past that reserve. I know some Americans who used to think that they had a tough time with the famous British reserve, and to be honest I would say that on the whole the two nations are very similar: a bit cool at first but when they warm to you, you know it. Of course there are always those individuals who break the mould in one direction or another, so you just have to take things as they come.

What is German public transport like?
Well that depends on where you are, cities like Berlin, Hamburg, München and even Nürnberg all have excellent systems where trams, buses and U-Bahn are all connected up in a network. The one I use the most was of course that of Nürnberg, and for a mere 62 DM you could get a *Mobikarte* which gave you almost unlimited travel for 30 days. I say almost because if you wanted to travel before 9am then you had to buy a different one at a cost of 83 DM, however, they are valid for two adults to travel and unlike the tickets bought from a machine you don't have to cancel them, so you can travel as much as you like. In other words you can travel as much as you like for 2 DM per day. The city systems reach out quite far too, on a trip to the Moritzberg (about 20 kilometres from Nürnberg) I spent a fair part of the journey back following a Nünberg city bus down winding country roads.

When travelling across country the trains really do take all the strain, the famous autobahns may have all the allure for those with fast cars, but you can get around just as easily and with less stress by train. It is also very handy for new arrivals, as most flights come into Frankfurt, and the airport there has its own station built in. The trip to Frankfurt am Main is about ten minutes, much easier than the 25 minutes by taxi, and cheaper too. On my first visit I was able to get off the plane and on the train in less than an hour, and get to Nürnberg in less than three hours. On another trip I was even able to reserve myself a seat on a train only two hours before I travelled, which was handy as German trains tend to be rather full, probably because they serve so many towns that the country has not developed a competing coach network.

Were you given accommodation or did you rent a flat?
I mentioned earlier that I had a friend living in Nürnberg and so the first month I was there I stayed in his spare room, he's a vicar and so had a house provided for himself and his family by the church. After that I managed to find a small flat for about 200 DM per week through the expatriate network, after having spent a few fruitless weekends searching through the *Süddeutsche Zeitung* property pages.

Have you any advice for anyone thinking of taking the plunge?
First of all brush up on your language skills, the Germans may well receive excellent English teaching at school but not all of them get much chance to use it, so they tend to be rather shy of speaking it. However, more often than not you will find that they really appreciate it if they find out that you speak their language. If you are not German it may come as a surprise to know that even they have problems with the German spoken by someone from another area, this is especially true in the smaller towns and villages. Another important point to bear in mind is not to hide within the expatriate community, unless you get homesick, although you can find yourself making more German friends through expatriate clubs than anywhere else, a not unusual experience.

Vacation Work publish:

	Paperback	Hardback
The Directory of Summer Jobs Abroad	£8.99	£14.99
The Directory of Summer Jobs in Britain	£8.99	£14.99
Adventure Holidays	£7.99	£12.99
Work Your Way Around the World	£12.95	£16.99
Working in Tourism – The UK, Europe & Beyond	£10.99	£15.99
Kibbutz Volunteer	£8.99	£12.99
Working on Cruise Ships	£8.99	£12.99
Teaching English Abroad	£10.99	£15.99
The Au Pair & Nanny's Guide to Working Abroad	£9.99	£14.99
Working in Ski Resorts – Europe & North America	£10.99	–
Accounting Jobs Worldwide	£11.95	£16.95
Working with the Environment	£9.99	£15.99
Health Professionals Abroad	£9.99	£15.99
The Directory of Jobs & Careers Abroad	£11.95	£16.99
The International Directory of Voluntary Work	£9.99	£15.99
The Directory of Work & Study in Developing Countries	£8.99	£14.99
Live & Work in Russia & Eastern Europe	£10.99	£15.95
Live & Work in France	£10.99	£15.95
Live & Work in Australia & New Zealand	£10.99	£14.95
Live & Work in the USA & Canada	£10.99	£14.95
Live & Work in Germany	£10.99	£15.95
Live & Work in Belgium, The Netherlands & Luxembourg	£10.99	£15.95
Live & Work in Spain & Portugal	£10.99	£15.95
Live & Work in Italy	£10.99	£15.95
Live & Work in Scandinavia	£8.95	£14.95
Travellers Survival Kit: Lebanon	£9.99	–
Travellers Survival Kit: South Africa	£9.99	–
Travellers Survival Kit: India	£9.99	–
Travellers Survival Kit: Russia & the Republics	£9.95	–
Travellers Survival Kit: Western Europe	£8.95	–
Travellers Survival Kit: Eastern Europe	£9.95	–
Travellers Survival Kit: South America	£15.95	–
Travellers Survival Kit: Central America	£8.95	–
Travellers Survival Kit: Cuba	£10.99	–
Travellers Survival Kit: USA & Canada	£10.99	–
Travellers Survival Kit: Australia & New Zealand	£9.99	–
Hitch–hikers' Manual Britain	£3.95	–
Europe – a Manual for Hitch-hikers	£4.95	–

Distributors of:

Summer Jobs USA	£12.95	–
Internships (On-the-Job Training Opportunities in the USA)	£16.95	–
Sports Scholarships in the USA	£12.95	–
Making It in Japan	£8.95	–
Green Volunteers	£9.99	–

Vacation Work Publications, 9 Park End Street, Oxford OX1 1HJ
(Tel 01865–241978. Fax 01865–790885)
Web site http://www.vacationwork.co.uk